# Crossing the Jabbok

Contraversions
Critical Studies in Jewish Literature, Culture, and Society

Daniel Boyarin and Chana Kronfeld, General Editors

1. *A Radical Jew: Paul and the Politics of Identity,* by Daniel Boyarin
2. *On the Margins of Modernism: Decentering Literary Dynamics,* by Chana Kronfeld
3. *Crossing the Jabbok: Illness and Death in Ashkenazi Judaism in Sixteenth- through Nineteenth-Century Prague,* by Sylvie Anne Goldberg, translated by Carol Cosman
4. *Foregone Conclusions: Against Apocalyptic History,* by Michael André Bernstein
5. *Founder of Hasidism: A Quest for the Historical Ba'al Shem Tov,* by Moshe Rosman
6. *Conversations with Dvora: An Experimental Biography of the First Modern Hebrew Woman Writer,* by Amia Lieblich, translated by Naomi Seidman
7. *A Marriage Made in Heaven: The Sexual Politics of Hebrew and Yiddish,* by Naomi Seidman
8. *Unheroic Conduct: The Rise of Heterosexuality and the Invention of the Jewish Man,* by Daniel Boyarin

# Crossing the Jabbok

## *Illness and Death in Ashkenazi Judaism in Sixteenth- through Nineteenth-Century Prague*

Sylvie Anne Goldberg

*Translated by Carol Cosman*

UNIVERSITY OF CALIFORNIA PRESS
*Berkeley · Los Angeles · London*

The publisher gratefully acknowledges the generous subvention provided by the Ministère de la Culture

Originally published as *Les deux rives du Yabbok: La maladie et la mort dans le judaïsme ashkénaze: Prague XVIe–XIXe siècle*


University of California Press
Berkeley and Los Angeles, California

University of California Press
London, England



Library of Congress Cataloging-in-Publication Data

Goldberg, Sylvie Anne.
[Deux rives du Yabbok. English]
Crossing the Jabbok: illness and death in Ashkenazi Judaism in sixteenth- through nineteenth-century Prague / Sylvie Anne Goldberg: translated by Carol Cosman.
p. cm. — (Contraversions: 3)
Includes bibliographical references (p. ) and index.
ISBN 0–520–08149–8 (alk. paper)
1. Mourning customs, Jewish. 2. Death—Religious aspects—Judaism. 3. Judaism—Czech Republic—Prague—History. 4. Jews—Czech Republic—Prague—Social life and customs. 5. Ḥevra kaddisha—Czech Republic—Prague. I. Title. II. Series.
BM712.G613 1996
296.4′45′0943712—dc20

95–2035
CIP

Printed in the United States of America

1 2 3 4 5 6 7 8 9

The paper used in this publication meets the minimum requirements of American National Standard for Information Sciences—Permanence of Paper for Printed Library Materials, ANSI Z39.48–1984 ♾

*To my parents*
*For my children*
*The chain of transmission*

# Contents

# Foreword

Goethe saw in what he called simply "The Cemetery"—a print of the Dresden version of Jakob van Ruisdael's great painting of the Amsterdam Sephardic burial ground—a cluster of gravestones that "in their ruined state point to something more than the past." "They are," he said, "monuments of themselves." The magnificent tombs in various states of disrepair are set in a landscape of broken trees and a ruined church, a fresh stream seeking a new path, the sun breaking through the clouds. A cluster of mourners in the background stands by a newer monument. The artist as poet, Goethe thinks, is telling us that "the past had nothing to bequest but mortality." But, according to Goethe, Ruisdael's allegory of transience is far from morbid; its "perfect symbolism delights, teaches, refreshes and invigorates." And it does so for all men. Despite the quite evident pseudo-Hebraic inscriptions on the tombs identifying this as a *Jewish* cemetery, Goethe demands that we regard this scene as an illustration of universal history.

But of course it is Jewish and was known to be so. Popular contemporary prints identify it correctly. John Evelyn, while a tourist in Holland, visited after a stop at the synagogue. (He was impressed with the stateliness and cost of the tombs.) The Amsterdam Sephardic communities of Beth Jacob and Newe Shalom in fact bought the land for the interment of members of their community in 1614, a date that brings it within the orbit of the late-sixteenth-century transformations in death practices among the Ashkenazi signaled by the founding of the *hevra kaddisha,* the communal burial society, in Prague.

Ruisdael's picture is topographically specific: the large marble tomb in the foreground is easily identified as that of the famous doctor Eliahu Montalo. And the subsequent history of the place is all too Jewish. By 1923 all the available land had been used. With rabbinic permission three meters of sand were ordered to cover certain eighteenth-century parts of the ground, thus ensuring that the Amsterdam community could bring its dead here, as it had done for three hundred years, at least until the 1960s. But of course the bones of those who laid these plans, and of their children, are broken, charred, and scattered around the death camps of Auschwitz and Treblinka. The pressure on this reclaimed ground is considerably eased; Goethe's universalizing impulse has taken a radically communal turn.

A similar sort of tension informs Sylvie Anne Goldberg's book. On the one hand, she wants self-consciously to find "in the study of the permanence and evolution of Jewish conceptions of death . . . the persistence of a singularity that existed before and survived the emancipation of the Jews." A singularity grounded, however, not in some essential trait but in the history of practices and experiences. This book is also intended to be part of a more general history, if not a universal one in Goethe's sense. As Yosef Yerushalmi pointed out in his 1988 introduction to the French edition, Goldberg is among the first of a new generation of Jewish scholars who are interested less in the eternal verities that define Judaism through the ages, or in the specifics of ethnography for its own sake, than in a history of cultural practices that articulates with other studies of death, suffering, and the body. This is a book that brings recent methodological developments of the French *Annales* school to bear on what has been a relatively insular tradition in Jewish studies. And conversely, it enriches this historiography by infusion with the dense and intriguing records of Jewish experience.

Goldberg shows that the death beliefs and customs of the Ashkenazi follow the contours of Western history more generally, albeit with a particular inflection. The evolution of the obligation to visit the sick—the notion of "disinterested kindness" (*hesed shel emet*)—developed, Goldberg says, as a result of specific contributions of the Lurianic Kabbalah in the sixteenth century. But this expansion of moral duty proceeds by virtue of a principle recognizably related to the notion of Christian mercy exalted by the Catholic brotherhoods. Although the work of historians of the Christian tradition—Caroline Bynum, Natalie Z. Davis, Eamon Duffy, for example—might lead some readers to wonder whether "Jewish conceptions of death confer a unique importance on the elevation of the divine soul, which separates from the body in order to rejoin the Shekinah," it remains fascinating that Jewish belief in such uniqueness produced the highly particular cultural practices Goldberg recounts. On the one hand, she finds that the development of religious conventions and beliefs predicated on a continuing community of the living and the dead, on the righteous dead caring for those who are left behind, is part of the "common evolution of Western mentalities in the monotheistic religions on the basis of universal 'popular beliefs.'" On the other hand, this book is full of detailed evidence for a specifically Jewish ethnography of death within the Prague community.

More fascinating still is the fact that Goldberg's narrative of the Jewish experience roughly tracks the general contours and chronology of the *long durée* offered by her teacher, the pioneering historian of death, Philippe Aries. For both, the two or three centuries after the first millennium of the common era mark a divide. For Aries, it is the end of death as a collective destiny and the beginning of its individuation, a stage in the history of the soul. For Goldberg, 1000 to 1100 C.E. signals the beginning of the Jewish cemetery and of customs that sharply define the Jews as a community, one among others, with its own destiny. For both, the Enlightenment signals increasing individualization and an emphasis on the here and now, even if for one the cause is secular philosophy and, for the other, citizenship and Hasidism. More generally, for both, death disappears from daily life, even if for Goldberg it remains as one of the critical occasions for communal practices among modern secular Jews. And finally, although they have traveled very different spiritual and political trajectories, they share a profound sense of loss for death as part of life, even if they do not share an aggressive dislike of modernity.

In wrestling with the problem of a specifically Jewish history Goldberg faces straight on the more general historiographical problem of how to write the history of cultural difference without recourse to essentialism. To some measure she shares the dilemma of postcolonial historians, the so-called subaltern school of Indian historiography, for example, who are trying to write a history from below knowing full well that the history they write is inevitably formed by a historicism, born of the nineteenth century, that neither those below nor their social superiors dreamed of before the coming of the West. In rejecting essentialism, Goldberg explicitly notes that she too must work to some extent against the grain of her sources, against their tendency to couch "every innovative element" in "the style, if not the rabbinic cultural tradition, of Jewish society." In an important way the history of Jews during her period is thus not like the history of women, the sick, or the poor, that is, of marginalized groups. It is the history of a group that self-consciously portrayed itself as living outside of the secular time of its neighbors.

In my view the great strength of this book arises not from how it resolves the tensions that inform it—from its struggles to define Jewish specificity—but rather in its luxuriantly detailed record of how identity was actually forged on the body in sickness and in death. Its real point is less to find the kernel of essential Jewishness—a profound and particular belief in a death as resurrection, for example—than to offer a historical anthropology of a community that is exemplary in its thoroughness and sensitivity.

And also, perhaps because Matthew Arnold's famous distinction between Hellene and Hebrew contains a hint of truth, perhaps because Judaism is more a religion of orthopraxy than of orthodoxy, Goldberg is able to offer us extraordinarily concrete glimpses into what it was like to confront epidemic, infirmity, and oblivion. A superb chapter on the relationship between popular and learned medical culture tells us, for example, that Rabbi Menahem of Speyer argued that it was perfectly fine to avail oneself of Christian incantations, potions, or exorcisms because, he said, "it is the tone of voice that heals, and not the words of the incantation," even if the name of Jesus is invoked. One could use impure substances as drugs if survival demanded—dried goat's blood, for example—and one could resort to magic if specific medications failed. And one's patient might resist. Gluckel of Hamel fell dangerously ill but told her physicians and family that she forbade them from "bring[ing] desperate measures into play," on the grounds that the Lord "can do very well without medications." Here the individual crankiness of the past makes its way through the abyss of time. Goldberg tells about how amputated limbs were saved and buried with the body because part of the soul dwelled in them too and separation from the main body would have disastrous effects in the afterlife. And there is, I think, no more harrowing account of the plague than the testimony of Moses ben Hayim Eisenstadt regarding the Jewish community of Prague in 1713: abandoned by its leaders, bereft of protection, the sick evicted from houses and living, until taken by the pestilence, by fires in the streets, proper burial impossible and in any case forbidden. This is very fine social and cultural history of early modern medicine. And it is the history of Jewish life in something like the untidiness in which it was lived.

But Goldberg's major claim is that death, suffering, and its commemoration define community: the Jewish community, of course, but I think the same case could be made for other communities outside that cultural core as well. It was the progress of Christianization that created the parish cemetery, the codification of rules for admissions, and hence the exclusion of Jews. The parish community gradually takes shape as *the* "natural" community within or outside of which Jews created the plantations of the dead that represented their claim to the earth to which all flesh returns. Thus from sometime after 1100 there come to be specifically Jewish places of death, their places as against the natural place of the ambient culture.

Names, especially the reading of lists of names of the dead, came as well to link their particular community of the living and of the dead. (Names in general hold a special place in the Jewish tradition. God called Jacob by his *name* and made him His. And on the level of the fantastical Goldberg records the practice of changing the name of a sick person so as to deceive the angel of death: "I am not the one you seek," the newly renamed might utter. "Moise? No, I'm afraid there is no Moise here," one imagines the conversation as the angel departs, foiled in his effort to claim the person once known by that name.) It was specifically the Crusaders' pogroms that gave rise to the memory books, those lists of the names of martyrs and, later, of ordinary folks that were read and remembered during a new prayer: the kaddish. Christians, of course, had such lists as well in the Middle Ages—the Libri memorialis—and they prayed for the dead. But these books singled out members of a monastic community or great donors; they did not define a whole community in relation to this world and the next. And masses or prayers for the dead were essentially a service for which survivors paid. But naming to join ghosts, kin, and progeny into one solidarity was a practice that would come to have especial resonance among Jews and subsequently among persecuted communities like the Quakers that produced "Books of Suffering" as did religious minorities in other countries.

And finally, there was the burial society, the Prague hevra kaddisha, which is the centerpiece of this book. Far more powerfully than the burial societies of the medieval and early modern guilds or even the various mutual self-help organizations founded among the working classes of the late eighteenth and nineteenth centuries to avoid the ignominy of the new category, "pauper funeral," it came to be the dominant institution of this Ashkenazi community. Readers will follow its political struggles: over membership, personnel (keeping the grave diggers in line was not always easy), religious questions, and indeed all those matters over which communities struggle and through which they continuously make themselves. But the critical point is that the warrant for this community is somehow mortality. The point is less that death rituals reflect other beliefs or serve as a prism through which to refract social evolution. It is rather that there could be nothing more serious at the heart of a communal enterprise.

Thomas W. Laqueur

# Acknowledgments

It is so common for French scholars to read works in Jewish Studies in English and to welcome their translation into French that I feel particularly grateful to Daniel Boyarin and Chana Kronfeld and to Stanley Holwitz of the University of California Press for giving me this opportunity to cross the Atlantic. And I am grateful to Carol Cosman for struggling with the many subtleties of the French language in her translation of this book into American English.

During many years of research I have accumulated a large number of intellectual and collegial debts. Without the help of Michael Silber for the documentation, Samuel Kerner for the translations from Yiddish, and Rabbi Édouard Gourévitch for checking rabbinical sources, this book would surely have suffered. And I hope this book reminds Alexandre Derczansky and Albert Ogien that without their constant criticisms and suggestions, *Crossing the Jabbok* would not have taken its final form. It is also a real pleasure to express my gratitude to the librarians whose assistance was invaluable: Yvonne Levyne in Paris, Jirina Sedinova in Prague, and Adassa Assouline and Yaakov in Jerusalem.

This book is based on a doctoral dissertation that acquired sharper focus under the direction of François Furet and Maurice Kriegel. They both followed in the footsteps of Philippe Ariès, who was a guide into the vastness of the realm of death.

I must also express my gratitude to Yosef Hayim Yerushalmi for his introduction to the French edition of this work and to my original editor, Nicolas-Jean Sèd at Éditions du Cerf. I was fortunate in receiving financial support from the Foundation Benveniste, the Memorial Foundation for Jewish Culture, and the Centre National de la Recherche Scientifique.

I remain in debt to all those who cannot read this book, those who preceded me and to whom it is dedicated.

# Translator's Note

In keeping with the methodology of the social historian, the author of this study cites the evidence of many different texts. Some of these are pioneering secondary sources, but most are original texts, both religious and secular, the testimony of famous rabbis and obscure travelers. I have used published English translations (or original texts, as the case may be) where these exist, and all quotations from the Hebrew Bible have been taken from the King James Version. There are a number of Hebrew and Yiddish texts, however, that exist only in manuscript form and were very difficult to obtain in the originals. The charters of the Prague Ḥevra Kaddisha fall into this category. In such cases I have relied on Professor Goldberg's French translations.

C. C.

“On watch for rebellion against the Society.” Statutes of the Burial Society (*Ḥevra Kaddisha*) of Kounice, Moravia, 1801/1817. From *The Precious Legacy: Judaic Treasures from the Czechoslovak State Collections,* ed. David Altshuler (New York: Summit Books, 1983), 163. Reprinted by permission.

# Introduction

Everyone was gathered in the sick woman's room and there they stayed. . . . The final agony began, the death rattle, the palpitations, the groans. . . .

"Repeat after me, my child," and he began to read the *Viddui*. . . . "My God and God of my fathers, I acknowledge that my recovery is in Your hands and likewise my death is in Your hands." Hearing this, everyone without exception remained silent. . . . Everyone, even the hardiest, had tears in their eyes and lumps in their throats, but all maintained a solemn and dignified bearing, and not a sob broke the silence. . . .

"You who weep in your houses of clay . . . He has given, He has taken away, blessed be the name of the Lord. . . ." Then . . . Esther Rachel entered the scene. After the nearest relations had been led away . . . , she approached the deathbed, leaned over the dead woman, and said:

"Holy soul of Nekhama, daughter of Moshe, return below, whence you came, and let your carnal envelope serve you until then." And she closed the dead woman's eyes, straightened her arms and legs, took the pillow from under her head, and covered her face. After doing all of this, she turned toward the mirror hanging on the wall, covered it as well, and said to those still in the room:

"Let us empty the water. . . ."

They did all that there was to do. They washed the dead woman in warm water, dressed her in a shroud, put a bonnet on her head as is fitting for a pious woman, all the while reciting appropriate verses. . . .

Afterward, two other bearers carried the body wrapped in a white sheet. . . . Then all the members of the family, relatives, neighbors, the entire female retinue . . . rushed toward the coffin and surrounded it; and from the tight circle, from the timorous and frightened women scrambling around the bearers . . . rose wild and multitudinous lamentations:

> "May good angels come to greet you!"
> "May the gates of heaven open before you!"
> "Intercede for us. . . ."[1]

Death has often served to shed light on the customs of the living. It was thought that Spanish Jews could be recognized by their ways of death and burial: if they turned toward the wall to breathe their last, they were heretics; if not, the converts could be buried in consecrated ground.[2]

When death occurs, the living set in motion ritual procedures that express their untiring inquiry into human origins and finalities. Funerary practices confirm our beliefs in the unknowable, in the infinite, and illustrate our perceptions of the afterlife.

Research on the configuration of mental dispositions in the Christian West has led to a definition of eras marking basic modifications in attitudes toward and beliefs connected with death.[3] Are these definitions relevant to the Jewish world? In our desire to investigate the ways of being Jewish and Christian in earlier times, shall we assume that people of both backgrounds participated in an identical culture? To hold an unqualified view of this kind, we would have to accept the notion that Jew and Christian have shared the same world of representations and the same body of attitudes. Yet a simple glance at Jewish and Christian beliefs connected with death reveal their respective originality: they differ on points that may seem minor but are nonetheless basic, points that generate obvious disparities.

The emergence of Jews as individuals in European national societies by the end of the eighteenth century marks a global transformation of the Jewish world that echoes throughout its religious universe. As the old way of life with its strict adherence to Jewish laws disappeared, the boundaries between Jewish communities and the surrounding world dissolved, leaving space for interpenetrations and a blurring of distinctive traits. Through the study of the permanence and evolution of Jewish conceptions of death, this book constitutes a search for the persistence of a singularity that existed before and survived the emancipation of the Jews.

PART ONE

# Itinerary

CHAPTER ONE

# From the Universal to the Particular

Questions about the origin and finality of the individual have haunted humanity over the course of its development. Hoping to find answers, human beings build temples and places of worship where they celebrate rites that ease their existential anguish. From animal worship through the cult of the sun to monotheism, the path of human development, and therefore of the human condition, passes through the anguish of origins and ends. In the organization of social life, death is rarely disregarded: it is not silenced by its ebb and flow in the commonplaces of language, nor can it be completely hidden. And while death may be organized, structured, even systematized, it is never tamed. The structures erected by the living to deal with their dead are only a reflection of their spiritual and organic society, whether it is real or ideal.

In our day, history is bent on delineating a multitude of social distinctions, but there is one that continues to elude it: the distinction constituted by the permanent presence of Jews in the Christian West. Membership in a given religion does not determine the entire spectrum of practices and beliefs in any absolute way. And conversely, cultural changes create attitudes that are reflected in religious practice. From this perspective, we would have to distinguish the relevant elements in a civilization at any given period: on the one hand, the realm of the sacred—that which concerns religious affiliation—and, on the other hand, general phenomena that are subject to mutations without any direct relation to Christian dogma or Jewish law. This commonsense distinction between "dogma" and "law" has long served to justify an apologetic vision of Jewish history. How should the historian resolve the problem posed by religious texts? It is difficult to leave aside the question of their "holiness" without betraying them through reductive secular interpretation, while still analyzing them from a historical point of view.

To sift out specifically Jewish conceptions of illness and death, I investigate, through practices indicated or described in the most familiar and characteristic works, the "commonplaces" of Jewish society. The connections between Jewish and Christian attitudes to be found throughout this book therefore issue from the period under scrutiny rather than from religious interventions. Moreover, an emphasis on the relation between Jewish and Christian worlds is bound to lift the history of the Jews out of its idiosyncratic cultural and social context.

The evolution of Christianization, then of Christianity, can be traced, localized, and occasionally dated through pontifical bulls or popular religious iconography. While a Holy Roman Empire at one time ruled all of Christendom, the history of Judaism lacks an equivalent centralized authority and uniformity. Rather, Jewish communities evolved region by region, according to the influence of local rabbis, and Judaism seems to have developed ritual realms characterized by the contributions of local custom, which were then grafted onto the common trunk of universally accepted Law. These local customs impart a uniqueness to the Jewish communities that lay claim to and define themselves by that Law. The systematic elaboration and maturation of Jewish ritual is thus marked by contributions from diverse sources, three of which can be designated as essential: (1) those depending on ritual that flows directly from biblical writings (from the Torah); (2) those originating in ritual established at a later period by rabbinic writings (Halakhah) that results from the interpretation of and commentary on Scripture; and (3) those issuing from ritual that derives essentially from the influence of the local setting and therefore belongs to what is called "custom" (*minhag*). For situating the modifications and evolutions of the religious life of Jews, only the last two categories are pertinent, since they allow us to distinguish the process of change in mental and social attitudes. The rabbinic literature will therefore provide the variations I intend to analyze.

The most important corpus of rabbinic writings is the *She'elot uteshovot* (responsa). It consists of the rabbis' epistolary exchanges concerning reception of rabbinic decisions. This corpus is divided into two groups, defined as follows:[1] *rishonim,* the "earlier authorities," which contain the responsa of French, German, and Spanish Judaism[2] from the late Middle Ages, and *aḥaronim,* the "later authorities," which are classified as such beginning in the sixteenth century and continue to our own day. The *She'elot uteshovot* treat all problems that might arise in Jewish communities at every level, from lofty ethical, scientific, or philosophical questions to minor matters of daily life, ritual detail involving the individual, or new situations to be envisaged from a rabbinic point of view. Over the centuries, these documents reveal important transformations of ritual. For example, the ban on polygamy in Ashkenazi communities appears in the responsa of the eleventh century, although the practice had ceased long before.[3] Similarly, a discussion is recorded that took place in the sixteenth century between Moses Isserles of Cracow, the Rama,[4] and Solomon ben Jehiel Luria, the Maharshal, on the subject of approval of secular studies such as philosophy, grammar, or, even, Kabbalah for all those who would like to pursue such interests.[5] These two examples of rabbinic responsa suggest changes in mores that influenced not only the meaning of respect for the Law but also the larger domain of "custom."

While it is possible to date practical changes in religious and ritual life, laws and rites nonetheless remain extensions of belief. The analysis, then, of material on the relation of Jews to death (whether in its imaginary or social aspects) must incorporate two decisive elements: on the one hand, beliefs specifically connected with death and, on the other hand, attitudes derived from these beliefs as they are reflected in the organization of Jewish society.

## THE HEREAFTER, BEFORE DEATH, AFTER DEATH

If Jewish belief rests on the principle of revelation,[6] that is, that Moses received the Torah on Mount Sinai and with it the essence of Judaism in the form of all possible laws, past and future, then the cornerstone of beliefs concerning death is faith in resurrection. Revelation and the resurrection of the dead are the two pivotal notions by which Judaism is articulated, and no study of Judaism, whether religious or social, can ignore them.

The notion of revelation invites continual exegesis because it is a system open to every reinterpretation; according to this cosmogonic principle, any future modification is now and forever an integral part of the original revelation. Hence past, present, and future form a single and unique entity: chronology is ignored so that revelation may be continually reenacted.

Belief in the resurrection of the dead, although disputed over the centuries,[7] is central to the attitudes of the living when they are faced with their end. Such belief is not situated in a clearly evolving framework, for modifications, such as they are, are perpetually reintegrated into the framework of revelation in accordance with the practice of normative Judaism; the Mishnah itself evokes an ahistorical situation par excellence, implying that history cannot influence the Law.[8]

The concept of resurrection originates in the Hebrew Bible. We find the most evocative verses in the Pentateuch, and these constitute Jewish commonplaces regarding the resurrection of the dead. These biblical verses, as well as the commentaries attached to them, are as much part of the daily service as they are of the holiday liturgy, and they play an integral role in the rituals of death, burial, and mourning.

The idea of the resurrection of the dead evolved from the first five books of the Pentateuch to the late prophets, gradually taking on the formulation and definitions that would be passed down through the centuries. Originally, man's finality lies in death: "And Enoch walked with God; and he was not, for God took him" (Gen. 5:24). Then, "'For we must needs die, and are as water spilt on the ground, which cannot be gathered up again; neither doth God respect any person, yet doth He devise means, that His banished be not expelled from Him'" (2 Sam. 14:14). And again on this subject:

> "O remember that my life is a wind;
> mine eye shall no more see good.
> The eye of him that hath seen me shall see me no more:
> thine eyes are upon me, and I am not.
> As the cloud is consumed and vanisheth away,
> so he that goeth down to the grave [*She'ol*] shall come up no more.
> He shall return no more to his house,
> neither shall his place know him anymore." (Job 7:7–10)

Rabba's[9] interpretation explains that this passage from Job leaves no place for the idea of resurrection ("'he that goeth down to the grave shall come up *no more*'"). In this case, death is without reprieve, and in it man discovers his mortality. Yet Deuteronomy, chapter 32, verse 39, "'I kill, and I make alive; I wound, and I heal,'" can be interpreted differently; in Pesaḥim 68a, this verse is analyzed as referring directly to the resurrection but only as it concerns the life and death of an individual.

Throughout the Bible, the "black" regions of She'ol stand in marked contrast to the realm of "life restored": "O Lord, thou hast brought up my soul from the grave, / Thou hast kept me alive, that I should not go down to the Pit" (Ps. 30:3). Or again: "Thou which hast shewed me great and sore troubles, / shalt quicken me again, / and shalt bring me up again from the depths of the earth" (Ps. 71:20).

In Isaiah, the tone is noticeably different:

> "Behold, for peace I had great bitterness;
> but Thou hast in love to my soul delivered it from the pit of corruption,
> for Thou hast cast all my sins behind Thy back.
> For the grave cannot praise Thee,
> death cannot celebrate Thee;
> They that go down into the Pit cannot hope for Thy truth.
> The living, the living, shall praise Thee,
> as I do this day." (Isa. 38:17–19)

In the Hebrew Bible, Sheʾol is also contrasted to the "light of the living," as in this passage from Job:

> "Lo, all these things worketh God
> oftentimes with man,
> to bring back his soul from the Pit,
> to be enlightened with the light of the living." (Job 33:29–30)

In the vision of Ezekiel, the idea of the resurrection of the dead is made concrete:

> The hand of the Lord was upon me, and carried me out in the Spirit of the Lord, and set me down in the midst of the valley which was full of bones. . . .
>
> And He said unto me, "Son of man, can these bones live?" . . .
>
> So I prophesied as I was commanded; and as I prophesied, there was a noise, and behold a shaking; and the bones came together, bone to bone.
>
> And when I looked, lo, the sinews and the flesh came upon them, and the skin covered them over. . . .
>
> . . . and the breath came into them, and they lived, and stood upon their feet, an exceedingly great army. . . .
>
> . . . Thus saith the Lord God: "Behold, O My people, I will open your graves, and cause you to come up out of your graves, and bring you to the land of Israel. . . .
>
> "And I shall put My Spirit in you, and ye shall live, and I shall place you in your own land." (Ezek. 37:1–14)

Though envisioned by Ezekiel, the concept of the resurrection of the dead is clearly defined only in the Book of Daniel:

> "And many of them that sleep in the dust of the earth shall awake,
> some to everlasting life,
> and some to shame and everlasting contempt.

> And they that be wise shall shine
> as the brightness of the firmament;
> and they that turn many to righteousness
> as the stars for ever and ever." (Dan. 12:2–3)

Materialized and subsequently defined, the idea of the resurrection of the dead is enriched in the prophecy of Daniel by a distinction between the just and the ungodly. In Ezekiel's vision, it is established that the resurrection will be corporeal (bones will be joined once more, covered with flesh, etc.), while beginning with the prophecy of Daniel the question of divine judgment becomes central. As the last verse of Daniel, "But go thou thy way till the end be; for thou shalt rest, and stand in thy lot at the end of the days" (Dan. 12:13) indicates, in this period of persecution,[10] death does not seem to be exclusively reserved for the ungodly sinner but touches all without distinction. The just, however, shall be distinguished from others and—lest their deaths seem gratuitous—rewarded. It is perhaps in this light that the end of the exile becomes a corollary to the concept of the resurrection of the dead. In this sense, posthumous reward is closely bound to Israel's return to and rehabilitation in the promised land.

In the course of the rabbinic period, exile becomes Israel's fate, and the concept of resurrection, indissolubly linked to the end of exile, will be considered one of the fundamental doctrines of Judaism. On this subject, the Mishnah *Sanhedrin* is supremely eloquent:

> All of Israel has a share in the world to come, as it is said (Isa. 60:21). And the people who have a claim to it, in the end they will inherit the earth. And he who says that there is no resurrection of the dead will forfeit his share in the world to come.[11]

This doctrine, here affirming faith in the idea of resurrection, is henceforth integrated into the daily liturgy at the beginning of the *Amidah,* formulated as "Blessed art Thou . . . who quickens the dead."[12]

The Jewish doctrine of the resurrection implies two assumptions: the notion of retribution and reward for Israel as a whole and not for the Jew as an individual; and the notion that body and soul are indivisible, equal, and essential in the constitution of human beings. This concept of carnal resurrection is fundamental; indeed, if body and soul form a "whole," their separation becomes problematic, and it is on these grounds that Jewish and Christian conceptions of the resurrection of the dead diverge. In rabbinic literature, numerous inquiries are conducted on this subject:

Will those raised from the dead have the same imperfect bodies they had in their former lives, or will they be perfect?

How will they travel from their place of burial to the land of Israel?

Will those raised from the dead awaken clothed or naked?

Such inquiries are found repeatedly in the Talmud[13] and, far from futile speculation, even seem essential as a starting point for the elaboration of death and burial rites:

If those risen from the dead take on their former bodies, they must be preserved intact at the time of interment. Consequently, the body must be buried carefully, with all its organs, including the blood it may have lost in the event of a violent death.

To facilitate the return of the departed to the land of Israel, wouldn't it be useful to bury them there in the first place?

If we have trouble imagining another world populated by naked people, we must then reclothe the dead, but how?

The rabbis' responses to these questions are translated into concrete ritual practices. We can trace them in daily rites as well as in those rites more directly connected to death and burial practices. Yet integration into rites and customs does not make these issues less perceptibly problematic.

The problems posed by belief in the resurrection of the dead are numerous, thorny, and even contradictory. The opinions of the rabbis, moreover, differ on this question,[14] and their judgments remain divided. Indeed, no dogma or canonical belief prevails when it comes to the Jewish concept of the resurrection of the dead. Are "resurrection" and "redemption" to be regarded as virtually the same state described in different terms, or do these terms qualify two distinct stages? And what is the precise nature of the world to come, the *Olam ha-Ba*? The talmudic sources also differ on the meaning of corporeal resurrection, some suggesting that only the "just" will be raised, others maintaining that Israel as a stable entity will be raised as such.

## ALL WILL RISE UP

Queries raised by the doctrine of the resurrection of the dead and redemption are at the heart of Jewish mysticism and the messianic

ssuing from it,[15] but they also define the extent to which
f diverges from initially identical Christian belief. In the
the distinction between Jewish and Christian concepts stems
relation to the idea of "salvation." For Jews the body and
n a necessary whole to be preserved intact even after death, while for Christians resurrection concerns primarily the spiritual body. The "hide" is merely corporeal—and hence secondary—clothing to be cast off by the dead upon their departure for the life hereafter. This element may well be responsible for the original differences in the relation of Christian and Jewish living to their dead and, by extension, for the separation of Jewish and Christian burial places.

As Philippe Ariès has shown,[16] while the early Christians evinced little interest in their own remains, asking only that they be buried someplace convenient and without particular ceremony, not until the fifth century did popular opinion dissociate the spiritual soul from the carnal body. The ideas current in antiquity of a grave inviolate and apart, of a separation of the world of the living from that of the dead (so present in Judaism), persisted, however, in connection with paganistic revivals of the cult of tombs. The Christian doctrine regarding belief in the resurrection of the dead, which involves the separation of the glorious body from the carnal body, assumes its full meaning in the funerary space with the concept of the "holy martyr." In fact, this concept will initially sanctify Christian burial space. But under the influence of the idea that the carnal body was not sacred in itself, the Christians initiated practices that were inconceivable to the Jews—for example, the practice of cutting open cadavers so that the heart or other parts could be removed and placed in the reliquaries of basilicas and chapels consecrated to the "saints."

Beyond such seminal beliefs, both the Jewish and Christian worlds of popular custom seem more syncretic. Surely we can cite similar practices among Jews and Christians living within the same geographic area because such osmosis would not necessarily depend on the basic tenets of a clearly defined religion and, even given canonical divergences, could affect general attitudes. These attitudes might in any case be the result of mutual influences issuing from a shared imagination of death, a product of "that abyss of time in which most beliefs seem to originate."[17]

Even if Christian and Jewish practices have evolved over the centuries, we can still ask whether they evolved in an identical fashion. A Christian burial of the Middle Ages—or even of the eighteenth century—can be clearly distinguished from a present-day burial, yet Jewish practices, by contrast, seem to have remained largely unchanged. From the time of the Mishnah and the Tannaim,[18] the basic elements resting on the idea of individual and corporeal resurrection have led to a ritualization that seems to have evolved without fundamental modification. These elements, bound to conceptions of the relation between the living and the dead body, have remained the same.

## REJOICINGS

The Talmudic treatise *Evel Rabbati* constitutes the classic rabbinic text on death, customarily and euphemistically referred to as *Semaḥot* (Rejoicings). According to Dov Zlotnick,[19] this tractate dates back to the third century. It represents one of the first works of mortuary and funerary codification, containing all the laws, customs, and practices dealing with dying, death, burial, and mourning.

*Semaḥot* belongs to the writings of the period defined by Mircea Eliade, after George Foot Moore, as that of "normative Judaism."[20] It is drafted in the form of questions and rabbinic discussions and grapples with each phase of an individual's final end, even the conduct of his entourage before and after death. One can follow in detail the practices of the time, the prevailing laws, and people's attitudes toward death. We can also find there practices that were subsequently abandoned and given no further mention in the rabbinic literature.

Certain customs simply disappeared, such as this one:

> One may go out to the cemetery for thirty days to inspect the dead for any sign of life, without fear that this smacks of heathen practice. For it happened that a man was inspected after thirty days, and he went on to live twenty-five years; and another went on to have five children and died later.[21]

Elsewhere in the tractate, we find within one sentence two practices that have since been abandoned. The first was rejected to prevent Jews from being subject to ridicule by their gentile neighbors: "The person in mourning must cover his face . . ." (with a veil, according to Moslem practice?); the other to forestall any suspicion of sorcery: ". . . and invert the bed." The commentary explains that the latter practice is not meant to aggravate the discomfort of the mourner but to signify the turning of the life cycle by overturning the place in which life is conceived.[22]

Two other customs were also abandoned because of the ridicule they might incur. One was completely relinquished and never mentioned again:

> Everyone should bare an arm at the death of a scholar or a disciple. For a *Ḥakham* [very learned man] who died, the right arm must be bared. For an *Av bet din* [the vice-president of the *Sanhedrin*] who died, the left arm must be bared. For a *Nasi* [president of the *Sanhedrin*] who died, both arms must be bared.
>
> Now it happened that when Rabbi Eliezer died, Rabbi Akiba bared both arms and beat his breast, drawing blood.[23]

The second custom was amended and involves the prohibition against the mourner wearing shoes after the burial. In the funerary practices established in the course of the following centuries, it is always specified that the mourner who must use a route taken by gentiles will take off his shoes only when he has reentered the Jewish quarter or his own house. These two customs are specifically concerned with the funeral procession.

One of the major preoccupations of the redactors of *Semaḥot* is to distance themselves through acts and customs from the surrounding idolators. Nonetheless, they do not systematically reject all local practices. It is obvious that a great number of customs were as much in use among the Jews as among the Greeks. Whenever the rabbis authorize a practice identical to a practice of the surrounding peoples, they anticipate and explain the reasons why the "pagan" custom is admissible. We have seen this with regard to inspection of the dead. The first seven paragraphs of one chapter are thus devoted to the enumeration of funeral customs that converge with pagan practices but must nonetheless be observed because of a theoretical basis valid for the authors of the period.[24] In this case, we are referred to practices that have since been abandoned: the wedding canopy must be erected for the burial of a married couple and decorated with fruits; on the occasion of a marriage, food and wine must be distributed to spread and enhance the joy; at the death of a king, a calf must be killed and burned on a stake as a sign of respect; the hair of a married woman must be unbound and the face of a husband uncovered, and they must be buried with some personal effects.[25]

The text then goes on to recount that Samuel the Small was buried with a key and his account book in his coffin, most likely an imported and ephemeral custom.[26] Two incompatible theories are used to explain such a practice. The first suggests that it was imposed on the Jews of Babylon by their neighbors and was brought to Palestine around the second century, when the Jews brought back their dead for reburial. The key symbolizes the "key to heaven" in cases where the deceased left no male descendant, in order to ensure his "admission to eternal life by other means." The second theory, running counter to this one, claims that the key and the account book are sufficient to symbolize that Samuel the Small was bringing with him his worldly possessions and leaving no one to inherit them.[27]

Certain injunctions serve to situate *Semaḥot* specifically in its time, such as the one addressed to the family of a crucified man to leave the city where he is until the flesh has fallen off the bones and he is reduced to a skeleton.[28]

Chapter 12, dealing with conduct at the ossuary, conveys practices going back to antiquity. The ossuary itself is not described, however, and to get some idea of its design we must refer to archaeological findings. The gathering together of bones was then current practice and did not need to be justified, but it was subject to strict laws.

The ossuary, so common in the ancient world, is found in Palestine as well. Most often it consists of a collection of vases and burial urns containing bones. Around Jerusalem the ossuary was in common use in the first and second centuries. The prevailing custom was to conduct two interments, the first at the time of death, the second approximately one year later. At the first interment, the body was placed in a funeral chamber or the substructure of the cemetery until its flesh was eaten away. As long as the deceased was still identifiable, no one was permitted to touch the body. After this period, which lasted approximately one year, the gathering together of the bones and their placement in the ossuary represented the final burial.[29] In the presence of the deceased's family, the bones were gathered one by one, put on a sheet, and deposited in small covered coffers made of limestone. These can still be seen in situ in the burial caves on the Mount of Olives in Jerusalem. These ossuaries date back to the period of the Second Temple. Although some of them bear inscriptions, most are laconic. Whether Hebrew, Aramaic, Greek, or bilingual, the inscriptions mention only the name or family status of the deceased: "Mama" or "Dostos, our father; do not open."[30] For final burial, the laws prescribed that close relatives repeat the rites of the primary burial and observe mourning practices for one day. Although the ossuary subsequently fell into disuse, the laws devoted to it continued to be applied to transfers from one grave to another.[31]

Bearing in mind the precepts of *Semaḥot* regarding the ossuary, can we liken the Jewish ossuary of the Tannaitic period to the Christian ossuary of the Middle Ages as it exists at the monastery of St. Catherine's in the Sinai desert, for example, or at the cemetery of the Capuchin church or Santa Maria della Orazione e della Morte in Rome, or in the catacombs of Palermo where the bones are mingled, arranged, and exhibited for the scrutiny of visitors? Apparently not, since the injunctions of *Semaḥot* are intended to preserve bodily integrity in accordance with the Jewish concept of resurrection. The Palestinian ossuary would seem to be related instead to those of ancient civilizations.

The laws governing the ossuary are described in *Semaḥot* as follows:[32]

1. The day one hears of a death is like the day of burial, so far as rending clothes and mourning, the precepts of *shiva* and *sheloshim,* are concerned. As for eating hallowed food, it is only like the day of ossilegium [the gathering up of bones]: both in one case and in the other, hallowed food may be eaten.

2. Rabbi Eliezer says: "On hearing of a recent death within thirty days, *shiva* and *sheloshim* must be observed. Beyond this, only one day need be observed."

The Sages say: "Whether one hears of a recent death or of a death long past, *shiva* and *sheloshim* must be observed."

It happened that when Rabbi Zadok's father died in Ginzak, Media, the news reached him after three years, whereupon he observed *shiva* and *sheloshim.*

3. Whenever clothes are rent for a person at the time of his death, they must be rent for him at the time of ossilegium.

Whenever clothes rent in the event of death may not be mended, they may not be mended in the event of ossilegium.

4. In the case of ossilegium, mourning must be observed for only one day. As a consequence, the bones are gathered only near nightfall. If while gathering them all that day, night falls, a man is released from the obligation of mourning on the very next day.

There should be no standing in line, and no comforting of mourners, but personal words of sympathy may be extended to them. The *ḥever ir* [members of the town assembly] should not participate in these rites, but may partake of the meal prepared in the mourners' house.

Rabbi Simeon ben Eleazar says: "If night falls while the comforters are going around the inverted beds offering personal words of sympathy, the beds need not be set upright."

5. This is what societies used to do in Jerusalem: some went to a mourner's house, others to a wedding feast; some to a circumcision, others to an ossilegium.

To a mourner's house or to a wedding feast?
The wedding feast comes first.
To a circumcision or an ossilegium?
The circumcision comes first.

The early Ḥasidim, however, gave precedence to the mourner's house rather than the wedding feast, inasmuch as it is said: "It is better to go to the house of mourning, than to go to the house of feasting; for that is the end of all men, and the living will lay it to his heart" (Eccles. 7:2).

What is the force of "and the living will lay it to his heart"? That whosoever follows the bier must say: "I, too, shall take this path!"

6. The bones of a corpse should not be taken apart, nor the tendons severed, unless the bones had fallen apart of themselves and the tendons of themselves had been severed.

7. A person may collect the bones of all dead except those of his father and mother. So Rabbi Johanan ben Nuri.

Rabbi Akiba says: "The bones may not be gathered until the flesh has wasted away; once it has, the features are no longer recognizable in the skeleton."

8. The ossilegium of two corpses may take place at the same time, as long as the bones of the one are put at one end of a sheet and those of the other at the other end of the sheet. So Rabbi Johanan ben Nuri.

Rabbi Akiba says: "In the course of time, the sheet will waste away; in the course of time, the bones will intermingle. Let them rather be gathered and placed in ossuaries."

9. The bones may be sprinkled with wine and oil. So Rabbi Akiba.

Rabbi Simeon ben Nannas says: "Oil but not wine, because wine evaporates."

"Neither wine nor oil," say the Sages, "because these only invite worms, but dried herbs may be put on them."

Rabbi Eleazar bar Zadok said: "Thus spoke Father at the time of his death: 'My son, bury me at first in a fosse. In the course of time, collect my bones and put them in an ossuary; but do not gather them with your own hands.'

"And thus did I attend him: Jonathan entered, collected the bones, and spread a sheet over them. I then came in, rent my clothes for them, and sprinkled dried herbs over them.

"Just as he attended his father, so I attended him."

10. A man may shroud and gird the corpse of a man, but not that of a woman. A woman may shroud and gird the corpse of a man or of a woman.

A man may attend another man suffering from intestinal illness, but not a woman. A woman may attend a man or a woman suffering from intestinal illness.

11. Abba Saul ben Botnit said to his sons: "Bury me at the feet of my father, and untie the purple fringe from my cloak."

12. A man may enter the bathhouse with everyone except his father, his father-in-law, his stepfather, or his teacher who had taught him wisdom.

Rabbi Judah says: "If his father is old or sick, he may enter and bathe him, for by this he honors him."

13. A body may not be carried out on a bier unless the head or the greater part of the corpse is intact.

Rabbi Judah says: "The spinal column or the skull constitute the greater part of the corpse."

All these pronouncements specifically concern the attitudes and duties of close family toward the deceased relative at the time of final burial. But outlined here as well is the corpus of Jewish law governing the body in general, that body which must be respected in its integrity, living or dead, but which must in addition be spared the gaze of family members (children and disciples) to preserve its dignity.

The ḥever ir mentioned in the text gives us a glimpse of one organizational aspect of ancient Jerusalem, the "societies" (*ḥavurot*), which I shall deal with in a later chapter. These societies, whose religious and charitable functions are not clearly defined, are considered by certain historians to be the source for the Jewish burial societies that later appear in Europe, first in Spain, then in the German lands and Poland. While it is not possible to define precisely the role these groups played in the Jewish society of ancient Palestine, we can nonetheless see that the fifth injunction implies their presence on specific ritual occasions: circumcisions, marriages, and burials. Indeed, it appears from the text that their presence marks the religious solemnity of these events. Moreover, it is specified that although the rites of the secondary burial do not require the presence of the ḥever ir, the sanctification of the first interment takes precedence over that of the second, and the people who go into mourning for the day of the gathering together of bones are considered mourners and must be provided with a condolence meal.

*Semaḥot* also touches on the duties of those who care for the dead, and later collections of mortuary rituals will preserve the essential features of these duties:

1. A person engaged in ossilegium or in guarding the bones is exempt from reciting the *Shema,* from the *Tefilla,* from *tefillin,*[33] and from all the commandments written in the Torah. Should he wish to exact more of himself, he may not do so, because of the honor due to the bones of the dead.

Rabbi Johanan ben Nuri says: "Let him withdraw four cubits and recite the *Shema.*"

Rabbi Simeon ben Eleazar says: "If they are with him on the same side of a boat, let him shift them and recite the *Shema.*"

Rabbi Isaac says: "If the bones are of his close kin, he is exempt from reciting the *Shema*; if of strangers, he is obligated."

Rabbi Simeon says: "On the Sabbath, he is obligated; during the week, he is exempt."

"If he is carrying his pack," says Rabbi Nathan, "he is exempt, for the obligation that is upon him is to guard the bones, not the pack."

2. Bones or Sacred Scrolls may be taken from place to place in a case, but not carried loose in a wagon, or in a boat, or upon the back of an animal, nor may one sit on them. If it is for the sake of the dead alone, or so that one might steal past customs, it is permitted.

3. While passing through a cemetery, one should not wear *tefillin* or hold a Sacred Scroll in his arm, this being mockery of the dead.

4. If while hollowing a *kok* [niche] in a tomb, the time for the recitation of the *Shema* has approached, one should neither recite the *Shema* nor pray, but withdraw to a clean place, recite the *Shema* and pray, and then come back.

5. Whosoever finds a corpse in a tomb should not move it, unless he is sure that this is a temporary sepulcher.

6. Whosoever finds bones in a tomb should place them in an arcosolium.[34] So Rabbi Akiba. The Sages say: "He should not move them from their place."

If he found them in a *kok* or in a loculus, he should not move them from their place.

7. Neither a corpse nor the bones of a corpse may be transferred from a wretched place to an honored place or, needless to say, from an honored place to a wretched place; but if to the family tomb, even from an honored place to a wretched place, it is permitted, for by this he is honored.

8. Two corpses may not be buried beside one another, nor a corpse beside bones, nor bones beside a corpse.

Rabbi Judah says: "Whomsoever a person may sleep with when he is living, he may be buried with when he is dead."

9. A tomb that has been cleared out may be used. It should not, however, be turned into a barn or a stall for cattle or into a woodshed or warehouse.

It is forbidden to use a *kok* that has been cleared out.

A tomb that was built for a living person may be sold; if for a dead person, it may not be sold. Stones that were hewn for a living person may be sold; if for a dead person, they may not be sold.

It is forbidden to use a coffin that has been cleared out. If it is of stone or clay, it should be shattered; if of wood, burned.

Whosoever finds boards in a cemetery must not move them from their place.[35]

In these laws enacted for the purposes of an obsolete funerary practice, we recognize the general characteristics of the Jewish attitude toward death as it has persisted since at least the third century. That most of the injunctions given in *Evel Rabbati* on conduct in the events of dying, death, burial, and mourning were reiterated in subsequent, much later mortuary manuals means that the conception of essential attitudes remained unchanged, fixed by fundamental, stable beliefs articulated around belief in the resurrection of the body.

While some customs in the mortuary ritual were lost over time, others made an appearance. But these later customs do not alter the basic stance toward the dead body that involves preserving its integrity while emphasizing its impurity. In this case, we must decide to what extent we endorse the hypothesis of a possible osmosis between the customs of the Jews and the population at large; and whether this would involve a reintegration of local customs through a prism that would make them acceptable or a straightforward absorption without the intervention of exegesis.

We shall see that the works of mortuary codification (despite a body of identical laws, rites, and customs) become quite distinct from one another over the course of time. The rituals of the seventeenth and eighteenth centuries studied below, then, will bear scarcely any resemblance to the tractate just presented. Variations will emerge not only in form but also in interpretation of the original text. These readings translate the cultural values of the period, the evolution of mentalities that reflect ways of life, scientific discoveries, and sociocultural interactions with the environment.

## THE HOUSE OF THE LIVING

In common parlance, the Jewish cemetery is given numerous designations, each with its own semantic nuances. In the Hebrew Bible, the cemetery is called the *beit kevarot* (the house of tombs): "the city, the place [in the Hebrew text, house] of my fathers."[36] Later the designation *beit olam* (the house of eternity), which appears in its Aramaic form, *beit almin,* in the commentaries, will be common usage in Hebrew as well as in Yiddish, but it can also be found in Ecclesiastes: "because man goes to his eternal home."[37] The phrase *beit moed le'khol ḥai* (the meetinghouse for all the living) is used in Job: "For I know that thou wilt bring me to death, and to the house appointed for all living."[38] In a more contemporary idiom, however, so as not to invite disaster, people employ euphemistic turns of phrase (which bear the mark of recent thinking), such as *beit ḥaim* (the house of the living, or the house of life) or, in Yiddish, *gute ort* (the good place).

The cemetery itself is a postbiblical institution. Until the talmudic period, tombs were installed on family-owned land or in the cellars and basements of dwelling places. As a general rule, prior to this period there were three kinds of burials that can be identified according to the custom followed. Hence, the *Jerusalomite* custom determines that the dead be placed in the basements of dwellings. According to the Palestinian custom, the dead are buried on family-owned land, while the Babylonian custom dictates interment of the body in open ground.

The marking of graves is mentioned in the Mishnah, but there it involves merely placing a whitewashed stone[39] (the *tsiyyun le-nefesh*) on the grave to signal the presence of a "soul." This marking, as far as we can tell from the evidence, served two purposes, both related to the impurity of the cadaver. First, it was proper to indicate to a *kohen*—a priest—that a corpse lay in a particular spot so that he could avoid it; second, the sign warned off any who would try to dig in this ground or walk on it. The whitewashed marker was renewed each year, even more frequently in cases in which it was effaced by seasonal rains. Funerary monuments and mausoleums dedicated to important persons are also frequently mentioned in the biblical and talmudic literature.

The cemetery as a communal site seems to have been the result of practical considerations (connected with the laws of purity) as well as the growing movement toward a separation of the universe of the living from the world of the dead. In the course of the talmudic period, the cemetery in effect became the site of superstition, the privileged place of demons. Thus, it becomes dangerous to the living, and the Talmud forbids passing through a cemetery at night.[40] Laws governing the separation of the realm of the dead were defined during this period. That the cemetery took formal shape at a distance from the town may well be due to the fear of resident demons. The minimal distance from the cemetery to the town is always specified in the texts: it must be fifty cubits from the nearest dwellings.[41] According to the Talmud, it must be guarded to protect against human and animal pillage, and this seems to be the origin of its surrounding enclosure.[42] The care taken with the cemetery was so assiduous that it was said at the time: "Jewish tombs are guarded more carefully than royal palaces."[43]

The first mention of funerary stele is found in Genesis, where reference is made to the monument Jacob erects on Rachel's tomb. The *matsevah* is often cited in biblical literature, but this funerary monument seems to be reserved for important persons. Detailed descriptions of tombs are also found in the book of the Maccabees, in which we find the decorated stele Simon the Hasmonean raised to his father and brothers.

Generally speaking, the headstone consisting of a simple tsiyyun lenefesh was a rather summary marker. It is specified in the Talmud, however, that any money left over from the cost of burial must be reserved for the erection of a monument, which should be engraved on a specific day, the fifteenth of Adar.[44] The Talmud also signals the existence of two types of monuments richer in ornamentation. One, the *nefesh* (lit. "soul"), is a closed construction with no opening; the other has an entrance leading to a room where a guard might have stayed.[45] In the course of the Hasmonean period, and perhaps under Greco-Roman influence, some imposing funerary monuments were erected (these are continually being discovered by archaeological excavations; the famous tomb of Jason in Jerusalem is one such monument). Yet already in this era ostentation in funerary matters prompted objections from religious authorities. Thus Rabbi Simeon ben Gamaliel declared: "One must not erect *nefashot* to the righteous, for their words are their memorial."[46]

Epitaphs on the headstones were rather laconic. As in the ossuaries, the name of the deceased appears, followed by the injunction not to open the tomb. The only mention of an epitaph found in the Talmud warns that "reading an inscription on a tomb" would be detrimental to study.[47] In fact, it seems that the epitaph was first formulated as a funeral eulogy. According to the biblical literature, the funeral lament seems to have been part of the ritual: "And he laid the body in his own grave; and they mourned over him, saying, 'Alas, my brother!'";[48] and again: "You will not conduct your mourning by crying 'Alas, the master,' and 'Alas, his majesty.'"[49] The tractate *Semaḥot* transcribes seemingly intact the funeral elegy pronounced by Rabbi Akiba at the burial of his son.[50] While we find numerous allusions to orations and funeral elegies accompanying the accounts of burials, the epitaphs as such are never mentioned, which would seem to indicate that they were not engraved.

The first Jewish epitaphs appear in the Italian catacombs. They date from between the second and sixth centuries C.E.. In Rome, Naples, and Venosa, certain Jewish inscriptions—in Greek or Latin—bear Hebrew words or characteristic symbols, such as the menorah or the lulav.[51] Their system of calendar dating combines the era of the creation of the world (maintained through the centuries) with the period of the destruction of the Temple (now in disuse). If we are to believe Ascoli,[52] the Jewish formulation of epitaphs is an abridged translation of oral elegies. The form and content of Christian epitaphs derive from Judaism, and the Christian epitaph, like the Jewish one, is the bearer of common pagan connotations.

With the emergence in Jewish texts of the notion of funerary space, the individual tombstone, and the dated epitaph, we have the three elements that define the "typical" Jewish cemetery of later periods. These cemeteries were set up slowly over the centuries and took their final form in the Middle Ages. Yet we know nothing of the constitution of ancient Jewish cemeteries. From the very first funerary spaces of the late Middle Ages, we have only fragmentary stones, such as the one from Narbonne, dated according to Moise Schwab's scholarly evaluation[53] as 24 November 687. The inscription is written in Latin and bears the doubtless much older Hebrew phrase, "Peace to Israel." Thanks to numerous fragmentary remnants found in Europe, it has been established that the Latin language was maintained in Jewish funerary inscriptions until the ninth century, and after this period it was increasingly supplanted by Hebrew. We might infer that after the Exile, Jews may have repudiated the use of the now "sacred" language of Hebrew to mark tombs—site of the impurity of the dead—and that they did this only when Latin became the official language of the Church. Nonetheless, the clumsiness in Hebrew usage would suggest that the Hebrew language had temporarily been forgotten and a cultural revival would be needed to renew it.

According to Joseph Derenbourg,[54] the definitive adoption of Hebrew on the headstones was linked to the confinement of Jews to their own communities, which led them, perhaps with some regret, to turn back to the sacred language. The hypothesis of a Jewish confinement at around the ninth century, however, hardly seems convincing in the light of the social situation in the European lands, especially in France. The flourishing of these communities would seem more relevant, especially in France and Germany, where rabbinic circles attained a degree of intellectual eminence and influence that left its distinctive mark on all of Judaism. And surely the use of the "sacred" language in epitaphs indicated the contribution of new conceptions of the duty of the living to the dead, specifically, a process of sanctification of the funerary space.

While there are enough funerary remnants scattered throughout Europe[55] to validate the hypothesis of the continuity of Jewish burial practices—an individual grave, headstone, and epitaph—there is, by contrast, no tangible trace of the Jewish cemetery before the eleventh century. The oldest all date back to this period, as do the texts of laws (whether pontifical, seigneurial, or charters of habitation) that indicate their existence, purchase, or destruction.

In the cemetery at Worms, considered the oldest surviving Jewish funerary space in Europe, the five oldest headstones date back to the eleventh century, as does the charter of residence accorded to the Jews of Speyer in 1084, which specifies,[56] "I give them for their cemetery a site that was Church property and to which they would preserve hereditary title." After the eleventh century, the Jewish cemetery is an objective given, a concept established as cultural fact to the extent that it is natural to offer Jews a burial site when they are welcomed into a city. The total absence of remnants or even mention of funerary space before this period is troubling, however, for while it is certain that beginning in the eleventh century the Jewish cemetery is present, organized, and accepted as a necessity, we know nothing of what preceded it.

The fragments of stones dating back to the late Middle Ages tell us nothing about the inception or disposition of funerary space. At best they authorize the hypothesis of a continuous tradition, though not without raising some questions. According to their epitaphs, it seems that these stelae were erected for community notables, and their location is unknown: they may have been on family lands, in open country, or in the center of town. With the exception of the Italian catacombs, which were not, as we know, exclusively reserved for Jews, there is no basis for answering these queries. For the period between the ninth and eleventh centuries, which has left no trace and leads us to the cemetery at Worms, one guess is as good as another.

All Jewish historians interested in this question have therefore postulated that sufficient evidence suggests the continuous presence of the European Jewish cemetery. But it may be equally plausible to advance the hypothesis that ordinary Jews were buried—not at the dump, as Gérard Nahon ironically puts it[57]—in funerary spaces shared by others and doubtless without the benefit of headstones, as was the custom in the *extra-muros* cemeteries of the late Middle Ages. I would suggest that the spread of Christianity among the peoples of the West ultimately led Jews to envision their own funerary space. By imposing stricter regulations and transferring the cemetery from outside the town (the ancient pagan necropolis) to the interior of the Church and its periphery, the Christians turned the cemetery into a funerary space that was increasingly sanctified. The result was that such burial places became both prohibited to Jews by the Christians and proscribed by the Jews themselves due to location and attendant rites. This hypothesis, which would account for the gaps in the source materials, can be further supported by a line of argument based on ritual. In fact, from the Jewish perspective, there was nothing to prevent the practice of burial in any kind of funerary field, as long as the prescribed ritual could be performed and as long as it was understood that in any case the cemetery was not in itself a sacred space.

From a strictly religious viewpoint, however, certain conditions had to be met. First, distance: "Remove carcasses, cadavers, and tanneries 25 meters from the town";[58] second, supervision.[59] There is no evidence to suggest that these two conditions were not fulfilled; we could therefore assume that there was no need for an exclusively Jewish burial ground. The idea of a funerary space shared by Jews and Christians later became unthinkable, due in part to Christians' increasing sense of the sacred, which extended to the bodies of the dead, and in part to irreconcilable differences regarding the conduct of the living at the cemetery.

If there were exclusively Jewish cemeteries throughout the late Middle Ages, how is it that there is no trace or mention of them? If fragments of headstones with Jewish symbols, a word or phrase in Hebrew, and some more extensive Hebrew texts are all that remain, should we conclude that these clearly indicate the presence of a "Jewish cemetery"? And in this case, would they have all been destroyed without a trace, even in the civic records?

Whether we accept or reject the hypothesis that Jews had been allowed burial in the extraurban cemeteries of the late Middle Ages, Jewish cemeteries could not suddenly have appeared in the eleventh century in such elaborate form. There must have been a progressive evolution of the notion of funerary space, accompanied by changes in the social condition of Jews. These modifications of the social fabric must have occurred between the ninth and eleventh centuries, a period spanning the appearance of Hebrew epitaphs in the catacombs and the existence of the cemetery itself. It is also possible that in the course of these two centuries, which correspond to the flourishing of rabbinic circles in Italy, Germany, and France, the ideas of Rabban Gamaliel with regard to funerary matters prevailed,[60] preceding those of Maimonides (1135–1204) and dictating that one must not erect headstones on the graves of the pious,[61] a notion that would explain their absence throughout this period.

While Ariès's formulation suggests that Christian death was definitively integrated into the "lap of the Church,"[62] the Jewish cemetery as a specific entity seems to be constituted only in the eleventh century—although its genesis remains unknown. And it would continue to exist in this spatially identical way until the opening of the great interfaith urban cemeteries at the end of the eighteenth century. Until then, however, there is not one text justifying residence of Jews in a place that does not grant them their own cemetery or authorizing them to be buried in the cemetery of a neighboring community. After the expulsion of the Jews, mention is also made of the destruction of their cemeteries, of the transfer of their cemeteries into pasturelands, or of the recycling of headstones. This was the case in Tours in 1359 and in

Perpignan in 1420, where headstones were put up for sale at public auctions.[63] From then on, Jewish residence would always be accompanied by the possession of a cemetery, and this would become one of the determining and essential factors of community definition.

## GREGORY AND PRISCUS

Jewish funerary space provides ample evidence of the modifications that took place between the ninth and eleventh centuries and were translated by the shift from the catacombs—an enclosed place common to Jews and Christians—to the cemetery—an open but unshared space. And we may well wonder whether this mutation was due to transformations that specifically affected relations between the living and the dead, or whether it also reflected transformations in the relations between Christians and Jews in the social world of the living. What actually happened between the ninth and eleventh centuries? What rupture occurred that might suggest a mortuary district shared by Christians and Jews had been possible until that moment and inconceivable afterward?

On the Christian side, this process of rupture coincided with the incursion of the Church into the lower ranks of the population. Texts from the late Middle Ages concerning the Jews are indeed rather scarce, but those we have bear witness as a whole to the Jews' integration into medieval society. Furthermore, these texts indicate a certain sympathy for the Jews that even seemed to generate some confusion between Christian and Jewish faiths. Council decisions from the fifth and sixth centuries attempt to alert Christians to guard against the influence of the Jews. They prohibit clerics and lay people from eating in Jewish company, take a stand against mixed marriages, warn of the danger of the observance of sabbath interdictions (on Sundays), and forbid Jews to mingle in Christian crowds during the Easter holidays.[64] These prohibitions were obviously meant to hinder current practices—otherwise they would not have been necessary. So we might simply reverse them to get some idea of the relations between Jews and Christians in the sixth century.

As they appear in the chronicles of Gregory of Tours[65] at the end of the sixth century, the Jews are well integrated into gentile society: they have typically Gallo-Roman names (Priscus, Armentaire, Julius, Gaudiocus); they bear arms and are welcome in the company of noblemen and even the king; they are often wealthy merchants and great travelers. When the bishop discusses theology with the Jew Priscus (Book 6), the man answers him on an equal footing, without fear of expressing his doubts about the legitimacy of the basic tenets of Christianity. Certainly, Gregory of Tours studs his narrative with a few pejorative qualifiers (race of unbelievers, treacherous nation, etc.), but his general attitude toward Jews is not hostile, and while he may be surprised by their unbelief he is not at all outraged. According to Anchel, the Jews of France even used the vernacular in religious services.[66]

In the ninth century, we have the anti-Jewish epistles of the archbishop of Lyon, Agobard, who, even as he testifies to the misdeeds committed by Jews, informs us of their influence and their privileged status in his city. He protests in particular against Jews and Christians sharing earthly and spiritual nourishment. Certain Christians, whom he qualifies as "ignorant," even go so far as to claim that Jews would make better preachers than the priests. Others share the Jews' sabbath meal and profane Sunday. Christian women work in Jewish homes, sometimes allowing themselves to be led astray. And, worse still, some see the Jews as God's chosen people and grant them the merit of observing a purer religion.[67]

It seems from these two examples that for the Christian population, Jews did not yet represent objects of horror or dread. In the Carolingian empire, the mixing of Jews and Christians appears to have been extensive and well accepted. The absence of documentary evidence of their encounters similarly bears witness to a peaceful life. The coexistence and conviviality that seem to have prevailed attest to a fluid social fabric still in the making. Yet we must not deceive ourselves about the numerical value of Jews in the heart of the European populace. In fact, we do not have access to any precise statistics on their numbers until the twelfth century. These are so few, however, that normal demographic growth would suggest the population would have been much smaller four centuries earlier. When speaking of "Jews" before the eleventh century, then, people are not referring to a clearly defined group but rather to individuals.[68] When people begin to evoke the Jews as "communities," they are implementing a political concept of social organization. And the emergence of Jewish cemeteries in the eleventh century can be considered the sign of this organization of Jewish communal entities in the feudal world.

While the text evoked[69] by the charter granting residence to Jews in the city of Speyer informs us that they will be accorded a cemetery, it also suggests that the Jews henceforth constitute a legal unity. Indeed, it says that

> in addition, as the ruler of the city judges the affairs of citizens, so the supreme authority of the synagogue would be charged with pronouncing judgment on all affairs arising among the Jews or involving them. . . . They would have responsibility, only within their own quarters, for [maintaining] fortifications, providing guard duty at night, and watchmen.

These clauses, articulated in these terms, seem to contain the germ of medieval community management. Elsewhere we can observe that Jewish "quarters" appeared simultaneously in various towns. They have been verified in Ratisbonne between 1006 and 1028, in Cologne between 1056 and 1075, in Worms in 1080, and in Nîmes between 1080 and 1096.[70]

It can be determined, then, that the emergence of the exclusively Jewish burial ground is inscribed in a more general process of differentiation that dates from around the year 1000. The Jewish community was established during the period when the European city was similarly taking shape through a more hierarchical ranking of social relations that became institutionalized in the feudal system.

CHAPTER TWO

# A Distinctive History

## *Specific Perceptions*

### THE YEAR 1000

Favorable conditions prevailed while the European Jewish communities coalesced as part of the social fabric, and Jewish groups spread out from France along the Rhine, reaching as far as Prague. For this geographic area, Judaism is chiefly considered to be "Franco-German." From England through the German lands and Bohemia and into Poland, we can find the French language in the glosses of the most eminent rabbis of the period.[1]

The era of the Crusades left a definitive stamp on the image and condition of the Jews. Even when committed by foreign hordes, the massacres that marked the path of the Crusaders, notably in the Rhineland, must have contributed to solidifying the paradigmatic image of the Jew as "infidel," "heretic," and "miscreant," while considerably undermining his social status. These massacres created a need for protection among the Jews that would indeed have grave consequences for their place in medieval society. Moreover, notions of the Jewish nation as "Christ-killers"—deicides—were created and disseminated by catechesis: accusations of ritual murder, of profanation of the host, and so on, would contribute, through the religious theater and mystery plays, to spreading animosity and a newly awakened hatred throughout the lower ranks of Christian society. If Jean Delumeau[2] finds it difficult to determine the role played by the Church in the explosions of violence against Jews committed in its name, he nonetheless notes in the stories of these accusations the corollary development of the cult of the "holy sacrament," which, along with the belief in transubstantiation, was specifically responsible for accusations concerning profanation of the host. Whatever the subsequent attitude of the Church, it would not succeed in restraining the reactions of its flock. When the "Golden Bull" promulgated by Emperor Frederick II in 1236, followed by the Bull of Pope Innocent III, attempted to absolve the Jews of ritual murder, it met with little success. These accusations would emerge with regularity in an almost cyclical fashion and would pave the way for the cults and confirmation of new saints.

These new conditions, which were certainly ideological but also economic and demographic, as Fernand Braudel has pointed out,[3] would provide the backdrop to which the trials of the Talmud and the epidemics of the Black Plague would add the finishing touches. Thereafter, the myth of the Jew as an "instrument of Satan" would reach its height, provoking a series of chain reactions: a variety of accusations followed by massacres and sporadic expulsions. In addition, to put an end to the general mingling that prevailed among Christians and Jews until the thirteenth century, measures of sartorial discrimination would be enacted against the Jews: the wearing of the yellow badge would be imposed to discourage mixed marriages and sexual relations between members of the two religions. Hatred of Jews would eventually reach such convulsive proportions that they would be expelled from England, then from France, putting an end to the period of "Franco-German" Judaism.

With its extinction, the cultural seat of European Jewry shifted progressively eastward. One group of French Jews reassembled and joined the Jews in the south of France; another distributed itself between Spain and Italy, thus joining the other cultural pole of Mediterranean Jewry. Those who came to swell the ranks of the "German" Jews would form with them a new cultural entity, henceforth known as Ashkenazi, in contrast to the Jews of the Iberian peninsula and the south of France. The Ashkenazi communities would constitute the Jews of the German lands. The juridical, political, and social condition of these Jews was subsequently of the utmost importance in the formation of Jewish community institutions and burial societies and, by extension, in defining the relation to death of Jews within this environment.

## UNDER PRINCELY LAW: FROM ARMOR TO THE YELLOW BADGE

Guido Kisch has devoted a major study to the books of laws and judicial decisions published in great numbers in the regions and provinces of the German lands.[4] He has demonstrated that these books shed light on the conditions of medieval life with respect not only to prevailing laws but also to the development of thought and the social life of individuals. Most of these codices concern the condition of the Jews, and if they offer precise data on their legal status, they also reveal how medieval Germans envisaged their relations with Jews and to what extent their attitudes coincided with contemporary ideas on this subject. One of Kisch's main points is that the juridical conception and historical basis of Jewish legal status were matters dealt with by jurists who were experts in medieval law.

The legal treatment of Jews varied according to time and place, as these materials accurately reflect. Some of them adopt or imitate the laws elaborated by the Canon with regard to the Jews, as is the case in southern Germany, while in others no trace of ecclesiastical influence can be found.[5] Among these books is the *Meissener Rechtsbuch,* which spread from Meissen to Thuringia, into part of Silesia, and especially into Bohemia and Moravia (an entire chapter is reserved for the Jews of this region).[6] Taking account of Jewish laws, it assimilates princely charters such as that of the Polish king, Casimir the Great.[7] Of all the books of Germanic law, it is certainly the most benevolent with regard to Jews, considering that "as subjects, they [ministerial officials] must legally treat the poor as they do the rich, the foreigner as they do the citizen, Jews as they do Christians."[8] Particular arrangements are made for offering Jews special legal protection, motivated by regard for their religious feelings and their institutions. Among these we find a paragraph establishing that no Christian can force a Jew to pay his wages "on festival days"[9] and that the sanctity of cemeteries and synagogues is placed under special protection of the penal law.[10] It is specified as well that in case of danger, Jews must receive aid from their Christian neighbors.[11] These measures show that the writers are not unmindful of anti-Jewish sentiment, which is why all possible cases of ritual murder are foreseen, even though anti-Jewish laws are quite moderate.[12]

As we have seen in the text of the charter of Speyer,[13] Jewish communities maintained their laws and their rabbinical courts throughout the Middle Ages. Subsequently, the clauses pointing in the direction of Jewish autonomy are integrated into all the law books, and the *Meissener Rechtsbuch* remains the most explicit on this subject. It specifies that except in certain cases, "the Jews must not accept any judgment or accusation elsewhere than in the *Shul,* or in front of the *Shul.*" It seems that in the fourteenth century, then, the power of the community was reinforced by the attitude of jurists and of Christian courts, which encouraged and favored Jewish autonomy.[14]

Arrangements concerning the public peace are of special interest to Jews in terms of their security. After the explosion of violence that followed the First Crusade, jurists determined that the Jews needed special protection. In the *Sachsenspiegel,*[15] as well as in the works it inspired, Jews appear among the *homines minus potentes*. Protection is extended to all Jews without distinction of locale or community; Jewish persons and property are thus placed under permanent protection. Violence against them is considered a breach of the public peace and severely condemned. Again, according to the *Sachsenspiegel,* anyone who violates this protection risks beheading.[16]

Yet it is in the chapter devoted to the right to bear arms that the Jews' progressive loss of status is most clearly expressed. The right to bear arms is based on the public right of the individual, but it is also a right that issues from membership in a social group, in a political entity, in a feudal society or judicial district. And it establishes a honorific right to participate in certain institutions. In the medieval state, the right to bear arms indicates that the possessors of that right have a superior status, and this right is closely bound to the concept of honor—hence withheld from outcasts or marginal persons. For those who have the privilege, this right implies in return a whole series of civic duties having to do with military obligations defined by the *Gerichtsfolge*. In the *Schwabenspiegel* this duty still involves the Jews, but its formulation suggests the reduction of their legal status: "Clerics, women, beadles, shepherds, and Jews must not participate personally in campaigns against the enemy, but they must contribute to these, whether by sending substitutes or by material participation."[17] In the *Sachsenspiegel* the first four categories are cited, but Jews are not included, which indicates that they were not exempt and could still bear arms.[18]

The bearing of arms is also mentioned in the Hebrew literature. In his narratives of the First Crusade, the anonymous author of Darmstadt recounts that Jews killed each other with their own swords so as not to fall into the hands of the Crusaders.[19] In addition, Solomon ben Samson recounts that in one town (which is generally identified as either Prague or Halle), the prince sent a thousand armed knights to fight against the Crusaders alongside five hundred Jews of the city who were armed as well.[20] This clarifies the pronouncement of Rabbi Isaac ben Moses of Vienna, in his *Or Zarua,* in which he stresses that it is not good for Jews to carry swords on the sabbath. He specifies that in Bohemia, Jews do not obey the (Jewish) law and remain armed on that day but that this is authorized in case of danger or when one must guard the city.[21] Rabbi Eliezer ben Yehuda of Worms describes the siege of Worms, during which Jews were authorized to remain armed, even on the sabbath.[22] Rabbi Meir of Rothenburg mentions in one of his responsa that some Jews pawned their arms and iron cuirasses.[23] Bernard Blumenkranz similarly verifies the participation of Jews in the military conflicts of the countries where they lived, in particular in the conflict at Zagragos (or Zallala) in 1086, "where an entire Jewish army, 40,000 men strong, it seems, fought in force on the side of Alphonse IV, while the Moslem army they confronted counted an equal number of Jews in its ranks."[24] In this case he stresses the Jews' lack of a particular political allegiance.

In the course of the thirteenth century the law prohibited Jews from bearing arms, but, in contrast to a similar law regarding the peasantry, no punishment was specified in case of infraction. In the early medieval period, Jews, like all citizens of towns, were subject to military duties: they were required to take part in guard duty and combat and to aid in fortification efforts and digging trenches. If we consider that riding a horse was common practice at the time, Moritz Güdemann's suggestion that Jews participated in feudal tournaments seems entirely plausible.[25]

The exclusion of Jews from the right to bear arms followed the same evolution as the exclusion of the peasantry but spanned a period of about one hundred twenty years. It was completed, according to reasonable estimates, by around 1103, when for the first time Jews as well as other social groups were placed under the ordinance of special protection, the "Territorial Peace of Mainz." This kind of protection would be a double-edged sword: protected by the law, their right to self-defense would become superfluous, and they would be prohibited from bearing arms. For the Jews to continue to arm themselves would therefore have meant the renunciation of this offer of special protection. This would explain why by the Second Crusade (mid-twelfth century) Jews took refuge in castles and fortresses and why we find no mention of the fact that they were armed.

Jews and clerics are included in the same category. But while clerics incur excommunication or eviction from their ecclesiastical order for bearing arms, in the case of the Jews the matter is posed in different terms. The law signals degradation according to the medieval code of honor, as expressed by the statements of Johan von Buch in his gloss on the *Sachsenspiegel*: "Let us affirm here one great difference: arms are forbidden to priests for the sake of their honor; and forbidden to the Jews because of their dishonor."[26] Thereafter, the juridical character of the protection of Jews was modified, for they had ceased to be full members of society. Consequently, the notion of extending protection to a social group in its entirety resulted not in the augmentation of the security of that group but, as the effect of a paradoxical historical mechanism, in its degradation.

From the time of the First Crusade, the cultural and social integration of Jews was reversed by a mechanism of exclusion that would be realized, locally and progressively, in the fourteenth and fifteenth centuries. The increasing incorporation of the Roman Canon into the legal system and into social attitudes as well would complete the social debasement of Jews. The result was their enclosure in communal autonomy, and this affected not only the way they were perceived externally but their internal functioning as well.

## THE JEWISH MARTYR

From the moment of rupture provoked by the Crusades, Jewish attitudes would undergo a change, as much in relation to the surrounding society as in Jews' own vision of their condition. Perhaps the most obvious of these changes would be translated into new contributions in the religious realm, particularly in the liturgy. These modifications initiated a process that would extend over several centuries, resurging during persecutions and becoming concrete in the fifteenth century in the writing of Joseph ha-Cohen, who would choose to define the history of the Jews as "The Vale of Tears" (*emek ha-Bakha*).[27] History becomes martyrology for the Jews because persecutions became an integral part of their life cycle and because martyrdom became one of the characteristic features of the Ashkenazi communities.

Although the Jews took pride in them, their martyrs did not have the same spiritual attributes as their Christian counterparts. The Jewish martyr was not considered holy and moreover was rarely an isolated individual. Generally entire communities perished by fire or sword, and the martyr was therefore a communal fact. To die as a Jew means, then, that one dies for the sanctification of the Name (*Kiddush ha-Shem*) after refusing final conversion. This new conception of medieval Jewish behavior is illustrated by the liturgy and reflects unexpected transformations in the mentalities of Ashkenazi Jews.

Grafting this onto the ancient tradition of collective suicide, medieval Jews identified their fate with the inhabitants of Masada;[28] in the event of assault and attempts at forced conversion, they glorified the attitude of Hannah,[29] who preferred to sacrifice her children one by one with her own hands rather than abandon them to a non-Jewish life. For medieval German Jews, conversion was the worst choice, and they no longer imagined this as a verbal conversion that would allow them to save their lives in a pinch and then either openly or secretly recant. If "Marranism" was not a temptation, this was because they valorized death as martyrdom, just as the early Christians did, reckoning that the blood of their dead would rest on the heads of the responsible parties. Death awaited them in any event, should they not surrender, and in this case they preferred to embrace it themselves rather than submit to the enemy's sword.

Collections of medieval prayers would henceforth include the blessings recited before embracing death or administering it to family members. These prayers were integrated into the *siddur* (the collection of daily rituals), where they stand side by side with the blessings before and after the meal. The idea of death became part of daily life to such a degree that it far surpassed the moment of imminent danger and became simply a conception of the daily life of medieval Jewry.

To keep alive the memory of communal tragedies, religious chants would be composed, such as the *Seliḥot* (penitential prayers, which smuggle in the note of hope) and the *kinot* (bitter lamentations). The purpose of these prayers is to express the desire for vengeance as well as the refusal to forget by recalling the names and communities of martyrs. Henceforth memory becomes an essential element of Jewish culture,[30] while simultaneously another mnemonic procedure is initiated which consists of buying back the sins of the dead with the religious acts of their descendants. In addition, messianic hopes were intensified; and messianic poems express the view that if there is no hope of immediate vengeance, it will be meted out when the heavenly realm is realized on earth. The ninth of Av, the anniversary of the destruction of the Temple that is observed by a solemn day of mourning and fasting, would henceforth take on enormous symbolic value, inscribing the privileged place of this new liturgy in Ashkenazi ritual.

## REMEMBER!

The appearance of the Memorbuch (Book of Remembrance) is the perfect illustration of the importance attached to remembrance. It would constitute one of the local collections of prayers in Central European communities and generally consisted of three parts: (1) common prayers recited before the Ark at the blowing of the Shofar, the reading of the Book of Esther, and so on;[31] (2) a necrology of important persons, either members of the community or Jews in general; (3) a martyrology of people and places where catastrophic events occurred.

After the massacres in the Rhineland at the time of the First Crusade, it became customary to read the list of names of victims of the persecutions. Subsequently, the names of those massacred by Rhindfleisch[32] were added to the list, and then the names of the deceased formed the litany of every subsequent tragedy. We find here, for example, the names of victims of the persecutions that followed the Black Plague epidemic of 1348–1349. It was customary to read the enumeration during the sabbath preceding the holiday of Shavuʾot[33] (the anniversary of the First Crusade). Included are several thousand names of individuals, all of whom died in tragic circumstances. This day would later be replaced by the ninth of Av, symbolizing all persecutions. In the fourteenth century, Rabbi Jacob Moellin, the Maharil,[34] declared the reading of this martyrology obligatory for the Rhineland communities where it had occurred, while others might confine themselves to recalling the list of their own localities.

*Memorbücher* all seem to be based on the same model; it is likely, then, that the book of the community of Mainz served as a reference for the later copies, although another hypothesis posits the Nuremburg book as the original work.[35] Throughout the Middle Ages, Memorbücher would include the names of victims of the massacres at Mecklenburg in 1492 and at Brandenburg in 1510; then those committed by the hordes at Chmelniecki in the Ukraine in 1648. In the course of the seventeenth and eighteenth centuries, the Memorbuch would be endlessly recopied. We can confirm, however, that to the list of victims in the *Kiddush ha-Shem* (those who died for the sanctification of the Name) were gradually added local necrologies and prayers that were equally local in origin and custom. The Memorbuch, or *Yizker-bukh* in Yiddish, translates much more than a simple dramatic litany; it becomes the communities' mnemonic device par excellence, gathering to itself all the local particularities of the Jews. However, while the oldest Memorbuch (with the exception of the one from Mainz) dates back to 1600, it was especially between 1650 and 1750, with the establishment of new communities, that these books proliferated. The Book of Remembrance, then, reflects the religious life of its community and follows it in its migratory wanderings: the Viennese refugees of 1670 brought theirs with them to Furth, where they found protection; those from Fulda brought theirs to Amsterdam in 1671.

## PANEGYRIC OF BITTERNESS

The practice of reciting commemorative prayers in honor of the dead is a very old one. It is already mentioned in the "Book of the Maccabees" during the Hasmonean Wars (165 B.C.E.), in which the narrative specifies that Judah Maccabee and his men recited prayers for the souls of their companions who died in combat and carried offerings to the Temple in Jerusalem to redeem the sins of the dead.[36]

Two marble tablets have been found on the island of Delos which date from the second century C.E. and bear the inscription of a prayer beseeching vengeance for the murder of two girls, Heraklea and Marinea; "The God of Gods and all beings" is called upon to avenge the innocent blood spilled on the day (evidently Yom Kippur, the Day of Atonement) "when everyone is occupied in fasting and supplication."[37] If we suppose that the death of these girls was commemorated on this particular day, it would not have been done exclusively for them, and the names of other murdered members of the community must have been recited as well. Yet, while the Aggadic literature makes frequent mention of commemorative prayers associated with the belief that the merits of the descendants can redeem the sins of the dead,[38] it is especially in the Ashkenazi ritual that commemorative prayer becomes central.

The liturgy involving the *hazkarat neshamot* (recall of souls) takes its full meaning from the Crusades. Although it was sporadically revived during the following centuries, its primary meaning was reactualized in the seventeenth century, when Jews once more died by the thousands in the course of persecutions. They were inscribed in the *Yizker-bikher* and the custom arose of commemorating the dead after the Torah reading and during the morning service on Yom Kippur and the three pilgrimage festivals. The essential part of this service begins with these words: "Let God remember . . . the soul of . . ." (Yizkor Elohim). The practice dictates, even in our day, that those whose parents are still living should leave the sanctuary of the synagogue when this prayer is recited in order to mark their difference from those who are recalling to God the names of their dead.

The second element of the commemorative liturgy that owes its development to the Crusades is the Mourners' Kaddish. An integral part of the daily liturgy, the Kaddish is recited either in its entirety at the conclusion of the service or in shortened form in all the services, morning, afternoon, and evening. The Kaddish appears for the first time as a daily prayer in the tractate *Soferim*.[39] In the *Maḥzor of Vitry* (twelfth century), a collection of all the prayers of its time for holidays and events of the life cycle—circumcisions, marriages, divorces, death, and mourning—the Kaddish is not an integral part of the mourning liturgy.[40] It is mentioned in the *Sefer Ḥasidim*[41] when Abba Saul ben Batnit asks a Jew who is dying to teach his son to recite it, but it seems to be codified in the mortuary liturgy only in the thirteenth century, at the time of the persecutions in the German lands.

The Kaddish is characterized by its abundance of blessings and glorifications of the name of God but especially—and this is what makes it the central prayer of mourning—by its explicit mention of the resurrection of the dead. It was traditionally part of the funeral liturgy: recited during burial, then included in the specific ritual of mourning, it invokes a reaffirmation of faith at the very moment of divine judgment.[42] Furthermore, it was recited daily during the eleven months following the burial of a parent, as well as on the anniversary of the parent's death (*yahrzeit*). In the Ashkenazi imagination, the Kaddish is intimately linked to the idea of death, so much so that in Yiddish, a model of popular language, the son is called the *kaddish,* and the current expression describing someone who dies without a son is that he died "without leaving a *kaddish*."[43] In this sense, the male child who recites this prayer for his parents takes responsibility for their sojourn in the realm of death and consequently for their resurrection in the world to come, the Olam ha-Ba.

This role attributed to the male child has deep roots in Midrashic literature and was revived in popular literature during the Middle Ages, as the following anecdote illustrates. It happened in the time of Rabbi Akiba that a man sinned with a girl on the day of Yom Kippur. As this girl was already promised in marriage, it was the equivalent of adultery. He was therefore stoned to death. Rabbi Akiba, traveling through this region, met a strange creature on the road bearing a burden so heavy no ass or camel could have carried it. To the rabbi's questions, the creature responded that he was from the other world and that because of his sins he was condemned to bear this burden of wood and burn with it three times daily until the end of time. Only a Kaddish recited by a son, if he had one, could save him. After some investigation

Rabbi Akiba discovered that he had indeed left a son, whom the community had refused to circumcise because of his father's sins. He took charge of the young man, had him circumcised, and taught him the Torah. When at last the son succeeded in reciting the Kaddish and those assembled in the synagogue had responded, the result was immediate: the father was transported from Hell to Paradise, so the story goes.[44]

Another prayer for the dead was introduced into Ashkenazi ritual as well. Originally, the *El Male Raḥamim* (God is merciful) was recited in memory of the victims of the Crusades and the massacres at Chmelniecki. Numerous versions exist which are utilized for the funeral service, for the anniversary of someone's death, and for prayers at the graveside, especially on the ninth of Av. In the Ashkenazi rite, the *El Male Raḥamim* is also part of the Yizkor service of Yom Kippur. A musical version of this prayer entered the practice of these communities and even became the symbolic center of the funerary ritual, nearly rivaling the Kaddish.

## REPENTANCE

From the time that death and its attendant rituals were inscribed in the most anodyne acts of daily life, accompanying the shifts in attitude that took place in medieval Ashkenazi society, a new mystical current appeared which would become extremely popular. The pietistic movement of the Ḥasidim (the pious, known as the *Ḥasidei Ashkenaz*—unrelated to the Ḥasidic movement that arose in Poland in the eighteenth century) is defined by its founding text, the *Sefer Ḥasidim* (lit. Book of the Pious). The chief figure behind this text, Yehuda the Ḥasid,[45] has been compared by Fritz Isaac Baer[46] to Saint Francis of Assisi. Baer compares the conceptions of the *Sefer Ḥasidim* with those developed by the Clunist Reformation in the Roman Catholic West. Gershom Scholem[47] claims it is "undeniable" that these movements share "popular religious and social ideas"; according to him, the social philosophy of German Ḥasidism was influenced by the ideas of its monastic Christian surroundings. Scholem stresses "the blessed state of the martyrs and the transcendent splendor of the coming Redemption."[48] Following his exposition, three qualities define the *ḥasid*: "Ascetic renunciation of the things of this world; complete serenity of mind; and an altruism grounded in principle and driven to extremes."[49] This implies that the *ḥasid* must, above all, be able to surmount ridicule and humiliation, even death, while continuing to fulfill the divine commandments. This mystical articulation was responsible for the popularity of the concept of the *Kiddush ha-Shem* among Ashkenazi Jews and for the avowal that "For love of You we are daily put to death."[50] The *Sefer Ḥasidim* also specifies that all those who die for the sanctification of the Name are immediately transported to Gan Eden (the paradise of the Just).[51]

Why must the individual repent in his daily actions? The popular medieval literature of the Jews expresses this in parables: "Rabbi Eliezer says: 'Repent on the eve of your death,' but his disciples reply, 'How can anyone know the exact day of his death?' The rabbi continues: 'That is why each man must repent today, lest he die tomorrow. For no one can be sure, even in the final hour, of the moment of his death.'" So that the reader firmly grasps what is at stake, the *Maasebuch* insists on repeating Ecclesiastes, chapter 9, verse 8, "Let your garments be always white," and telling the following story. The king had told his liege lords that he was inviting them to a banquet without specifying the day or hour. The wise made immediate preparations and donned their most beautiful attire, while the foolish judged they would have time to make preparations later. The moment arrived, and the king sent for them instantly; the wise presented themselves in immaculate garb, and the foolish came in their soiled garments. The parable is meant to explain that death is a royal invitation, that repentance is represented by the immaculate appearance of the wise, and that the foolish remain in clothing soiled by their misdeeds at the moment of the supreme summons.[52]

Another aspect of Ḥasidism, the notion of penitence, had a strong influence on the concepts of Judaism. The thirteenth century witnessed the development of the idea of penitential penalties by both Christians and Jews. The *Sefer Ḥasidim* distinguishes four categories of punishments:[53]

*Teshuvat ha-baa* (immediate penitence), which concerns the fact that one has not taken the opportunity to avoid a sin previously committed;

*Teshuvat ha-gader* (preventive penitence), which is a system of prevention against occasions to sin;

*Teshuvat ha-mishkal* (penitence proportional to the sin), which considers that the sum of pleasure produced by a sin will be weighted in proportion to the penitence imposed;

*Teshuvat ha-katur* (supreme penitence of excision), which is the ultimate punishment for sins meriting "the extermination of the soul," which means being cut off from the community of men, for the soul retains its divine essence.

In practice, these penitential penalties led to ascetic "mortifications" of the flesh, which had previously been rare. The popular narratives are riddled with the punishments certain ḥasidim inflicted on themselves: sitting in the snow or ice in winter until they were taken in, and in summer exposing their bodies to ants and bees, or lying down to be trampled underfoot at the entrance to the synagogue, and so on.[54]

This system of penitence is elaborated as a function of an individual's estimate of human failure. It remains the personal responsibility of the penitent, like his death, for the sanctification of the Name. The pietistic movement nonetheless inaugurates the collective character of Jewish spiritual life by developing notions of isolation from the world; by religious regroupings along sectarian lines; by imposing the charismatic personality of the rabbi, director of consciences and lives; and by making conceptions of an ascetic model of the Christian type an integral part of Jewish mysticism.

CHAPTER THREE

# When the Specific Is the General Rule

## THE CASE OF PRAGUE

Death in itself is final; it has no history. The history of death would, in fact, consist only of the relations the living imagine they have with their dead. In keeping with the ideas of Norbert Élias, for whom "death is a problem of the living,"[1] it follows that if we wanted to attempt to articulate a history of death during a given period, that history would reflect only the certainties and doubts of the living, as well as the limitations of their culture and their scientific knowledge.

Generally, history of mentalities omits all mention of contemporaneous context, taking for granted that its general outlines are well known to everyone. Yet when dealing with the history of the Jews, which is usually unfamiliar in its particulars, recourse to context is inevitable, for their conceptions and their cultural models are inseparable from their history. To this end, I have decided to analyze Jewish funerary institutions in one representative community as a way of indexing the function and complexity of such institutions in the Ashkenazi world. For Jews, relations maintained with the dead were also determined by the possibilities offered to them by local authorities. Save for Halakhic rituals, the enjoyment of a local cemetery, for example, was an important prerogative, as were community buildings where Jews were allowed to prepare their dead for burial. Yet not every medieval Jewish community possessed its own cemetery or, of course, its own community center. These conditions were defined by the circumstances of their residence, in accordance with the legal "privileges" granted by the towns where they lived.

In feudal society, the condition of Jews was defined by their service to princes and kings. They are considered in the texts to be *servi camerae,* servants of the Chamber. This implies that their autonomy as a community was marked by an ambiguous judicial status. This particular condition was defined by Pope Innocent IV, then revised and adapted by different princes for their own uses. A communal book from Bohemia published under the title *Herewith the Rights of the Jews,* dated 1330–1340, lists those celebrated "privileges" that make this juridical notion quite explicit:

> No Christian may force a Jew to accept baptism; if one amongst them wishes voluntarily to become Christian, and his devotion is evident, then let no one prevent him.
>
> Let no one disturb them on their holy days, neither with sticks nor stones.
>
> If a Christian wounds a Jew, he must give twelve gold marks to the king, and twelve silver marks to the Jew, and over and above this he must pay the doctor's fees.
>
> If a Christian beats a Jew to death, let his punishment be commensurate and let his goods be allotted to the king.
>
> If a Jew wishes, in accordance with their beliefs to transport a dead Jew from one city to another [for burial], let him pay no customs duty, and if someone even so would force him to pay something, let him be punished as a thief.
>
> If a Christian profanes a Jewish cemetery, or if he digs up a grave, let him be condemned to death and his property allotted to the king.
>
> If someone performs a criminal act against a synagogue, let him give two livres to the Jewish Council.
>
> Let no one accuse them of imbibing human blood.[2]

What does the "service" of the Jews involve? The Jews benefit from certain kinds of legal protection, but their service is formulated in terms of their status as property of the court, in the image of a material possession retained by princes. In exchange, certain considerations must be extended to them, notably concerning their religious requirements. The document just cited indicates only religious requirements concerning funerary practices. It is tempting to infer, therefore, that the most singular feature of medieval Jews was their burial practice.

The final warning against accusations of ritual murder affords us a glimpse of the gap between law and punishment. Beginning in the thirteenth century, the Church launched a crusade against sorcery and heresy; from then on, accusations of blood libel proliferated against the

Jews. The thirteenth century is indeed the century in which the concept of the "diabolical Jew" was elaborated,[3] yet in the course of this period the Jews were defended as vigorously as possible by pontifical and royal authorities. Still, in the German lands massacres under various pretexts, such as the profanation of the host and the murder of children, were frequent and reached a height during the epidemic of the Black Plague that ravaged Europe in the years 1348–1349. On this subject, Jean Delumeau establishes that the massacre of Jews accused of poisoning wells sometimes preceded by several months the effective spread of the Black Death to the heart of a city.[4] Pope Clement VI, in a special bull, expressed surprise that responsibility for this epidemic was attributed to the Jews given that the plague raged in places where no Jews were to be found or where Jews were as much affected by it as Christians.[5] If the protection of these servants of the Chamber was real, it was nevertheless ineffective, as one chronicler, Pelzen, describes: "They had in fact burned alive two thousand of these unfortunates, and confiscated their property. At this period people behaved very cruelly toward the Jews all over Germany, and they burned them by the hundreds, accusing them of spreading the Black Plague."[6]

Jews perished by the thousands all over Europe. Whole communities, like those of Basel and Cologne, went up in flames; in Worms, the Jews set fire to their own quarter to preempt the populace. Elsewhere, as in Prague, they were subjected to humiliating conditions: Jewish men and women were obliged to wear distinctive garments and had to stay indoors during Easter and to suffer other such constraints.[7] Yet in 1357, the Jews of Prague received the right to carry the banner that would continue over the next several centuries to be the symbol of their autonomy, and, as shown in sixteenth-century engravings, the community would march with this banner through the streets on great occasions.[8]

In the year 1389, for reasons that are unclear, the Jewish community of Prague, like many others, was beset by tragedy.

> The houses of the Jews were broken into, their goods pillaged, the houses burned, and for two hours neither women nor children were spared and they laid waste to that unfortunate nation. They struck down several thousand: the mercy of good citizens saved a great number of small children, who were favored with baptism. The Jews are beset with calamities among the Christians.[9]

After this pogrom, Avigdor Kara[10] composed an elegy entitled *Et Kol ha-Tela'ah* (All the Trials), in which he recounts as eyewitness testimony the sad fate of his community. This text is integrated into the collection of the *Seliḥot* of Prague and is read every year on the day of Yom Kippur. Kara calls for divine vengeance and tells us that this pogrom began on Passover eve, under the pretext that Jewish children had thrown filth on a priest.[11] During this pogrom, the mob "freely ransacked the building at the site of our fathers' graves, they uncovered the remains of the dead and destroyed headstones."[12] Do these actions by the populace reflect the extreme singularity of Jewish cemeteries? Or is it that in the midst of a massacre, killing the living was not enough to assuage murderous passions which could only be satisfied by the desecration and pillaging of the cemetery?

While these facts are noteworthy, they do not provide us with an adequate picture of daily life among the Jews in Prague or of their relations with their Christian neighbors. Nor do they give us a sense of the possible cultural interactions between the two societies. This Judeo-Christian coexistence, with all its implications, both positive and negative, was self-defined by the history of the Prague community. One of its most essential features was the continuity of a Jewish presence throughout the Middle Ages; this locality can therefore serve as a reference point for a model of Jewish life uninterrupted by the rhythm of recurrent expulsions. It is not surprising, then, that during the period under consideration, the Jewish community in Prague constituted the most vibrant Jewish community in Central and Western Europe and in a way represented its capital. Prague is still a mythical city to many, with the Jews figuring among its notable aspects. And the central figure in a number of the narratives about Prague, the Maharal—the celebrated Rabbi Loew—remains in the contemporary imagination a Czech national treasure. Indeed, beginning in the medieval period, the Jews participated in the legendary history of Bohemia. They are part of this national imagination, not as foils but as actors. According to legends in books compiled by the chroniclers,[13] the arrival of Jews in Bohemia coincided with the formation of the state in the ninth century.

Princess Libuse, the mythic founder of the city of Prague, had a dream predicting that one day a group of people would arrive seeking asylum and protection in her principality. These people, her dream indicated, would affect the destiny of all her subjects by bringing them prosperity if they came to the wanderers' assistance. According to the narrative, on her deathbed she conveyed instructions to her son on this matter, and he passed them on to his successor. It was to this successor that Princess Libuse appeared, warning him that the moment for the realization of the prophecy had come. In these years, the Wendes invaded Lithuania and Moscovy and drove out their inhabitants, including a Jewish community that must have wandered a dozen years before arriving at the gates of Bohemia. They asked the prince for asylum, promising to become loyal subjects if they were welcomed. The prince, heeding the advice of Princess Libuse, granted them a part of the city situated on the left bank of the Moldau. Around the year 900, again according to legend, their numbers had outgrown this space, and they were allotted a quarter on the right bank in the "Old Town" of Prague, on the site that became the "Jewish Quarter."[14] A century later, another legend tells us, under the reign of Boleslav II, the Jews proved their patriotism by participating in a revolt led by the Bohemians, helping them to drive the pagans of Prague outside the city walls.[15] Another, older narrative affirms that the Christians massacred the Jews of Prague in 1140. One century later, around 1240–1241, when the German crusades reached Bohemia, King Wenzel armed the Jews and blocked the progress of the Crusaders, and a hundred Jews were killed.[16] Legend also feeds on commonplaces. Cosmas's commentary on the events of the year 1091 records this dialogue between the Moravian sovereign and King Wratislaw: "Nowhere else will you gain as much wealth as in the neighborhoods of Prague and in Wysserhad Street [the main street of the Jewish Quarter]. There live Jews who trade in gold and silver; here are to be found the richest slave traders in the whole world and the wealthiest money changers." After a pillaging of the Jewish quarter in 1098, he exclaims, "What incredible spoils were taken from these Jews; such riches hadn't been amassed even in Troy."[17]

The late medieval sources make only brief mention of the Jews and historical data are meager. As for Jewish sources from this period, they are nonexistent; those that may have existed were burned in the great conflagration of 1389, which destroyed documents, acts, various texts, even Torah scrolls.[18]

## MILITARY CONVULSIONS

Is the Jewish community of Prague an ideal type? The history of the states of Bohemia and Moravia is so singular and so troubled that in some ways it remains quite exceptional. The tribulations of the Moravian and Bohemian lands that began in the late 1300s buffeted all of Europe for two centuries and influenced all of Christianity to such an extent and so effectively that they merit a digression. Originally, the religious struggle of Jan Huss involved only the Church and the way of life of the clergy and the parish. He affirmed the principle that Christianity should not go beyond the values preached by the Gospel and consequently that ecclesiastical power could not be embodied by prelates who oversaw real or capital wealth. Ecclesiastical wealth, according to Huss, constituted a virtual turning away from the vocation of the Church. His preachings condemning the Church attracted a crowd of the poor to his pulpit at the Bethlehem chapel, where he enumerated the Church's exploitive ways:

> From cradle to grave the poor have been forced to pay priests and prelates for the baptism of a child, for marriage, for the blessing over eggs and salt, for intercessions with the Saints. . . . They pay for confession, burial, absolution, prayers. That swindler of a priest takes the last red cent the grandmother tied up in a corner of her kerchief for fear of brigands or thieves.[19]

When in 1412 Pope John XXIII sent legates to Bohemia to sell plenary indulgences to finance his war against Ladislas of Naples, Huss condemned what he considered to be a flagrant abuse. He was excommunicated and forced to leave Prague; the people took up arms to defend him. His presence in any city meant the suspension of all ceremonies of the Church there: no Masses, baptisms, marriages, or burials wherever he was given asylum. Summoned to the ecclesiastical Council of Constance, he was arrested, then remanded to the Inquisition. In July 1415, he was burned as a heretic. The Hussite epoch was about to begin.

The revolt led by those who claimed authority from Huss succeeded in rallying together in a single struggle social groups as disparate as the many peoples of Bohemia. Their motives, which led to the Hussite wars, were numerous and varied. They were united around a common hatred of the papacy, and that coupled with hatred of Slavs and Germans fueled the energies of ambitious lords, oppressed peasants, discontented itinerant knights, and rivalries of all sorts that prevailed in the towns between classes as well as nationalities. The suffering of Huss consecrated him as a saint and martyr: important popular gatherings took place on the hills, while preachers rose on all sides. The insurrection began in Prague: thousands of people, beggars and the poor, put to death members of the municipal council. The revolt spread to all quarters of the city where the insurgents rushed to the monasteries, drove out the monks, and confiscated their property. From that moment, every Hussite victory was marked by the confiscation of ecclesiastical holdings and the expulsion of Catholic priests. The set of demands for religious reforms was symbolized by the chalice, which defined communion in two forms and represented resistance to the Roman Catholic Church, to the clergy, and to the aristocracy.[20]

Two parties coexisted within the Hussite movement: the party of the severely deprived, beggars and serfs, who formed the most radical group and instituted a mode of communal life, claiming authority only from the Old Testament; and the party of the rich, the bourgeoisie and petty lords, who were more moderate and not necessarily committed to the absolute eradication of the Roman Church. Although they were rivals, they managed to agree on a truce so as to fight the Crusaders sent to defeat them. After a first victory, the moderate Calixtines (or Utraquists) armed themselves against the beggars and succeeded in dismantling the troops of Taborites and Chiliastics.[21] While they stifled the particular aspirations of the serfs, the Hussites continued nonetheless to symbolize the hope of a more just society for the poor, who still rallied to their side from all directions. They would go from victory to victory, operating beyond their borders where they were warmly welcomed by serfs and poor citizens, who in anticipation even expelled the local clergy and confiscated their goods.[22] The heresy thus gained ground, and the Hussites seemed to prevail in Bohemia.

Five times Rome sent armies against them, in vain. The Council of Basel, however, which opened a discussion on dogma and thereby seemed to ratify the Hussite movement in 1431, marked the beginning of its end. Indeed, while negotiations were pursued from Basel to Prague, the Calixtines rejoined the Catholic Church.[23] In 1434, at Lipany, the Hussite armies were defeated on the field of battle.

Yet while losing territory on the ground, the Hussites preserved the doctrinal advantage, which had far more impact than the annihilation of their troops. The Utraquist Catholic Church may have been recognized by the priesthood, but it represented only a tiny minority of Bohemians. It was open season on heresy, while rivalries once more raged in the towns. The essential modification, due to the Church's recognition, lay in the constitution of two Churches, one of which became Reformed. The differences between the Utraquist or Calixtine Church and the Roman Church were numerous and fundamental: the Utraquists united defiance of the pope with a rejection of beliefs in such things as purgatory and the intercession of saints. And they continued to reject monastic life as well as the use of Latin in the service.

Amid all these upheavals, what happened to the Jews caught in the civil war? It would seem likely that the Jews watched with a certain satisfaction as battles raged throughout the country against their old enemy, the Church. While the Jewish attitude toward Hussism has been the subject of many studies that need not be reviewed here,[24] several aspects of this attitude should be emphasized to establish, in a summary fashion, what sorts of relations were possible between the "unbelievers" and the "heretics."

The Jewish attitude toward the Hussites leads us into a recurrent debate among Jewish historians on the acceptance or rejection of the Jews by their host societies.[25] It seems clear that the Jews must have been concerned with struggles over religious freedom and thought; and this being the case, they would surely have taken the part of freedom. Situated at the epicenter of these persistent and frenetic struggles, which spared neither their quarters of town nor their houses, the Jews of Prague would have been hard put to maintain an indifferent neutrality.

Certain Hussite sects were accused of Judaizing. It seems that, indeed, many of the Hussites would have preferred conversion to Judaism to what they considered absolute apostasy or recantation: an acceptance of Roman Catholicism. One might suppose, as certain Jewish contemporaries of the Hussites did, that Judaism was but a short step from a theology claiming authority of the Old Testament, denying the Church any form of power, rejecting the idea of the celibacy of priests, and delegating the right to preach to those who seemed most able. Despite this, the Hussites remained, above all, Christians.

There are certain elements that suggest the active participation of the Bohemian Jews in the Hussite movement. As I have noted, the Hussites were accused of "Judaizing"—an accusation that was quite usual against Christian sects. According to the writings of an anonymous Jewish chronicler of 1470, however, Kara[26] was one of the favorites of the court of Wenceslas IV and a close associate of Huss. It was said that Kara's polemics on Judaism and Christianity may have inspired a number of Huss's theological principles.[27] Haïm Hillel Ben Sasson maintains that one of Kara's poems on the unity of God was used directly by Huss.[28] Whatever the case, the Jews were accused by the Catholics of providing weapons to the Hussites and were subjected to massacres and expulsions as measures of retaliation. They were expelled from Austria in 1421, from Bavaria in 1422, and from Jihlava in 1428. If this accusation cannot be verified, the Jewish records of

Prague attest nonetheless to the participation of Jews in the retrenchment efforts under Wysserhad in 1420. With such facts in mind, Jewish historians generally conclude that this participation was constrained rather than voluntary,[29] but the question cannot be settled definitively.

The Jewish literature is much concerned with Hussism, and its vagaries are closely followed and commented on by contemporary chroniclers as well as their successors.[30] On the Hussite side, we might take pause at the meaning of a treatise of the sort published by Jacobellus de Stibro, *De Usurae,* which appeared in 1414 and was applied to solving the Jewish problem. As a moderate Calixtine, the author preaches the assimilation of the Jews by means of their economic emancipation. He suggests that they should be made to participate directly in productive labor, such as agriculture, animal husbandry, or cottage industries of some sort. From his point of view, this would be the best way of dispelling the popular jealousy of the Jews that leads to pogroms. These theories virtually prefigure those usually advanced by the philosophes of the eighteenth century.[31] But the shift from theory to practice was not made, and these exhortations proved to be a dead end.

The attitude of the rabbis toward Hussism seems to be sympathetic: the most eminent rabbinical authorities of the era were deeply engaged in their relations with the Christians. Judeo-Christian polemics were quite common. Through the responsa of personalities such as Israel Isserlein,[32] Israel Bruna,[33] Jacob Weil,[34] and especially Yom Tov Lipman Mülhausen,[35] it seems that the philosophical or theological aspects of Hussism were addressed by the Jews and, moreover, that this movement seemed to inspire hopes for the future.

With the crushing of the Hussite movement these hopes were dashed. Yet at the dawn of the Renaissance, considered the "golden age" of the Prague community,[36] the dialogue between Jews and Christians was well established. Cultural and social interactions would contribute to the flowering of the community in a climate that seemed particularly favorable until the institution of a new political policy toward the Bohemian states.

The condition of the Prague Jews seems thus to have been inseparable from that of their fellow countrymen, the inhabitants of Bohemia. In a climate of religious and cultural turmoil, with various and complex ideas advocating the general amelioration of the human condition, the attitude toward the Jews and their relations with their Christian neighbors took a positive turn. By way of illustration, we could cite Konac of Hodislav,[37] a Calixtine who published a series of dialogues on the situation of Bohemia in which he defended confessional freedom for all, including radical reformists, Jews, and all non-Christians. From this time on, the Jews' relations with sectarians would be easier than with the adherents to the Counter-Reformation. In Bohemia, religious struggles would inevitably exacerbate national rivalries and political conflicts. The peace signed at Kutna Hora in 1485 for the first time guaranteed the confessional freedom of the two parties and proclaimed the principle of respect for individual faith. Religious freedom was still merely an empty concept, however, since the partisans of the most radical reforms were excluded from these accords. At the same time, political power totally slipped from the hands of the crown. The affairs of state were directed by the nobility and the towns. The noblemen shared all important functions; the Royal Council was dominated by the states, and religious conflicts were always sporadically in evidence. With the arrival of the Catholic nobility to the Diet, Catholic priests and monks once more took up residence in the towns, reopening the monasteries and convents. The religious peace was signed against a backdrop of rioting.

In sixteenth-century Bohemia, feudalism was still at its height. The nobility outranked not only the people but royalty as well. Without the agreement of the lords, the sovereign no longer had confiscated property at his disposal. Thus deprived of its most important resources, notably, of Jewish tithes,[38] the monarchy's power was dealt a harsh blow and lost the support of its natural allies; it was sovereignty in principle only. The clergy, whose possessions had been seized, had totally disappeared as a political entity. The guilds had also lost all power; trade with neighboring countries was hard hit by the breach in relations. In the towns, the expulsion of the Germans and the arrival of the lower classes in overwhelming numbers constituted "an irreparable blow to prosperity."[39] Religious conflicts were allied with ongoing struggles between the power of the towns and that of the nobility (who wanted to preserve their economic and political interests), and the royal cities were trying to preserve their privileges (deriving from a monopoly on cottage industries and trade) in opposition to the lords; in this extremely complex situation, the monarchy would once again be the loser. At this time the Diets controlled the crown and chose the king. The king wielded only such power as was granted him by the states. Furthermore, the king was bound to his realm by a "bilateral contract," which, while guaranteeing the privileges of the various classes, released the subjects from their oath of loyalty in case of an abuse of power. In this way the Diets of Bohemia held their king in absolute dependence. They voted on taxes and the administration of feudal properties, and through the jurisprudence of the Aulic Council they managed administrative power, economic goods, and the Jews.

When Ferdinand of Hapsburg was unsuccessful in his attempt to claim the crown, he had recourse to the decision of the Diets: he was elected only after accepting all conditions. He promised to maintain the "compactats," to name an archbishop to Prague who would respect its customs, to grant only Bohemians responsibilities of the realm, to maintain the privileges of all orders already established, and to suffer no confiscation of territory or reduction of tithes without the country's consent.[40] Despite these commitments, Ferdinand had other ideas about monarchy. He managed, after his election, to centralize the functions of the Diets and to consolidate royal power. As a fervent Catholic, he consolidated his dynasty's alliance with the Roman Church and succeeded in keeping the Turks outside the borders of his kingdom. Solidifying the agrarian system, he would even manage to turn the situation to his advantage by reversing the balance of political power, cutting the nobility down to size and once again limiting the power of the Diets to parliamentary and regional democracy.

When the Castle of Prague burned in 1541—and with it the country's archives containing all civic records—Ferdinand would ask the states to give up the system of free elections, forcing a recognition of his wife's hereditary right to the crown. At the same time he would take up residence in Vienna, issuing all orders of the Aulic Council from there, and would insidiously reinstate German as the administrative language. But elsewhere, despite Ferdinand's Catholicism, the Lutheran Reformation swept Bohemia, which became the seat of all religious uncertainties: "Beliefs varied from town to town, a multitude of nuances and interpretations established an uninterrupted chain between the orthodoxies of Rome and Wittenberg."[41] Was this due to the Lutheran Reformation? A rebellion was always brewing against the Hapsburgs. Ferdinand, ignoring the Diets, which refused to help him, allied himself with his brother Charles V to combat the Protestant states. An insurrection broke out in Prague, which considered itself released from its bilateral contract. The city's rather rapid surrender would mark the end of the quasi-"republic" of Prague; henceforth the king alone would reign. In a sweeping decision, he asked the town to remit to him all documents, arms, communal property, and city revenues. Autonomy was broken by the nomination of a royal officer who directed the police and presided over the council. After the execution of those accused of sedition, the benefits gained during the Hussite wars would be lost, and the towns, like the Diets, would be in thrall to the king. Assured of his political power, Ferdinand would try to reorganize the Catholic faith, with drastic results.

The divine service was suspended, and the hounded Utraquist priests took flight. The churches were closed. Meetings were forbidden, and the chief centers of the Unity of Czech Brothers reverted to the king. Their banishment occurred in 1548. Yet despite the influx of Jesuit brothers in 1556, the heresy was resurgent and more Lutheran than ever. Between 1552 and 1575, Bohemia swung completely toward Protestantism.[42] Despite Ferdinand's insistence, the pope refused to make any dogmatic concessions: the most common religious practices of the country would remain heretical.

The edict of 1602 ensured the triumph of the Catholics, and all nomination to the curacy not submitted to the archbishop was proscribed. Anyone suspected of heresy was stripped of his possessions, teachers were replaced by Jesuit priests, and all holidays and ceremonies of the Protestant cult were prohibited. The pastors could be expelled on any pretext. On ecclesiastical lands or lands belonging to Catholic lords, all the inhabitants were required to attend mass or vacate their living quarters. The right to burial in the cemetery was refused to all who had not received the last rites. This repression would extend to writings: printers received orders to refuse anything that came from Protestants. Municipal functions would be inaccessible to non-Catholics; to practice the professions of teacher, notary, physician, bookseller, or printer, among others, one had to accept whole cloth the dogmas and canons of the Roman Church.

Under the reign of Rudolph, Bohemia nonetheless underwent a considerable flowering. The reestablishment of the court in Prague gave a new boost to trade and industry as well as to all aspects of consumption and cultural life. The brotherhoods created in the fourteenth century intensified their activities and aided the spread of piety and instruction, an enhancement of the divine service, and the supervision of teaching. There were sixteen schools in Prague at this time.[43] A literary movement developed, books multiplied, numerous translations were published. At the university astronomy was the privileged discipline, and eminent personalities such as Tycho Brahe and Johannes Kepler were invited to lecture. Medicine developed as well: the first dissection was done in Prague by Cornelius Jansenius. In addition, the city witnessed the birth of linguistic studies: scholars collected popular proverbs and published dictionaries and grammars.[44] A law school opened, and while law became a scientific discipline, historians also gained serious recognition.

This cultural explosion was accompanied by a brilliant economic upsurge: foreign merchants took up residence in Prague, formed colonies, and received corporate privileges for the construction of synagogues and churches. This society, which could not have been more cosmopolitan,[45] was extremely lively, as the decree of sumptuary laws in 1618 attests: peasants and their wives were forbidden to wear fabrics of gold or silk, bright clothing, or "high top" boots.

The reign of Rudolph is often associated with legends that circulated about his person as well as his court. He was suspected of being mentally disturbed and of surrounding himself with alchemists, magicians, and enchanters of all sorts. Among these legends, the one about the "Maharal of Prague" has a privileged place. Rabbi Yehuda Loew was supposed to have had a secret meeting with Rudolph on 16 February 1592,[46] and though this cannot be verified, legends persist, nonetheless, in linking this meeting with the miraculous creation of the Golem.[47] According to Ernest Denis, superstition reigned supreme at the court, and the Hradschin was "the Eldorado of prestidigitators . . . inventors of marvelous potions." As for Rudolph, he "pursued the elixir of life and the philosopher's stone."[48] This is also the recorded period of witchcraft trials, the flourishing of cultural, scientific, and artistic life, the baroque era when indeed mythic Prague was at its height.

On the political level, however, things deteriorated for Rudolph. In 1606 his monarchical powers were ceded to his brother Matthias, because of "Rudolph's mental indisposition, which rendered him incapable of exercising authority."[49] The country immediately plunged back into civil war as Matthias promised to guarantee religious freedom. The *Majestat Rudolphina,* granted in the guise of a compromise, authorized non-Catholics to govern their own administrative centers, and indeed Catholics and Protestants were equally protected under the law; freedom of conscience seemed to be accepted. The king abdicated all religious authority to the states. In the wake of these events, the Reformists claimed the university and the consistory, and sects proliferated. There was widespread jubilation in Prague after the promulgation of the *Majestat,* but the Jesuits ordained forty hours uninterrupted, penitential prayer to "entreat the Lord to protect the Christian faith against the fatal project of the heretics."[50] Preachers harangued the crowds, while the ultra-Catholics renewed the decree stipulating that every member of the council, institutional director, and teacher must follow the procession of the Holy Sacrament.

In an attempt to reestablish his authority, Rudolph appealed to a foreign army. Once again the country was torn by the violence of political and religious strife. The end of Rudolph's reign triggered a cycle of insurrections, riots, and pillaging. The population rushed into the churches, shattered images, and massacred anyone who looked like a member of the clergy. Bands of beggars roamed the countryside, attacking and killing soldiers. While Protestants and Catholics were busy killing each other, the crown passed definitively to Matthias in 1611, and the court returned to Vienna. Prague had become a vassal city.

When Ferdinand of Styria assumed the throne, his aim was to reestablish the Roman Church. With the Catholics on the offensive, the Protestants became outlaws. The Evangelicals were insulted, their books were proscribed, Reformed chapels and cemeteries were confiscated. Children whose parents were married by pastors were declared bastards; orphans and non-Catholic children were raised by the Jesuits; people were obliged to attend Catholic ceremonies. Those who resisted were expelled or thrown into prison.[51] The priests condemned tolerance and refused absolution to those who attended the heretical cult; mixed marriages were forbidden. But the Protestants still formed the vast majority of the population, and numerous lords tried to free themselves from all dynastic subjugation. Moravia allied itself with the Bohemian states and drove out the Jesuits. The Confederation of Bohemian States committed itself to the mutual defense of the provinces, and aid was expected from the Reformed lands. The confrontation at "White Mountain" would return Frederick V and Ferdinand in quick succession, but while it was seen as a decisive victory over the heretics, it ensured the crushing of Protestantism in Bohemia. The war would spread throughout Europe.

The restoration of the Roman Catholic faith gave way to a virtual crusade launched by the priesthood. Volunteer priests from every part of Europe were sent into Bohemia. Germans, Belgians, Italians marched in: "The country is inundated by robes of every cut, by coats of every color, Augustinians, Carmelites, Barnabites, Dominicans, Servites, Franciscans."[52] All the Protestant churches were closed in 1622. After an eclipse of two centuries, the Latin language was reestablished in the service. The Jesuits, back in force, once more took possession of the university; henceforth they alone could teach in the schools of theology, and they would be chosen as professors of medicine and law as well. Rectors and chancellors would depend directly on the order's superiors. The Jesuits, then, were the masters, exercising censorship and inspecting booksellers and printers to verify that no prohibited texts were circulated.

Heretics would be hunted until the end of the reign of Maria Theresa, in accordance with a 1624 decree that "[forbade] the exercise of any religion other than the Catholic faith, not only in Prague but in the whole country."[53] All those who did not accept the ruling faith were declared outside the law. Citizenship was now granted only to Catholics, who alone had the right to practice the professions. Heretics would no longer have the right to marry and were subject to the confiscation of their property. In 1626, the Counter-Reformation was officially over. One year later, a decree directed the lords who refused conversion to leave the realm. Orphans or children under guardianship were handed over to the Jesuits and had no right to leave the country. In the years following, burghers, noblemen, and knights went into exile in great numbers, but this was not an option available to the common people, who had to convert, voluntarily or by force. While war continued to rage, the émigrés joined together in Reformist armies in an attempt to recover their families and their property. Yet all their offensives ended in defeat, for these troops, whose violence and pillaging made them no different from the papist armies, did not manage to gain popular support. In 1648 the Swedes were in Prague, in the neighborhoods of the Left Bank. When news of the peace reached the combatants, they fought under the Charles V bridge, which provided access to the Old Town. The peace treaty definitively settled the religious question, leaving Bohemia papal and Catholic under Hapsburg rule.

## JEWS AND CHRISTIANS

The religious wars had brought considerable change. The Jews were no longer the only miscreant people, sworn to exile. The numerous Christian sectarians had suffered their share of indignities and persecutions. While this shared fate led inevitably to a transformation in relations between Jews and Christians, it was also the price paid for sufferings commonly endured during the offensives of the Counter-Reformation.[54]

In sixteenth- and seventeenth-century Bohemia, the circumstances and aspirations of the Jews were clearly ambiguous, as can be seen from the conflicts and developments of this murky period. The Jews were deeply interested in the movements of Catholic reform, and no doubt some were eagerly searching for signs of the birth of the messianic era that would change the face of humanity. Yet their status as subjects particularly bound to the crown incited them to seek protection from the sovereign: the stronger his authority, the greater their guarantee of security. Under the reign of Rudolph, the community had also benefited from the general cultural and economic flowering, thanks in part to the "court Jew" of the period, Jacob Bassevi. Through him[55] the Jews of the empire had obtained the right to conduct trade in large and small goods, buy houses, name rabbis, establish synagogues, and purchase lands for their cemeteries.[56]

By European standards, Prague had become an important metropolis and cultural center, home to illustrious personalities and wealthy merchants; and for the Jews, Prague was a principal crossroads. It was a meeting place for Jews from Italy, Germany, Poland, and Hungary who settled there, temporarily or permanently, to study with Rabbi Loew or to tend to their business affairs. The Jews of Prague imported leather and furs, and they were also involved in the metals trade, particularly in silver. In 1585 they received authorization (which merely ratified a de facto practice) to enter the cottage industries. After this they practiced nearly all the civic trades, becoming not only businessmen but also furriers, tanners, silversmiths, and so on. The prosperity, indeed the extreme vitality of the Prague community, is exemplified by the figure of Marcus Sax Meisel. A rich merchant and burgomaster of the community, he obtained permission to build the city hall, two synagogues, and several houses and even to pave the main streets of the Jewish Quarter.[57]

During the period when the city of Prague was in conflict with the empire, the situation of the Jewish community remained more than ambiguous. The autonomy of the Judenstadt was preserved because the Jews depended on the jurisdiction of the king and not on the civic authorities. But the burghers continually tried to interfere in this particular governance. In the eyes of the common people, the Jewish Quarter seemed to conceal "an inestimable treasure";[58] social inequalities and consequently the extreme poverty of some were hidden from general view. The civic authorities, who were struggling with intractable financial problems, watched enviously as Jewish contributions fell directly into the imperial coffers, and rather than relinquish this treasure, they called unceasingly for the expulsion of the Jews.

Very few historians have specialized in the history of the Prague Jews, yet most of them, like Otto Muneles, assume that at the beginning of the seventeenth century anti-Jewish feeling was ubiquitous. Yet David Ganz testifies at the end of the sixteenth century that in no era were the Jews as well off, "nor had they found as much grace in their [the Christians'] eyes." He adds, however, that "we are among gentiles and strangers, residing with them."[59] Anti-Jewish feeling is one of those historical elements particularly difficult to evaluate because the criteria for defining a condition always perceived as a priori unfavorable to the Jews can be questioned without a flat denial of the situation.

During the Thirty Years' War the Jews were exclusively exempt from exactions for the soldiery, yet they did not escape so easily: "The States' army arrives; a disagreeable visit, and to amuse themselves in their free time the soldiers mistreat the inhabitants, loot Jewish shops, ransack the synagogue, spreading out through the surrounding villages, marauding, burning houses."[60] Given the complexity of this context, research into a specifically anti-Jewish sentiment would seem hazardous.

The social exclusion of the Jews can be defined on the basis of their geographic localization, as we read in this description of the ghetto by Muneles: "But the [Jewish] quarter . . . remains within its walls, with four gates, isolated from the rest of the world. These gates were closed if need be. Save in exceptional circumstances, Jews and Christians could freely enter and leave the ghetto."[61] Yet reading descriptions of medieval Prague, we realize it was composed of four distinct cities, each with its autonomous administration, special privileges, and high defensive enclosure. Prague was composed of the "Hradschin," the castle quarter; the "Mala Strana," the lower town, also called "The Little Way," extending along the Moldau and connected to the Old Town by the Charles bridge; the "Altstadt," the Old Town, capital of the realm; and the surrounding "New Town" created under Charles IV. Seen from this perspective, the Judenstadt, situated in the Old Town, with its autonomous administration, its special privileges, and its own defensive walls, was not so different from the other quarters that formed the city of Prague.

Considering the events that affected the life of the Jews in the course of the Thirty Years' War, we can see how they must have found themselves caught between rival parties and tried to use chance contingencies to ensure their security or derive advantages that might mitigate their situation. But during the whole period of the Counter-Reformation they were not the focus of attention: they were not the object of the religious wars, and the Church was more interested in its own dissidents than it was in the Jews. Yet in such an atmosphere of inquisitorial fanaticism, the Jews could not seem other than victims singled out for persecution. That the burghers continued to perceive them as special subjects of the Catholic Chamber while the Jesuits simply saw them as more potential candidates for forced conversion simply reinforced this perception.

Upon the election of the Calvinist Frederick V as head of the realm (in 1618), the Jews, like the burghers of Prague, were heavily taxed by the Palatine Elector, who was trying in his way to sustain his mercenary armies "without pay or sustenance."[62] Historians vary in their opinions on the effectiveness of this imposition: "The burghers and the Jews of Prague provided silver only with much ill will," Victor-Louis Tapie suggests.[63] Maurice Popper estimates that the Jews offered gifts to the king and accepted the imposed loan of 30,000 florins. In spite of this, one Friday evening when the Jews were at the synagogue, all their houses were pillaged. The Jews turned to Emperor Ferdinand, who wrote to the commander in chief of the armies to use the same consideration toward the Jews as toward the Christians of Bohemia. By virtue of this order, the Jewish Quarter would be spared during the sacking of Prague.[64] This fact is further attested to by Rabbi Yom Tov Lipman Heller, who composed two elegies commemorating the battle of White Mountain.[65] In the introductions he describes the causes of this battle and specifically says that the emperor protected the Jews from pillaging.[66] These *seliḥot,* which are part of the Prague Purim holiday, celebrate the entrance of imperial troops with a daylong fast and evening festivities.

The difficulties encountered by the Catholic clergy in their efforts at Counter-Reformation can be deduced from several conflicts that set them against the Jews—who were not, however, their chief targets. In 1630 Ferdinand II ordered that all the Jews of the empire must listen every Saturday to a Jesuit preacher in their synagogues "without talking or sleeping."[67] Clearly, this was inspired by the hope that the Jews would be forced to heed the voice of Christian faith. But it was quite different from the conflict with the butchers that took place in the same period. Forcing the Christians to keep Lent, Archbishop Harrash forbade butchers to sell meat during the specified days. The Jewish butchers, who did not feel subject to this interdiction, attracted a clientele of Christian Reformists, who refused to practice the fasts. Prompted by the protests of the cohort of butchers who were losing customers, the archbishop extended his interdiction to Jewish butchers as well.

In the course of the Saxon invasion, "preaching to the Jews" was suspended, as were the most spectacular activities of the Counter-Reformation. Yet despite the peasant and popular insurrection that welcomed the Saxons and exiles with cries of "Death to the papists!," Prague was bled dry, and its people were ultimately dissuaded from joining the Reformist armies. One month before being crushed by the imperial troops led by Wallenstein, the Saxons sacked the city, indiscriminately pillaging Catholic, Jewish, and Reformist communities. And like their towns, the individual religious communities would all emerge devastated from this experience in 1631.[68]

In 1636 the city was again under imperial protection. The Jews were once again summoned to listen to Christian preachers who tried to convert them in Hebrew.[69] During the same period, the Jesuits relentlessly converted Jews and Reformists, taking children to be baptized, hunting them down in the streets, and shutting them up in cloisters despite the protestations of surprised parents.

During the Swedish invasion, the plague raged throughout the land. In 1639 the death toll was counted at 18,000 among the Christians and 10,000 among the Jews,[70] who were nonetheless accused of poisoning the city's wells.[71] If the number of Jews is surely exaggerated, it still gives us a glimpse of the losses suffered from the ravages of the plague.

In 1641 a new conflict arose between the Jews and the Catholic clergy. This time the issue was Jewish musicians who, like the butchers before them, were often employed by Christians because the constraints of Lent did not prevent them from practicing their art. But the cardinal forbade this practice.[72] The Jews protested to the emperor, who lifted the ban: once again they could play on Sundays and holidays, except on particularly solemn Church days. The conflict dragged on for ten years, but the Jews would obtain the imperial privilege allowing them to play for Christian marriages and baptisms.

The last years of the war were very hard on the population. The permanent sieges, pillages, and repeated assaults by various armies, not to mention the ravages of the plague, created a desperate situation for protagonists on all sides. And pillaging and killing went on indiscriminately, without regard to religious affiliation.

Prague then effected a decisive turnabout. This city, birthplace of the Protestant offensive, became a bastion of Catholicism so as to rebuff the Swedish troops. In 1648 Jews fought alongside Christians. They dug trenches and participated in fire brigades and guard patrols. During the final assault, Jews staked out defensive positions around the wall of the Old Town. For the duration they organized a force of one hundred men by day and three hundred by night supplied with "pokers" and "dampened hides."[73] The Jewish community's assistance in the defense is marked by "the Jewish fortification," a term that continues to be used. Jews, moreover, discovered common ground with the Guild of Students. A respected member of the Jewish community would distinguish himself on the students' side during the siege. Wolf Arzt had taken the lieutenant of the guild into his home, gave him his bed, and shared his bread with the starving soldiers. After the proclamation of peace, his friends did not forget him and asked that he be elected to the Jewish Council.

Bearing in mind these disparate elements, the question is whether specifically anti-Jewish attitudes can be distinguished in the course of this period. We may rather, in fact, be dealing with presuppositions. This hypothesis can of course be supported by sufficiently numerous attacks, even brutal ones, against Jews: a Jewish woman was actually burned at the stake in 1642. But it seems more judicious to conclude that Jews suffered no more than Catholics or Protestants did for their respective religions. Similarly, it is impossible to determine whether their active participation in combat was forced recruitment, as is often thought, or voluntary. Moreover, if the autonomy of the community was reduced after 1635 by its subjection to the monitoring of an imperial officer—"the inspector of the Jews"—similar measures were taken against all the guilds and even against the university.

The Jews were nonetheless subjected to punitive treatment in the economic sphere. They were able to continue practicing their trades, but the guilds of locksmiths, clockmakers, and arms makers obtained the privilege of barring their professions to Jews. Jews were especially affected through taxes and residence requirements. Until 1627 Jews were not more heavily taxed than other inhabitants of Bohemia, who suffered equally. After this date, however, the emperor sporadically instituted special contributions for Jews. The inequality between Christians and Jews was defined by the age of eligibility. Christians were taxed only from the age of twenty, while Jews paid the tax from the age of ten.[74] In 1636 the Diet mentions a consequent disparity in the price of rent paid by Jews: 10 *schoks* were exacted annually from Jewish houses, while others were required to pay 1 schok, 18 *gros*. This is explained, however, by the density of the Jewish Quarter, which led people to share houses: individually, the burghers—Jews or Christians—probably had to contribute additional sums, but the multiplication of tenants made the tax on Jewish houses higher.[75]

Professional rivalries between Jews and Christians appear in the Prague municipal archives, where the burghers and the guilds are constantly protesting against the privileges of the Jews: fencing masters must no longer teach Jews and should not teach them their secret thrusts;[76] all the guilds are closed to Jews.[77] Yet despite this antagonism, Jews and Christians maintained mutual solidarity during the Thirty Years' War. The Jews found refuge with their neighbors when their quarter was pillaged. Conversely, they sheltered the goods of those threatened with confiscation.[78] These activities, which can be considered exceptional, nonetheless indicate that Jews and Christians seemed to feel they were companions in misfortune and to choose mutual aid in cases of danger. These small incidents, which may seem quite trivial, raise one of the basic and recurring questions posed by Jewish history: Was the exclusion of the Jews within host societies a real and generally widespread fact implying absolute ostracism, or did it depend on juridical and social conventions that could evolve or vary according to circumstance?

If the "Jew" represented that demonized animal, horned, stinking, and monstrous, as he is complacently described in certain works, it would have been inconceivable to draft him to participate (or even to accept his inclusion) in battles in defense of the town. And even more tellingly, Christians would have been embarrassed to welcome their Jewish neighbors in moments of distress or entrust them with their goods. Yet it is true that the image of the Jew that Martin Luther offers us in the last years of his life underscores the idea that even baptism is powerless, in the case of Jews, to modify their satanic character.[79]

These statements are not meant to minimize the obvious importance of the magisterial analyses of medieval anti-Semitism found in works such as those of Joshua Trachtenberg[80] or Léon Poliakov.[81] Yet a monograph from the community of Prague would certainly demonstrate, in the face of stereotypical notions of anti-Semitism, that this analytic model of relations between Jews and Christians is not applicable to the case at hand. The image of the malevolent Jew indeed existed in the Christian imagination and is corroborated by the accusation made against the Jews for spreading the plague during the terrible epidemic of 1639; yet at the time, this accusation had no untoward consequences.

The participation of the Prague Jews in the upheavals of this era, in particular their support of Ferdinand of Hapsburg, also seems to challenge the systematic analysis of Jewish society as a society closed in on itself. As a reward for their courage during the battle against the Swedes, Ferdinand III reiterated the Jews' right to carry their own banner. In 1650, during the ceremonies organized to celebrate the peace (two years after its proclamation), the Jews marched through the city along with the other burghers. It is told that on this occasion some of them wore shrouds and prayer shawls and even brought out the Torah mounted on a palanquin.[82]

Did the Jews of Prague benefit from exceptionally privileged conditions? If that were the case, others would have flocked there in droves. It is said, however, that Luther's theoretical about-face on the subject of the Jews was prompted by learning that in Bohemia, "at the instigation of the Jews, the Reformists Judaize, celebrate the sabbath, and some even have themselves circumcised."[83] If this assertion is well founded, we should note that the attitudes shared by the Jews and Christians of Bohemia were the result of two centuries of theological upheavals. These attitudes, moreover, which had developed from Hussism (it has been suggested that the Jews contributed to its emergence), persisted until the end of the Counter-Reformation.

Whatever the case, relations between Jews and Christians were not exceptional. The rabbinic literature informs us that Jews regularly frequented taverns kept by Christians. Yaʾir Bacharach even recounts, in the monumental collection of his responsa,[84] that in Frankfurt a tavern was kept jointly by a Jew and a Christian. And the rulings of the Jewish Council of Moravia forewarn that "in every community great care must be taken that men do not go to the taverns (houses of the gentiles)."[85] The frequenting of Christian taverns by Jews must have been a common fact, for the prohibition against going to such places is reiterated even in the statutes of the burial society of Prague in 1702: "Let no member of the Society of Gravediggers go into an inn or a non-Jewish house" [to drink or to play cards, a translator specifies].[86] According to Herman Pollack,[87] the Christian taverns where

Jewish students ate even became favorite meeting places for business transactions.

The variety of possible relations between Jews and Christians is suggested by the events following the so-called French torching of the Jewish Quarter of Prague in 1689. This murderous fire ravaged the quarter in the course of a day, with 318 houses destroyed and others rendered uninhabitable.[88] The fire abated, the Jews found themselves in the street, and the populace fell upon them to grab the little they had saved from the flames. Resettling among the burghers of the Old Town, they developed a harmonious life that so frightened the bishop that he would complain to the emperor of Jewish proselytizing and demand an end to this communal life. Consequently, on 29 November functionaries of the state went to inspect the houses of burghers in which Jews were living so as to pronounce judgment on these complaints. A schedule of punishment was even established for Christians suspected of Judaizing: eight days in prison for a minor offense, fourteen for a case in which Jews had fitted out a room as a place of worship.

It was compulsory to rebuild the houses in stone and to surround the quarter with a high wall, and so the reconstruction of the Jewish Quarter dragged on and decrees for the removal of the Jews were not enforced. It was nearly ten years before they were reestablished in their quarter of the city: in 1698 the Jews presented a petition to the city requesting that the debris be cleared away. Yet in an attempt to limit the Jewish presence, the authorities proscribed the establishment of newcomers, particularly from Poland,[89] and made it illegal for native Jews to marry foreigners.

## THE AMBIGUOUS COMMUNITY

A document from 1522 indicates the presence in Prague of a community of six hundred souls. A list of taxpayers from 1528–1549 records 171 Jews. In 1549, 976 names appear on the lists, numbering among them 132 heads of families with their household members and 184 impecunious Jews exempt from taxes.[90] If we accept these figures, and considering that a family consisted of six persons on average, we can estimate that the real population of the Jewish community in 1540 would have been between 1,100 and 1,300, and in 1546 around 2,000. The sixteenth century, then, marks a demographic expansion that, momentarily halted by the expulsion of the community between the years 1543 and 1549, would be vigorously revived by obtaining "safe conduct" in general and an unconditional residence permit, the *Glejt.* The immigrants who then arrived in Prague, beyond those simply returning to their homes, hailed from countries where the Jews had been expelled, such as Spain and Portugal, but also from the neighboring regions of Germany, where at the beginning of the sixteenth century they were banished from almost all the important towns; and to these must be added the many Jews who were expelled from the royal towns of Bohemia.[91] From this time Prague was transformed into a center of trade, a transit point en route to the Polish provinces. The limits imposed on their residence, however, obliged a great number of Prague Jews to seek recourse in emigration. Under these conditions of perpetual coming and going, of mingling populations and cultures, the community had to be vigilant in maintaining its prerogatives. But what were they?

Beginning in 1515, the subjection of the Jews to the Royal Chamber was transferred by Vladislas II to the burghers of Prague. The municipal authority possessed a right of inspection over what was commonly called, in this period, the Judenstadt: the Jewish Quarter. As a consequence, the Judenstadt enjoyed a certain juridical and legal autonomy. But as Kisch[92] has emphasized, the self-government of the Judenstadt reflects the social and legal inequality of the Jews in feudal society. The "elders" who represent and govern it are chosen by members of the community, but the final decision is submitted for ratification to the external civil authorities. In effect, if the elders protect community interests, they are nonetheless the instruments of an external sovereignty: they must collect taxes and other "contributions." According to the sources,[93] five elders were delegated by the city of Prague alone; five others represented the Jewish population of greater Bohemia. Only eminent members of the community participated in the vote. For candidates and electors alike, wealth was a determining factor, since those who represented the community had to control and sometimes advance great sums of money that were the surest guarantees of the community in case of litigation or conflict.

In practice, the role of the elders was quite broad. They decided all internal affairs of the community. They designated rabbis and sat equally on the Beit Din, the rabbinic tribunal. Concretely, the Beit Din dealt only with current commercial matters; on the one hand, recourse to this tribunal prohibited any later appeal to the municipal courts, and on the other, it could inflict only spiritual punishment. This would explain why the Jews themselves voluntarily applied to the municipal courts rather than to their own jurisdiction. But to do this, the case had to be investigated from the beginning, and a person could not alter the investigation once it was initiated. Serious offenses or cases of criminality necessarily had to be adjudicated by the municipal court, which alone had the competence to decide a case and pronounce a sentence of corporal punishment or imprisonment.

The elders were also responsible for community employees. Even before 1541 we find mention of two administrators, of the hospital and of the cemetery, who agree in 1518 to pay 50 schoks in Bohemian money to the burghers of Prague as a pledge of protection for the cemetery and the bathhouse.[94] The community also employed scribes for official communications, most often composed in Yiddish, and for religious texts, in Hebrew. These scribes could, should the occasion arise, serve as witnesses to oaths or in cases of litigation. There is no trace of the lesser community occupations, but the community certainly utilized the services of gravediggers, guards for the gates to the city, nightwatchmen, hospital inspectors, and so on. Similarly, there must have been a *mohel* (ritual circumciser), a *shoḥet* (slaughterer), and officials who presided at the ritual baths.

In the *kehillot*—the communities—the center of gravity was the houses of study and the synagogues. The site of worship as well as social life, the synagogue functioned as a community center and a cultural and educational institution. This was where men studied, discussed problems of all sorts, or just met their cronies. Students sometimes even slept there.[95] Indeed, above all, the Jewish community was, by definition, a religious community. It also took charge of the social needs of its members, although given the community's multiple responsibilities, these were not always adequately met.

Yet outside the Jewish Quarter, individual needs were addressed by various social structures. There were the professional guilds, the religious or secular charitable orders that managed the social system.[96] Medieval corporate society is perfectly described by Aaron J. Gurevitch.

> The behavior of city dwelling was in effect fixed and defined in the corporate urban codes. Along with rules that governed production and other aspects of economic life, we find, among other things, articles concerning aid to indigents, the procedure for the baptism of children, the types of clothing

permitted to apprentices, and even the enumeration of oaths with an indication of the fine incurred for the use of each one.[97]

In Jewish society it is the community that represents the structure and system of social, but also political, organization. The community assumes the autonomy of the group by exercising the functions of a corporation, a system of jurisdiction, a charitable institution: it metes out justice, oversees ritual, and levies taxes.

Among the many problems posed by an attempt to define the community, estimating the number of its members is not the easiest. The figures for Prague, for example, are quite confusing. If we accept the figures of the Judenstadt, of 2,000 persons in the sixteenth century[98] and 11,517 in 1703, with the Christian part of town accounting for 11,618 persons,[99] we are faced with an astounding demographic explosion in just two centuries. In the interval, the available figures seem to convey only sketchy information. If we are to believe D'Elvert,[100] at the beginning of the seventeenth century there were only 400 Jews to be found in Bohemia. According to Gotlieb Bondy and Franz Dvorsky,[101] again 400 Jews were named on the tax lists of Bohemia for 1619, and 800 Prague Jews would have participated in the fire brigades of 1620. According to Popper,[102] however, a population census of 1653 verifies 129,882 inhabitants of Bohemia, of which 2,619 were Jews over twenty years of age and 970 over ten; this gives us a total of 3,589, to which we would have to add, according to Käthe Spiegel,[103] women and young children. However, in 1635 the Chamber levied contributions on the Jews based on a figure of 14,000 individuals residing in Bohemia. If we rely on the Jews themselves, this estimate would have been greatly exaggerated, and they protested vehemently against this number that increased the burden of their financial responsibilities. Contributions were imposed on the community in a contractual fashion, so they cannot shed any light on the real number of individuals taxed.

In the wake of complaints from the community, the fiduciary administrator and the owner of the vineyards were designated to take a house-to-house census of all the observable inhabitants: Jewish men, women, and children living in Prague. Unfortunately, no trace of this detailed accounting remains, and no one knows if it could have been done.[104] In 1653 the elders of "the ruined Jewry of Prague" presented a petition to the government of Bohemia in which they enumerate their financial difficulties. They explain that before the war, the few wealthy families of the time were able to contribute more taxes than the entire present community.[105]

In the seventeenth century the life of this community was characterized by numerous excommunications and the impoverishment of various rabbis, which indicates the extent of its divisions and internal problems. It is true that the elders and the chief rabbi had to assess taxes among the members of the community for purposes of allocation. Insofar as possible, people were taxed according to their means, based on a contractual sum fixed by the external authorities, either the Aulic Chamber or the City Council. The Jews had to get along among themselves, then, to discharge the debt. If the majority of the inhabitants of the Jewish Quarter had scarcely enough to survive and so could not pay their share, the task was incumbent on the more prosperous families, and this was a fatal source of permanent conflict. The chief rabbi was personally responsible for this assessment and therefore found himself the prime target of suspicions of dishonesty and foul play in the administration of his duties.

Governing the Prague community was an arduous task for the rabbis, and we get some idea of this from the problems encountered by Rabbi Yehuda Loew, the Maharal, who was twice forced to depart for Poland. But the difficulty of being a rabbi in Prague might better be exemplified by the experience of Yom Tov Lipman Heller, who composed the famous elegies celebrating the battle of White Mountain. An erudite scholar named assistant to the chief rabbi of Prague at the age of eighteen,[106] he occupied this post for twenty-eight years, between 1594 and 1624. In his autobiographical narrative, *Megillat Eyvah,* he tells of the mishaps he endured in Prague. At the end of 1624 he was offered the post of chief rabbi in Nikolsburg, in Moravia, then in Vienna. During 1627 he received a summons from Prague offering him the post left vacant (voluntarily or not) by Moses ben Mendels. Despite attempts made by the Viennese community to keep him, Lipman Heller decided to return to Prague. After only six months, however, there was an explosion of opposition against him. The pretext for the quarrel was one of his most recent writings, *Ma'adanei Melekh,* which aroused such polemics that the rabbi resigned. But his enemies were not content with his resignation and denounced him to the Imperial Court for having insulted Christianity in his writing and preaching. Within the community he was suspected of electoral and/or financial fraud. Popular legend has it that Rabbi Yom Tov had been implicated in the departure of his predecessor, who had then foreseen that Yom Tov's turn would come as well, and he too would have to leave his community "in shame and disgrace."[107]

Whatever the case, the consequences of this denunciation were considerable: the rabbi was arrested, then imprisoned in Vienna. At the trial instituted against him in July 1629 he was condemned to death. Although his punishment was commuted, he had to forfeit the exorbitant sum of 10,000 florins and see all his writings censored. Jacob Bassevi, his friend, helped him raise the money;[108] after forty days in prison, the rabbi, a broken man, returned to Prague and then emigrated to Poland to live out his final days. According to Popper,[109] the departure of Rabbi Yom Tov put an end to the illustrious rabbinate of Prague, which thereafter "lost all brilliance." His successors maintained an appropriate mediocrity for almost a century.

In the community, however, calm was far from reestablished. Most communal problems centered around the rabbinical court. Conflicts arose from outside the community as well as within. Outside, the Christians wanted to be able to intervene in the trials of the rabbinical court when one of their own was involved. They obtained a ruling from the council of the Old Town decreeing that a magistrate could sit in on a trial involving litigation between a Jew and a Christian. Within the community the Jews were not satisfied with electoral laws that made nearly absolute the power of the elders and the chief rabbi. The presiding Jewish magistrate in a trial could demand prison sentences, but he could also, most crucially, pronounce a sentence of exclusion from the community: the *ḥerem,* or excommunication. The exclusion could be relative, running from a light sentence of eight days to an average of four months, or it could extend to several years or life.[110] In this last case, the incriminated person was condemned either to emigration or conversion. The ḥerem, which severed the individual from his community, made living within it impossible. Deprived of all rights, with no more access to schools or synagogues, to community aid or the *ḥevra kaddisha* (holy brotherhood, burial society), the excommunicated Jew was at the very least socially dead. He was considered a "non-Jew," and his sons no longer had the right to be circumcised; neither he nor his family could be buried, and his food and his books became prohibited to others. Moses Isserles, the Rama,[111] specifies that one must cut the fringes of the prayer shawl of the excommunicated Jew and take the mezuzah off his door.[112] It was even acceptable to consider the excommunicated effectively dead and not uncommon to see fathers go into mourning for one of their excommunicated children and perform all the pertinent rites. Were the Jews merely following the example of the Catholic church?[113] In any case, excommunications were frequent in all the Jewish communities of Europe.

Beginning in the last year of the Thirty Years' War, the Prague community was so divided that sentences of excommunication proliferated. Two factions dominated the community, and each had all the members of the other excommunicated. The "Terror," as Spiegel defines it, was such that the Bohemian Chamber decreed in 1630 that anyone punished by excommunication by the rabbinical court would be paid a compensation of 1,000 ducats.[114] This measure did not prevent the internal crisis from lasting several more years, until the community's electoral system was completely reformed. The internal situation was so strained that in 1649 a text of excommunication was established to be applied in case of electoral fraud. After being pronounced by the tribunal, the ḥerem was publicly invoked at the synagogue in quite a spectacular fashion. The sentence was read in front of the *bima* (pulpit) in the presence of the Torah scrolls and to the sound of the shofar (ram's horn), while candles burned that were then symbolically extinguished once the excommunication was duly proclaimed. This text of excommunication read as follows:

> By invocation of the Almighty, who created the heavens, the earth, the grass, and all that lives, who delivered the people of Israel from Egypt and who has given us the Ten Commandments on Mount Sinai, by invocation of the heavenly tribunal and the earthly tribunal, and with permission of the Chief Rabbi: let him be placed under interdiction and cursed, any man or woman—in the manner of the interdiction pronounced by the son of Isaac on the city of Jericho and comprising 613 maledictions—who, on the occasion of this new election of the Council in the Jewish community of Prague, foments factions, cabals, secret intrigues, written or verbal fraud, or who provokes such things in any way in thought or speech, whether he does it himself or prompts another; all this is forbidden and rendered void under pain of the aforesaid interdiction and all the maledictions comprised in the five books of Moses. If anyone, man or woman, commits such a transgression, let him be cursed, anathemized, and swallowed up like Korah, Dathan, and Abiram; let the divine punishment of leprosy strike him like the sting of a whip, let God Almighty efface his name under heaven, and let him be separated from the rest of [the people] Israel. Let God strike him with the worst calamities and shorten his life and that of his wife and children. As for those who refuse to join these factions and these intrigues, who respect God and conscience, who leave aside their personal interests, envy, jealousy, and hatred, who do not show themselves to be enemies of

the community but are honest and decent folk, let them be protected against all evil and sheltered under this malediction. Let God Almighty grant them all the blessings announced in the Pentateuch; let Him prolong their life and that of their near ones; let Him give them happiness, salvation, and all that is good. Amen!

Signed: Rabbi Israel Brandeis, Rabbi Simon Bonatus, Rabbi Simon Jeiteles, Rabbi Joel Karpeles, Ventura Sax, Herschel Lazarus, David Sacerdote, Solomon Moses, Bernard Fonta, Abraham Jodels.[115]

This document demonstrates that, far from abating, the conflicts were becoming exacerbated to such a degree that excommunication was extended to the violators of community laws. Until then, excommunication was pronounced only for essentially religious or moral reasons, against those who put their community in peril. This text also expresses the secularization of this punishment, by which the exceptional becomes commonplace.[116] We can read in the rules of the Moravian Council that the ḥerem becomes the usual punishment imposed on persons implicated in fraudulent bankruptcies and in the receiving or selling of stolen goods.[117] These cases of "social death" decreed by rabbinical proceedings are highly revealing of the problems posed by communal life that would persist throughout the eighteenth century. The ḥerem would become so widespread as to be almost anodyne.

The authority of the elders was therefore unreliable, and even the chief rabbi could be stripped of his duties. Indeed, he could be denounced and either imprisoned or expelled. Community power was clearly difficult to master. In Prague, after the dismissal of Rabbi Yom Tov, the post of chief rabbi remained vacant until 1640—nearly ten years. The election of Aaron Simon Spiro, a native of the community, did not reduce the dissention, and he barely managed to escape imprisonment. Despite continual complaints against him, Simon Spiro occupied the post of chief rabbi until his death in 1679, but once again ten years elapsed before a new election took place to find a successor.[118]

Thus in opposition to the legal power that was, significantly, under the constant surveillance of the external authorities and with which the Jews did not seem to identify, an entity arose beyond political divisions which would unite the community in its social organization and would become the communal organization par excellence: the ḥevra kaddisha.

PART TWO

# Taming Death

CHAPTER FOUR

# The Institution of Death

Until the sixteenth century in the communities of the Ashkenazi world, the domain of death was limited to the cemetery. The communities of the German lands were more or less effectively assured of the presence of gravediggers, and the people themselves were organized to deliver the last rites to their family members in accordance with Halakhic precepts.

It was not until 1564 that the first Jewish philanthropic organization was created in Prague, and then other communities increasingly followed suit. Is the emergence of this new institution the fruit of a sudden need for philanthropy, or does it rather reflect cultural transformations under way throughout the Ashkenazi community as a result of changes in their way of life and in certain religious and social practices?

In the cultural domain, changes are indicated by the sudden explosion of works codifying the laws that fix ritual and good conduct in all circumstances. There could be many reasons for composing works of this kind. Perhaps in the towns, where immigrants from all corners of the Jewish world gathered, the diversity of customs was so openly expressed that the absence of strict codifications was keenly felt. Rather than a vacuum, it may have been the very scope of the rabbinic corpus of Ḥalakhah that led to variations in the customs practiced by the communities. Moreover, the language used in the numerous tractates, hence their contents, made them accessible only to the learned. Maimonides was already conscious of the problem posed by the multiplicity of laws.

In writing the *Sefer Ha-Mitzvot,*[1] then the *Mishneh Torah,*[2] he set himself the task of providing a systematic compendium of laws and commandments[3] so that everyone could have knowledge of what was authorized or forbidden. It was only in the course of the sixteenth century, however, that Joseph ben Ephraim Caro would succeed in accomplishing this plan with the publication of the *Shulḥan Arukh,* containing the vast sum of all the positive and negative commandments governing human life.[4]

In the course of the same period, the *Sifrei Minhagim*—Books of Customs—would proliferate in all the communities of any importance. These works, which are less ambitious and more limited in scope, generally confine themselves to a description of customs and practices most commonly found in the communities. They chiefly treat holidays, marriages, birth, and death.

The sixteenth century, then, seems to mark an important turning point for more reasons than one. The personalities of the time, whether rabbis or scholars, bear witness to a lively interest in new developments in universal knowledge, scientific as well as geographic,[5] while projects of historiography are equally absorbed by the Jewish world.[6] At the height of the period sometimes called the "era of the ghetto,"[7] then, when the gates to the Jewish quarters seemed to be voluntarily closed, Jews displayed an evident curiosity about the sciences and secular subjects and kept an attentive eye on the outside world.

In addition, the arrival of exiles from Spain and Portugal, carrying with them a specific culture, particular ritual practices, and a traditional body of knowledge different from that of the Ashkenazis, had important ramifications. This is as noticeable in Jewish thought in general—through the development and influence of the Kabbalist School of Safed[8]—as it is more locally in the communities that welcomed these immigrants. Within the Jewish community as a whole we find the awakening and animation of an entire series of debates and discussions, sometimes over fundamental issues. Inquiries were conducted into the education of children and the principles of Jewish learning,[9] as well as the validity of customs, notably through the elaboration and publication of reference works. These varied investigations would similarly influence the internal politics of the communities, which were subsequently transformed as a result.

When for the first time in the Ashkenazi world the Jews of Prague established a burial society, or ḥevra kaddisha, it was meant to attend to the ultimate necessities of life for members of the community. The ḥevra's vocation was to fill what seemed to be a void in the community structure. The creation of a social institution within the community must have provided both relief for the enormous social demands of the needy of all orders—vagabonds, the impoverished, the ill—and an extension of the authority of the elders while reinforcing it, thanks to a new compilation of rights and duties strictly legislated by the texts of duly enacted regulations.

The document we shall read here in extenso, in a literal translation, comes from a copy, itself established from a later transcription, of the original text of the founding charter of the ḥevra kaddisha of Prague. The three paragraphs of the text were composed over successive periods: they were conveyed as a supplement in order to justify the reproduction of the initial text in the wake of fires that successively ravaged the Jewish Quarter, endangering the validity of institutions through the loss and destruction of original documents designating communal authority. These documents contained lists of authorized residents or various acts legislating relations with the external civic authorities.

> As our former masters have said, the just and cherished commandment must be kept by the members of the Holy Brotherhood, *Gomlei Ḥasadim,* toward the living and the dead from time immemorial, from the lineage of Eli—eminent, exceptional persons who have displayed their generosity in order to maintain the purity of this commandment. The leaders of the generation, treasurers of the community, have supported their effort, and how great they are, the rabbis of this land, paragons in their time, and who are in the land of the living. They fixed the date on the Sabbath of . . . , and in this Brotherhood they have signed with their own hands the list of statutes, new and old, passed on from generation to generation, as well as the practices ordained by the masters: the different records and acts. And they all answered unanimously that it is good to follow the well-trodden path: "In the house of mourning rather than the house of marriage." And the sons will walk in the ways of the fathers. Thus, after all the trials and tribulations of the times that have unfolded over the years. And these have been more difficult of late than in former times.
>
> In the year 514 [1754] there was a fire in which texts and written documents, including acts, were destroyed. And [of which] none remained in our hands, for there was only a single tablet on which were inscribed the statutes and acts of the GOM [*Gomlei Ḥasadim*]. The signs of the day of the year, the basic elements of the Holy Brotherhood from earlier years, and several particular records were not devoured by the flames. But the main body of material is missing, the very ancient vellum signed by the directors of the Brotherhood, and after them those who signed in their name until this day. And this document is full of signatures [without which] truth will be absent and forgotten by the generation to come, which will turn

aside from it. The foresight of the heads of the *Gomlei Ḥasadim,* with the support of the Elders, [allowed] this letter to be renewed a second time [accompanied by] a recopying of statutes and recommendations, and the signatures of the masters who are above in order to maintain this commandment in the name of Heaven; and surround it by a majestically decorated border for every generation of those to come. Made in 20 days of the month of Shevat, since the first day of the month of Shevat, in order to accomplish Good and Truth.

Copy of the Act

In the year five thousand three hundred twenty-four [1564] of the Creation of the World, when we are returned to the houses of our fathers from the four corners of the world. After the expulsion in the year 321 [1561], there was a destruction of the fortification of our community, and through the covetousness of our enemies, the community was devastated. This was overcome with great effort in the month of Nisan 322 [1562]. From this land people departed for other lands, and among those [who remained] a great number died, and among the members of the Holy Community in their affliction rose a tumult of sighs. For no one remained to bury the dead, save two hospital caretakers. And when someone died, whether he was important or not, they imposed on the relatives to give them an enormous fee for burial. And anyone who asked for someone to collect the deceased from his house for transport to his final resting place was forced to pay a huge sum to these two caretakers, who moreover did not conduct themselves with the respect owed to the dead. They cavorted and amused themselves on the way to the grave. This was so offensive to members of the community that they loathed their own existence; and they had to pay fees to these caretakers even though they were still alive, in good health, and in the flower of youth, and anyone who could not satisfy their exorbitant demand was left to groan many days and nights, so that bearing the dead to his grave became, for his friends and relations, a trial worse than death. And the indignation in our community was so profound that anyone who would agree to fulfill this duty would receive wages from the leaders. Thus came forth the faithful, the virtuous, and the pious, and they took their lives in their hands and presented an elaborate reply to the leaders of that generation that they desired to perform the desire of their Maker, according to the commandment: "I am the Lord who buries the dead." But on the condition that the leaders of the Jewish Quarter pay them wages, and that this remuneration serve no common use but that they should set up a charity fund that would serve to defray the expenses of burials, distribute wood to the poor each year, and hand out charity to the poor twice a year, on the holidays of *Pesaḥ* [Passover] and *Sukkot* [the festival of booths], to distribute to the worthy poor as they see fit. And what is left over is to be deposited in the communal house to provide for three goals of our community:

—first, for the needs of annuling the expulsion and for avoiding all possible misfortunes that might result;

—second, for buying land to enlarge the cemetery of our community, or for anyone of our brothers of Israel who might come from any town where they live to ask for aid for their cemetery, not to fill their pockets, but to give them a small or large amount, according to the time and circumstances;

—third, in case of war, if it should happen unexpectedly, one must refer to the Law, which is committed to taking precautions against the adversary. Or to feed the poor in a period of quarantine and anything else.

Then the leaders, blessed the Lord, these honest men whom the Lord had inspired to do good for their people, and the Lord rewarded those who are good and honest, and He has given them an eternal law that must not be transgressed. The charity collectors decided that a third of the money from the funerals of every son [and daughter] of Israel taken to his final resting place will be put into the large charity fund of our community. And if there is a rich person, the community will ask him to contribute a certain sum, according to its estimate. All those who are to be buried will be obliged to give a certain sum to the community fund. And a quarter of the amount that the Council has estimated. Thus the princes of the community pledged to them that all this would remain binding for us and our children, and for all the generations of Israel that settle in the community of Prague.

Eliezer Ashkenazi, son of Rabbi Elia Roffe;
Mordekhai, son of Gershom Ha-Cohen;
Ḥayim, son of Isaac Ha-Cohen;
Abraham Moshe, son of Yeḥiel Winternitz;
Menaḥem, called Mendelika, son of David;
Yehuda, son of Gershom;
Schraga Feibl, "Gaf" Ha-Cohen;
Shmuel, son of Avner of Weisswasser, of the family Altschul;
Meir, son of Moshe Brandeis Ha-Levy;
Petaḥia, scribe, son of the martyr Rabbi Joseph, scribe of the community of Prague;
Ḥayim, son of Shmuel, beadle and faithful of the community of Prague.

The content of this document is recopied from an ancient copy, dated the year 449 [1689]. After the great fire that took place in the community, which burned all the documents and privileges, and in which only a single record remained after the fire was extinguished, and it was small and worn, and given its state could not have been preserved without being reproduced. And even this copy was torn and damaged, so it was written on parchment for the generations to come.[10]

Reading this charter, we immediately notice indications of a factual and ethical kind concerning the Prague community. The first paragraph is dated 1754 and explains that the community has just been ravaged by a terrible fire in which all its official legal documents were consumed, including the founding charter of the "Brotherhood," the

Gomlei Ḥasadim—those who provide charity—which was partially damaged. So it is understandable that the elders wanted to take advantage of the opportunity provided by this fire to revise several elements of its statutes: "In this Brotherhood they have signed with their own hands the list of statutes, new and old." Numerous ethical considerations regarding the necessity of keeping vigil at the deathbed to provide last rites for members of the community and transmitting to future generations the profound meaning of those practices that seem vital are expressed. In this paragraph, which serves as an introduction and justification for the retranscription of the act, it seems important to convey as well the human chain that authenticates these rulings from the time of the founding of the society. "But the main body of material is missing, the very ancient vellum signed by the directors of the Brotherhood, and after them those who signed in their name until this day, and this document is full of signatures [without which] truth will be absent and forgotten by the generation to come, which will turn aside from it."

The second paragraph, which reproduces the original document, is dated 1564. Information of a historical nature legitimizes the founding of the Brotherhood. It is clear at the outset that the community endured serious acts of discrimination: first an expulsion,[11] then pillaging, accompanied by the partial demolition of the wall surrounding the Jewish Quarter. The text adds again that probably for this reason a great many members of the community emigrated, and those who remained or returned to Prague may have suffered through an epidemic; in any case, "a great number died." Further on we learn as well, "For no one remained to bury the dead." Whether the gravediggers were among the exiled or whether they died, we do not know. The fact remains that only two were left (if indeed there had been more), and these abused the situation and demanded exorbitant sums to do their jobs; moreover, they did not do them in accordance with the "respect owed to the dead," as religious convention prescribes. This situation does not, however, seem to be the result of a specific recent event, for "they had to pay [the people of the community] fees . . . even though they were still alive, in good health, and in the flower of youth."

Following this narration come the objectives the brotherhood set for itself: in addition to the primary vocation of dealing with the dead, the members intend to create a general charity fund on the basis of contributions from members of the brotherhood as well as the gravediggers' fees, making them, in effect, unpaid workers. The Brotherhood is committed to addressing the needs of the poor by overseeing the distribution of wood and alms. And they have three other aims as well: (1) a permanent fund for paying exceptional taxes, for example, in case of a decree of expulsion; (2) a permanent fund meant to ensure the upkeep of the Prague cemetery or, this failing, that of other communities; and (3) a permanent fund reserved to provide for extraordinary social needs, in case of wars or epidemics.

The rest of the text, in the flowery and metaphorical language of the period, evokes measures of internal discipline. To ensure the smooth functioning of the society and so that everyone should be obliged to join, the text indicates that anyone who comes to settle in Prague, whatever his financial status, must participate in this community fund according to his means. The chain of continuity is ensured and certified by the report of the former signatures of the ḥevra kaddisha's founding members.

Several lines of the final paragraph attest that the transcription of 1754 was made on the basis of a prior copy, itself dated 1689. On this date a fire had already destroyed the Jewish Quarter, along with its precious official documents. The whole of the text is embellished with two lions who frame the document on each side according to classical practice.

As it is described by the founders of the ḥevra kaddisha, the situation of the Prague community seems by 1564 to have reached a critical stage in its internal functioning. Indeed, the bond between members of the Jewish community seems to be based on their unified observance of religious precepts; after all, membership in a Jewish community means first and foremost sharing the same faith, respecting the same precepts and ritual tasks. And the commandments and prohibitions dealing with death seem to be of the utmost importance. The question is whether to conclude that the situation as described bears witness to an unexpected change in attitudes toward death, or whether it reflects a momentary malaise.

This document could suggest that during certain periods Jews demonstrated less rigor with respect to the ritual prescriptions and prohibitions of death, so much so that the last rites were left to individual initiative. In this case the creation of a burial society may indicate that new requirements were emerging in the beliefs linked to death and in ideas related to the resurrection. Or it may confirm the painful nature of an intermediary situation associated with factual circumstances.

According to ritual practice, the dead must be buried as soon as possible, within twenty-four hours of demise, as much out of respect for their corporeal integrity as out of concern that they should not pollute their environment. Texts devoted to establishing and commenting on the impurity of human remains are abundant[12] and very strict on the subject: persons and utensils that have been in contact with a cadaver become impure, as does the place where they have lain. So allowing the dead to lie "many days and nights" represents a serious breach of the spirit of Jewish laws concerning the deceased and his family. One sentence from the text is particularly revealing: "Bearing the dead to his grave became for his friends and relations a trial worse than death." Taken literally, this could mean that a cadaver left for several days without particular attention is trying to others, notably to the family. It must be remarked, however, that this sentence reproduces word for word a citation from *Moed katan*[13] which Naḥmanides quotes in the *Torat ha-Adam*[14] in the paragraph devoted to the way one must "dispose" of a cadaver. This talmudic anchorage in the narration does not obviate its entire meaning but invests it with yet another. When Naḥmanides uses this citation,[15] he specifies that "in the beginning, disposing of a dead person was, for his kin, a worse trial than his death," because, he says, they deposited him at the cemetery, then fled, and this was the case until Rabbi Gamaliel proposed the custom of covering the whole dead person with a piece of linen. Naḥmanides thus reveals a transformation in funerary practice: disposing of an uncovered cadaver was no longer current practice after the era of Rabbi Gamaliel, in the first century.

The founders of the Prague burial society may have appropriated this citation to describe an ahistorical situation in preparation for their announcement of a transformation. They anchor the transformation in the past by recalling the societies of ancient Jerusalem that chose to visit "the house of mourning rather than the banquet hall."[16] In this way the difficult situation of the Prague Jews is not something new; it was already described in the Mishnah[17] with great acuity: to bear a cadaver several days old is painful to the family, who are thus confronted by the decomposition of a loved one. Whether such a thing actually happens or not seems, at the moment described, quite secondary. The allusion to the burial societies of Jerusalem is again meant to show that the creation of a burial society is not an innovation: "It is good to follow the well-trodden paths: 'in the house of mourning rather than the house of marriage,' and the sons will walk in the ways of the fathers."[18] In so doing, the founders ground themselves in the continuity of the Jerusalem tradition, and the burial society is thus following in the path already trodden by the Mishnah, anchoring itself in the Jewish past.

We may well wonder about the Jewish burial society anchoring itself in a tradition of charity and about its possible transposition of a Christian model. Among historians, this issue remains unresolved. Some see its origin in ancient Palestine,[19] where such an institution would have existed from the time of Bar Kochba.[20] Others are more persuaded by the influence of the Christian guild on the Germanic model than by a hypothetical talmudic genealogy.[21] Yet we do not know a great deal about the organization of ancient societies. We do not know if the gravediggers did their work gratis or received remuneration. We do not know if all the townspeople participated in the burial, or only a certain number of them. Nor do we know if these societies were responsible for the purification of the dead person, for putting him in the coffin, or only for digging graves and actually burying the deceased.

Rashi participates in these inconclusive inquiries in his commentaries. In one he states[22] that these societies were numerous and that each one concerned itself with the burial of its own members, but he does not establish whether these societies were closed or organized by district, depending on the size of the town. Elsewhere[23] he advances the hypothesis that the beadles were responsible for burying the dead. In ancient rabbinic texts, however, we find elements that can pass for the rudiments of the ḥevra kaddisha, in particular where we read that every person residing in the town nine months or more must make a contribution for burial of the dead;[24] but it is especially the paragraph that deals with the transfer of moral responsibility for the dead person and his family to a society[25] that is most frequently cited by defenders of the hypothesis that the burial society was common among the Jews from talmudic times.

Is it really useful to engage in the disputes of the last century?[26] It hardly matters whether the ḥevra kaddisha is a pure creation of the sixteenth century or whether it dates back, with some interruption, to the Palestinian period. It seems more to the point to distinguish the underlying discourse of the founders, the elements characteristic of the tradition, of its ideas or mentality at the moment of creation. In this regard Jacob Rader Marcus,[27] whose work on the Jewish societies is still the most complete and erudite, judiciously remarks that the typical phraseology employed by the members of these institutions is talmudic in origin: the terms used are *gemilut ḥasadim,* for the dispensing of benefits and charity, and *ḥesed shel emet* (true kindness), for the activity of burials but also to designate the functions of the societies or name them in their own right. It seems of primary importance to integrate every innovative element into the style, if not the rabbinic cultural tradition, of Jewish society.

In other words, we might think that it is not so much history that matters as its eternal process of recurrence. This would suggest that the communal situation depicted does not necessarily correspond to a real state of affairs but is rather inscribed in an ahistorical order, leading to the simple revival of a community institution already active in the more distant times of the Palestinian era. By extension, the creation of the ḥevra kaddisha would not be a purely human creation imposed by social necessity but would take on its biblical meaning of gemilut ḥasadim and ḥesed shel emet, that is, the performance of "acts of piety." And we might situate in the same intellectual process the impulse of the directors of the burial society to revise the statutes that seem out of date while specifying that they are preserving a portion of the old laws.

Yet in consulting other texts that describe the creation of burial societies during the same period and in other places in the Ashkenazi world, we can confirm that the problems are identical and that what happens in Prague is repeated elsewhere. Thus Joseph Yuspa Hahn,[28] after articulating his reasons for writing his book of "customs," identifies himself as one of the founding members of the ḥevra kaddisha of Frankfurt, established in 1517. He comments on and justifies this creation by specifying that formerly, "there were many dead, groaning like abandoned corpses,[29] who had no one to bury them." And he adds that "those who performed this task did not know the required ritual procedure." These remarks are embedded in an autobiographical narrative that offers no supporting evidence. We might conclude, nonetheless, that his description illustrates the behavior of his contemporaries. He would thus confirm the prevalence of a real carelessness in the burial of the dead, probably the poor, and an ignorance of death and burial ritual. After concluding this narrative, Joseph Hahn articulates the role of the ḥevra kaddisha: on the one hand, to make sure that all members of the community can be buried decently and according to prescribed practice, and, on the other, to oversee the education of members of the burial society in matters of funerary ritual.[30]

If we simply stick to the facts set forth in either the 1564 Prague text or the Hahn narrative after 1597, we can verify the rupture that took place in Jewish society with the founding of a corporate institution meant to assume responsibility for the final moments of life. It seems clear that in previous times the last rites had been left to the individual initiative of families as much as to the goodwill of professional gravediggers. The transformation in the social fabric of the community wrought by the ḥevra kaddisha's erection of a hierarchical structure would have many consequences, not the least of which was the emergence of an effective moral power exercised by the group over the individual. But we can be sensitive as well to the evident intention to endow the Jewish community with the same categories and institutions as its environment and at the same time to the constant care taken by the composers of the founding charter of the Prague ḥevra to situate this society solidly in a tradition that would be specifically Jewish in order to express its perpetuity through—or in spite of—its evolution.

## THE PERIOD OF RUPTURE

In addition to circumstantial and anecdotal conditions, a multitude of other factors influenced the creation of the burial society. Marcus[31] is convinced that the ḥevra kaddisha was established on the model of the Germanic guilds. He sees it, rightly, as introducing a system of corporate hierarchy copied, in his view, from the guild model, especially its characteristic convivial aspects, such as the well-known corporate banquet. Yet his highly detailed analysis of the inception of the burial societies convinces him of an obvious connection between the expulsion of the Spanish Jews and the appearance of the burial societies in the Jewish communities of the German lands. While in the Ashkenazi world no specific organization seems until then to have managed philanthropic activities, on the Iberian peninsula the community model more closely mirrored that of Christian society, and Jewish mutual aid societies were created in Spain contemporary with Christian societies of the same kind. Some of them specialized in social activities as early as the thirteenth century and set as their objective to oversee the "last rites." The *Confratrias, Confrarias, Ḥevrot,* and so forth, proliferated, especially during the fourteenth and fifteenth centuries, in step with the expansion of the Christian brotherhoods. We can take as an example the community of Arles, under pontifical authority, which in 1401 created the society of Malbishei Arumim—those who clothe the naked.[32] Its vocation consisted of dispensing money to the poor on a weekly basis, whether or not they were part of the society, visiting the sick, escorting funeral processions, and consoling mourners.[33]

This highly structured model of social assistance seems totally unknown in the Ashkenazi world of the same period. Yet if the ḥevra kaddisha emerged only in the sixteenth century among the Ashkenazi Jews, it was not for lack of an existing model. In the German lands the Christian guilds certainly existed, though without any apparent influence on the Jews until the sixteenth century. Yet the affiliation of the burial society seemed to follow the path traced by the exiles from Spain or Portugal. Thus Jewish burial societies arose in the towns of Italy where these exiles gathered: first in Ferrara, then in Modena in 1516, where the society Ḥevrat Gemilut Ḥasadim[34] was created with a mission to visit the sick and deal with funerary matters. It took half a century, however, for the first institution of this type to appear in Prague in the Ashkenazi community. Marcus reckons that before this period, philanthropic needs were easily met because of the size of the communities, which did not justify a structure more elaborate than the structure of the community itself. He remarks, nonetheless, that certain towns such as Worms and Mainz contained several hundred Jews,[35] which might have justified this type of social organization. For him, however, it was chiefly through their contributions to theology and philosophy that the Sephardic exiles helped to transport the idea of the burial society to the Ashkenazi world.

If it were necessary, then, to find a Spanish influence in the propagation of new attitudes concerning the spiritual and material responsibility for the dead and dying, the diffusion of ideas from the school of Lurianic Kabbalah of Safed would seem to offer fertile ground. Indeed, it was in Spain at the beginning of the thirteenth century that the Kabbalah found its center, in particular with the Gerona School,[36] which was later revived and re-created after the expulsion of the Jews and the relocation of the kabbalists to Safed, in Palestine. Based on the themes of resurrection, atonement, and the individual life of the soul—similar in this respect to certain points of Christian doctrine—the Kabbalah manifested its influence in the appearance of a characteristic spectrum of attitudes and innovative religious practices in the management of illness and death. Indeed, it can be confirmed that between the sixteenth and eighteenth centuries there was a virtual explosion of books on death rituals containing the liturgy for the "deathbed" which until then did not exist in an exhaustive or specific form.

Gershom Scholem demonstrates in his work (which is not specifically on death)[37] the extent to which the kabbalists influenced Jewish mentalities, in particular their conceptions of death. The kabbalistic doctrine of man and his soul is supported by the eschatological view that after death the soul passes across a river of fire (evocative of a kind of purgatory) to arrive, purified, at the earthly paradise; from this place the soul heads toward the sublime pleasures of celestial paradise and toward the realm referred to by the ancient kabbalists by the term *tseror-ha-ḥaim*—the knot of life, that means eternal life, a phrase mentioned systematically at the end of epitaphs, particularly Ashkenazi ones. This eternal life is sometimes synonymous with the earthly paradise and sometimes refers to a "sphere" to which the soul would return and where it would share the life of the divine essence.

The Kabbalah is specifically concerned with representations of heaven and hell. Scholem reckons that the number of eschatological themes on this subject rivals those of Islam and Christianity.[38] The kabbalists of the twelfth century, notably in the *Zohar,* indulged in lengthy speculations on this topic. They brought considerable attention to bear on such subjects as the clothing of the soul in paradise,[39] the nature of its perceptions, and the expansion of its consciousness, as well as the apprehension of the Divine: the unification of the highest level of the soul with God, or *devekut.* From these elements, notions of punishment and retribution became the fate of the soul, the *neshamah,* and the breath, the *ru'aḥ.*

The Kabbalah distinguishes three parts of the soul that form the whole while the individual lives but are separated at the moment of his death. After burial, the corporeal soul, the *nefesh,* remains for a time in the grave, floating around the body, while the ru'aḥ rises toward the earthly paradise, according to its merits; and the essence of the soul, the neshamah, returns directly to its original home, the divine substance or presence, the *Shekhinah.* One of the fundamental spiritual values of Lurianic Kabbalah is represented by the concept of exile. The redemption of Israel is "one" with the redemption of God himself from his mystical exile.[40] This notion is elaborated in the verse "The salvation of the Holy One, blessed be he, is the salvation of Israel."[41] The exile of Israel is tied to the sin of Adam, which resulted in the scattering of the holy sparks that together form the divine essence, the Shekhinah, and of the soul of Adam, which according to tradition forms the general spark of the future souls of humanity. When the sparks, or the vessels containing them, were scattered among the descendants of Adam, the mission to reunite them in preparation for the day of redemption became incumbent upon Israel. In terms of this definition, exile is not a punishment or a trial but rather a mission to be accomplished—an end in itself. The Messiah cannot appear while the good of the universe has not been completely separated from the evil. The conceptions of the kabbalists of Safed led to the will to overcome the exile: by aggravating one's torments so as to achieve the "night" of divine exile, the communities might be brought back to repentance, which alone could lead to redemption.

Though an extremely simplified summary, this explanation of certain elements of Kabbalah should allow us to follow the innovative paths of Lurianic Kabbalah through Jewish society, at least as concerns our subject. For if the Kabbalah influenced the life of the Jews, this was chiefly evident in the areas of prayer, customs, and ethics. This is confirmed by Scholem, who judges that from the eighteenth century on, kabbalistic motifs were integrated into the daily prayers[42] and reached into every Jewish home. He adds that the Kabbalah was thus the source of particular liturgies associated with specific ritual occasions.

The center of this new mortuary liturgy developed in and expanded outward from Italy with the work of Aaron Berachia of Modena: the *Ma'avar Yabbok,* a book of death and burial ritual, whose title, *Crossing the Jabbok,* is a direct allusion to the notion of the purifying river of fire mentioned above.[43] Two other works also had a considerable influence on their contemporaries, Moses Zacuto's *Tofteh Arukh,* a dramatic work recounting the torments of the soul in its grave,[44] and Nathan Nata Hannover's *Sha'arei Tzion* (The Gates of Zion), a collection of kabbalistic prayers based on the doctrine of Isaac Luria. Published in Prague in 1662, the latter work was one of the most widely read books in the Jewish world.[45] Of these three works, two deal specifically with death and the third grants it an important place, which would confirm the fascination with death and its influence on the doctrine spread by the school of Luria. And indeed, Scholem verifies this, noting, "Death, repentance, and rebirth were the three great events of human life by which the new Kabbalah sought to place man in blissful union with God."[46]

With this new interest in death, concepts such as "repentance"—which is now distinct from its meanings and implications for the German ḥasidim of the thirteenth century[47]—become the focal points of human conduct. The principle of repentance is linked to the human condition and in particular to the doctrine of *gilgul,* which was generally widespread. Gilgul, or metempsychosis, represents exile in the higher sense, exile of the soul, which is embodied in the transmigration of souls. Exile issues from the fall of the soul of Adam, which contained all the souls of humanity and was thus divided and shared out among his descendants. The idea of metempsychosis is thus equivalent to the idea of the perpetual reincarnation of a single soul that, according to Scholem's formula,[48] *expiates its sins.* But every individual through his acts provokes in his turn supplementary reasons for renewing this exile indefinitely. Humankind's mission in the universe is thus charged with meaning, for every soul that would fulfill the commandments would find itself disengaged from its individual existence and would take its proper place in the divine essence. Gilgul would therefore be the cycle of fulfilling the commandments and consequently a means of accomplishing the ultimate reunification, *tikkun.* Hence the emphasis on individual consciousness: the process of transmigration—and therefore the duration of the exile, both earthly and mystical—can be shortened by the execution of certain rites, including penitential exercises.[49]

Beginning in the sixteenth century, then, repentance was perceived through the kabbalistic lens of Isaac Luria and his disciples. This doctrine implicates Israel as a whole and would explain why the penitential acts of the German ḥasidim were replaced by new exercises recommended by the kabbalists, who are much more oriented toward collective acts. Their exercises can be distinguished from Christian acts of penitence as well: communal fasts and processions would replace individual practices. But it must be noted that in the spirit of the new Jewish penitence, the individual saw himself as granted real power to affect his fate—and thereby the fate of all Israel—which spurred him to spiritual action. The *Midrash ha-ne'elam* is precise on this point: "I swear to you, if they return to penitence, the heads of the community, or a community, through their merit the diaspora will be gathered in."[50] A new but crucial factor in this perception of repentance, *Teshuvah,* now depends on confession, *Viddui.*

Since death can strike at any moment, certain kabbalists of the sixteenth century even practiced daily confession.[51] These ascetics confessed to each other, which was, under the circumstances, a radically revolutionary initiative but would be only a temporary and unique one. Usually confession was reserved for Yom Kippur, when it was recited collectively in the name of the whole community through prayers such as the *ashamnu* (we have sinned), called the *viddui katan* (minor confession), and the *al ḥet* (for the sin), considered the *viddui gadol,* or major confession.[52] But basically, and this is Maimonides' recommendation,[53] individual confession continued to be reserved for the deathbed.

Among the noteworthy innovations in the domain of death rituals and customs established under the influence of Lurianic Kabbalah is the popular practice of studying the Mishnah in the house where the seven days of mourning, or shiva, are being observed in memory of the deceased; this is done because the letters of the word Mishnah form the anagram of neshamah. The Kabbalah also influenced the customs of forming a circle around the dead person and forbidding children to follow their father's funeral ceremonies.[54] But even more important are the prayers, many composed at this period, that were transformed by the new doctrine. New attitudes and customs issued from this modern current with messianic ambitions, and they generated global transformations within the very structure of the community. Thus the creation of the burial society was not exclusively an indication of the circumstantial or political history of the community. It would mark a decisive evolution of ideas current in Jewish society concerning its relation to death and, by extension, to everything associated with it. This would be reflected in social practices in the medical realm, in cases of illness, and also in daily life, for which the ḥevra kaddisha would take organizational responsibility. Through this accumulation of missions, the burial society would become, in a way, the chosen vehicle for the spiritual growth of the whole community.

The primary vocation of the Jewish burial societies was to provide for charity and the mortuary needs of the community. This mission was based on ethical principles propagated by the Kabbalah and equally prevalent in Christian society. It may be, as Marcus suggests, that the ḥevra was modeled on the Christian guilds,[55] at least in its structure. If his comparative analysis of their respective structures is convincing, however, his interpretations of the phenomenon are less so. He makes two rather contradictory suggestions. On the one hand, he confirms that when the Jewish burial societies were being created in Italy with the arrival of the Sephardic immigrants, Christian guilds with identical vocations were in the process of full expansion. This would indicate, in his view, a common evolution within the framework of the Counter-Reformation. On the other hand, he points out that in the German lands the Catholic guilds were in decline because of the Reformation, which in this case would have "morally" authorized the Ashkenazi Jews to use a model the Christians had abandoned.[56]

The situation of Christianity, caught between the Reformation and the Counter-Reformation in Italy and the German lands, would have encouraged the Jews to avail themselves of a model that had been tried and found effective, and, at the same time, it would have provoked them to embrace an outdated model. The argument does not seem adequate to explain the sudden proliferation of burial societies during this period throughout all the regions of the Jewish world. If we consider the case of Prague, with the first Ashkenazi institution, we can observe that this çommunity exists in a Catholic country and in the midst of the Counter-Reformation but also in the midst of the Lutheran crisis; the creation of the burial society cannot, then, be accounted for solely by its geographic location. There were close contacts between Prague and Italy via Venice, through intellectual and commercial exchanges between the Prague and Venetian Jews. In addition, the Prague community was all the more open to external influences because of its recent expulsion and because its members had resided in foreign territory, sometimes for many years, before returning to the city. In addition, during the second half of the sixteenth century, the community engaged in intense cultural activity, which favored the flowering of conceptual transformations. And perhaps Eliezer Ashkenazi,[57] whose name heads the list of signatories of the founding members on the charter of the ḥevra kaddisha, played a crucial role in this matter before leaving to end his days among the kabbalists in Safed. Following Prague's example, burial societies sprang up in all the German lands: in Frankfurt in 1597, in Worms in 1609, in Metz in 1621, and so on.[58]

Jewish burial societies were generated by an internal process that must have appropriated an existing model and yet created from it a mutation specific to the Jewish world, allowing it to adopt, perhaps rather belatedly, the ethical conceptions of the surrounding culture. But we should not hastily conclude that the ḥevra kaddisha was a pure creation of the kabbalist movement. When the burial society was constituted in Prague, Lurianic Kabbalah was far less widely diffused among the populace than it later became. Its essential texts were not yet published, and only from the seventeenth century on did it become a more popular movement.[59] The seeds of its conceptions, however, spread through the orientations and injunctions of the rabbis and thinkers of the communities who had experienced or witnessed the expulsion of the Spanish Jews as "the night that must precede redemption."[60] The currents generated by Lurianic Kabbalah and the ḥevra kaddisha flowed from the same development: the former was its spiritual issue translated into new attitudes, a new liturgy, and new rites; the latter its material issue embodied in a new communal institution, the burial society.

## THE COMMUNITY AND THE BURIAL SOCIETY

The text of the statutes of the ḥevra kaddisha (see the Appendix) is twice dated: it was composed from rules established in 1692, then repeated and augmented in 1702. Like the founding charter of the burial society,[61] the original document disappeared in the "French" fire of 1689. The text examined here defines relations between individuals and the burial society, foresees conflicts that might arise and ways of resolving them. In this sense it fixes the specifically communal role of the institution. If its vocation is hardly mentioned, this is because it is now an organization whose existence no longer needs legitimation; its functions and its internal operations, however, must be regularly redefined to keep it running smoothly.

The authority of the burial society was exercised, to varying degrees, over all members of the community. For a Jew of the seventeenth century, it was inconceivable to abstain from participation in the ḥevra kaddisha. Just as excommunication made it impossible to remain in a community, the refusal to participate in the burial society in some fashion inevitably led to the severing of social life. Access to the cemetery may have been a chief factor, but this did not represent the only or ultimate aim of this participation. For the life of the community revolved around the structures of the burial society and was marked by the rhythm of its activities. If, however, the burial society's ascendency affected everyone, each person did not participate in the same way. The *kavranim*—the gravediggers—according to the label current in the rules, were admitted by election within a strictly hierarchical system. Indeed, the regular payment of dues to the society was not in itself adequate to confer the status of "member." In addition, if we are to believe article 6, a classification of gravediggers divides them into three distinct groups: lowest in rank are the "host" members, the *Aufgenommener,* who carry out the work of the burial society but cannot vote or be elected. They form the group of candidates during a probationary period lasting one or several years. Access to the status of permanent member of the ḥevra is obtained by passing a public examination (article 21), in the course of which the candidate must answer very precise questions concerning funerary rites. If he qualifies, he must still be elected before acceding to "permanent member." If he is not, he will remain a candidate or "probationary" member for the following year and must then submit to a new competition.

Then come the *ḥatumim,* literally the inscribed, who form the bulk of the permanent membership. They have the right to participate in elections and eventually, after several years of tenure and irreproachable conduct, to be elected to the title of elder and participate in the management and administration of the society.

As in the community, the elders form the ḥevra's elite and its pool of candidates eligible for director. One can, however, obtain the honorific title of elder without its prerogatives (article 19). This distinction between the purely prestigious status of elder and that of elder of the burial society marks the ḥevra's independence from community structures. This is why an elder who might have the privileges of this title in the community would not automatically benefit from them in the framework of the society.

The members of the directorship of the burial society are the *gabbai'im* and the *mevorarim.* They are elected each year from among the elders and by them. They may represent authority, but this too is highly stratified: the *gabbai* must first (article 15) graduate from the status of *mevorar* for at least two consecutive years before hoping to acquire this title. At the head of the directorate is the *gaon.* He is someone who has already passed through all the previous stages of the hierarchy. He was first a candidate on probation for (at minimum) eight years, then he would have been admitted to the title of "permanent member" for an additional eight years before gaining the title of elder, thanks to which he was elected mevorar, then gabbai. Having passed through every stage as a member of the burial society, he is familiar with its functioning at every level; in principle, he can respond to any problem that might arise.

Direct responsibility for the society falls alternately to different administrators, designated from among the gabbai'im as "administrator of the month": the *parnas ha-ḥodesh.* According to article 31, this person cannot hold the office more than two consecutive months. His role consists of managing the treasury (article 31), distributing charitable donations to the poor (article 24), and exercising the power of decision in cases of litigation or particular problems (article 26); in addition, it is his duty to delegate tasks and issue immediate directives.

The mevorarim represent the committee of the elected members, and under this rubric they share the general responsibilities for arbitration and are entitled to execute decisions made by the gabbaiʾim and the parnas ha-ḥodesh. The lower-level administrators are the *vokhn man,* officials of the week, and they are assisted by the *vokhn layt,* assistants of the week, and by the *shammashim,* the beadles, who are salaried employees of the burial society.

All the inhabitants of the Jewish Quarter had to pay dues for the "services" of the ḥevra kaddisha, insurance that they would receive the last rites as well as a place in the community cemetery, yet the burial society had only a limited number of permanent members. Article 16 specifies that no more than forty candidates are accepted "on probation" each year. Furthermore, only four men a year can be admitted as permanent members. In practice, then, the ḥevra functioned as follows: the day after the festival of Shavuʾot,[62] the gabbaiʾim and the mevorarim would gather in the major synagogue—in Prague, the Altneuschül—and draw lots of seventeen names from among the elders (article 12). These elections had to be done under the vigilant eye of the av bet din, the president of the rabbinic court, the chief rabbi if there was one in office. They had to choose ten of the seventeen elders to form the committee of gabbaiʾim and mevorarim for one year (article 20), but article 12 specifies that these seventeen elected must form the "members of the synagogue" whose function is to vote and to elaborate the regulations of the society. Article 13 governs the rotation and provides that each year seven persons will be replaced in this group of the elect while preserving a majority among the former members.

The general admission of candidates on probation and of permanent candidates took place each year on the day of the burial society's banquet. On this day, the members of the ḥevra fasted and formed a procession that ended at the cemetery for the *meḥilah,* or rite of forgiveness. There they asked the forgiveness of the deceased for all errors of commission and omission made against them in the administration of the burial rites. In Prague, according to article 11 of the statutes, this ceremony took place on the first day of the month of Shevat which generally falls in January, and was followed in the evening by the society's great banquet. This banquet, which was the community's annual event, monopolized a significant portion of the society's resources. Thus article 32 specifies that the sums dispensed by candidates to the society, whether probationary or permanent, must be used essentially to defray the costs of this banquet.

The revenues of the burial society came from various sources. Every candidate paid an entrance fee, and in addition, all members, whatever their status, paid annual dues, to which were added the dues of the "nonmembers" of the community. These fixed revenues were supplemented, on the one hand, by sums collected in the alms boxes that circulated in the synagogues and were also brought out on special occasions such as burials, marriages, or other ceremonial events, and on the other, by revenues resulting from fines imposed for the smallest infractions in the discipline of the society. Article 29 specifies that people must also pay a certain sum to the society on the death of family members. The society received gifts as well and even sold headstones and cemetery plots.

The ḥevra kaddisha exercised its power by the same means the community employed: the threat of exclusion. Thus recalcitrants and offenders could be deprived of their status. Article 6 recommends demoting members in case of prolonged absence from burials, but when the offenders are only members on probation, they are simply excluded from the society. The ḥevra reserved the right to settle disputes with its members by having them declared "rebels" at the synagogue (articles 2, 3, and 4). Exclusion from the society was not irrevocable; the "rebel" could make amends honorably and be readmitted to membership, but this recourse is authorized only once (article 3). If a man who had been declared a "rebel" and excluded was then readmitted, he could recover his previous title only by repeating the entire procedure for candidacy. Motives for exclusion varied, from the simple failure to fulfill one's duties as a member of the society—lack of attendance at burials, for example—to inflicting injury or brawling or refusing to pay one's dues. A man excluded from the ḥevra kaddisha incurred the refusal of last rites, which meant not only that members of the ḥevra would refuse to attend his sickbed and recite prayers for the dying but that it would be difficult, if not impossible, for him to obtain the services of those who prepared the body for burial, to purchase a coffin, to engage persons to recite the burial service, and even to purchase a place in the cemetery—all services monopolized by the ḥevra. These conditions prevailed for all members of his family as well. Indeed, if he was absolved from community duties, he was also stripped of the benefits of its assistance (philanthropic community aid in cases of illness or imprisonment). The ḥevra kaddisha had at its disposal utterly powerful and effective means of coercion, for life within the community was very carefully channeled by the structures it had put in place.

Beyond its funerary vocation, the ḥevra kaddisha took up a variety of tasks. The rules of 1702 mention only two of them: the distribution of charity to the poor (article 24) and the organization of the society of *sandakim,* godfathers. The *sandak* holds the newborn male during the circumcision, and practice dictates that one of the most highly respected members of the community should have this responsibility. He was supposed to provide the circumcision cloth as well,[63] and therefore only rather well-to-do persons could be sandakim. According to articles 14 through 17, this subsociety depends directly on the ḥevra kaddisha: if a man no longer has the trust of its members, then he no longer has the trust of the *hevrot ha-sandakim*. Moreover, the election of sandakim is voted on by the gabbaiʾim and the mevorarim of the ḥevra kaddisha (article 17), which defines the close relationship between the two "societies," one being, in fact, merely an extension of the other.

To explain the extent of the ḥevra kaddisha's authority over the community, a number of factors must be taken into account. First and foremost is the elimination of potential personal conflicts through the system of rotating those representing authority, which prevented the perpetuation of dissent. When, for example, a conflict arose with the parnas ha-ḥodesh, everyone knew that his authority would not extend beyond his two months in office. In addition, the evident democracy of the elective system, as well as the collegial power sharing, also granted greater internal freedom to members of the society.

In contrast to the community power represented by the elders, who had to be accepted by members of the community as well as by the council members of the Bohemian Chamber, the power of the burial society issued exclusively from its members, who were the sole judges presiding over the choices of their own to positions of responsibility. The people chosen from within the ḥevra were not responsible for resolving potential problems between the Judenstadt and the Christian city of Prague, nor did they have to levy regular or occasional tariffs on their coreligionists. They therefore attracted less animosity than the official representatives of the community. The numerous conditions to be fulfilled before attaining positions of authority, however, seriously limited democracy—as we understand it—within the burial society. Those who attained the status of gabbai had reached a respectable age, and among the men conceivably eligible for selection, the rotation was perforce made within a closed circle. Furthermore, the elders of the community had to have been drawn from among the elders of the ḥevra kaddisha, for it seems highly unlikely that a person of irreproachable morality and sufficient wealth to be one of the community notables would not be a prominent member of the burial society as well. In both cases the title is linked as much to wealth as to the morality and citizenship of the individual. The distinction between these two memberships was limited to the nature of the relations maintained with the world outside the Jewish community: the burial society enjoyed its autonomy in order to distinguish itself from the larger community; its chief sources of revenue could be borrowed by the Jewish community in case of need, and this conferred on it a considerable financial and juridical "veto power" and allowed it to exercise a right of inspection over decisions or elections. In short, the hypothesis could be advanced that the ḥevra kaddisha represented an intermediary structure, but one quite as powerful as—and perhaps alternative to—the official structure of the community.

The text of the statutes of the Prague burial society can be taken as the model for those of other cities. While the internal workings of the societies might differ in detail, their principles were similar. The Prague society, then, represents an archetype of the Jewish burial society in the seventeenth and eighteenth centuries. The common basis of all the burial societies rested on an original constitution, governing members occupying honorific positions, salaried officiants, codified rules of general conduct, methods for collecting funds, regular meetings of administrators and members, set fines for penalizing violations, general measures concerning the sick, the dying, and the dead,[64] and, of course, annual elections of the executive committee and the annual banquet. The essential difference between one burial society and another lay in the procedures for admitting new members. The rules are more strict or more relaxed depending on the importance of the community. In Prague—a very important community where candidates must have been numerous—the status of "titular member" was granted only after a long period of probation. In Koenigsberg this status was conceded only to married men—after a year for those whose fathers already belonged to the ḥevra and after a minimum of two years for those whose fathers were not members.[65] Certain burial societies did not offer the status of member unless one of their number passed away, leaving a place vacant.[66] In the statutes of Boskowitz, in Moravia, we find that the candidate must be married for at least six years and that acceptance is limited to two candidates per year, except in case of a vacancy resulting from the death of a member of the ḥevra.[67] In Eibenschitz (Ivancice, in Moravia) a candidate had to have been on probation for four years and married at least three,[68] and this holds for

Neu-Raussnitz (Kaunice, in Moravia)[69] as well. Nevertheless, the societies generally used a selection process based on the ranking of assigned status, as in Prague. This is why in practice the majority of the members of the ḥevra kaddisha have a lesser status: they have neither the right to vote in elections nor the right to enact the rules they must follow. Yet they perform all the tasks of the society, visiting the sick, washing the bodies of the dead, collecting alms, and attending burials to constitute the *minyan,* the quorum of ten men, for prayer.

At two levels, then—one for full members, the other for potential members—the society allows for the rather speedy elimination of persons who do not suitably fulfill the duties of gravedigger, or who cannot pay their contributions, since probationary members are purely and simply excluded should they be remiss. The direct consequence of this system was the creation of an institution based on oligarchy but whose concrete functioning depended on all its members.

CHAPTER FIVE

# The Rhythm of Death

## THE SPIRITUAL POWER OF THE BURIAL SOCIETY

While Jewish historians have applied themselves to defining the ḥevra kaddisha either as a specifically Jewish structure dating back to the talmudic period or as the result of an integration of corporate models from the surrounding Christian world, they have not tried to analyze the subtle differences that distinguish it from the Christian guilds. The guilds functioned by the regrouping of a social and professional category of associates who became its members. And the social and spiritual "power" the guild exercised over its members combined privileges and constraints. As for the Christian societies devoted to works of charity, these "confraternities" were very close to the ḥevra kaddisha in their secular vocation as the "institution of death," according to Ariès.[1] Yet while they "provided assurance regarding the afterlife" by enshrouding the bodies of the dead and reciting prayers, they remained the religious arm of the usual corporate model, so doubling its primary vocation.

The ḥevra kaddisha is situated midway between these two models. On the one hand, it regrouped the Jews—on the basis not of profession but of citizenship and religion—while practicing a rigorous selection of its executive members; on the other hand, it enjoined all its members to behave in conformity with the rules it instituted, without transgression or exception, on pain of exclusion. The effective power of the burial society was therefore based on the conjunction of a juridical and spiritual body of law that assumed the acceptance of a social and moral power based on death. In this way daily life was organized around everything that constituted the end of the individual, and this became in a sense the motivating force and catalyst of communal life.

Members of the ḥevra placed primary importance on the act of faith, which is a spiritual exercise. Faith tacitly defines the internal functioning of the burial society. When Israel Abrahams studies the life of Jews of the Middle Ages,[2] he cannot define that life outside of daily religious practice and the conjectural contingencies imposed by the surrounding society. H. Pollack[3] may situate his study within a larger social framework, but he nonetheless resorts to the same type of analysis. This similarity of methodology occurs because until quite recently, Judaism represented a way of life. If the burial society therefore appropriated a power that allowed it to become a "state within a state,"[4] it was assured that this resulted from the polarization of the spiritual or religious universe translated by seemingly unrelated daily actions. Yet in the text of statutes governing the Prague society, spiritual exercise seems to be largely absent. Only article 27 mentions the reading of the *Maʾavar Yabbok* at the bedside of the dying, and article 1 requires that members of the ḥevra attend the synagogue mornings and evenings. The rules of societies in other cities are more specific on this subject. Notably, the society of Steinitz in Moravia indicates that "any person who mocks or slanders the occupations of the *ḥevra* on the subject of *tohorah* (mortuary purification) or visiting the sick . . . that person has sown rebellion against the *ḥevra*. . . . He has thus abused the divine commandments."[5]

To the extent that life and death depend on God, who "heals the sick and revives the dead,"[6] the organization of the burial society inevitably became the human intermediary not only between the divine will and the sick or dying but also between the divine and those in good health, for "he who fulfills the commandments of ḥesed shel emet (which define the mortuary and charitable functions) lengthens his days and his years, and he who does not disqualifies himself before heaven."[7] In this way the ḥevra kaddisha was "untouchable," for any person who tried to rebel against its authority was immediately punished for "mocking" the divine commandments. Not to participate in the society was equivalent, from a communal perspective, to social exclusion and, from a spiritual perspective, to refusing to fulfill the laws or commandments, the primary basis for the practice of Judaism.

As intermediary between the community and its members, the ḥevra kaddisha also seems to have been intermediary between God and man. It is therefore more tempting to compare this society to the Church than to a Christian religious order, despite certain shared features. This is even more striking when we learn from the Steinitz statutes[8] that the recitation of the Kaddish[9] and the *tehillim*[10] were put up for sale. The selling of the Kaddish was, however, neither innocent nor anodyne, for Jewish popular tales say that the soul of someone deceased can be saved by a special recitation of the Kaddish.[11] In this case, such a sale would be equivalent to the selling of indulgences—a confirmed bond between temporal and spiritual exercise. The text written by the scribes of the burial society is intended more to establish its limits and its internal administration than to define its field of action, which was no doubt so well known that it needed no explication. We shall have to turn to their mortuary practices for information about the specific activities of the ḥevra kaddisha with regard to attendance at deathbeds and the provision of mortuary and funerary "services."

## READINGS AT THE "DEATHBED"

With the exception of the talmudic tractates, the first specific compilation of laws and practices with regard to death and dying was done by Moses ben Naḥman, Naḥmanides, commonly known as the Ramban. *Torat ha-Adam,* which appeared in the thirteenth century, was the first exhaustive work treating laws relating to illness, death, and mourning. His compilation is based, of necessity, on talmudic and tannaitic sources, to which the Ramban added customs current in the Spanish and Ashkenazi communities of his time. Broadly repeated by Joseph Caro in his *Shulḥan Arukh,*[12] the precepts laid down by Naḥmanides were subsequently repeated in the general *Sifrei Minhagim* (Books of Customs) of the various communities, as well as in works specifically devoted to death.

In the seventeenth and eighteenth centuries, the most widely read works in the communities were the *Maʾaneh Lashon* (Expression of the Tongue), the *Sefer ha-Ḥaim* (Book of Life, a classic Jewish euphemism for death), and particularly the *Maʾavar Yabbok*. Of these the *Maʾaneh Lashon* is considered to be the oldest. It was published around 1615[13] and would be continually reissued, in Hebrew as well as in Yiddish, until the nineteenth century. It takes the form of a collection of prayers to be read at the cemetery, most often intended as pleas to the dead who had been "just" during their lifetimes to intercede on behalf of the living as well as the dead. Like a great many works of this period, it also contains a whole series of prayers meant for individuals in delicate situations or evident danger, such as pregnant women, women in labor, or sick children and adults; it also includes recitations for warding off demons or the evil eye. The *Ma'aneh Lashon* also contains the formulaic confession of the dying, the *Viddui.*

The *Ma'avar Yabbok,* composed by Aaron Berachia ben Moses of Modena in 1626, is a much more exhaustive work. It includes not only the complete ritual for dying, death, burial, and mourning but also prohibitions, cautions for the dying and the dead, and all the prayers in current use. In its abridged form, the *Kitsur Ma'avar Yabbok* (published in 1682), it was disseminated throughout the communities, sometimes under variants of the original title, as a small, handy manual for the sick or dying.

The *Shnei Luḥot ha-Berit* (the two tables of the covenant), written by Isaiah Horowitz, commonly known as the *Shelah* (the acronym of his book's title), was published in Amsterdam in 1649. Without being exclusively devoted to death, it nevertheless exerted a great influence on its contemporaries in the area of ethical practice toward the sick and dying.[14] The parts of this work concerning illness and death were largely integrated into later mortuary manuals.

The works cited constitute the common corpus found among the vademecum published by the communities. Between the seventeenth and the nineteenth centuries, works of this sort proliferated to such a degree that it is impossible to account for all of them, as almost every community published its own. The *Yosef Omets,* commissioned by the Frankfurt community from Joseph Hahn,[15] is one of the most typical of these books of customs, an amalgam of talmudic precepts, practices, and recommended prayers. It also describes practices specific to this community that were determined by conditions of life in the city of Frankfurt.

Faced with this abundance of writing and the many reissues of such works, we are tempted to wonder what such publications mean. Who was their intended audience? Should they be seen as manuals reserved for members of the burial societies, or do they formulate "the art of dying well" to be read by anyone who would not be taken unprepared by the arrival of death?

If it is difficult to gauge the use individuals made of these works, it is still more difficult to evaluate their real impact. Were they in fact read? If so, by whom and on what occasions? This is still an open question. The numerous reissues of these manuals over the course of two centuries, however, suggest that they had a definite influence on generations of readers. Moreover, several answers are provided by the works themselves, by their literary style and their method of writing. For example, Horowitz's work, the *Shnei Luḥot ha-Berit,*[16] reminds its readers that always, in all circumstances, life and health are in God's hands, and they can be taken at any moment; the *Shelah* adds that the individual must constantly think of death "as if he were on his deathbed"—which recalls the exhortations contained in the *Artes Moriendi.* Nonetheless, these pious inducements are not addressed to everyone. The author's refined and often lyrical style would not be intelligible to the average reader: the numerous citations and kabbalistic formulas are drenched with an esoteric mysticism that keeps it from being a popular work.

The case of the *Ma'avar Yabbok* is quite different, and so too is the Sefer ha-Ḥaim. These works imitate the two types of writing usually found in books of the period: the specific use of Yiddish writing, the *vaiber shrift* (dubbed "women's writing" because women were not supposed to read Hebrew), for the explanatory discussions of ritual and Hebrew writing, including vowel points, for the parts to be recited. The Hebrew portions were found in all prayer books and were clearly meant to be accessible to the greatest number of people. The edition of the Sefer ha-Ḥaim that serves as a reference here also contains a nonrecitable translation of the text into Yiddish,[17] clearly to make it available to readers who had no grasp of the Holy Tongue. If all this does not give us a specific count of the readers involved, it does allow us to confirm that those works were composed in order to be read and understood by everyone interested in doing so.

If the *Ma'avar Yabbok* deviates from the funerary ritual with its kabbalistic interpretations (and accompanying customs) and represents a kind of Lurianic breviary of death and the beliefs associated with it, the Sefer ha-Ḥaim is more specifically a handbook of prayers than a complete work of ritual. It must have been widely disseminated, for very few individuals in the course of their lives can avoid attending a funeral or praying for someone deceased, for a woman in labor, or for a sick child. This work also contains prayers for the education of children, and it furthermore exhorts a husband to prevent his wife from "falling asleep while nursing her child," to "put it to sleep in its bed near her" for fear she might suffocate it. This last and singular warning indicates that this collection must have reached a wide audience.

If the Jewish mortuary liturgy presents a great number of daily prayers that seem to be part of the quotidian preparation for death, their function does not seem a priori to correspond, like a Judaized echo, to analogous works in Christian society. It would seem that the Jewish mortuary manuals were more specifically meant for the burial society, and for individuals in need of their help and able to summon it, than for ordinary folk. The distinction in the use of these works is related to the distinction established between the complete collections, like the *Ma'avar Yabbok* and the *Torat ha-Adam,* which were specifically conceived for members of the burial societies, and the abridged or pocket versions, such as the Sefer ha-Ḥaim and the *Kitsur Ma'avar Yabbok,* which found wider circulation.

## CROSSING THE JABBOK

The ḥesed shel emet, that is, the charitable acts necessary for the completion of the *mitzvot,* the commandments, begins with caring for the sick. Naḥmanides defines the importance of this commandment, for even "God buries the dead, visits the sick, and consoles the afflicted." *Bikkur ḥolim,* visiting the sick, is a bedrock value, for "he who does not visit the sick is like he who sheds blood," and he adds that the person who visits a sick man thereby intercedes in favor of his cure.[18]

The *Shelah* again defines the role of the visitor: he explains that according to the *Zohar,* he who watches over a sick man and encourages him to repent is an "angel who brings good."[19] But the basic function of the visitor is to read from the Torah, for "in every portion [of the Torah] there is a portion of the world to come."[20]

The Sefer ha-Ḥaim reckons that visiting the sick is necessary for three reasons: first, so that the visitor can eventually learn how to heal the sick person; second, to provide for all the needs of the sick; and third, so that the visitor may pray for the sick person, including him in "all the afflicted of Israel" by recalling the notion of the entity of Israel (the people of Israel), which is inscribed in the Jewish perception of the universe.

In the *Ma'avar Yabbok,* Berachia explains that the *gemilut ḥesed* also concerns the living and the dead and that visiting the sick is part of it. The visitor prays to ask grace for the sick person, which implies that he who would approach a sick man without praying that he might live is not completely fulfilling the commandment to "visit the sick."[21]

The second element formulated by the duty of bikkur ḥolim is the value of life itself. It is necessary to visit the sick, especially on the sabbath, says Horowitz, because "the sabbath is [in itself] an entreaty and hastens the cure."[22] Naḥmanides specifies that illness suppresses all the prohibitions connected to the sabbath for someone whose life is in danger, for life takes priority. Therefore it is one's duty to light the fire if it is cold, or to make and bring something to eat if this is advisable. Citing his master Maimonides, he adds, "One does everything necessary for a sick man, even on the sabbath; and especially for a woman in labor. For the danger of death takes precedence over all else."[23] While he advises that everything must be done to cure the sick person, however, Naḥmanides specifies that one must avoid the temptation to cure him by magic or sorcery.[24]

The notion of visiting and caring for the sick is nonetheless a late addition to the vocation of the burial societies, as shown by the Prague texts of 1692 and 1702. This function is mentioned only in article 27, which requires that one read the *Ma'avar Yabbok* to the dying. It is only in the second half of the eighteenth century that the burial societies devote themselves equally to the sick. Until then their mission was limited by their title, "gravediggers."[25] The burial society of Steinitz is the single exception and a pioneer in this area: beginning in 1655 the gabbai is in charge of human life and must see to the needs of the sick, visiting them daily without regard to whether they are rich or poor. He is also responsible for deciding whether the ḥevra should pay for the care of an indigent sick man and for delegating one of the members of the society to care personally for someone ill. On the sabbath, all the members of the ḥevra must get together to make morning visits to the sick. Imagining every possibility, however, the rules specify that an enemy of the sick man who would begrudge his recovery is exempt from visiting him.[26] In the statutes of Triesch, dated 1687, we find that the gabbai "must not be allowed to abandon" a sick person, but there is very little emphasis on this mission of bikkur ḥolim, which hardly warrants a whole paragraph.[27]

Horowitz established three levels in the accomplishment of ḥesed shel emet, "for the Holy One, blessed be He, blesses the married, heals the sick, and buries the dead."[28] He explains this definition by stating that the first level of piety involves the celebration of marriage but that visiting the sick represents a higher level because the sick person does not know if he will live or die, "and if he dies, he will pay nothing back." The third level, the highest of these values, consists of burying the dead without expecting any payment. These three levels of the concept of "service" or "kindness" circumscribe, according to Horowitz, the beginning (marital union), the middle (the uncertainty of life), and the end (death) of the life cycle.

In all these texts the emphasis is on the final confession, the *Viddui*. As Horowitz explains, "If visiting the sick is very important for the needs of the body . . . one must also attend to the needs of the soul and make certain that the sick man asks correctly for meḥilah [absolution]."[29]

Naḥmanides compares the sick person to a man who must be judged before being sent to the scaffold: "If he has good advocates, he is saved, otherwise he is not." He adds that a man's best advocates are found in the confession. Furthermore, the confession is recited to the *goses*—the dying—so that he or she will not die.[30] Isaiah Horowitz thinks that the individual must be warned that he is in danger, without waiting "for the soul of the sick person to float away, thus preventing him from repenting in full consciousness and utter sincerity."[31] Berachia in his turn relies on the *Zohar* and holds that recitation of the *Viddui* leads one's sins from the upper to the lower regions, thus whittling them down, and that in addition the confession "closes Satan's mouth" so that he cannot slander the dying man in Heaven.[32]

The Sefer ha-Ḥaim provides all the formulas of prayers to recite at the sickbed, depending on whether the speaker is a close or distant relative or a stranger. It advises visitors to make pleasant conversation with the sick person while reassuring themselves that he will not leave unfinished business behind, such as unpaid wages or debts. It also advises testing him before he is too ill. Two formulas of confession are suggested: the first for a sick person asking to be healed, the second for someone preparing for his imminent entrance into the Olam ha-Ba, the world to come.

All the mortuary manuals caution that women and young children should be sent away before the recitation of the confession. Naḥmanides writes that after reciting the Shema,[33] attendants must refrain from weeping and lamenting before the dying man, and those who cannot stop groaning must be sent away.

Berachia specifies that the dying man must donate money for charity, then wrap himself in his prayer shawl and recite his confession in

Berachia adds that "the higher life" depends on these three commandments, which incarnate the *sod,* the essential secret or mystery of life. The moment of birth is therefore crucial, for the *sefiroth* (spheres) are thus attracted here below: the life of the mother and that of the child are in danger.[46] But if the woman should die in labor, even on the sabbath, "one takes a knife, opens her belly, and removes the child," Naḥmanides tells us.[47] Naḥmanides, again citing the *Evel Rabbati,*[48] declares that when several burials must be ordered, the sage takes priority over the disciple (as a sign of honor), but when it comes to a man and a woman, the woman must be given first burial because she is "closer to decomposition."[49]

The connection between the woman in danger and the candle mirrors the link between impurity and light: if the woman does not respect the prescriptions of the laws of purity,[50] she puts herself as well as her child in danger, for, says the *Ma'avar Yabbok,*[51] "they [women] are all beneath the rod of death," and death is intrinsically "feminine"—*nekevah*. This triad associating woman, birth, and death evokes universal notions of conception.

When death has done its work, the witnesses recite psalms and must perform the *keriah,* that is, they must tear their clothing above the heart. The torn garment is the external sign of mourning for the Jews.[52] Naḥmanides recalls that a man also tears his clothing when a Torah scroll is burned in order to express the violent rupture of the universal order.[53] Horowitz comments on this act by assimilating it to the "breaking" of the Tablets of the Law, to which he compares the dead man. As we have seen, death modifies the place granted to the human being, and the torn garment also expresses this breach between the dead body that becomes the seat of impurity and the soul that flees from it by consecrating the effective disunion between the human entity (the body and its soul) and the cadaver (the body alone). The *Shelah* insists on this human entity, which is "like five and five that make ten," namely, the ten fingers of God.[54]

At the hour of death, says the *Ma'avar Yabbok,* a human being knows the dead, whom it encounters along with the "light and glory of the *Shekhinah,*" for, if disencumbered of the body, it sees and understands through the perceptions of the soul. Berachia adds that "his tutelary Angel," that is, the angel personally assigned to him, stays by his side, "and he sees the Angel of Death who fills his eyes." This reminds us, he says, that we have tasted of the fruit of the knowledge of good and evil. At this moment the son (if he has one) closes his father's eyes, for "the dead man has seen the *Shekhinah*" and must see nothing more.[55]

One must be particularly vigilant, Horowitz specifies, that no limb of the deceased should hang over the bed, for "all that hangs over the bed will be neither reassembled nor buried (in the higher sepulchre)." He notes as well that the bed represents the sphere of the *malkhut Shekhinah,* the kingdom of the Divine Presence, and is thus the receptacle of souls. Every limb found outside the bed would be touched by the impurity that is rampant around it, and this would compromise the integrity of the soul. For this spiritual integrity is also guaranteed by corporal wholeness, hence "the guardian of the soul remains far from the *Shekhinah,*" that it shall not become whole without having an unbroken vessel on the day of the resurrection.[56]

According to these sources, after the deathbed ritual the object of subsequent practices shifts. The dead person is treated only as a cadaver, *nevelah* or *gufah,* and the last rites now concern only the living, who are divided into two categories: those who must administer the last preparations for burial and all others, close relatives of the deceased who must follow the laws of mourning for the coming year.[57]

## THE SECRET OF THE TREE OF LIFE

As soon as the death throes begin, the family notifies the ḥevra kaddisha, which sends some of its members to say prayers composed for this purpose in the *Maʾavar Yabbok.* Except for Naḥmanides' work, written in the thirteenth century and before the creation of the burial societies, all the mortuary manuals mention the ḥevra kaddisha. Those present suggest that the dying person offer gifts to charity, and works heavily influenced by Kabbalah methodically calculate, according to the *gematria* (numerical equivalents of Hebrew letters), the numbers corresponding to these offerings, for according to the hallowed formula, "charity saves from death."

When the dying man has breathed his last, the congregation recites psalms as well as the traditional prayer, the Baruch Dayyan ha-Emet. The mourners tear their clothing, while the eldest son, if there is one—otherwise a close relative—closes his eyes. At this point, the ḥevra enters the scene.

The administrator of the society designates members to prepare the body for burial, make the coffin, and dig the grave in an appropriate place at the cemetery, depending on the deceased's social rank. During this time, the mortuary ritual is organized around the body.

The *Ma'avar Yabbok* recommends that the son scatter earth on his father's eyes.[58] Then the face is covered. After waiting at least a quarter of an hour,[59] the deceased will be put on the ground, on earth or sand, or on a straw pallet. Berachia explains that the ground is impervious to the impurity of the dead; this is not the case with a bed or table, which retains evil spirits. The sheet used to cover the deceased serves to isolate him from the sight of the living, who must not see the mystery of death.[60]

Then the windows are thrown open,[61] and custom dictates that all water found in receptacles in the house of the dead, as well as in those of the closest neighbors, must be thrown out. This water must be spilled onto the earth, for again, the earth cannot absorb impurity. Berachia illuminates the meaning of this practice by indicating that anyone who drank this water poisoned by the Angel of Death would be in grave danger.[62]

While the members of the burial society are busy digging the grave at the cemetery, the mortuary purification in the house of the dead (or in the building designated for this purpose) must be seen to; this is called the tohorah. Vigil must also be kept to make sure that the deceased is not left alone, even for a moment, and thus attendants must be notified who will take turns at the bedside until his burial. The deceased is particularly vulnerable to evil spirits that could take possession of his remains and is rather like the couple about to be married, who must not be left alone in the hours before the ceremony.

The tohorah is performed by the members of the ḥevra. The body must be completely washed in a precise way, without ever being completely uncovered. The order of purification begins on top—seat of the Divine Presence—and proceeds toward the bottom—seat of the world of "husks" that cover matter. Each of the gestures executed during the purification has its own significance. Those who fulfill this duty must see to it that no speck of dust or impurity of any kind remains, either on the body or in the hair, which is carefully washed and combed.[63] Every operation is accompanied as well by a specific liturgy composed of verses from the Bible, especially psalms. It is recommended that disciples should be responsible for the tohorah of their master, but a son cannot perform this ritual for his father. Once the purification is complete, the deceased must be clothed, for on the day of resurrection

..e dead will arise clothed. According to Berachia, the dead man will first be completely covered by a shroud of white swaddling and then wrapped in his prayer shawl, for "the soul of the body" must be clothed as well as that of the "breath."[64] The *Ma'avar Yabbok* thus makes a distinction between these two souls sundered by death: the bodily soul and the divine soul, which will be reunited once more only at the resurrection.

According to the *Zohar,*[65] the undergarment is that of the animal or bodily soul. The prayer shawl represents the dress of the divine soul, which is united with the Shekhinah whenever a man dons it to pray with devekut.[66] This indicates the extreme importance given to clothing the dead, for a man must leave the burial vault just as he has entered it.[67] But if this is the case, why not dress the dead in their best finery, in their sabbath clothes? Because, the answer goes, this difference in dress marks the distinction between the profane body one dresses for the sabbath and the holy body that rejoins the "Divine Royalty" after death.

The attitude of those involved in mortuary purification, coffin construction, and gravedigging must be free of any profane thoughts, out of respect for the dead. These injunctions, already inscribed in the *Evel Rabbati,*[68] are also found in all the mortuary manuals as well as in the regulations of the burial society.

> Let the *gabbai'im* [the administrators] take care that those who dig the grave do not behave frivolously, that they are not negligent in any detail, that they do not eat or drink in the cemetery, and that they do not quarrel or joke among themselves. Let them conduct themselves with dread and fear of God in every thing, and let this stand as well for the construction of the coffin and for the *tohorah*.[69]

The vigil that must be kept over the deceased applies equally to his grave. From the moment it has been dug, it can also be invaded by evil spirits or by impurity that would attack the cadaver.[70]

After death, the soul leaves the body only gradually and only after the burial has been completed, for this separation is a wrenching and painful process. The soul watches all the acts performed by the living around its remains.[71] If the soul is present, it sees, perceives, and hears everything that is done and said around the body it has inhabited.[72] This is why the body of the dead must not be treated negligently and vigil must be kept over it to preserve its dignity, for if the integrity of a dead person can be damaged by contempt, it can, in turn, harm the living.[73] It is therefore out of respect for the dead, who cannot chant any blessing, that those who keep watch are exempt from the recitation of the Shema as well as from other positive commandments bound to prayer.[74]

The necessity of burying the dead in the ground is based on the fact that man comes from dust and must return to dust. The cadaver, then, must have earth "under" it and "over" it to realize the original union of the body with the earth, as well as that of the divine soul with the Shekhinah. A man who is buried in the land of Israel is as if interred beneath the Temple,[75] and he is thus doubly sanctified; this is his eternal home since all the exiles will be gathered here on the day of the resurrection. Jews practiced the custom of sprinkling a little of Israel's earth on the eyes of the dead to recall its presence; this served both to chase away the impurity of the lands of the exile and to hasten the decomposition of the cadaver and hence the process of reuniting body and earth, soul and Shekhinah.

It is also out of respect for the dead that the recommendation is made not to let the deceased spend the night without burial. In Prague, for example, the regulation of the burial society specifies that every person who dies should be buried that very day, until 3:00 P.M. in summer and until 2:00 P.M. in winter.[76] The problem posed by holidays (or the sabbath) requires that burial be delayed—because of the interdiction on any act relating to work (and therefore on digging a grave or carrying the bier). But as any delay may affect the integrity of the dead person, the officiant is charged with deciding whether or not he has reason to authorize the burial outside regular hours.

A place in the cemetery is not, however, obtained gratis. The price of the grave varies depending on the communities and the age of the dead. Distinctions are established, sometimes between babies and children, as in Raussnitz,[77] or between children under the age of twelve and adults, as in Steinitz.[78] In Triesch, the difference in price is evaluated according to whether the dead person is an adult, an adolescent, or a child under five years old.[79] It is notably the case, moreover, that when the burial societies establish a price list for places in the cemetery, which does not happen in Prague, they are establishing a distinction between individuals depending on whether or not they are registered with the ḥevra. In Triesch the gabbaʾim are entreated not to ask more than the price indicated by the rules of the country.[80] The burial societies also reserve the right to take pledges from families who are not registered with the society and to sell them in cases where the debt incurred by the heirs is not repaid: the Triesch ruling specifies that this reimbursement should be made during the thirty days following death.[81]

When the members of the ḥevra kaddisha have performed the tohorah, when they have recited the customary prayers for each stage of the purification of the body, when they have spread an egg beaten in its shell (symbolizing the life cycle) on the head of the deceased, he is then dressed in mortuary clothes of white wool that the women have sewn for this purpose, wrapped in his prayer shawl, and covered with a shroud. He must then be put in his coffin. The dead person is thus in his mystic dress, which will accompany him in the upper worlds, and he knows the secret of "the tree of life."[82] After undergoing the ritual purification and being dressed in celestial garb, the symbolic status of the deceased changes once more: the dead person is transferred to the side of the divine and therefore is no longer an object of impurity. If the deceased is one of the "Just," a *tsaddik,* he rejoins the glorious meeting of the upper worlds where the other *tsaddikim* await him, as is evoked by the words of the Shema Yisrael [Hear O Israel]: "the Lord our God, the Lord is one."

The dead man must then be borne to the cemetery, where those in attendance will proceed to the *hakkafot.* The coffin will be raised and carried at shoulder height. The ritual will be slightly different depending on whether the deceased was or was not a *ba'al Torah,* a learned man. If he was, the last ritual duties will be performed in the room where he used to study Torah, for the tsaddikim fill their dwelling place with holiness, and this holiness, kedushah, is a permanent thing. The coffin is carried on its bearers' shoulders while the attendants recite appropriate songs and verses.[83] Carrying the bier in this way is symbolically analogous to the way the Holy Ark was borne before Moses: the deceased thus becomes the equivalent of that supremely precious object, the divine Ark.

In principle the whole community, or at least all the members of the ḥevra kaddisha, is present as the body is borne to the cemetery. No one must precede the bier, and the family walks behind it. For the burial of a "great man," they proceed as if leading a couple under the wedding canopy, for the soul of the deceased rises toward the Ark of glory, and one must witness this splendor.

The bier that supports the coffin is led by the angel Michael,[84] who accompanies the soul of the deceased toward the Holy Temple. Berachia compares burial to the different mystic levels of the soul: the cemetery is related to the upper sepulchre in the same way that the death of the body is allied to the higher life, for the soul rises toward the seat of the dead in the upper worlds, while its "husk" remains in the lower world, the cemetery.[85]

On the way to the cemetery, inside it, and on the way out, men and women must form two separate groups, the men walking in front, the women following, and they must not mingle or walk together. The cemetery must not be disturbed by men gazing at women, for this would represent a transgression that would put their very lives in danger. Moreover, the women's weeping and lamenting weaken the song of the seraphim, who rejoice at the arrival of the deceased. The "forces" that might be unleashed during a burial must therefore be carefully controlled.[86] The rules of the burial societies indicate the seriousness of the preoccupation with separating men and women. If we are to believe the particularly harsh arrangements made in Prague for enforcing this rule, its observance must have been highly problematic. If the women stray from their section in the procession, their cloaks are taken as a retaliatory measure and given to the poor; and as this is obviously not an adequate deterrent, article 25 cautions that beadles will be hired to spray water on those who would approach the procession of the other sex. In Triesch, the beadle must march between the two groups to mark their separation, and he is authorized to use any means possible, even stone throwing, against recalcitrant citizens to ward off "the danger of death" that mingling would provoke.[87]

The interment takes place as follows: if the cemetery is at some distance from the Jewish quarter, the deceased is brought by cart as far as the entrance. At the gate of the cemetery he is placed on the ground, the designated psalm is recited, and the procession is formed. First comes the bier supporting the coffin, borne by men chosen by the family of the deceased: sons, disciples, parents, friends, or members of the burial society. According to the Sefer ha-Ḥaim,[88] the family walks immediately behind the bier. Then come the dignitaries of the community and the burial society at the head of their membership. The women come last, with family members leading the way.

The funeral procession will stop seven times on the way to the grave to mark the seven levels of the universal order. The coffin is placed before the open grave, and the ceremony proper begins. This is led by a dignitary of the burial society, whose importance depends on the rank of the deceased.[89]

The prayer said specifically for burial is the Tsidduk ha-Din—which means literally "justification"—but the most solemn moment of the urials of this period surely must have been the hakkafot. Seven times the coffin was circled, each of these circlings punctuated by a particular blessing and a gift of charity to the poor, for which the alms box was held by a member of the burial society or by someone honored with this task.[90] The mortuary manuals indicate that at the same time pieces of gold or silver money, or lacking these, stones, were cast onto the deceased and buried with him as a sign of "sacrifice." This done, the cantor left the ranks to chant the prayers asking for mercy, to which the congregation responded in chorus.

The hakkafot were not always performed in the cemetery itself. They could also be performed, according to local custom, in the house of the deceased, before the raising of the body. Berachia recommends in his introduction that they are best done at the cemetery, right after the Tsidduk ha-Din. This practice is not mentioned by Naḥmanides,[91] which would indicate that it did not exist in the thirteenth century. Berachia, however, devotes two paragraphs to an explanation of its underlying meaning,[92] relating the seven circlings to the seven symbols of the universe according to the order of the "spheres" (sefirot). The hakkafot are meant, then, to reaffirm the union of the soul of the deceased with the upper worlds. They symbolize, in addition, the dancing and rejoicing God will grant to the Just in paradise. Barachia recalls that the city of Jericho was conquered by such hakkafot, encircling the forces of impurity below and on high. In the same way, the hakkafot will protect the dead from harmful powers.

Finally, the coffin is taken in the arms of the gravediggers, as if "in the arms of the Universe,"[93] and placed in its grave. After the recitation of the Sanctification, the Kaddish, the congregation passes by the grave in the same order as in the procession and throws three shovelsful of earth taken from a receptacle held by the beadle. Those present again put alms in the charity box, for the adage inscribed on it tells them that "charity saves from death."[94]

When the gravediggers have filled the grave, the funerary ritual is complete. The family then begins the period of mourning, which is marked by the immediate removal of their shoes. Close relatives stand in line, men and woman always separated, at some distance from the grave, and the congregation presents the customary condolence: "May God console you among the mourners of Israel," recalling the cosmogonic unity of Israel and the universe and also reiterating the previous inclusion of the ill among "all the afflicted of Israel."

To leave the cemetery, the separate processions of men and women are reassembled. The *Ma'avar Yabbok* asks the women to be patient for a quarter of an hour before starting off toward the gate, so that the men have time for completing the rituals for leaving the cemetery.

In leaving the burial ground, people must again disengage themselves from its resident evil spirits, impurity, and devastation. To do this, they will first stop three times to pull up fistsful of grass, which they will throw over their heads, behind them, and skyward. This gesture is an allusion to the resurrection of the dead, "who will be raised up with a pure body."[95] Then, heading toward the gate to the cemetery, they punctuate their progress seven times, or three, depending on local custom, by sitting on the ground and reciting prayers meant to scatter the destructive forces that accompany the deceased on his way to Heaven,[96] for when they are seated, says Berachia, "they are saved." He entreats people to stop seven times and not three, for the "husks" of the dead are accompanied by six destructive powers, bad female spirits who attack the human being. These forces represent the spirit of evil, the *yetser ha-ra,* and also Satan. To banish these definitively, it is necessary to sit seven times and on the seventh to recite the Shir Shel Pegu'im, which symbolically combats them.

At the cemetery gate, or once back home, depending on local practice, people must wash their hands three times without either drying them or reciting the blessing that usually accompanies this act, to eliminate any impurity. According to the mortuary works, this marks the conclusion of the funerary ritual proper. The prescriptions that come afterward describe the rites of mourning.

At this juncture several important concepts emerge in terms of Jewish mentalities, and certain elements are evident which might serve as cultural guidelines. The first observation concerns the place of the Kabbalah in the mortuary manuals examined here. Indeed, its fundamental works, such as the *Sefer Yetsira,* the *Zohar,* and the *Midrash ha-ne'elam,*[97] are frequently cited and serve to explain, comment on, or establish the ritual that determines the attitudes formed by Jewish custom and belief in the course of these two centuries. The custom of hakkafot, for example, seems to be a particular element in kabbalistic literature, which is the likely source of these contributions to funerary practice.

Reading these Jewish mortuary manuals, we might postulate that the "mystery of death" is resolved by the interpretation of the mystic mystery: the sod of the Kabbalah. According to these texts, the hidden forces of the universe, which seize the individual upon his death, are responding precisely to the universal "rupture" that is continually reenacted in the rupture occasioned by individual death. We can equally confirm that the sick and the bereaved (in the literal sense, the Hebrew term *avelim* means "the afflicted"), must be reunited through ritual with the cosmogony of Israel, like the dead in the prayers and services of commemoration: the Yizkor and the Kaddish. According to this principle it seems indispensable to include the sick, as well as the bereaved, who are then reentering the category of the sick, according to the *Shulḥan Arukh,*[98] in the entity that represents Israel. The adage concerning the "bereaved of Israel," then, cannot fail to recall the allegory of the "bereaved of Zion," symbolized by the seven angels who weep each night for the destruction of the Temple. The *Shelah* encourages all its readers to join these angels in their recitation of the nocturnal psalm: "By the rivers of Babylon," one says each night, "the world is as in death, and souls rise and float in the universe."[99]

If death incorporates the supreme rupture of the universe, according to kabbalistic interpretation, it is an inherent part of it, and daily ritual will not allow this to be forgotten: the Jew commends his soul to God each evening by reciting the Shema Yisrael, which will also be the final prayer of his life. Berachia distinguishes, however, "great death," the real thing, from "little death," or sleep, which is the "soul's rest." Citing Moses Cordovero, he indicates that when a person sleeps, the soul, the breath, and the essence receive their vitality from the *sefirah* of the *bina,* in the image of its fate after death, as the Midrash explains: "The *ru'aḥ* rises and descends, and while man sleeps the *neshamah* rises and breathes in the life on high."[100]

Horowitz specifies that the human being is subject at any moment to the divine will that legislates whether we "live or die" and that he must think of his death "as if he were bedridden and in mortal danger."[101] For Christian society beginning in the sixteenth century, the appeal is identical, as Ariès writes: "We must at every moment in our lives be in the state the medieval *Artes Moriendi* recommended for the dying: 'in hora mortis nostrae.'"[102] This shared perception of life as before-death, or as preparation for death, can also be correlated temporally and chronologically with the subtle evolution of *Artes Moriendi*; Ariès tells us that these manuals for dying well increasingly became "a new category of pious literature for the devotions of everyday life."[103] The Jewish mortuary manuals must surely have followed the same development, otherwise we could not explain why the Sefer ha-Ḥaim includes recommendations connected with maternity in a work of prayers for the sick and the dead.[104]

Are such exhortations the result of an evolution, or do they spring from secular injunctions that date back to the sources of Judaism? The importance granted quite clearly from the beginning of the sixteenth century to the notion of ḥesed shel emet—disinterested kindness—would favor an evolution of attitudes, influenced, among the Jews, by the specific contributions of Lurianic Kabbalah within the context of a general tendency toward transformation in Western mentalities.

Indeed, the insistence on the notion of charity—which might seem to be the source of the creation of the burial societies—suggests, through the practices of the societies, a very progressive mutation of this notion. The meaning of charity was increasingly directed toward the needs of the living. From a single focus on final duties to the dead, the burial societies would extend their activities to the sick, then take responsibility for the poor as well, by virtue of a principle identical to the notion of Christian mercy exalted by the Catholic brotherhoods.

Jewish conceptions of death confer a unique importance on the elevation of the divine soul, which separates from the body in order to rejoin the Shekhinah. The soul and Shekhinah thus evoke the image of a mystic marriage based on the analogy between the situation of a betrothed couple and that of the dead. The *Evel Rabbati*[105] already posed the question of which takes priority, a marriage celebration or a funeral (the middle or the end of the life cycle). And the mortuary manuals maintain that since the "dead" and the "betrothed" are equally vulnerable to malevolent forces, they must be protected in a similar fashion: by constant vigilance, until burial in the case of the dead, until the celebration of marriage in the case of the betrothed. Furthermore, the concept of ḥesed shel emet implies the identical sanctification of marriage, illness, and death by the intermediary of the "Holy One, blessed be He, who blesses the betrothed, heals the sick, and buries the dead."[106]

This notion of death as a mystic marriage exists simultaneously with the duality that operates against sanctification. With the final breath, the body is separated from its divine contents, the soul, which will progressively escape it and, if deserving, rejoin the Just who welcome it to the higher sepulchre where it will happily await the resurrection of bodies and souls. Although the cadaver must be treated with the respect due its supernatural powers, death has removed its "holiness." Only its essential corporeal integrity must now be overseen, without any intervening notion of sacralization.

Yet once beyond death, the living and the dead can still speak together in the universe of prayer, for the soul remains attached to the place where its remains reside. We can see in the idea of this permanent bond the reason that practices in which the living ask for the intercession of the dead were so frequent in Jewish societies during this period and were always situated in the cemetery. This represented the symbolic and central site of the breach between the human and the divine, the bond between the eternity that remains tied to the body, though dead, and the divine realm where the Just gather: the outer limit defining the boundary between the forces of evil and the divine essence.

## FROM AFFLICTION TO SORROW

In Judaism, the loss of someone close is an unusual event. Those who survive enter a sort of private space, whose limits contain, even while embracing, the violence of intense emotions that can be unleashed by the death of a loved one. The rupture provoked by death is accompanied by a suspension of the exercise of positive commandments and an interdiction on sociability that thus allows the expression of sorrow, guilt, and the desire to die even as these feelings are carefully channeled. The extreme ritualization of the period following a death establishes a distinction between practices devoted to the fate of the deceased and those reserved for the family. And the exegetical texts insist on the mechanism that maintains the deceased and those who survive in a spiritual interdependence that goes beyond the moment of death. Because all the descendants of the deceased are considered in danger, stalked by the Angel of Death, they must initiate a detailed ritual procedure that, at the end of one year divided into five distinct phases, will allow them gradually to rejoin the life of the community.

From the moment the last breath is drawn, laws strictly codify the conduct of the family of the deceased. Mourning applies only to close family and is assumed for the seven closest relatives: father, mother, son, daughter, unmarried brother or sister on the father's side, as well as the wife or husband.[107] Halakhah makes a semantic distinction between two stages of mourning, the first before and the second after burial. How, it asks, shall we differentiate the *aninut* that precedes burial from the *avelut* that follows it?

> *Aninut* represents the affliction of the heart, the internal suffering of the soul, as indicated by *ben oni (Vayishlah,* Gen. 35), son of my suffering; *avelut* represents true mourning and is recognized as such, defined as [being] *overcome with sadness and the head covered* (Esther 6:12), [and] the clothes of mourning: *and they did not pray during mourning but lamented, for there is no lamentation that does not come from the heart* (*Sanhedrin* 46).[108]

When death occurs, the period of *onen* begins—which I shall qualify here, arbitrarily, as "of affliction," although the Hebrew root implies complaint and lamentation. First, those present at the deathbed tear their garments, then the mirrors are covered with a cloth or turned against the wall. Numerous commentaries interpret this practice, so common in the societies of those days, and one explanation is based on the creation of man in the divine image: upon the death of one of his creatures, God's integrity is diminished, for the decrease of a man is equivalent to an interruption of relations between the living man and the living God. As man's dignity is conferred on him only by this reflection of his creator, so that the image of the Creator himself is diminished by the death of a human being. The moment of death is thus also a moment of destruction of the divine image, and the mirror that serves to reflect the human image must no longer serve.[109] More pragmatic reasons are also proposed: people will come to pray in the house of the deceased, and to diminish the risk of bowing before one's own image, it is forbidden to pray before a mirror,[110] which reflects and serves as an intermediary between vision and perception.[111]

According to custom, one or many candles are lit around the dead body, and the explanations proposed for this practice are equally varied: according to *Ma'avar Yabbok,* the demons that swarm in the darkness flee from light;[112] furthermore, the flame of the candle symbolizes man, as it is said: "The soul of man is a divine flame."[113] Finally, to warn the neighbors that a death has occurred in the house, bringing impurity and initiating the period of mourning, a glass of water is thrown out the window.[114]

During this stage, which must be as brief as possible, the afflicted is responsible for his dead: he must notify the ḥevra kaddisha to make all the necessary arrangements for the funeral garments, the coffin, and the grave. But while the "affliction" lasts, he must not take the time to wash or tend to other affairs, and he must eat standing up, in haste. While the dead man is in his house, the onen must not perform any positive commandment: he is not to put on phylacteries, he is not to recite daily blessings, and he is to abstain from eating meat or drinking wine. Once the ḥevra takes responsibility for the funerary procedure, however, and all the details are in order, the afflicted can resume eating complete meals.

It is only when the grave is closed that mourning actually begins. Avelut is initiated at the cemetery, and the first prayer of the bereaved consists of the recitation of the mourner's Kaddish before the tomb, which differs from his daily recitation by the addition of a paragraph specifically devoted to the resurrection. The bereaved must symbolically bare their hearts by tearing their garments and then remove their shoes. Already in its time the treatise *Evel Rabbati*[115] understood that going without shoes might occasion the mockery of gentiles and allowed the mourners instead to put a little earth in their shoes until returning home.[116] The first expression of avelut is the practice, observed annually on the day of Tisha b'Av,[117] of including the mourning for the deceased in "all the mournings of Israel," as symbolized and remembered in the mourning for the destruction of the Temple. Thus the bereaved dresses in the black "mourning cowl" and sprinkles ashes on his head, according to the custom of the "bereaved of Zion."[118] When the second stage of mourning, the shiva, has begun, the interdiction on performing the commandments ceases. The bereaved hasten to the place "of the execution of judgment," if there is one in the cemetery, or go home to recite the other daily services. When the avel is allowed to resume praying, the members of the community must provide him with tokens of consolation, for according to Berachia, the bereaved is under the blow of divine judgment, the Tsidduk ha-Din, which has just been recited, and the consolers must soberly repeat to him that his consolation will also come from Heaven.[119]

As its name indicates, the shiva lasts seven days, in the course of which the family must remain secluded with its pain in the house of the deceased. After returning from the burial ground, the bereaved may not eat their own food.[120] The "first meal" must then be brought to them by neighbors or more distant relatives untouched by the codifications of mourning. The "condolence meal" must be provided by a third party: "For the *avel* is disturbed by the death in his family, he scarcely thinks of eating as his desire is to die; that is why he must be fed by others."[121] Custom dictates that this meal should include bread and hardboiled eggs or lentils, which are "the food of mourning"[122] because these foods are round like the life cycle[123] and have "no mouth," just as "the mourner has no mouth."[124]

The family observes mourning, if possible, for seven days in the house of the dead. A candle is lit—the *ner neshamah,* or candle of the soul—and the bed of the deceased and all the chairs are covered with sheets.[125] During the entire week, the bereaved must sit on the ground and must not sleep in their beds (even if they go home for the night), following the example of Job: "So they sat down with him upon the ground seven days and seven nights, and none spake a word unto him: for they saw that his grief was very great."[126] Shiva can be considered the period of the public observance of mourning: the bereaved is exempt from all work, as well as from all the usual obligations of civility. He can remain silent, speak to no one, and must neither greet nor be greeted by anyone in anticipation of his state. During these seven days he does not change his underclothes and permanently displays the tear in his garment made at the cemetery. His ablutions, just as on Yom Kippur or Tisha b'Av, must be as summary as possible. It is incumbent on the community, however, to visit the bereaved so that they are not isolated in their sorrow, and people must act as their "consolers." But during the first three days, which are reserved for tears,[127] no one is to speak to them unless spoken to; no one is to ask them for news of their health, and no one is to make any statement to them about anything whatsoever. Berachia insists on the importance of these days of weeping, for "the body knows great suffering in its grave," and one must weep in order to attract divine compassion to the deceased, for the soul leaves its carcass and mourns for itself in the course of the shiva.[128] While the soul roams around its house,[129] the minyan—the prayer quorum—meets there for the daily readings of the Mishnah and the recitation of all the services, in which the bereaved is to serve as officiant for the recitation of the Kaddish. The seven days must be reserved for *hesped*—eulogy—which, even while recalling the actions of the deceased, would open the upper gates to him, for during this period the soul cannot rejoin the Shekhinah and wanders between its house and its tomb.[130] This is why the Torah should be brought to the house of mourning, so that the bereaved and the soul of the deceased may benefit from its reading.

In her memoirs, Glückel of Hameln described very simply the shiva that took place after her husband's death.

> Sunday, the 24th of Tebet, 5449 (January 16, 1689) he was buried with all honor. The entire community was struck with horror and grief at the sudden blow of it. With my children gathered around me, I sat upon the ground for the seven days of mourning, and a sad sight it must have been

> to see me. . . . We immediately secured our ten men to pray for the daily prayers in the house of mourning, and we engaged scholars to "learn" the Torah day and night through the whole year—be it not to my reproach! And the children diligently said *Kaddish* for their departed father. And there was not a man or woman who did not come, daily, to comfort the bereaved among us.[131]

The sabbath or a religious holiday interrupts the public mourning, whatever the day. In this case—and in the course of a week there is always a sabbath—the bereaved must change his outer clothing and wear a garment that is not new or holiday dress but is untorn. He must, like anyone else, take his place at the table and not sit on the ground during the entire holiday. Externally suspended, mourning still persists within, for the avel nonetheless continues to wear the same undergarments, and the dim light that must shine for the entire period of the shiva is relit before the holiday and preserves its spirit.

The Talmud confirms[132] "three days of weeping, seven of eulogizing, and thirty for the beard and hair." After the shiva come the *sheloshim,* the thirty days that continue to be counted from the day of burial, in the course of which the avel must resume his normal life. He puts on his shoes, signifying his return to sociability; abandoning his torn clothing—which he must nonetheless save—he continues his mourning in private. Although the consolers no longer come to visit him, he will express his mourning by washing only summarily, not cutting his hair, shaving, or cutting his nails.[133] He will wear no holiday clothes, nor will he attend any joyous occasion. At the synagogue he will change his place, while officiating every day for the Kaddish.[134] The thirty days are a transitional stage for the bereaved between the brutality of the rupture provoked by death, expressed by the shiva, and the integration of the work of mourning that will allow him, at the completion of the year, to be once again made whole. But if in the course of the shloshim a religious holiday should occur, then this stage is terminated, "for the essence of mourning yields to the judgment of the soul, and since the soul is freed by the holiday there is no reason to resume mourning."[135]

Mourning is pursued throughout the year that follows: the son will recite the Kaddish at the daily services, and the bereaved will not attend joyous occasions such as marriages or banquets, for twelve months if he has lost his parents and thirty days if he has lost someone other than a parent.[136] Naḥmanides specifies that the bereaved can go into the banquet hall, but without rejoicing, eating, or drinking.[137] All signs of joy, such as song and dance, are proscribed during the year of mourning. In the same spirit the bereaved must not dress in new clothes.[138] The thirtieth day and the last day of the twelfth month are marked by a visit to the cemetery. A minyan is assembled at the grave of the deceased to recite the Kaddish.

As we have seen,[139] this series of sanctifications accompanying mourning is integrated into the mortuary ritual from the time that Halakhah established it was possible to obtain the salvation of the soul in the torments of purgatory, for it is understood "that there is no one who has not sinned." The emphasis on this redemptive aspect grew stronger over the centuries, and it was thought that during the entire year of mourning divine judgment weighed heavily on the family. Because of this, the thrice daily recitation of the Kaddish before those assembled for prayer became fundamental because it provoked a remission. "As we know, the meaning of the *Kaddish* is to annul Gehenna and release benevolent forces. Thus the son, by reciting the *Kaddish,* brings his father out from the depths and sends him to the Garden of Eden."[140] But this recitation can also preserve the mourner from danger,[141] that is, from any sort of divine decree. If it represents the prayer of the son par excellence, those who leave this world without a son must nevertheless be provided with someone to recite the Kaddish. Anyone masculine can take responsibility for reciting it for a relative, and failing that, the family can even pay for the services of someone from the outside.[142] But if there is a son who refuses to fulfill this duty, "he is not worth a *prutah,*" that is, a penny.[143] The day when the avel ceases the recitation of the Kaddish, he is called to the Torah to mark the end of his mourning. According to certain commentators, the sojourn of the soul in Gehenna lasts twelve months for "ordinary" sinners,[144] so that the year of mourning could correspond precisely to the sojourn of the deceased in purgatory. Only those who have committed particularly grave or heinous acts toward others—like rejection of the doctrine of the resurrection of the dead—are condemned to remain there forever.[145]

Mourning is ended on the anniversary of the death, the yahrzeit. That day, the votive candle is relit and the bereaved take up the practices of mourning for the day. Every year on the anniversary of the death of a father or a mother, custom dictates fasting:[146] "The law dictates that one afflict oneself, for father and son are but one body, and the sons must be saddened"[147] and feel the weight of the actions of the deceased.[148] Children, then, are obliged to afflict themselves, to pray, to recite the Kaddish, to light the yahrzeit candle, and to visit the cemetery.[149] One must also study the Torah and give alms. One can be called to the Torah, if it is a day when the Torah is read,[150] and say the *El Male Raḥamim*.[151] The candle lit in memory of the deceased must not be used for any other purpose, nor for light, and it must be left to burn out by itself.[152] On the day of Yom Kippur it is also the custom to light a ner neshamah for the dead,[153] for this day is also called Yom ha-Kippurim: the Day of Atonement, in the course of which pardon is granted to the living and the dead;[154] and since the dead, unlike the living, cannot repent, they are simply pardoned.[155]

In the annual holiday ritual, the memorial service of Yizkor is incorporated on four occasions: on Yom Kippur, on the seventh day of Sukkot, and on the final days of Pesaḥ and Shavuʾot.[156] Practice dictates that during the service for the "remembrance of souls," the hazkarat neshamot, those whose parents are still alive leave the synagogue for fear of the "evil eye," because "[if] your father and your mother are alive [and] you say that they are no longer, they will die."[157] One must thus "remember the souls" of the departed all one's life. But if a widower or a widow remarries, out of regard for the present spouse he or she must be restricted to lighting a votive candle. A certain fear justifies this abstention, for the Sefer ha-Ḥaim cautions that in case of remarriage, the survivor runs the risk of great danger by visiting the grave of the former spouse.[158] The meaning of the "remembrance of souls" is also explained in the Midrash.[159]

> They return, they are cast out like the arrow from the bow, this is why we have the custom of remembering the souls of the dead on the sabbath, so that they will not return to Gehenna. . . . Forgive Your people Israel, those who live ransom the dead, so that the living must pay for the dead. And thus we have the custom of remembering the dead on *Yom Kippur* and give charity for them.

According to the Aggadah, the dead "suffer all the days of the week, but on the sabbath they rest."[160] A person who has a yahrzeit during the week will recite the *El Male Raḥamim* the preceding sabbath and on the day itself, if it is read that day.[161]

Berachia suggests that the death of a close relative involves the creation of an opening between the previously self-enclosed worlds of the living and the dead. Indeed, a person who has recently died does not have immediate access to the world of the dead. The three elements of his soul are still wandering together; they are present, witness the burial, and remain perhaps until the end of the first seven days.[162] In sum, the first three days of the shiva, while the deceased encounters the infinite torments of separation, the seven days when the deceased bears witness to his own mourning, and the year that follows, which equals the time spent in purgatory, seem to mark a period of dialogue between the living and their departed. When a parent dies, a transfer of responsibilities takes place since the eternal repose of the deceased now depends, in part, on the attitude of his children. But if a form of life persists (though the "breath" has escaped) which allows the departed to experience what happens here below, another source of perception is manifest which allows souls to communicate. This is why Berachia specifies that the place of burial is important: one of the Just will be interred near another of the Just so that their souls might converse, and the son will be buried near his father. For this reason, too, when the funeral eulogy is recited, the parents of the departed are remembered by name so they may welcome their child, for "those who have cared for someone during his life will care for him in his death."[163]

In the seventeenth century, then, in the beliefs of Jewish society, death seemed increasingly crowned with divine glory. The burial society perforce saw its role all the more magnified. No doubt this is one of the reasons that the ḥevra kaddisha became an elite organization legitimized as much by the filling of a "void" in community structures as by new contributions in the mystic realm. Issuing from religious laws, the spiritual element would be transformed into a form of moral action resting on the principle that Judaism is a way of life and not a confession, contrary to its self-definition at the end of the nineteenth century. The ḥevra kaddisha's power is exercised on the basis of the notion of ḥesed shel emet. This allegorical notion, to the extent that it was systematically applied by an institution, had a significant effect on the order of the community's social life.

Despite the contradictions that emerge between the original function of the ḥevra, its oligarchical organization, and its efficacy in the field of its spiritual and social prerogatives, it seems to have been the true pillar of community life in the seventeenth and eighteenth centuries. The social empire of the burial society developed through the "moral action" it exerted, and its legitimacy rested, as a last resort, on the possibility of refusing the last rites and religious burial. If, moreover, the ḥevra rejected the use of penal constraints for purposes of internal discipline when addressing itself to the soldiery to frighten people,[164] it was nonetheless authorized to refuse the full right of religious burial to those who refused to grant its prerogatives.

It seems that this threat alone was enough to discourage sedition, for it was evidently implemented only on rare occasions. The ḥevra sometimes anticipated for its purposes a special enclosure in the cemetery reserved for delinquents and their families.[165] But as a general rule, the system of fines minimalized rebellions,[166] and no one could doubt that at the end of his road he would find the ḥevra kaddisha.

Fourteen of fifteen paintings from a cycle commissioned by the Burial Society of Prague, ca. 1780. Oil on canvas, each 55 × 110 cm. From *The Precious Legacy: Judaic Treasures from the Czechoslovak State Collections,* ed. David Altshuler (Washington, D.C.: The Smithsonian Institution, 1983), 154-155; reprinted by permission. Courtesy Jewish State Museum, Prague. Photos by Quicksilver Photographers, Takoma Park, Maryland.

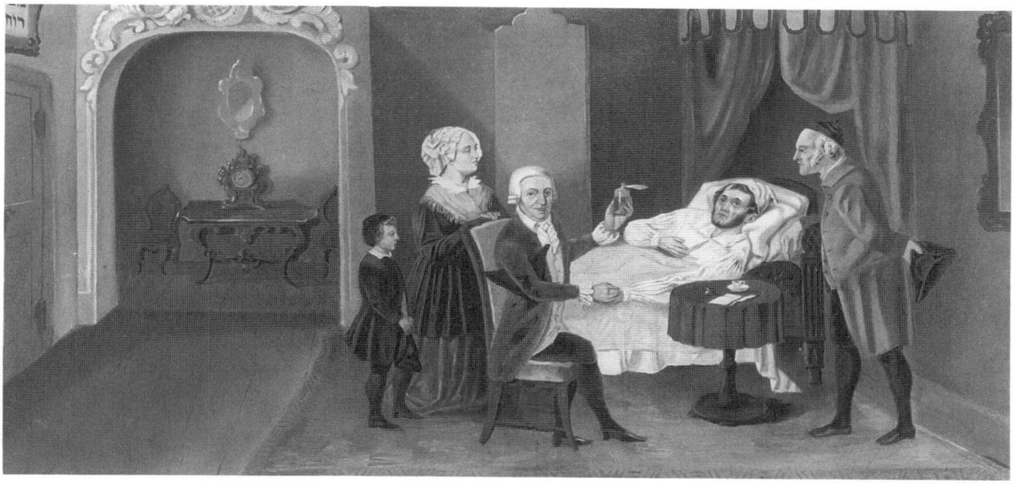

1. *Visiting the sick man.*

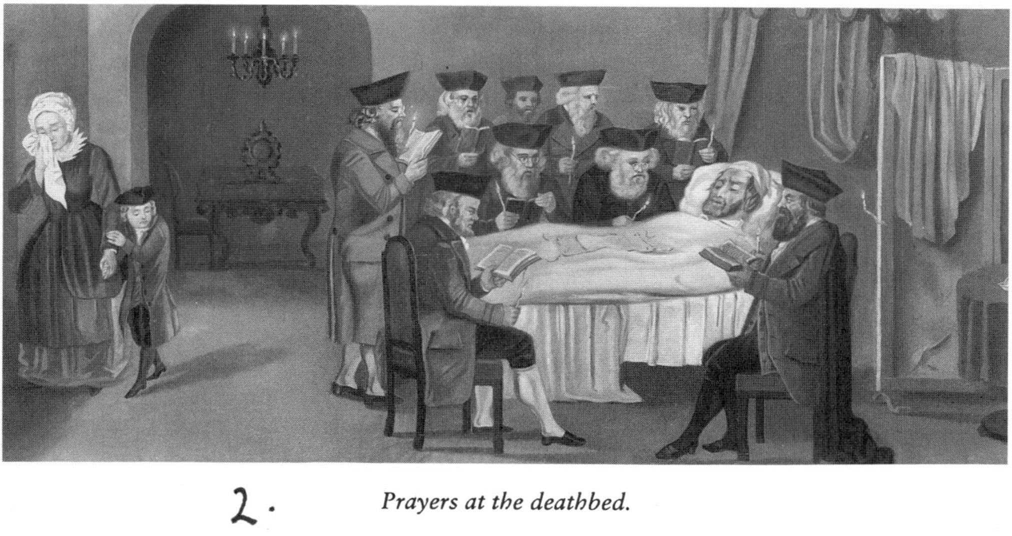

2. *Prayers at the deathbed.*

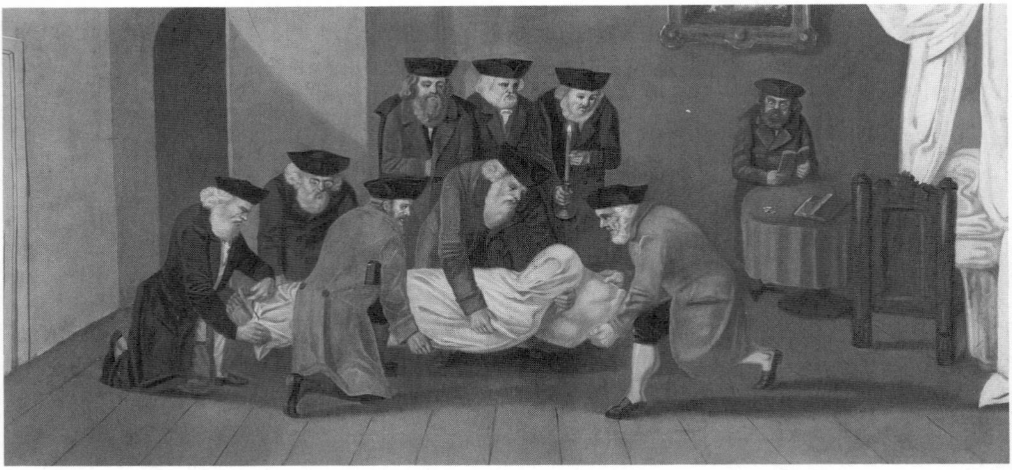

3. *Taking custody of the dead man.*

4 *The making of the shroud.*

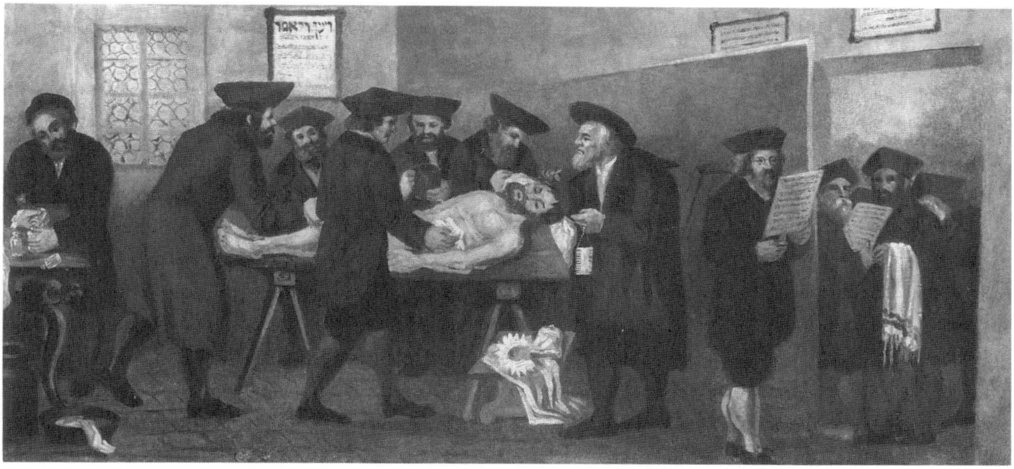

5. *The washing of the body.*

6. *Carrying the body out of the house.*

7 *The digging of the grave.*

8 *The entrance of the burial procession into the cemetery.*

9 *The oration over the dead man.*

10 *Carrying the body to the grave.*

*The making of the coffin.*

*Lowering the body into the grave.*

13 *After the burial.*

14 *Washing hands upon leaving the cemetery.*

Burial Society beaker, Prague, 1798/1799. Faience, painted under glaze, 14 × 22 cm. From *The Precious Legacy: Judaic Treasures from the Czechoslovak State Collections,* ed. David Altshuler (Washington, D.C.: The Smithsonian Institution, 1983), 204; reprinted by permission. Courtesy Jewish State Museum, Prague. Photo by Quicksilver Photographers, Takoma Park, Maryland.

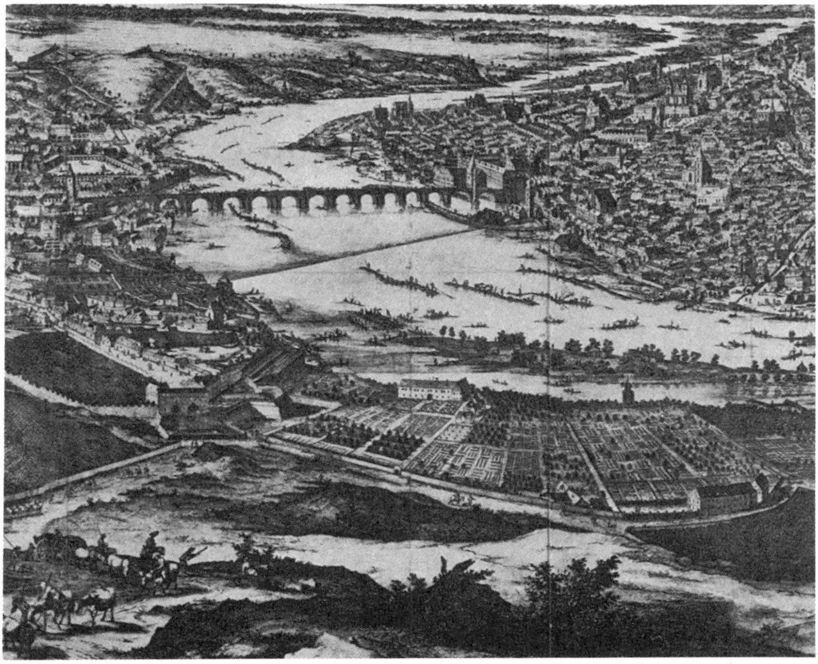

View of Prague, from castle side of Vlatava River, 1685. From *The Precious Legacy: Judaic Treasures from the Czechoslovak State Collections,* ed. David Altshuler (Washington, D.C.: The Smithsonian Institution, 1983), 75; reprinted by permission. Courtesy Jewish State Museum, Prague.

Death with unknown persons (Jews) and painter. Self-portrait by N. Manuel, Bern, sixteenth century. Courtesy Bibliothèque Nationale, Paris.

*Hakkafot,* ritual circling (Portuguese rite). Engraving by B. Picart, 1723. Courtesy L'Alliance Israelite Universelle, Paris.

Statues of the Burial Society of Prague, 1754. Courtesy Jewish State Museum, Prague.

Title page, *Kitsur Maʾavar Yabbok,* Moravia, eighteenth century. Courtesy Jewish State Museum, Prague.

Membership roll of the Burial Society of Halberstadt, Sunday, the 27th of Nissan, 5456 (1696). Courtesy The Central Archives for the History of the Jewish People, Hebrew University, Jerusalem.

PART THREE

# From Precept to Custom—Learned and Popular Religion

CHAPTER SIX

# The Law and the Letter

A mingling of laws and customs formed the seamless whole of death and burial ritual. Yet transformations signaling divergences of time and place are evident in the difference between precept, which stands for law or doctrine, and custom, which is subject to local or general modifications. The evolution of Jewish beliefs and mentalities, then, may be read through established practices. The margin between the law and its literal practice might be related to the acknowledged differentiation between "learned culture" and "popular culture," considering that for the Jews, what is known as learned culture represents the dimension of their distinctiveness, and what we call popular culture represents a penetration into their environment. Yet the practices that are an amalgam of precept or strict codification that may be modified by minhag, or local custom, challenge such a differentiation and resist our best efforts to disentangle their constituent parts.

Although there is an apparent distinction between the rabbinic discourse of learned religion and practices based on custom that would constitute popular religion, none of the existing sources suggests any validity to this differentiation. Indeed, it is not clear that the rabbinic discourse as it can be read in the corpus of responsa is really the vehicle of "learned" culture; it may rather be a mediation between laws and customs, sometimes secular, and their actualization. For if we were to admit the principle of a learned culture, we would have to be able to compare it to a culture that is not learned. And clearly popular custom can sometimes be imposed by the intermediary of scholars and rabbis; in this sense the resulting minhag may be systematically considered a phenomenon that contradicts the intangible separation between these two kinds of knowledge.

> When someone is very sick, a candle and alms are given to the nearest synagogue. The sick person is measured with a thread, and then a candle wick is made from it. The candle is brought to the synagogue and buried in the cemetery, wrapped in a shroud. Instead of measuring the sick person, the cemetery may be measured.
>
> The length and breadth of the cemetery are measured with canvas. Then the canvas is distributed to the poor.
>
> The family of the sick person goes *aynraissn di shul,* that is, goes to the synagogue: there the Ark is opened and during this time the family weeps and calls upon God to heal the sick.
>
> Then they go to the field [burial ground], to the tombs of deceased relatives, and pray for them to intercede with God, that the sick person might recover his health. They take a spool of thread and measure the entire length of the cemetery. This is usually done by two people: one takes one end while the other helps the first by holding the thread.
>
> They make a wax candle the size of the sick person, give charity, and distribute bread to the poor or to pious students at the rabbinical school. With the thread a candle is made that is brought to the synagogue.
>
> If the sick man's name is changed, he can be cured. Another name is given to someone gravely ill. A name will be chosen for him that indicates health: Alter, Zeide, Baba, Ḥaim, Ḥaya, so that the fatal decree should not be placed on the new name.
>
> A candle is molded in the shape of a man and buried, that the dying man might be saved.
>
> A person can save someone gravely ill by offering him years. However, he who has offered his own years will live a few years less.
>
> If a person speaks to no one en route to the cemetery, and goes directly to the dying man and pulls off his shirt, he will recover his health.
>
> If a person gives all that belongs to the sick man to the poor, he will be cured.[1]

This long list of practices performed to ward off illness and death is not part of any ritual. These are ways whose origins are now lost—products of the local environment or of an age-old Jewish tradition. Whether passed on through popular or learned culture, such customs form the spirit of a civilization. By investigating three of these practices, I shall try to delimit more precisely what aspect of the Jewish attitude toward death comes from the religious realm and what from the realm of the profane.

## CIRCLING

This custom seems to have been unknown in the Jewish communities at the time of Naḥmanides, but two and a half centuries later its practice was an integral part of the funerary ritual, at least as it is described in the *Ma'avar Yabbok*. Indeed, while Aaron Berachia discusses whether it should take place in the house or cemetery, he does not seem to doubt that it should take place, as do the tohorah and the recitation of the Shema, ancestral practices having the force of law.

The custom of circling the dead person seven times before burial, each time throwing stones or silver coins, does not come from Halakhah but from Kabbalah. This minhag is not found in any work of legal codification, whether in ancient or more recent texts, or even in those produced by the Kabbalah.[2] The custom seems to have appeared with the generation that emigrated after the expulsion from Spain. Traces of it are found in several collections of Spanish prayers in poetic form, *Raḥemna alav,* which beg mercy for the deceased and are composed in seven rhymed stanzas, each corresponding to a circle of the hakkafot.[3] There seems to be a certain discrepancy, however, between the requested clemency for welcoming the deceased to the world of the dead and the spiritual basis of the argumentation of the *hakkafah*—the circling—that Berachia provides in the *Ma'avar Yabbok*. In the *piyyut,* the poem, no allusion is made to the Kabbalah: as an inducement to God to be magnanimous toward the departed, virtuous acts are recalled that might lead the deceased to Gan Eden. The last stanza suggests that the soul is faced with the "seven groups of the Just and the Pious," which is reminiscent of Berachia's "seven forces," but conversely, since in the *Ma'avar Yabbok* these are forces of impurity.

For Berachia, the reason for performing the hakkafot was different: he belonged to that generation of kabbalists who interpreted the illicit relations of man with Lilith as the moment when evil spirits are conceived. Meir Benayahu recalls that the hakkafot for the dead are linked to the custom of sitting seven times while leaving the cemetery and to the interdiction prohibiting the child from following his father's burial.[4] Each of these three customs was meant to banish the deceased's illegitimate offspring, who come to the cemetery not only to claim their share of the paternal inheritance but also to harm him—knowing that their interference will prevent the dead man from receiving divine grace. Furthermore, while these demons have no physical incarnation, being a part of nothingness, they live and die like human beings[5] and therefore seek to meddle with human bodies. But each of these practices has an independent origin: the custom of sitting seven times, for instance, goes back to the period of the Babylonian exile, when one had "to rise and sit seven times" to mark the difference between the living and the dead.

These customs are connected with the evolution of symbolic practices meant to separate the realm of death from that of the living, the cemetery from the synagogue, through the mediation of burial. But the meaning given to the hakkafot is not the subject of any rabbinic codification, and it is merely the transposition of a custom brought by the Spanish Jews and subsequently spread throughout the Ashkenazi communities by the mediation of the Sephardic kabbalists. According to Benayahu, these hakkafot were performed in Spain without any mystic content[6] and were later incorporated into the rabbinic world by the diffusion of Kabbalah. To support this assertion, he cites the variety of explanations given by the first authors who mention the practice, all of them kabbalists coming from Spain and Portugal, before Aaron Berachia incorporated it into the accepted funerary ritual.[7]

Isaiah Horowitz also describes the hakkafot performed to banish the adulterous and satanic offspring that the deceased could have procreated through relations with Lilith. Ten men purified by the ritual bath circle the dead man and place him in his tomb.[8] Horowitz cites his source, the *Ta'ame ha-mitzvot,* by specifying that this was a custom practiced in Palestine, without indicating whether it must be performed at the cemetery.[9] According to Benayahu's analysis, this is a local practice whose meaning is limited to the plea for mercy for the deceased; scholars then integrated it, through a prism of more elaborate commentaries (i.e., to banish demonic children), into the general ritual codifications. In this case the theological assumptions—their authors' simple invention[10]—would have served to confirm spiritually a custom conveyed from one place where it was familiar to other places where it was unknown.

Yet what do we know about the actual practice of the custom of hakkafot? An engraving by Picart contributes a solid indication of its reality in the Portuguese community of Amsterdam at the beginning of the eighteenth century.[11] It is mentioned earlier, in the *Ma'avar Yabbok,* one of the most important mortuary reference works read in numerous communities, as well as in the *Shnei Luḥot ha-Berit.* It is easy to locate the piyyut on which Benayahu bases his analysis in the Portuguese works of ritual.[12] When Glückel of Hameln describes the death of her husband, she indicates that on his deathbed, he reads the work of the *Shelah*. As for the burial ceremony itself, she simply says that her husband was buried "with honor."[13] Obviously, the most common practices are rarely spelled out.

In fact, there is no formal indication that the communities performed the hakkafot. Furthermore, when Horowitz mentions the practice, he never says he has seen it done, either in the course of his tenure as rabbi in Prague or elsewhere,[14] but that he has found indications of it in his readings. Keeping strictly to what is described in the ritual works, we can infer that the hakkafot were observed everywhere the *Shnei Luḥot ha-Berit* served as a "breviary." Yet among the numerous engravings we have from Bohemia representing the various stages of burial,[15] none exists depicting this practice. We can see the mortuary purification, the funeral procession, the eulogy, the interment, the departure from the cemetery, but not the hakkafot. It would surely be reasonable to conclude that in the eighteenth century this practice was part of the minhag of only some of the communities.

Since the practice of hakkafot was well known in the Polish communities, where it was still recorded at the beginning of the twentieth century,[16] and was also mentioned in modern Ashkenazi Jewish literature,[17] it seems likely that customs that may have been unfamiliar elsewhere but in use among certain communities—for which they had the force of law—can be differentiated from precepts. This conclusion can again be supported by the introductory quotation on the title page ornamenting the second part of the *Sefer-ha-Ḥaim* of Sulzbach.[18]

> There are many things done with dead persons for no particular reason, and there is no sense writing about them except as they touch on the *minhagim* of our fathers. . . . But what the Sages have written must be done for the dead, be it only a *minhag,* it must not be changed, for the *minhag* of our fathers is Torah. The Torah [in the sense of doctrine] of life, *ḥesed shel emet.*

The problem posed by the legitimation of custom is discussed by the rabbis. We read in Yair Bacharach, commenting on the fact that a man had asked his daughter to recite the Kaddish when he died (a request the community had accepted), that it is dangerous to see anyone stray from spiritual authority and mount his own pulpit.[19]

## JEWISH CUSTOMS AS SEEN BY ANTON MARGARITA

Margarita, a notorious Jewish apostate in his time, took the trouble to examine the practices and beliefs of the Jews in order to mock their absurdity, hence the title of his work, *Der gantz judisch Glaub*.[20] To this end he claims to describe his own experiences; this, notwithstanding the disagreeable aspects of caricature, would make his narrative a kind of "ethnographic report" on Jewish practices of the sixteenth century. In the chapter devoted to death, "Von der Todten," he presents Jewish customs he claims to have observed in Prague, where he says he had occasion to stay with his father during his youth, at the end of the fifteenth century to the beginning of the sixteenth century, before his conversion. This narrative, which is often quite precise in its detail, contributes useful information on the practice of certain rites, for the works of ritual or rabbinic exegesis may provide information but do not guarantee that they were actually performed.

Margarita describes confession in this way:

> The Jews confess to one another. . . . If a man is not learned, he cannot perform his own penitence and writes his sins on a piece of paper. He admits his guilt and asks for penance: he does not write his name on it, he puts the piece of paper in a book or in the armchair where the rabbi sits. . . . The rabbi writes his answer and the penance on another piece of paper, which he puts in another place in the house that must be discovered.

On mortuary customs:

> And when he is dead, he is laid out on the ground on straw. Whether it be night or day they light a candle by his side and keep vigil over him . . . [then] they throw out any water found in the house and knock on the neighbors' doors. And they [the Jews] say that this is because Satan washes his knife on his way out.

Popular belief on this subject, according to Margarita:

> On the subject of the water, the old Jews write that since the most distant times, when a man dies, Satan ostensibly appears carrying a heavy sword.

Taking out the body:

> When death has done its work and [the dead man] is cold, he is stitched up and dressed in the white robe he wore on "the long day" [Yom Kippur]. He is wrapped in his talit [prayer shawl] and then laid out on a plank and transported from the house to their cemetery. His children and friends follow the plank, crying out, weeping, and shouting. When the dead man

leaves the house, those who live in the same house throw a pot into the street to break it . . . and dissipate the sadness.

Ritual purification:

Then they carry the dead man to their cemetery, to the little house.[21] They place him on a long table, wash him with warm water, smear him with egg and wine, and put on his white robe and his talit. Thus washed, the body is again laid in its coffin. . . . Close friends take a candle and measure themselves with it, as tall as they are, and write their names on this candle, which they put beside the dead man in the coffin.

Popular belief on this subject:

They think that with this, death might relent and will not then claim someone else in another house. [Then] they place the coffin in the soil of a freshly dug grave. His friends must throw earth on him. . . . The closest [relative] stands above the tomb and tears his clothing on the left side, near the heart.

Departure from the cemetery:

And when this is done, they all leave quickly, moving with great haste.

Popular belief on this subject:

For they say that when the dead person is covered with earth, a mouse comes and bites his nose, and that this bite is so painful that one can hear a cry. And he who hears it will die in thirty days. This is why they hurry away, so as not to hear the voice of death and die. . . . And in this flight they turn around three times, pulling up grass, throwing the earth and covering their heads. . . . After this they all go to wash their hands and sit three times on the ground as well.

As described by Margarita, Jewish mortuary customs correspond, on the whole, to those cited by the mortuary works. Of course, I have omitted from this description most of the malicious and more or less obsolete comments. We can observe, however, in the example of "the mouse that comes to bite the dead man's nose" that Margarita attempts to support his comments on the rites of the Jews with statements that seem to have been taken from the midrashic literature but come, rather, from his inspiration as an anti-Jewish theologian.

Among the inventory of customs that were cataloged and are found elsewhere, three seem unusual and deserve some scrutiny. In the first case, the "request for penance" after the public confession, the *Viddui*,[22] was effected by the mediation of a confidential piece of paper transmitted to the rabbi, which Margarita claims to have seen performed by his father, the rabbi of Strasbourg, and his Prague cousins. Although this practice is not indexed, it might be inscribed in the spirit of Jewish tradition, sparing the "penitent" from publicly unburdening himself of particular omissions at a critical moment. Moreover, although in the formulation of the *Viddui* the al ḥet contains all possible sins of "act and thought" that may have been committed "voluntarily" or in "total unawareness" and should therefore mitigate the embarrassment of mentioning them individually, the written enumeration of sins and the request for penance need not be inscribed in the works of codification to have been performed and may once have been current practice.[23]

The minhag that consists of throwing an earthenware pot into the street "to break it . . . and dissipate the sadness" might contain a reference to man's origins in dust—the earthenware pot—and breaking it may mark the ineluctability of his end. However, it is mentioned neither in descriptions of burials that we find in the literature nor in the ethnographic questionnaire on the subject of death established by An-Ski,[24] and not even in the reference work of Joshua Trachtenberg.[25]

The custom that would have the close relatives of the deceased measure themselves with a candle, then bury it in the coffin, seems less credible than the others. This practice may evoke the custom of "measuring" the cemetery in case of danger, or burying the dead with the thread used to measure the body for the fabrication of the shroud—for this thread has touched the dead man and belongs to him—but it is not really related to any of these practices, nor does it correspond to any known practice dealing with the Angel of Death.

Should we doubt the reality of these three practices? We might characterize them as pure inventions on Margarita's part, but they may simply have fallen into disuse over the course of time. Indeed, the abundance of truthful details that he provides confirms the transmission of certain practices over time and space. For example, the custom, typical of the Jewish quarter, of knocking at the doors of neighboring houses to announce a death in one habitation is also described by Glückel in the seventeenth century[26] and recorded both in Alsace in the nineteenth century[27] and in Poland at the beginning of the twentieth century.[28] It is quite possible that among the variety of behaviors connected with death in the Jewish communities, customs that were not adequately described in the written record could have disappeared without leaving any trace.

## RENDEZ-VOUS IN THE CEMETERY

Processions to the cemetery took place mainly on four occasions: the two evenings of Rosh Hashanah, Yom Kippur, and the day of Tisha b'Av, which marks the end of the period of mourning for the destruction of the Temple. To these three religious dates were added the annual procession instituted by the ḥevra kaddisha to ask meḥilah, or pardon, of the dead who might have been offended in the course of death or burial rites. In this category, however, we must distinguish two different practices and one that is related to them. The first type of Jewish procession consisted of "circling" around the cemetery, three or seven times depending on local custom;[29] in the second sort, the cemetery was measured by a wick whose length would then be used to make candles for the synagogue.[30] The term used to designate these customs is *hakkafot,* and, as with the funerary hakkafot, one must circle three or seven times depending on local custom. Related to these is the custom in certain communities whereby the men lie on the graves of the Just during the night of Tisha b'Av.

This tradition of "visiting the cemetery" seems deeply anchored in Judaism: it is already mentioned in the Talmud and the Midrash,[31] although Meir of Rothenburg in the thirteenth century questions its merits.[32] The procession to the cemetery has a double objective: on the one hand, it involves praying for the deceased to intercede in favor of the living; on the other, in the case of the procession of the ḥevra kaddisha, it involves asking the deceased for absolution so that they will not take revenge on the living. The evenings of Rosh Hashanah and Yom Kippur are responses to the annual sessions of divine judgment, and Tisha b'Av marks a day of mourning for the destruction of the Temple; these symbolic meanings would have encouraged the observance of such days of "meeting with the dead."

To the anticipation of the resurrection, Judaism would add a particular connection with the dead, who continue to exercise a role quite beyond their corporeal finality. The understanding of this eternal bond between the living and the departed, this secular Jewish assurance that can be read in the Midrash based on biblical exegesis, is found in a great many civilizations. We have the example of medieval Christianity, which lavished on its "patron saints" a devotion proportional to the benefits the individual hoped to receive. This, of course, poses the problem of interpenetrations, even as it provides evidence of a common evolution of Western mentalities in the monotheistic religions on the basis of universal "popular beliefs."

Mortuary ritual stresses the way that those who attend and care for the dying experience the progressive modification of their perception of them. Thus the sick, even the dying, are still considered wholly alive, but demonic forces surround them, attempting to take possession of them. Once dead, the individual is split into two parts: the cadaver—an object of impurity—and the three levels of the soul, each of which has its own destination and symbolic meaning in the relation between the living and the dead. While the neshamah rises toward the Shekhinah, the nefesh is left in its wake, wandering between house and grave for seven days, then departing, though it is not entirely gone until one year is up. The ru'aḥ, for its part, never detaches itself entirely from its terrestrial garb, or from its husk, which is found at the cemetery and is inhabited by malevolent powers of the soul.[33] This explains why the cemetery is the seat of impurity, where the destructive forces of death reside, and a place of terror for the living, for it is permanently inhabited by "spirits." Despite this dreadful aspect, and although it is a domain reserved for death, the cemetery is also the privileged place for demanding intercession to revoke divine decrees. We may not be able to situate the origins of processions to the cemetery, but we can follow their continuity throughout the centuries and down to our own day.

Until the nineteenth century these processions were an integral part of the ritual volumes that anthologized both blessings to be recited at the cemetery and formulas for requests of the dead. Horowitz thus describes the annual processions: "There is the practice of visiting the cemetery on the evening of Rosh Hashanah and the evening of Yom Kippur, and circling around it."[34] Then he adds, "It is told that a woman whose son was ill circled to obtain help, and from there it seems that many [people] go there [to circle around the cemetery] to find help." This last element of the description suggests that the procession was done with the purpose of asking the dead to intercede in case of specific danger. In a period of epidemic or in times of imminent danger, it was the custom to visit the burial ground in an attempt to modify the impending divine decree. It was to this end that in Frankfurt the cemetery served as a refuge during the great fire of 1711.[35] In Prague it served the same purpose during the "French fire" of 1689; then, during the decree of expulsion of 31 March 1745, the Jews again went to the cemetery in solemn procession.[36]

Concerning the night of Tisha b'Av, Horowitz informs us,

> I have also found that they visit the tombs to lie upon the graves of the Just, as if to say, "if You do not take pity on us, we are like the dead," and there is again a meaning to our lying on the graves of the dead: that they may ask mercy for us.[37]

For his part, Naḥmanides wrote,[38]

> There are those who go on the evening of Tisha b'Av to lie on the graves, and the "crier" goes before them; and the next day, the "crier" goes out and says: "Let the living be separated from the dead, and let the living return to their houses to recite lamentations," and they go in their *talit*.

There is no particular dogma in Judaism regarding the hereafter, and the canons of belief are therefore those established by the rabbis. Trachtenberg believes that these demands for the intercession of the dead echo Christian practice.[39] He bases this pronouncement on an erroneous citation from *Taanit*,[40] according to which one goes to the cemetery the evening of Rosh Hashanah and Yom Kippur, and "if there are no tombs of Israel [in other words, no Jewish cemetery] one goes to the tombs of the gentiles," therefore to any cemetery even a non-Jewish one. The question is effectively posed in this treatise for Rashi, who comments on it and answers resolutely in the negative: when the dead are not Jews, it is impossible to ask them to intercede. Despite the numerous testimonies and descriptions of processions, this custom does not receive the approbation of the rabbinic authorities. Meir of Rothenburg declared on the subject that the Jews must pray to God without any mediator, like Abraham, for "only dogs lie on tombs."[41] The position expressed by Moses Mat would be characteristic of the rabbinic attitude. In his ritual work, *Mateh Mosheh*, he describes the practice of visiting the cemetery on the day of Tisha b'Av and mentions the processions in terms almost identical to those employed by Horowitz:

> It is customary to visit the cemetery and circle around it, thus it is reported that a woman whose child was ill had circled [around the cemetery] and had been helped. Whence the custom of circling around the cemetery and giving alms to the poor.[42]

Apropos the customs of Yom Kippur, he adds,

> And then [after the *Kapparot*[43]] they go to the cemetery to lie on the graves of the pious, to signify "if You do not have mercy upon us, we are like the dead." And it is also said that we lie down thus on the graves of the dead

> so that they may intercede in our favor. It is a fact that many people lie on the graves of the fathers. And the dog lies down on the graves as well.

The last part of this citation poses a problem for the reader. In Hebrew, the same three letters are used for the word *kelev* (dog) and the name Caleb, so the meaning will be different depending on which translation is chosen. If we opt for the first reading, the final sentence contains a veiled criticism: without seeming to linger over it, Moses Mat adopts the argument of the Maharam. But if we choose the second reading, the biblical legacy is invoked, for Caleb went to seek compassion at the tombs of the patriarchs. Yet despite the criticism reiterated by certain rabbis,[44] the custom persisted, evidently touching sensitive issues of belief among the Jews and their relations to the dead.

In addition to the religious processions, people individually had the habit of visiting the cemetery to ask counsel or help from the deceased, and the ḥevra kaddisha also adopted this practice by instituting as part of the "day of the ḥevra" an official procession of meḥilah, followed in the evening by the banquet and the inauguration of new members.[45] The processions seem to be of the "schema type" of popular custom, which, despite the criticisms they provoked, were perpetuated by ancestral tradition without benefit of rabbinic justification. As a result, this minhag rests, on the one hand, on a secular practice mentioned in the Midrash and the Talmud—which would tend to legitimize it—and, on the other, on periodic reenactments through reinterpretations, which, whether they encourage it, like Horowitz, or stigmatize it, like Meir of Rothenburg, in any case cannot prevent it from being part of community life.

## THE DANCE OF DEATH

The practice of the "dance of death" among the Jews cannot be classified among the customs verified by descriptions or mentioned in works of ritual. Suppressed or unnoticed by Jewish historians, it does not appear and is not described as either ritual or minhag. It was practiced, however, in certain Jewish communities, though it is impossible to establish exactly when or where, or even on what occasion. In the Christian West, the *danses macabres* are above all known for their symbolic iconography in books of hours, frescoes, or scenes that illustrate Death's battle with the living. And, of course, Death conquers all, without distinction, as Ariès has written:

> The dance of death is an eternal round in which the dead alternate with the living. . . . Each couple consists of a naked mummy, rotting, sexless, and highly animated, and a man or woman, dressed according to his or her social condition and paralyzed by surprise. Death holds out its hand to the living person whom it will draw along with it, but who has not yet obeyed the summons. The art lies in the contrast between the rhythm of the dead and the rigidity of the living. The moral purpose was to remind the viewer both of the uncertainty of the hour of death and of the equality of all people in the face of death. People of all ages and ranks file by in an order which is that of the social hierarchy.[46]

Sometimes, as in the fresco in Berne, a Jew is depicted following death, coiffed in a pointed hat and wearing the yellow badge defining his condition.[47]

In the Jewish universe, the "dance of death" is not an iconographic convention since there were no painters in the communities who would metaphorically inscribe their beliefs and customs. In fact, only two meager narratives inform us that this practice existed in a Jewish setting. Glückel of Hameln, an inexhaustible source, cites it as a banal and familiar performance, already somewhat obsolete. She does not pause to describe it in detail, since this is not her aim; she is recounting the festivities that took place at the marriage of her oldest daughter, Zipporah, to the son of the eminent court Jew, Elie of Cleve:

> Then appeared performers who bowed prettily and played all manner of entertaining pranks. They concluded their performance with a truly splendid Dance of Death, something that has become quite rare in our days.[48]

The other mention of this dance, later in time, comes from a surprising testimony by Shlomo Rubin.[49] He recounts that during his travels through the regions of Russia and Poland-Volhynie in 1863, he had gone into a little synagogue in Ostrog to pray on the eighth day of the holiday of Sukkot, on which the memorial service, or "recall of souls" is performed. After this service, while the cantor intoned the "priestly blessing,"[50] Rubin heard a kind of "strange" melody whose "strident sound pierced the ears" and was taken up by the *kohanim* in a tone of lamentation, like "owls in a deserted land." Surprised and intrigued by this, the visitor inquired of the cantor the meaning of this chant. The cantor then answered that it was music from the "dance of death," which the community was accustomed to singing on the occasion of this commemoration, but he admitted, after close questioning, that no one knew its source. We can hardly claim the "dance of death" was a customary practice, or minhag. Though this holds true for the narration of the dance performed at the marriage of Glückel's daughter, it is a different matter with the story of the Jews of Ostrog. There we can assume that local minhag incorporated the melody of the dance of death into the liturgy of the ceremony of hazkarat neshamot and that this was still the case in the nineteenth century.

Following Herman Pollack, we may conclude that the dance of death, after spreading through the Christian world, was adopted by the Jews, first as an entertainment in Germany, as it is presented in Glückel's narrative, then in the ritual of religious holidays in Russia, as suggested by Rubin.[51] The popularity of this practice among the Jews is confirmed by the recording of the "barber's dance" performed on the holiday of Purim,[52] which is directly related to the "dance of Doctor Faust," itself classified as a customary dance of death.[53]

From the rabbinic point of view, the problem is the dance proper: mixed dancing is strictly prohibited by Halakhah.[54] And how was the dance of death performed? A young man—or woman—entered, masked and announced as death, and went to embrace the other dancers, who represented the living.[55] In the fifteenth century it was described in this way by an eyewitness on the occasion of another marriage in the region of Hameln:

> The dance begins with joyous music and couples dancing with great animation. The music stops, and the dancer symbolizing death appears. He is accompanied by the plaintive music of a funeral march, he collapses on the ground, as if dead. The music continues, young girls appear, surrounding "death" and embracing him. When the last woman has embraced him, he quickly returns to life and the dance is over.[56]

Generally, in the course of marriages and other joyful festivities, men and women danced alongside each other without mingling. However, to judge by the numerous criticisms and warnings of the rabbis, it seems clear that on these occasions in the seventeenth and eighteenth centuries, men and women regularly violated this prohibition. The records of the community of Runkel, in Hesse-Cassel, testify to this: "We have observed during ceremonies of marriage that men young and old dance with strange women, and young men and women spend the night in the same room."[57]

Are these "strange women" the masked figures who represent death in the danse macabre? Nothing specific can be cited in this regard. When Ezekiel Landau condemns the behavior of the Prague Jews during marriages, he refers quite specifically to mixed dances.[58] Somewhat earlier, Shabbetai Sheftel Horowitz had exhorted men and women not to dance together, even face-to-face, for they make "Satan dance between them."[59]

It seems that there is a symbolic connection between the custom of performing the dance of death at marriages and the practice of clothing the betrothed in "mourning cowls" on their wedding day. Indeed, this practice, well known in Frankfurt and Worms,[60] was widespread in the German lands beginning in the fifteenth century, according to Jacob Moellin.[61] Was it to temper the joy of marriage by recalling the ephemeral nature of time? Was it to prevent the Angel of Death from attending the celebration? Death and marriage always seem to be intimately entwined, and their respective rituals again reinforce this analogy. First the bride is led under the canopy—the *ḥuppah*—by women carrying lighted candles; then she circles seven times around the bridegroom. Death is surely present here as the enemy: to defend against it, no chair can be left empty for fear that death might sit; a marriage must not be celebrated if there is an open grave in the cemetery;[62] again, to ward off death, the betrothed visit the cemetery to announce their marriage and invite deceased family members to the ceremony so they should not come and disturb its progress. Much Jewish literature was inspired by this theme, as An-Ski was in *The Dibbuk*.[63] When an epidemic or grave danger was imminent, it was customary in Poland at the beginning of the century to marry the orphaned at the cemetery so that the dead, as witness to this charitable act of the community, should intercede on its behalf.[64]

CHAPTER SEVEN

# Body and Soul

I have tried to distinguish between the categories of Jewish popular culture and the learned culture of rabbinic pronouncements, while demonstrating the unreliability of this distinction when applied to the history of the Jews. Two examples of customs linked to death have allowed us to establish that Jews could have incorporated the popular practices of the surrounding society by reinterpreting their meanings. The Jews of a small Russian community were found at the end of the nineteenth century to have incorporated the dance of death, so popular in thirteenth-century France, by adopting its musical theme for their memorial service and thus diverting the exorcising function it performed in Christian society in the preceding centuries.[1] And we have seen that the custom of clothing the bridegroom in mourning dress on the day of marriage confirms that German Jews and Christians alike attempted to ward off or remember death on this occasion.[2]

There is one realm that offers a clear indication of the parts played by learned and popular culture, and that is medicine. Indeed, the treatments and therapies used for various complaints were intimately involved in the preparation of the living body as it became the dead body. This accounts for the importance of healing practices based on spiritual means; these were characteristic of the period, as were practices that seem macabre to us today but that embodied current ideas on illness, which was systematically perceived as divine punishment, and on the supernatural power of the dead. We have already found evidence of the belief that the dead could intervene on behalf of the living, and we shall see, too, that the dead were thought to possess curative powers.

In contrast to attitudes toward death that involve particular rites, conduct in the face of illness in part escapes codification. Beyond religious differentiations, this conduct refers to a universal meaning of the "sacred" determined by its time. In this sense, Jewish medicine allows us to approach an order of concepts and practices commonly shared in the West.

## THE MASTER OF NAMES AND THE APOTHECARY

In 1518, in a lecture before an audience of students, Moscellanus, rector of the University of Leipzig, encouraged the study of Hebrew in these terms: "The libraries of the Jews contain such a great treasure of medical knowledge that it is unsurpassed by works in any other language. The secret of this treasure cannot be discovered without knowing Hebrew grammar."[3] This citation should serve to illustrate the medieval cliché of the "Jewish doctor," whose prototype is Maimonides. Although a central figure in Jewish thought, he practiced medicine at the court of the sultan of Cairo. Thus, in addition to essential theological writings, he has left medical treatises on subjects as varied as the circulation of the blood, medications, asthma, and poisons.[4] Whether or not medicine was really compatible with the role of rabbi,[5] many rabbis added it to their community functions. The Church regularly tried to forbid Christians from seeking care from Jewish doctors (because they were often rabbis), but this never prevented royal or influential people from becoming permanently attached to the services of the most reputable among them.

As medical literature and practice go hand in hand, the beginning of the sixteenth century witnessed an explosion of medical works addressed to practitioners or meant for a popular readership: illness, care, and treatment are part of everyday life. In the Jewish world, these works relied at once on the acquired knowledge of popular medicine and practical Kabbalah—which was becoming widespread—and on medical information contained in the Talmud. Furthermore, numerous translations of important contemporary works that circulated in the communities, whether in Hebrew or in Yiddish, in particular the famous *Canon* of Avicenna,[6] bear witness to the new interest in universal medical knowledge. The importance granted to medical practice and to the role of the physician is obvious in rabbinic writings of the time: Yair Bacharach, Jacob Emden, and Ezekiel Landau deal with it at length and seem familiar with the essential medical literature.[7]

In the rabbinic texts themselves, the role and duties of the doctor are amply examined and evaluated according to the ethical criteria of Judaism, as the following queries indicate.[8]

—Is the doctor authorized to give a sick infant a treatment that might make him sterile?[9]

—Can the doctor administer a remedy to an acutely ill person that could cure him but might also kill him?[10]

—Is the doctor responsible for the death that his treatment might have induced?[11]

—Should the doctor be banished who may have mistakenly administered a dangerous remedy to a patient and caused his death?[12] In other words, can the doctor be considered a murderer in case of an error on his part, banishment being the usual punishment?

—Can the doctor treat a patient during the seven days of mourning, when he does not have the right to work and receive remuneration?[13]

—Does the doctor have the right to receive remuneration for care given on the sabbath?[14]

—Can a doctor violate the sabbath for a non-Jewish patient?[15]

—Can a doctor who is a kohen visit a dying patient?[16]

—Is a doctor who may be a kohen, and so contaminated by contact with a cadaver, nonetheless authorized to carry on his activities as priest, reciting the blessings and being the first called to the Torah reading?[17]

—Can a doctor officiate for the court, even though he is paid for his work, which can be considered "deriving a profit from a dead man," something that is strictly forbidden?[18]

—Is the doctor who must visit a sick person on the sabbath authorized to take a carriage or a boat?[19]

—Is a surgeon authorized to operate on his own father, if the father trusts only him and will accept no one else, despite the prohibition on the son from seeing his father's nakedness?[20]

These recurrent questions in the responsa define the limits assigned to the notion of "saving human life," which releases anyone from the obligations and prohibitions of Halakhah. They also highlight the problem of medical responsibility, placing the activity of practitioners in its human perspective. Although the term *doctor* refers to the person who performs medical acts, many designations are used which indicate the spectrum of functions performed by these practitioners.

The doctor is usually designated by the term *rofeh,* which can also be used for the surgeon, but he can be given many other titles as well, such as officiant, specialist, generalist, or court physician. Those doctors who are admired for their religious qualities are described by complimentary epithets, such as doctor-king, illustrious and sympathetic, eminent and exceptional,[21] exceptional in Torah,[22] or eminent in Torah and piety.[23] Mention is also made of dentists,[24] gynecologists,[25] and even ophthalmologists.[26] The practitioner, thus designated by his various tasks, would be related to the "physician," whose position defines a scientifically recognized medical status conferred either by his studies at the medical schools[27] or by apprenticeship with a reputed master. However, the existence of this first highly valued category does not discredit the others, whose healing art is honed by empirical practice.

Female medical practitioners are often mentioned in the rabbinic literature. As in the Christian world, they were the bearers of traditional medical knowledge transmitted by women, from mother to daughter. In his French translation of Glückel's memoirs, Léon Poliakov designates them in circumstantial terms: "healers," "midwives," or "experienced women." Glückel herself used only the Yiddish term *royfeanes*—literally, the bone setter.[28] As the representatives of popular medicine, they prescribed remedies based on incantations or inhalations.[29]

The midwives, and it is not always clear if they are Jews or Christians, are sometimes denigrated in the responsa and accused of unhygienic practices and negligence.[30] In the medical world, however, they are the objects of a critical consensus, universally taxed with "dirtiness, clumsiness, and superstition."[31] When, toward the end of the eighteenth century, the medical establishment as a whole was agitated by the malpractice of midwives, holding them responsible for the deaths of women in childbirth,[32] it was decreed in Turkey that henceforth only midwives who had studied or had been educated by master doctors would be authorized to practice. The problem of midwifery is found in this period in the responsa of Moses Sofer, in Hungary, who was asked to make a knowledgeable pronouncement on whether Jewish midwives, who alone fulfilled the new criteria for professional legitimation, were authorized to serve non-Jewish women in childbirth, even on the sabbath.[33] Hirsch Jacob Zimmels judges that despite the general outcry, the rabbis must have persisted in their high regard for midwives, who, in certain regions, were often the only purveyors of medical care.[34]

The label "barber" appears very frequently, and when they are called *rofim,* doctors, without being distinguished from the *rofeh mumḥeh,* the specialist, it is difficult to differentiate them from their legitimate colleagues. These distinctions are nonetheless taken up by Poliakov: "He agreed, then, to see Abraham Lopez, a Portuguese who was a barber-surgeon. . . . Thursday, I brought another surgeon and two doctors."[35]

According to the sources, Jews did not hesitate to consult anyone who could provide them with medical care, including Christian priests. Their healing specialties were incantations and exorcisms but also sympathetic remedies and potions. It might be surprising that Jews had recourse to the representatives of an alien faith who used Christian formulations in their medical treatments. For Rabbi Menaḥem of Speyer, in the thirteenth century, the problem is not, however, posed in these terms: "It is the tone [of voice] that heals, and not the words of the incantation; so that a Christian is authorized to care for a Jew, even if he invokes the aid of Jesus and the saints in his efforts."[36] But Rabbi Samuel Aboab, in the seventeenth century, considered these practices proscribed. Consulted about calling in a priest to exorcise an epileptic possessed by demons, he adds to his negative response that this question has been posed many times, indicating that it was current practice.[37]

Recourse to magicians and sorcerers is widely discussed in the rabbinic literature. The rabbis questioned on this subject were determined to define the limits of magical practices. If Zimmels is to be believed, most often magicians and sorcerers were not Jews. He cites, however, the case of a seventeenth-century Polish Jew who had a reputation as a magician. He treated people with herbs, baths, and magic.[38] But Jewish magicians usually fell into another category.

The *ba'alei-shemot,* or "Masters of Names," designates practitioners who were adept at practical Kabbalah. Their supernatural power was generally attributed to the use of the *Sefer Yetsira* (the Book of Creation). The names or divine attributes were also used therapeutically. Rabbi Akiba Egger (end of the eighteenth century and beginning of the nineteenth century) indicates that the ba'alei-shemot were particularly consulted in cases of mental illness.[39]

The rabbis and tsaddikim who made "miracles" arise from a tradition deeply anchored in Judaism. They challenge earlier distinctions, for they combine rabbinic knowledge with medical science while having recourse to traditional therapeutic practices. They treat their patients by prescribing herbal potions and infusions of all sorts, by performing incantations and exorcisms, and sometimes by using practical Kabbalah as well.

## FROM HUMORS TO THE DEMON

Just as medieval medicine rests on an almost undifferentiated mixture of science and superstition, illness is perceived as the result of a confluence of physiological agents, like humors, heredity, and contagion, and supernatural factors, such as demons, sorcery, and divine punishment. As the first is intimately bound to the second, illness is often considered just one of the manifestations of demonic agency. For just as illness insinuates itself into a deficient or weakened body, evil spirits penetrate the human body diminished by its misdeeds, or by malign forces. Thus illness signals a rupture, a mental and physical disorder that affects the integrity of the human being.

Dominated by the doctrine of Hippocrates, medical science until the seventeenth century[40] based its notion of corporal harmony on Galen's theory of the equilibrium of the four "humors," which correspond to the four elements: earth, air, fire, and water. They determine the balance of bodily fluids as well as their color: red for blood, white for phlegm, black for black bile, and yellow for yellow bile. These humors thus define the balance of hot and cold, wet and dry, which together form the general equilibrium of the human body; when the humors are unbalanced, illness is the result.

The configuration of astral bodies, which can provoke a corruption of the air and cause miasmas, is considered another pathogenic factor. The responsa express the belief among Jews that it was dangerous for anyone to drink water during the periods of the equinox or solstice.[41] Epidemics were generally considered the price of miasmas; plague, cholera, and other diseases were thought to be generated by astral vapors that could be associated with demonic machinations. The most commonly designated pathogenic agents were demons and their human agents, sorcerers. Since antiquity demons had been held responsible for human illness; this belief is found in the Talmud[42] as well as in the New Testament,[43] where we read that Jesus gives his disciples the power to banish the demons causing illness, and Augustine declares that all illness affecting Christians could be attributed to demons. Demons and sorcerers are regularly mentioned, then, from antiquity until the beginning of the nineteenth century. According to Jewish sources, malign forces are often associated with filth: evil is malodorous, and demons prefer to inhabit latrines, empty houses, and dark corners. Satanic illnesses are spread by contamination and lack of hygiene.

In addition to the forces of evil, supernatural factors transmit illnesses in the guise of divine punishment for sins committed by individuals or whole groups. In this case, it is angels who are the epidemiological agents. Among the extraordinary factors are the malign spirits of the dead, introduced in the fourteenth century:

> Why do evil spirits act on the sabbath eve? Because the evil spirits are not [that day] in Gehenna, furthermore, evil spirits are harmful and it is permitted to harm those bearing the illness . . . and there is no human remedy against these malevolent spirits for the one who is affected by them, only the Creator can heal him.[44]

In fact, for relieving an illness caused by sorcery, it seems that the only recourse was to commend oneself either to God or to a magician. When the Jews hesitated to call in sorcerers and magicians, in view of biblical prohibitions, they sought the opinion of the rabbis, who found themselves in a rather ambiguous situation, for the Torah specifies:

> Let no one be found in your house . . . who practices enchantments, who studies auguries, divination, magic; who uses charms, who might have recourse to evocations or enchantments or who questions the dead.[45]

Yet the sheer number of citations or explanations of these practices suggests that recourse to the assistance of practitioners of the occult must have been quite common. Israel Isserlein provides information particularly relating to magic.

> In order to answer your question, can a sick person consult a magician, know that we have found no explicit prohibition on this subject, the biblical restrictions as to sorcerers do not apply in this case.[46]

Solomon Luria is even clearer: "If a serious illness is caused by magic or an evil spirit, one can call in a non-Jewish magician to cure it."[47]

Since healing the sick person is primary, the duty to save human life gives the doctor latitude to prescribe whatever seems to him most effective. Jacob Coblenz says it quite clearly: "The doctor must do whatever possible, save committing idolatry, incest, or murder," which are absolute prohibitions.[48]

## THE ARSENAL OF THE ORDINARY

In the doctors' struggle against demons, the idea of medical care was based on the concept of repulsion, according to the principle that dictates the following: "If nauseating treatments disgust humans, they must have the same effect on demons."[49] To try and dislodge the demons from their human habitat, medieval medicine concocted the most revolting potions on the principle that "what is bad for demons must be good for the patient."[50] And if medical works of the seventeenth century contain recipes for philters and extracts made from dog's urine, donkey's blood, flesh, excrement, and fur of all sorts,[51] the Talmud was not unaware of these therapeutic practices and also recommended this type of treatment.

We might be surprised that animals considered Halakhically impure for consumption can be used as curatives if they have been reduced to powder, unguents, or potions. Jacob Reischer and Eliakim Goetz discussed this through interposed responsa. In order to determine cases in which this kind of treatment could be prescribed for the sake of health, Goetz interrogates Reischer on his reasons for authorizing a patient whose life is not in danger but who is suffering to be treated with "frozen and dried goat's blood." In his response, Reischer argues on three points. He first explains that popular customs have the force of law. Then he adds that the compromised blood, being frozen, has neither taste nor liquid and that furthermore an illness must always be considered a serious case, since one has the right to profane the sabbath to prepare a remedy for the suffering.[52] Goetz is consulted by someone who is advised by "specialists," although his illness does not seem fatal, to take the bone of a cadaver and make a bath of it, or, if this is not possible, to replace it with a used shroud. Goetz answers that in a case where the patient's life is not at stake, Halakhah must not be violated. Under the circumstances, the use of the bone from a human cadaver or even a shroud that has touched a dead person cannot be justified.[53] However, when it is a matter of "saving a life," Menaḥem Mendel Krochmal, in the sixteenth century,[54] and Jacob Emden, in the eighteenth century,[55] may hesitate to authorize these medications but tolerate such cures as remedies of last resort. Emden even required a medical opinion that a patient's life was really in danger before he would be permitted to use a carcass.

Saving a human life under these conditions could involve compromising the intact, dignified resurrection of someone else, whether by removing a bone or unwrapping a shroud. We do not know how the rabbis dealt with this dilemma, or how they resolved it, but in any case the shrouds disappeared, as Glückel attests.

> Soon after, her body was robbed and the shroud taken from her. She revealed the outrage to someone in a dream; the body was exhumed and the robbery confirmed.[56]

The narrative clearly says nothing about the thieves, or their religion, or whether they meant by this theft to clothe a corpse or treat a sick person.

Related to the cure with bones is a treatment that involves the "mummy," discussed by Rabbi Eliezer Ashkenazi.

> It is known in our day [sixteenth century] that sometimes when a man is on his way in the wilderness and is attacked by a sandstorm from which he cannot escape, he is covered by sand. When, after a certain time the corpse, uncovered by another wind, is found by wanderers, it is taken to drug merchants, and this corpse is termed "mummy." Dessicated bodies of this kind are used in medicine.[57]

In the fifteenth century, Ibn Zimra was questioned on this subject.

> What is the religious warrant permitting people to employ as a remedy the flesh of corpses called "mummies," and this not only to cure dangerous cases, but even to engage in trading in them? This is, of course, prohibited, for we know that one should not derive benefit from a corpse.[58]

The *Radbaz* responds that there is no prohibition against absorbing mummies since these creatures are reduced to the state of "dust." He adds that the sale of mummies is authorized and that their bodies may be used not only as a plaster but also taken internally. This is because one is not deriving any benefit from the cadaver in itself but only from the medication it contains and, moreover, that nonembalmed flesh and bodies are of no therapeutic use.[59] In the seventeenth century we find mummies in the responsa of Mordecai ben Judah ha-Levi concerning the problem of the purity of the kohen who comes in contact with them.[60] This curative vogue surely began with the direct importing of mummies from Egypt, but in the course of time this source must have been replaced by a local, more prosaic trade in dried cadavers.[61]

It must surely have been easier for the rabbis to authorize the prescription of mummies than to condone using bones from neighboring cemeteries—Jewish or non-Jewish. Medieval theories on sympathetic or antipathetic remedies expressed the correlation between the nature of the treatment and the person treated. Various colors were supposed to act on parts of the sick body according to their relation to unbalanced humors, just as these could be reestablished by external contact with a body, whether human, animal, or inanimate, on condition that it was of the same nature. So it was no simple matter to be treated by the bone of a stranger, whose good qualities might be incorporated along with his faults.

In the medieval view, the notion of the body was not limited to its living and animate state: everything that touched it or was part of it belonged to it forever. When a limb was amputated, it was not buried but preserved while its owner lived. People must have believed that a limb interred before its former owner would lead him quickly to the grave. Upon the death of the amputee, care was taken to bury the limb beside him. Among the Jews this practice was influenced by ideas concerning resurrection, as we read in the *Ma'avar Yabbok*:

> And as it is said, because the soul is bound to the specific bones that existed in this world, care must be taken that all the limbs are with him [the dead man] in his tomb and that there is no exchange.

Berachia notes that it was the usual practice to bury the dead with everything that might have been detached from them, whether jaws or an amputated limb.[62] Any corporeal exchange of parts was now deemed dangerous.

> It happened that the noses of two gentiles were cut off. Unfortunately they got mixed up and were wrongly affixed by the doctor. When one of them died, his original nose, although in the process of healing on the other man, withered.[63]

The person conceived that his corporeal limits included his clothing, his jewelry, his aura—which reflect his identity, his character, and his individuality. It was even said that if a cat drinks human blood, this changes the person it came from.[64] In the same way, the cow is thought to suffer when men boil its milk.[65]

There were numerous remedies available in the daily practice of medicine. These consisted of products in a pure state, like goat's milk,[66] fish oil,[67] animal blood consumed immediately after slaughtering,[68] the milk and urine of humans or donkeys,[69] hot animal bile,[70] or even snake soup;[71] or of pharmaceutical preparations, often involving different waters mixed with all sorts of ingredients, like water boiled with marinated apples,[72] barley water prepared with sugar and spices,[73] or water mixed with peeled almonds.[74] The responsa also mention beer,[75] *agua ardiente* made with herbs, special wines,[76] and even coffee.[77] In this category as well are various brews and mixtures, such as "pills made of different ingredients, with the pulverized ashes of human skull."[78] Certain remedies are directly associated with particular pathologies: donkey's milk is used for treating attacks of asthma and when the patient is spitting blood;[79] jaundice is treated by the ingestion of either one's own urine[80] or eight strands of one's own hair.[81] A person must eat snake to cure the spitting of blood,[82] and it is reputed to be even more effective in its roasted form as *polvere viprina*.[83]

Amulets are an integral part of the pharmacopeia and have above all a preventive function. They defend those who wear them against the "evil eye,"[84] demons,[85] and miscarriages.[86] But amulets can also be used to obtain positive results where demonic illnesses are concerned, as in epilepsy,[87] dementia,[88] fevers,[89] or poisonings.[90] They were often made according to kabbalistic practice with a parchment inscribed with holy names, but they could also be composed of herbs that cure fevers.[91] To treat hysteria, women were advised to wear a "wolf's heart" amulet,[92] while Tobias ha-Cohen recommended that women in labor wear a belt made of human skin.[93]

Samson Morpurgo was one of those famous rabbi-doctors in eighteenth-century Italy. He was aware of new directions in medicine due to recent discoveries in anatomy, as well as of the reforming influence of Paracelsus,[94] and he offered his reflections as a practitioner in the following text.

> Some remedies are individual ones. They have the power, nature, and individual quality of affecting a particular limb of the body and curing its diseases. The body is influenced by them through occult qualities, according to the ancient view, or through their entire substance, according to the view of later doctors. But though they seem to act only sympathetically, they are complete remedies, because they have a natural, clear, and well-known cause. . . .
>
> There are some remedies which the intellect cannot grasp, for example, many roots, leaves, herbs, metals, animal entrails, fowl, fish, excrement, and urine, which are hung on the neck or arm of patients suffering from fever, from dysentery, jaundice, epilepsy, and similar disorders. . . . These are, according to the views of all doctors and specialists, not completely known remedies, but only *segullot*. They declare unanimously that they are

> *segullot,* working on the principle of love and hatred, by "sympathy" and "antipathy." They have included them in their medical books and sometimes they employ them, for experience has often confirmed their potency. Sometimes the doctors using them know and admit that they are no remedies but only specifics, for example, the heart of a wolf that women suffering from hysteria hang upon their necks, and all different kinds of live fish that are put under the soles of people suffering from jaundice.

What is the difference between a "real" medication and a *segullah,* which is clearly valuable but also mysterious and highly specific? One answer can be found in the proposed explanation for the remedy that consists of ingesting snake.

> This is not only a *segullah* but a well-known and famous remedy, confirmed by experience and reason. It belongs to the group of remedies which cure in a natural way. A proof of this is that in medical books of ancient and modern doctors it is prescribed for many kinds of diseases caused by damage to the white humour. This cannot be maintained for other things, which cure by occult virtue alone. They are only of use in a particular illness to which the *segullah* in question applies.[95]

While we can see the attitudes of physicians and rabbis shift, depending on whether they have to administer a treatment as a last resort or as medicine for an illness that is not too serious, it is rare to find the patient's behavior recorded in the available writings. Here again we may thank Glückel:

> I fell dangerously ill . . . and the doctors, doubting of my recovery, wanted to bring desperate measures into play. . . . I told my husband and my mother I would not submit to them, whereas they informed the doctors of my decision, and although the physicians meant well and did their best to persuade me, I said to them: "Talk as much as you please, I'll take no more of your physicking. If the dear Lord minds to help me, He can do very well without medicines. If not, what good are all the medicines in the world?"[96]

Considering Glückel's behavior when confronted with certain prescriptions, we may well doubt their automatic acceptance. Indeed, Glückel is a pious woman who represents above all the ordinary German Jewish bourgeoisie at the end of the seventeenth century and the beginning of the eighteenth century. Her testimony may indicate a common reticence with regard to radical treatments. Besides, this is the only circumstance in which she refuses a prescription: when the doctors or barbers propose plasters, balms, or unguents for her, her husband, or her children, Glückel rarely hesitates.[97] Assuming that numerous patients would have reacted in the same way in the face of "desperate measures," it is likely that doctors must have had to be content with using less draconian methods. And since "the medicine of this period had only two effective remedies: mercury for venereal diseases and quinine for fevers,"[98] patients must have been, for the most part, commended to the grace of God. In fact, both doctors and patients did indeed turn to the heavens. But this was not a matter of submitting passively to divine fatality: actual treatments were undertaken to call upon divine aid, which was the only really effective medication. Apart from remedies in which the power of the segullah worked in "an occult fashion," a whole therapeutic world was elaborated on the virtues of spirituality. This consists of fasts, prayers, and alms, as well as the analysis of dreams, exorcisms, and the changing of the sick person's name.

Purely spiritual medicine, based on fasts, prayers, or alms, requires neither medical mediation nor recourse to rabbinic authority. In this sense, it may have been the first step toward self-healing. When Glückel's husband fell ill, she says, "And I fasted and I prayed . . . and otherwise gave myself, as best I could, to penitence, prayer, and deeds of mercy. And God, too, took mercy on us."[99] Thus the adage "charity saves from death" was taken literally, and if there was never any lack of occasions for distributing alms to the poor, all the more reason to do so when someone's life was in danger. Fasting was also considered an effective means of obtaining forgiveness for sins committed, so that charity, fasting, and prayers were often practiced as preventive measures: before undertaking a journey, in order to treat an illness or a simple discomfort or to transform one's fate or gain release from a vow.[100] Days of collective fasts were decreed in the communities in order to bring rain, guard against a pogrom or an epidemic, and so on. Women in labor were particularly helped by the wearing of amulets, as well as by the recitation of Psalm 20, "The Lord hear thee in the day of trouble; / The name of the God of Jacob defend thee."[101] Amulets were also indicated for preserving the lives of newborn males, who were prey to Lilith for the first eight days and especially on the night preceding their circumcision.[102] According to Yuspa Schamach, the practice in Worms held that a circle should be drawn on the ground in which were inscribed the names of "Lilith, Adam, Eve, Sansanus, Samiglof."[103] The circle was considered effective protection against Satan. Notions of practical Kabbalah are reflected in the amulets and in recourse to the circle, which was sometimes used by healers who drew it around the ailing part of the body to isolate it from the rest of the healthy body and prevent the disease from spreading.[104] If amulets can be classified as segullot, occult and specific therapy, according to Morpurgo, they are also part of spiritual medicine when they are elaborated from the verses of religious works like the Bible or the *Sefer Yetsira,* or based on mystical invocations.

Another prophylactic practice was the interpretation of dreams, for dreams can be the product of various pathogenic factors. When food is richly spiced, says the *Sefer Ḥasidim,* it leads to sensations of warmth, which have an influence on dreams.[105] Daytime thoughts are reflected oneirically and translate cerebral activity, but dreams can especially issue from the soul and constitute a kind of prophecy. This may be trivial, the activity of "idiots and children," whose intelligence is limited and who project in dreams analogies with the events of the real or future world.[106] But the peregrinations of the soul in the course of the night are inexhaustibly fertile, for "the souls of the Just who are deserving rise and the gates are open to them and they go up towards the holy . . . place where all souls stand before the Holy One, blessed be he."[107]

Dreams, then, can result in these journeys in the upper worlds. At night one can encounter the souls of relatives who are geographically distant or even dead. Numerous narratives report encounters with the dead and departed. Thus Eliakim ben Joseph visits his son-in-law and acknowledges an error of judgment concerning a ritual decision;[108] Meir of Rothenburg helps a student, though not one of his, to clarify a difficult talmudic passage.[109] Rashi explains to his grandson the exact pronunciation of the Tetragrammaton.[110] Less celebrated but just as convincing is Glückel's story of the woman who in a dream communicates that her shroud was stolen.[111]

The visions sent to people during sleep can be celestial messages, transmitted by herald angels; but they can also be the products of demons coming to outwit miserable creatures powerless to escape their nocturnal grasp. It is more against this eventuality that one must arm oneself. A personal projection or a decree from on high? The attitude toward dreams is ambivalent. According to the Talmud, it seems that dreams are often inconsequential and must not be taken seriously;[112] yet when someone dreams of an excommunication, either of himself or of someone else, a quorum of ten people must be brought together to annul it. When dealing with dreams, medieval rabbinic literature attempts to determine the specific cases that should properly be taken into consideration, depending on which of the two attitudes defined by the Talmud is adopted. Fasting is recommended to avoid the influence of bad oneiric journeys. The rabbinic discussions focus, as a result, on defining the circumstances of these fast days observed as penance after a dream or as a defense against demons: the *Taanit Ḥalom*.[113]

It is especially at night that man is vulnerable to demonic attacks. When he is in their possession, can he be held responsible? Generally, if a man or a woman confesses to being outwitted by demons who took on the appearance of a husband or wife, the rabbis consider them neither blameworthy nor adulterous.[114] However, certain illnesses like dementia, epilepsy, impotence,[115] limping, blindness, or *plica polonica*[116] are considered virtually demonic illnesses, and it then becomes necessary to free the possessed person through exorcism.

As therapy, exorcisms are a combination of many methods: amulets, charms, and incantations are used more or less in equal measure, and a prayer quorum is gathered to banish the offending demon. The recitation of the Shema Yisrael also has the power to discourage demons. The kabbalists elaborated formulas of particular prayers to recite at night, in self-defense, against the assault of bad spirits.[117] These prayers are based on biblical verses or psalms, the recitation of the "Holy Names" of angels, repeated three or seven times: "All Israel refrains from drinking, eating, or talking after the reading of the Shema, which is recited in bed," says Horowitz.[118] In the *Sefer Shaʾare Tsion*, the majority of the prayers, based on Lurianic Kabbalah, are devoted to combating demons. Here we find prayers for the night, prayers to be recited in bed to bring on sleep,[119] prayers to banish Satan when someone dies,[120] and prayers reserved for pregnant women from the seventh month on, "for many enter labor in their seventh month."

In Jewish belief there is a fine line between demonic sickness and possession. Beginning in the sixteenth century and as a corollary to the spread of Lurianic Kabbalah, cases of possession multiplied in the communities. We find the appearance of the *dibbuk*, a demon or departed and sinful soul that slips into the body of a living being, takes over his voice and thoughts, and incites him to change his behavior. It would be difficult to deny that the idea of possession is closely linked to the doctrine of gilgul, the transmigration of souls.[121] For if the souls of sinners cannot find rest in the afterlife, they are obliged to seek refuge in this world; they will then attack the most vulnerable human beings, or those who, being sinners themselves, give them an opening into their body or soul. To check this assault, it may be enough to "buy back the soul."[122] This "buying back" might also be translated as "redemption" and can be effected in many ways, the most common being the employment of an expiatory victim, the *kapparah,* the cock or hen, sacrificed in the name of a person mortally ill,[123] or of a family whose members are dying for no apparent reason.[124] Sometimes satanic dreams also require recourse to an expiatory victim, which will be sacrificed as "penitence of the soul" and whose flesh will then be distributed to the poor.[125]

Tobias ha-Cohen suggests that an illness can be cured by transferring it onto other entities, whether animal or vegetable.[126] This illness can also be transferred to others and even sold through a commercial transaction.[127] However, one of the most widespread customs in case of illness consists of changing the sick person's name. The principle is a simple one:

> Thy will be done, may the name of such a person be changed to annul all bad decrees and all fatal judgments made against him on high. And if death has been decreed for such a person, may this decision no longer be decreed, for he is now someone else, a new creature, like a newborn entering a happy life and long years, full of days.[128]

According to the Talmud,[129] name changing is one of the four most effective ways of invalidating a divine decree. Israel Isserlein even thought one must choose a new name that contains no letter appearing in the old one and has a greater numerical value than the old one.[130] This practice illustrates the certainty that death and illness are sent to men as punishment. One can therefore induce the angels entrusted with carrying out the divine punishment to make a mistake by modifying the name of the sick person according to the formula of Moses of Coucy, which specifies, "I am not he whom you seek, I am not the one who has committed the sins you charge me with."[131] Through the illness or death of children, the parents are punished. And in the case of children sought by the angels because of their parents' sins, whatever name the child is given, he or she will be found. Should all the names in the family be changed, then? According to the responsa, only the name of the child is changed, but it is also sometimes symbolically sold to other parents, whose healthy children bear witness to their irreproachable conduct and the angels' good intentions toward them. At the dawn of the nineteenth century, the case was presented to Moses

Sofer of a sick child who had been sold to the ḥevra kaddisha.[132] It is noteworthy, too, that sterile couples changed their names in an attempt to improve their chances of procreation.[133]

Depending on time and place, the new names could be drawn by lot or chosen for their meaning; preference was thus given to Ḥaim (life), Alter (old one), or Zeide (grandfather), and these were feminized for women. Doing this increased the chances of prolonging the sick person's life. The ceremony of name changing took place in public and was a solemn occasion. At the least a quorum of ten was gathered, and the officiant recited the prescribed formula while carrying the Torah scrolls. When the new name was proclaimed, the ritual involved announcing it to the heavenly authorities while requesting that this modification be taken into account.[134]

## PESTILENCE

If Jews could call on barbers, surgeons, or ba'alei-shemot, depending on the organic or demonic nature of their illness, in an outbreak of epidemic these therapeutic measures proved useless. Diseases that indiscriminately affected all the members of the community and for which there was no effective remedy were perceived as exemplary divine punishments. Until the carrier of pestilence was discovered,[135] Jew and Christian alike regarded the plague as a heavenly scourge sent, like the plagues Moses called down upon Egypt, to punish sinners. In the fourteenth century, when the terrible epidemic of the Black Death spread over Europe, Christians massacred the Jews, whom they regarded either as poisoners of wells and spreaders of sickness or as the incarnation of sin. So when Margarita explains how Jews, like Christians, are vulnerable to illnesses and even to the plague, we understand that his intention is not to demonstrate that Jews are merely human beings and similarly subject to illness but that because Christians regard them as the incarnation of sin, they are even more subject to illness than others.[136]

In his *Journal of the Plague Year,* Daniel Defoe's narrator relates that while refusing to succumb to the terror and "hallucinations" that gripped his contemporaries during the great epidemic of 1665, he could not help seeing the plague as a divine punishment:

> I saw both the Stars; and I must confess, had so much of the common Notion of such Things in my Head, that I was apt to look upon them as the Forerunners and Warnings of God's judgments; and especially when after

> the Plague had followed the first, I yet saw another of the like kind; I could not but say, that God had not yet sufficiently scourg'd the City.[137]

Similarly, when the plague raged in a Jewish community, the acknowledged cause was inevitably the accumulation of collective sins. The entire community would then try to implement measures of moral cleansing to appease the divine wrath, according to the testimony of Moses ben Ḥayim Eisenstadt.[138]

> Almighty God, in the Heavenly realm, You always come to our aid when we are in peril: You brought us out of exile in Egypt and out of exile in Babylon, You have preserved us from all evils.
>
> Merciful God, in the third exile, again You defended us, and in the fourth exile You will also protect us.[139] Our hopes turn toward You, and we hope in these times that You will not try us so harshly.
>
> A terrible fear and a great terror are come upon us. My soul weeps and moans over my tale of the woe that has befallen our holy community. This misfortune came upon us on 29 Tammuz [June–July] because of our many sins.
>
> In the year 5473 [1713] since the creation of the world, from the moment it began the plague fell upon us because of our many sins. In the community we still had no one ill nor bad air in the country.
>
> Unfortunately, a great change came about on 22 Tammuz. How did things deteriorate until evil gripped the holy community, and we grew anguished? Six people in one house fell ill at the same time.
>
> And the plague struck hard: after three days, three were already dead; others were beginning death struggle, and in two days they, too, died.
>
> In the community, as soon as anyone caught it, a terrible fear gripped us. Everyone wanted to flee, to escape.
>
> Many people went to the authorities, who took them under their protection in the countryside. And here they were seen everywhere packing and departing, from every street and every corner [of the city]. All day long they were seen carrying cases, and what are they to do, the poor who remember seeing all the rich people leaving to save their own skin? We, we are compelled to stay behind in misfortune!
>
> This evacuation occasioned a great, heartbreaking turmoil in the community. And a great fear seized the people. All the porters and coachmen around were inadequate to the need.
>
> Thousands of people thus made arrangements [to depart]. So effectively that no more rich people remained in the community, nor scholars or other people of means: everyone had departed.
>
> You who pass along the roads, see what has happened to us and may you be spared! The president of the rabbinic court and the leader of our community have left, and we have seen them. The beauty and light of so many years, we have seen depart. Who will protect us now?
>
> Young people had come from the four corners of the earth, and as they wanted to escape the plague, they left when it began and returned home.

These young people studied and upheld the grandeur of the Torah; how could we have suddenly lost everything? [In other times] in all the streets and all the houses one heard nothing but the Torah, and formerly they also studied.

It is through the merits of the Torah that we are maintained in life, and because of our many sins, death has begun. Great misfortune is very near! Not even a whole night was now granted to any Jew in the country.

Our sins took precedence over everything; and we measure how terrible is God's anger that fell upon us. How the poor have been harshly struck! On 22 Menaḥem[140] all our streets were closed because of the extent of our sins.

Many people fled, if [however] they had not been seized here by the ravages [of the epidemic]. For several days the roads were full; but it was no longer possible to find refuge.

Heaven took the Just from among us, the great preacher and rector of the *yeshivah*.[141] God took them all from us! How misfortune fell upon us because of our sins! May Heaven forbid it: that such a just man should meet such misfortune!

I would still like to tell how this calamity came to pass, even until this day. And how so many people died of the plague because of our sins. At first it was thought that this fire could be put out, but it grew into an epidemic.

So the leader made a rule: when someone was suspected of being in danger, he had to be taken out of his house and laid in a hut.

All others from the same house who were still healthy and feeling well might stay at home, it was suggested. And this is how the world began to turn upside down.

Most of the babies died. As the plague began to tear a great number of infants from their mothers' bellies, because of all our sins, they perished. And the plague immediately hounded our children [to the tomb].

During the day, mothers and infants died. It often [happened] that the father and the other children died as well. Three of the dead were carried on a single stretcher. This was seen in every street and on every corner.

Cries rose up to God in this great misfortune that befell us and which our eyes beheld. More than twenty new stretchers had to be constructed to carry [the dead], and as our sins were so numerous, this still did not suffice.

Many people left their houses to live in the streets. There they slept and ate in booths. Their houses were contaminated, and they thought they would thus be spared.

The first to come were the seriously ill, to whom God could grant nothing. Who could witness such misfortune? All the booths in the street were full of [people] lying down.

And those who found a shop to lie down in ought to have felt very happy, because they could not stay at home and because the others had chased them out.

In this state of cruelty, people rose up against each other. Even wife against husband; father and mother turned against their own child.

And even a child could rise up against his own father and mother; and even if he was a good person, as soon as someone was suspected of sickness, people fled from him; for their lives were at stake.

Some could say to others: "Rid us of yourself." When they saw a dead person carried out of a house, no one could perform the *gemilut ḥesed* [mortuary ritual], for fear of being infected himself.

I cannot be silent about what happened then, how people began [to tear] each other to pieces. People's minds did not perceive the warning, and the dead multiplied because of all our sins.

More than eighty, ninety, even one hundred eighteen persons died in a single day. How did they drag themselves along, diseased and destroyed? Certain people thought they could stay in the homes of others, but the bitter death they harbored in their own homes caused the others to chase them away.

Let me continue to report what happened, what I saw with my own eyes: every week we had to distribute several hundred thalers, for the poverty became dire.

Generally, the sum of money distributed could not be augmented, but for such indigence nothing could have sufficed, and even more than what was distributed each week [would have still been inadequate]. We cooked daily for the poor.

Day after day great fires were lit in the empty streets and the poor flocked around them. There, people cooked several hundred pounds of meat and fowl for the poor. And on the sabbath as on other days of the week.

Day and night we heard nothing but "Alas! We must bring food to the sick at the bathhouse and the huts. For among them are many who are alone, and a great number who will not recover and will depart." For because of all our sins the sick were too numerous.

There were eight hundred sick, and sometimes this number rose to a thousand at once. How could the nurses, the barbers, and the provisions suffice? All the huts and the bathhouse as well were overflowing, for it was here that the poor were lodged.

I must continue and begin by [saying] what was done about the burial of the dead. To our misfortune, an order was given by the [royal] authorities which we had to follow scrupulously.

When someone would die, he could not be buried in the nearest cemetery but had to be driven or carried to the lazar house. Who could have looked upon such misery and such unhappiness! The *Kahal*[142] ordered three large wagons.

Each wagon would carry about twenty [bodies], and every night they passed three times in front of the door. There the dead lay many days, until two weeks were up, and then one could no longer drive them there by cart.

When someone would die, two bearers of the dead were needed to carry him to the cemetery, but there he was still not interred; no interment was permitted before the wagons had gone out.

A great number of dead were transferred from one cemetery to another.

Like me, people were busy, for they were gathering [cadavers] in this place. In three nights, seven hundred fifty cadavers were transported to the lazar house.

As many as fifty corpse carriers were hired. Let such a calamity never befall us again! Who can write or tell of such misfortune? Each time, two bearers of the dead carried a stretcher.

In every street and in every corner you saw nothing but people dragging wood to carry [the dead]. Who would not have wept and wailed to witness such carnage? [To look upon] this destruction that befell us?

My dear good friends, let us lament and weep over this desolation! Day and night we saw only people transporting the dead. Sometimes, we saw five or six groups of them at the same time. Let everyone weep and wail over this desolation!

The sabbath and the holidays were disrupted by it. Who ever heard of such a thing in his life? As the precept has it, one must always cook for the sick, on the sabbath as on other days of the week.

We also had to dig [graves] day and night, on the sabbath and on holidays, as well as transport the dead by wagon. The number of dead multiplied so that nothing frightens me but the telling of it.

Up to one hundred people were busy sawing planks day and night. All those who could work came to help. Several hundred women were busy sewing shrouds. How the eye rebels at this sight!

No more planks were found for the coffins, so those who had cupboards and chairs were asked to contribute them for mortuary purposes, and [were told] that the *Kahal* would pay for this.

In the same way, it was not enough to work on the shrouds day and night, as well as on the sabbath and holidays. Therefore, those who had finished shrouds were asked to contribute them. People who had enough white linen threw it out the windows: they believed that in this way they could avoid the grave.

There were several hundred people digging [graves] at the lazar house, and more were needed. With good words the people of the *Kahal* implored the poor to come work as well:

"Dear ones, do it in the Name of God, and for these holy souls, for one day you too will be buried. Look at what misery our holy community suffers; and you will be paid doubly for it."

With these good words and double wages, the poor people were convinced and they came to the gate of the lazar house. There was more work here than in the whole country. That night they buried almost two hundred people.

The misery suffered by the dying cannot be told or written. They had to lie nearly ten or fourteen days. For certain of them, the poison made them swell in height or girth. And sometimes nothing of them remained.

Some of them were left in pieces. Who could describe all these horrors? For some a hand, for others a foot, sometimes the head came off the body. Let us lament over these men and women!

These limbs had to be gathered together and stitched to others. Those full of worms could not be reattached; the drivers who brought the dead here kept [the detached limbs] in sacks, and each time they had to choose which one to take out.

Most of the dead were no longer recognizable. Those who could be given a name were rare, usually those on whom a paper was found. Any corpse that was whole was given a proper burial.

Let us cry out to God, my good friends, and with all our heart, that He may preserve us in the future from such sorrows! I write all this so that you shall remember, and will no longer desire to sin.

The pious chief rabbi Taini Neueschatl was not spared by God's terrible wrath. He, too, was lost in this misfortune. And he was a man of the Torah! In all the community there was no better man than he.

A day after *Yom Kippur* it was the turn of the illustrious Rabbi Moshe. Everyone went before his bier. Now the Great Synagogue was touched by sorrow, the cries must have been heard even to the heavens.

The day after 25 Tishri, it was the illustrious chief rabbi Shimon, brother of the great rector of the *yeshivah,* who died; and a certain number of pious men from the Great Synagogue departed. The whole community laments them, the great as well as the small.

Nor can I forget the celebrated cantor Rabbi Wolf, and the illustrious cantor Rabbi Naḥum. Who could still eat or drink? There was no cantor to equal them. And the disaster did not spare them.

We must lament such pious men, that we should see such pious men carried off by such a scourge to the grave. We heard that the death of the just was honored, and immediately the whole synagogue was in a turmoil.

During the *Days of Awe,*[143] the greatest misfortunes befell us. May such important victims be sacrificed! May our beloved God reunite your soul to those of the living, and may the angel Michael bear them to him as a sacrifice!

During *Yom Kippur* and *Rosh Hashanah* there was great suffering in the synagogues. Who could rejoice? Even when we heard the divine hymns intoned by the cantors. Who would now instruct us?

Heavenly God, see what is left of our joy? How did they pass, the *Days of Awe*? No one had the heart to [welcome] the holidays, while most of the women mourned and dressed in black!

Am I still going to tell how we spent our *Simḥat Torah*?[144] And how a new calamity began? The distinguished and beloved leader, Rabbi Nathan Roiznih, died. The illustrious leader, Naḥum Karpeles, was also taken from us.

They were, both of them, beautiful trees. In all our holy community there were none better than they. Wherever they went, they would have been pillars of the *yeshivah*. Tragic! They returned to dust so young.

Among the magistrates of the *Kahal,* the celebrated chief rabbi Abraham Lichtenstadt was also tragically carried off by death. How the community felt this loss! He had always been a father to us, and, alas, he was not spared by this misfortune.

It is truly proper to weep and wail over such catastrophes. For these tragedies happened to us during our lifetime. Who has [already] seen the holidays in our community? Such a person cannot stanch the flow of his tears.

Dear friends, awaken your hearts and weep sorrowfully over these sainted souls: three thousand and several hundred are on the list of the departed. And unfortunately, they left this world so soon.

How could you want consolation, o holy community of Prague? And on what merits can you rest? Forever on the merits of your Just? They are all beneath the ground!

In other days, the holidays were the best time. Everyone who used to rejoice on these days has vanished like smoke. Now everything is upside down, our holidays are disrupted.

*Tisha b'Av* and the other holidays are all the same. No one can distinguish rich from poor; everyone goes around with their heads covered. No one knows whether we will be allowed [to live] until tomorrow.

In the nearby synagogues, they set up great prayers. No doubt Heaven will take pity on us. For the pandemonium and weeping of the poor people must surely have reached to Heaven.

Nearly eleven hundred children, who had committed no sin, were thus taken because of their parents. Were our sins, then, so great? Infants perished at their mothers' breasts.

My eyes cannot stop their tears. Eight or nine hundred dead are stretched out on the ground at once! They were uprooted in good health. At this sight, my eyes fill with tears.

Must I recall the betrothed who departed in this tragedy? Their number was more than one hundred twenty, and this figure will be included in the list.

We have yet to mention the newborns, for this is truly cause for lamentation. There were so many who departed at once. Ah! If only we had been able to find a plot of virgin ground for them.

A grave was made by digging very deep. During this time, the women in childbed [women who died in childbirth] lay in the sun. They had all been placed in the shade, [but] the drippings stained their shrouds.

Because just at this time, it was very hot. Even the dead perspired, and they were roasted by the sun. Has such a thing been heard of before?

An actual event also happened in which I was involved, along with others. They came with me to carry out the body of a woman who had died in childbirth, and while we were bearing her toward the grave, we heard the baby moan and cry.

My dear good friends, what can I add to this, when infants moaned in their mother's body over such misery? All the more reason that we should pray, great and small, that Heaven save us from such tragedy.

The sick were carried to the cemetery and laid next to the dead. The sick man must have been terrified. Under him and over him he saw the dead on stretchers. What did he feel then?

Shall I go on to report what we endured, what our community was subjected to? How we have suffered from this [epidemic] attack, when even the rich man was affected.

Can the deepest wells be dried? Would all our money be enough for food? Even when we are in good health, all the more reason when there is such sickness!

All the money was spent for barbers, nurses, and apothecaries. How could the poor manage? The *Kahal* could not take care of them for long, where would it have found money?

It had arranged nearly two hundred beds for the poor and [medicaments] from barbers and nurses, lemons and other food stuffs, as well as medicines for the poor. Our *Kahal* had spent its money on this.

A lot of money was also spent on the gravediggers of the lazar house, and still more to feed the sick. All that was available was given to the sick, or to healthy people so they might be nourished and survive.

The streets were closed for so long that no one could earn a living, even one *tsalmer*. Many honorable people who used to give generous daily alms now had to beg to find a few *groschen* to live.

And you had to see what went on at the apothecary's! It was impossible to get in; people had to line up for more than three quarters of an hour to get inside.[145]

And anyone who wanted medicines at the apothecary's, or something to eat for a sick person, had to pay plenty. And he thought he was keeping the patient alive.

The world should know what our pious folk and the president of the *Kahal* have done: his name is Samuel Taussig. His reknown is already so great that half the world knows him.

[. . .] Holy community of Prague, you must do penance! And remember this punishment for many years to come; and let us pray to God whom we love and in whom we hope, that He may never again send us such punishment.

For all chastisements are not the same, and this one affected the rich as well as the poor. You can escape almost any punishment, but not this one, for it is death.

And let us see what the Book of Samuel says: in it Heaven tells David to choose between three [punishments]. And he chooses the plague, which was the worst of all.[146]

[. . .] And he chose the plague, this is what the Book of Samuel tells us. And he spoke this way to put himself in God's hands rather than man's. For the cry to God for mercy can be very great.

This is why, in the end, we pray to God from the bottom of our hearts. That we might henceforth be spared this kind of sorrow and others, in the present and the future, for all time, we live in Thy mercy.

[. . .] I still want to note several useful pointers, in case this scourge should return, may God preserve us! For with God's help one might protect oneself from this calamity in the world.

1) Hold solemn services and supplications to Heaven, for it sent us this punishment. We beg Heaven to cease its wrath.

2) And let Him cease His punishment immediately. And if ever [this should begin again]—may God preserve us!—flee as soon as possible, right away.

3) And if one cannot leave, then let people stay with their families in their houses as much as possible, and especially at the hour of midday, and let them not go near the door when it gets dark.

4) When going out is unavoidable, it would be useful to wash your face and hands in vinegar, and also hold a sponge soaked in vinegar to your nose and mouth until you have returned home.

5) And if someone catches the plague, then let him immediately take a fresh brown egg and with the point of a knife insert into it sulfur, half a peppercorn, rye and camphor, let him mix it all up and heat it thus, then drink it hot and perspire.

6) A measure of peeled pepper, drink hot and perspire.

7) Do not have him bled.

8) When constipated, abstain from obstructive foods.

9) A good plaster, well tested and proven, is the following: take a piece of sour pastry the size of an egg, and if you have none, take rye flour. Add to this a spoonful of honey, a whole fresh egg, a drop of linseed oil, and of saffron; you then have an unguent. Spread it on a piece of new linen, and if you haven't any, do it with old linen. You must keep the plaster throughout on the surface of the lesion.

10) And when you have availed yourself of all possible remedies, you must appeal to Heaven, that He may include you in all the sick of Israel.

In Prague, as in Mantua, Padua, Marseilles, and elsewhere, when the plague claimed its first victims, everyone fled who could, as the narrator, Moses ben Ḥayim Eisenstadt, advises his readers to do. This imperative, however, does not prevent him from being outraged by the flight from community obligations, although that was hardly unusual.[147] This exodus exacerbates the dread of social inequalities, and it is in a community bereft of its civic and religious leaders that this struggle against the plague is conducted. The disease spreads in a calamitous way: in no time at all the dead pile up and the sick litter the shops, which are turned into public hospices. When the disease becomes evident, the community does not seem to be caught off guard, although it is quickly overwhelmed by the extent of the mortality. A draconian management of the disease is put in place with a swiftness that suggests the familiar frequency of these epidemics.[148] From the moment a sick person is diagnosed, the victim is brought into the buildings preassigned or requisitioned for this purpose. The city authorities forbid customary burials, and we gather that the prevailing measures require, as is customary practice, that the bodies be covered with quicklime until they are decomposed: "The dead lay many days until two weeks were up."

Like all the survivors of the epidemic, Eisenstadt describes the ghastly spectacle of the heaps of dead bodies, the familiar carts relentlessly transporting their awful load. But despite the general poverty, which made help difficult, the author emphasizes communal organization: he details the quantities of food furnished daily to the unfortunate around the great fires of purification lit in the streets[149] and relates in detail the general commitment to mortuary needs of "more than a hundred people," despite the horror provoked by the slightest contact with infected persons. The Italian chronicle of the Plague of 1630 provides similar testimony.

> In the year 5441 [1680], in the beginning of the month of Tishri, the plague stopped in Prague. . . . In Heshvan the plague had raged around our neighborhood, and many Jews had died from it. In some villages all the male population died out, and only a few women were left. No one was there to take charge of the dead, who could not be buried, for it was winter and the earth was as hard as marble, and there was a heavy snowfall in those parts; so they only covered them with snow, and often wolves came and ate the corpses, and sometimes dogs scratched the snow off the bodies. May God have pity on their souls.[150]

This description of the plague is typical. But it is surprising that at a moment when mortuary rites could no longer be performed, the Jews of Prague devoted themselves to the macabre assembling of the detached parts of cadavers in order to reconstitute the remains insofar as they could: "These limbs had to be gathered together and stitched to others." We find in this description a notable difference from those of the comon charnel houses covered with quicklime and exposed to the elements. This must surely be seen as concern for the preservation of the body in view of the resurrection, for "any corpse that was whole was given a proper burial." As ghastly as the gravediggers intent on reassembling bodies must have been the fate of the sick, transported to the lazar houses along with the cadavers. But it is noteworthy that despite their quantity, the dead are treated in Prague, in similar circumstances, with the greatest possible respect. The landscape of the plague is the same wherever it raged, but the Jews made sure that their dead were not deprived of shrouds—for which people stripped themselves of their linen—or of coffins—for which they gave whatever wood they had. This picture is quite different from the one presented by the epidemic of 1680: No one was there to take charge of the dead, who could not be buried, for it was winter . . . but often wolves came and ate the corpses.

Such careful attention to burial procedure, even in a period of epidemic, is not unusual, as the Jewish community of Mantua also carried its dead to the cemetery.

> In this time, in the month of Nisan [March–April] of the year 390 [1630] a great epidemic began. . . . In the beginning, three or four among the children of Israel died daily, but the epidemic gathered strength around the holiday of *Shavuot,* and more than twenty died day after day. And the ghetto was closed, no one could come or go, only a few Jews were authorized to go to bury our people's dead in the cemetery, and they were always escorted by soldiers who protected them, in accordance with the Duke's law. The epidemic ceased on a Monday, the sixth day of the month of Av [end of July–beginning of August], and at the end of this day, at twilight, all the Jews came to the great synagogue and recited the great *Hallel* [psalms of praise], and blessed the name of God. And to combat the epidemic, they made good and important arrangements for our people, [they called in] reputable physicians, and they prepared beds, chairs, and tables in a large building to meet the needs of the indigent sick who could no longer care for themselves. And the leaders of the Holy Brotherhood cared for them, and each one voluntarily made a charitable contribution until there was no longer a single poor person completely destitute. Let God remember the souls of the Just. Amen![151]

The remedies considered most effective against the plague were, according to the sources, plasters made of eggs and flour, spiced with camphor, sulfur, alum, or pepper, and also sprinklings of vinegar. In any case, in the rabbinic literature mention is made of other medications of a sympathetic nature, like an amulet carrying the retranscription of the Tetragrammaton in blood from a circumcision,[152] which was reputed to be effective against the plague. It is also noteworthy, as Tobias ha-Cohen reports, that people especially tried to protect themselves from airborne contamination.[153]

> I had to keep all the windows closed . . . without ever opening them; if a window or a door had to be opened, the room had to be thoroughly fumigated with the aid of rosin and tar, sulphur, cannon powder, and other products of the same kind.[154]

Among the collective behaviors observed during plague years, one is particularly striking: certainty that the epidemic was a divine punishment incited the Jews to seek out and banish presumed offenders, as they did in Prague by excommunicating the prostitutes in 1612 (see Appendix). Yet if the emphasis is on penitential prayers and demands for divine mercy, we find no trace of huge processions like the "columns of the Plague" in Marseilles;[155] or of public confession as it was practiced by the flagellants of the fourteenth century—both common responses among the Christians. By contrast, we find collective fasts and great prayer services: "And in all the holy communities a day of fasting was decreed on the eve of *Rosh Ḥodesh Kislev* [December], and prayers on the day of *Rosh Ḥodesh*."[156] Delumeau has shown that the necessity for expiation among the Christian populations generated an acceptance of the divine scourge, making it an obligation to expose oneself to death by refusing to flee or submitting voluntarily to the contagion.[157] Such an attitude seems unknown among the Jews, who, on the contrary, ask God "that He may immediately cease his punishment."[158]

## THE HERE AND THE HEREAFTER

For anyone interested in the transformation of Jewish mentalities and attitudes, it is a mistake to frame the question in terms of openness or resistance to outside influence. It is inconceivable that profound changes affecting perceptions, beliefs, customs, a whole vision of the world, were accomplished over brief periods, as if it were a matter of a simple shift from one autonomous system to another. My approach to the emancipation of the Jews is rather to consider the slow movement of transformations within Jewish society. As we have seen, the Jews were well informed about the scientific, geographic, and medical discoveries of their times. And as for attitudes, their categories of thought were the same as those of their contemporaries, so it is not surprising to find in Jewish literature assertions such as this one, formulated by Benjamin of Tudela in the twelfth century:

> In the church Saint John of Lateran there are two bronze columns taken from Solomon's Temple, on which are engraved "Solomon, son of David." The Jews of Rome have told me that every year on the 9th of Av, these columns secrete a substance like water.[159]

Or to read Joseph Hahn's account of the laws of sympathetic connections:

> If there is a murder and the murderer is not known, let all the people be brought before him [the dead man], and when the murderer is before him, the wound will reopen.[160]

These two examples must surely evoke Christian imagery of bleeding hosts or weeping crucifixes. When Joshua Trachtenberg[161] asserted that the Jewish processions to the cemetery echoed Christian practice, he implied there may have been a symbiosis between the two societies. It is just as plausible to posit a coexistence preceding or presaging acculturation. Yet if we leave aside questions of religious belief, are the Jews really so distinct from the Christians when it comes to attitudes toward sickness and death?

In his study of fear, Delumeau characterizes the period from the fourteenth to the seventeenth centuries[162] as washed by a "tidal wave of Satanism." For him this "obsession" was manifest in two forms: "infernal imagery" and "the frequency of innumerable traps and temptations" produced by the devil to seduce human beings. The Jews are hardly exempt from these fears—far from it. But despite everything, Jewish and Christian beliefs about satanic powers are quite distinct. Indeed, if historians and ethnologists have been able to support Michelet's hypothesis of an ancient pagan cult that persisted throughout the Middle Ages and developed among an imperfectly Christianized population,[163] a study of demonology in the Talmud would show the continuity of Jewish conceptions of Satanism without any suggestion of such an "incomplete" conversion.[164]

The omnipresence of Satanism in medieval ideas is suspended for one day each year among the Jews. The numerical value of his name (*ha-Satan*), which is 364, is interpreted by the Talmud to signify its impotence on Yom Kippur.[165] Satan is often mentioned in the Talmud as "the Accuser"—*Satan ha-meqatreg,* he who slanders human beings in the ears of God.[166] He is frequently encountered in this guise as well in works such as the *Zohar,* the *Shenei Luhot ha-Berit,* and the *Ma'avar Yabbok.*[167] In the *Sefer Ḥasidim,* Satan awaits his hour, which is the death of the human being. Elsewhere, according to the Talmud, "It is Satan who [diabolically] created the Angel of Death."[168] This means that Sammael—the Angel of Death—and Satan are a single malevolent being who, like Janus, has two faces: the Angel of God, and the Angel of Evil. When his two faces are merged, the demon carries out God's will, the death sentence, while laying claim to some of the malevolent acts that are uniquely his own.

In ordinary times, the numerous protective measures taken by the Jews against Satan adequately express the deep feeling of real danger he inspires.[169] Indeed, if the Jews sometimes call the adversary diabolical when they are dealing with occult forces, they always take care to specify that "magic" is forbidden. In effect, medieval rabbinic authorities continue to recall the biblical prohibitions, and Jewish practices distinguish black magic—forbidden—from white, which is exercised without being called by that name. Thus the Jews always employ euphemisms to qualify their magicians, who are the "masters of names," or their practices, which are merely segullot. When the sorcerer appears in medieval Jewish literature,[170] it is to signal the presence of a Christian magician or to stigmatize someone devoted to black magic.

If "the distinction between the terrestrial and the unseen world" is not clearly established in the medieval vision of the universe,[171] it is nonetheless apparent that Jewish and Christian conceptualizations, while sharing a foundation, follow divergent paths. Thus the common belief in the resurrection leads them to implement quite opposite practices with regard to the dead; their relations to Satanism and magic also differ. Despite the interdictions on magic, Jewish society never banished sorcerers, which would indicate an attitude based not on an implicit recognition of demonic powers but on a will to maintain a modus vivendi. These magical practices, without being encouraged, were exercised within limits that were constantly redefined, as Joseph Hahn recalls, with the establishment of a list of acts authorized as segullot, not sorcery.[172]

A mystical doctrine like Kabbalah, which perpetually links the temporal world to the "higher worlds," necessarily bears on the concrete events of daily life. The work of Menaḥem Ziyouni on magic and demons is a perfect illustration of this point:[173] mysticism, Kabbalah, and magic are closely intertwined. Around the fifteenth and sixteenth centuries, the Christian world discovered the speculative universe of Kabbalah. For Christian theologians, its exploration opened doors to certain mysteries of the Catholic faith. They thought that they would be able to prove the Trinity or the Incarnation with kabbalistic axioms.[174] The inquiry into intellectual and speculative hypotheses, however, elaborated to establish the validity of the order of the spiritual world in its Christian form, was supplanted by a basic interest in practical Kabbalah, as a work like Cornelius Agrippa's *De occulta philosophia* demonstrates.[175] From that time on, the Christian world identified the Kabbalah with sorcery or numerology. The Christian Kabbalah, of course, followed its own development, which incorporates occult practices familiar in both societies. Hence the well-known figure of the vagabond wandering from town to town supplied with "strange-looking phials covered with Kabbalistic signs, a crystal globe and an astrolobe, followed by an imposing scroll of parchment inscribed with mysterious Hebraic-looking characters,"[176] who was an intimate part of the landscape of medieval Germanic society. According to the narrator, he would "probably drive a roaring trade amongst townsmen in love-philters, cures for the ague and the plague, and amulets against them, horoscopes, predictions of fate."[177] Is this a Jew who would sell the secrets so jealously guarded by the closed circles of the kabbalists? The question would be trivial if the answer were not an immediate negative, for these kabbalistic signs, so openly proferred, are in absolute contradiction to kabbalistic practice. But this description suggests just how widespread were current clichés about the Kabbalah (and the vagabonds): parchments, Hebrew signs, astrolabe, crystal ball, and so on, are the tools of ordinary magic.

During the entire Middle Ages, as long as the human spirit was haunted by the devil and his domain, the sorcerer was identified in the Christian mind with that mythic Jew in constant dialogue with Lucifer, whose attributes, Hebrew and kabbalistic signs, are the very language of Satanism.[178] So the rabbinic warnings against sorcery reflect the danger actually incurred by Jews indulging in such exercises. It should be noted in this regard that the number of Jews called before the tribunals of the Inquisition for sorcery was, in fact, insignificant.[179] The absence of black magic among the Jews would therefore have to be attributed as much to imminent danger as to the prohibitions of Halakhah.

Although the Jews did not accept identification with a satanic alter ego, they participated, with their own beliefs, in the same mental universe as the people who stigmatized them. Satan is integrated into their folklore, and in this sense their system of demonological elaboration is not substantially different from that of their environment.

> He says that he had violated the religion by engendering numerous children [with Lilith], and when he died and was buried, an angel came and revived him. And living, he stood up from his grave. And he said to him: "Wretch! What have you done? How will you be judged now?" Then all at once came destructive angels who looked like toads, and they ate his flesh until he died of it. Then, he immediately got up. Then came bad angels who looked like rats, and they ate his flesh until he died of it. Then came destructive angels who looked like dogs. Then came malevolent angels who looked like wolves, and then came all sorts of creatures who fell upon his body and devoured its flesh. And between each [episode] he was dying. . . . And after that they led him to the threshold of Gehenna. And when he arrived there, all the children of Hell cried out: "Leave this place! Why do you come to pollute us? You have no reason to come among us!" And the malevolent angels said to him as they led him: "Wretch! You have no reason to go to Gehenna, now you are sent into the sling of the catapult."

> And the spirit says to the rabbis: "Gentlemen, do you know what the sling of the catapult is?" The pious Rabbi Hirsch tells him: "I have heard that two bad angels stand guard at the end of the world, one on each side, and he who is sent there is put between the catapult and sent back and forth from one to the other." The spirit added: "That is not exactly the way it is! Two bad angels stand guard on each side, and each of them touches the ground. One of the two swallows him until he falls at his feet and breaks all his limbs, for he really does fall, from heaven to earth. Then he is broken by the second angel, in the same way. And the second swallows him, then vomits him into the mouth of the first." And this is done for eighteen years. He never saw the light of the world, except once, when at the end of several years he was vomited out, he saw it then in something like an opening, an angle in the void. He saw his father and his mother, who was crying: "Oy! Alas, alas for that hour when we conceived you, my husband and I! Alas for that moment when he begot such a son!" Then came one who was responsible for leading him to another place. And he dropped him in the dirty waters of the street. And the girl passed by, indeed, by this water; the angel who was appointed to him gave him the authorization to inhabit the young girl. And it was not because of her sins that he inhabited her, but because of the sins of her father and her mother.
>
> [. . .] And the rabbis told him: "Leave that place and we will pray for you! Each of us will pray every day for you, and will say a *Kaddish* for you." But the spirit answered: "Whatever you do is useless to me, since I have spread the semen that begot an alien people." And so he remained, he did not leave until the girl's death.[180]

Medieval hauntings are clearly articulated in this narrative: the sin of the flesh, which may be different from the Christian concept but is nonetheless present; and the infernal bestiary to torture the dead man, which is utterly characteristic of the medieval imagination. Yet while the Jews may have incorporated the "diabolization of the flesh and body in the Middle Ages, assimilated to a place of debauchery,"[181] the Christian version of this concept, which "denied all dignity to the body," according to Jacques Le Goff,[182] is once again contrary to the Jewish notion. Indeed, among the Christians the "tabernacle" of the body is compelled to chastity or marriage, while among the Jews it is, of course, associated with marriage, but especially with the essential value of procreation. That is why for Jews the sin is not so much the act of the flesh in itself as sterile copulation, a source of bastard children who will increase the number of demons. Within a vision and perception of an identical universe, Jews and Christians pursued different itineraries that are nonetheless marked by the familiar themes of the medieval world.

CHAPTER EIGHT

# Sickness and Death

## *The Wager of Emancipation*

### THE ERA OF REFORMS

When the empress Maria Theresa decided, in 1745, to drive the Jews out of Bohemia, Moravia, and Prague, what might have remained a local affair provoked the violent censure of foreign governments. The European Jews had grown used to a certain tolerance; in Great Britain and Holland some had acquired political positions that gave them access to power over their own fate and that of their coreligionists. When Maria Theresa's decision was taken, decrees of expulsion had not been enacted against the Jews of Europe for nearly a century, and since such a measure did not correspond to the "spirit of the times,"[1] numerous indignant protests were raised, coming especially from the English court. For this was an attack on one of the oldest and liveliest Jewish communities, which since the medieval period had represented "the center of gravity of Judaism and the study of the Torah."[2] This impromptu banishment posed a fundamental challenge to the relations established between Jews and Christians, as well as to the patriotism of the Jews toward their countries of residence. The empress justified her decree by declaring that the Jews were enemies of Christianity, but there is no doubt that the expulsion was meant to punish the Prague Jews for "taking sides" with the Prussian adversaries of the empire. If the official accusation against the Jews ended in a resort to medieval practices, the official reason bears witness to a radically different attitude. The decree of expulsion of 1745 was a political event that can be said to mark the formation of modern anti-Semitism as it would manifest itself at the end of the nineteenth century, notably with the later publication of the *Protocol of the Elders of Zion*.[3]

Despite European diplomatic pressures, Maria Theresa did not retract her decision, but she was nonetheless forced to readmit the Jews of her empire in 1748.[4] The failure that followed this expulsion underscores the new character of the Jewish presence in international political life: Jews were now in a position to influence decisions that concerned them and to rouse outside interventions in their favor in a way quite beyond the power of the former medieval intercessor, as Josel of Rosheim has represented him.[5] The return of the Jews to Prague marked a clear diplomatic victory; it did not, however, entail their emancipation, since it was accompanied by the payment of higher taxes than those of previous times;[6] and unlike the Jews of Vienna, who were allowed to dispense with the yellow badge by the end of the seventeenth century, Prague Jews still had to wear it outside the boundaries of the Jewish Quarter, whether on a ruff or affixed to a shoulder, hat, or veil.[7] Moreover, the restrictions imposed on the residence of Jews in imperial territory resulted in a revival of Jewish wandering between the German lands and Poland.[8] It was only after the advent of Joseph II, in 1780, that the general situation of the Jews began to improve in a concrete way, although his reforms were by no means construed positively by the interested parties. After suppressing legislation condoning religious discrimination in his empire, Joseph II dealt with the Jewish question. In May 1781, the *Judenreformen* appeared, which were intended, in the spirit characteristic of the latter part of the eighteenth century, to make the Jews "happier" by making them more "useful."[9] The wearing of the yellow badge was abolished along with the payment of the poll tax.[10] For the first time these reforms aimed at strongly encouraging Jews to integrate professionally into the larger society by becoming or remaining craftsmen, and a general education in German was offered to Jewish children. In January 1782, the celebrated "Edict of Toleration" was promulgated, granting the Jews of the empire, for the first time in Europe, equality of duties to the state and a rough draft of something like citizens' rights.

To implement his ends, Joseph II simultaneously enacted authoritarian measures addressing the traditional Jewish way of life: in 1781 he suspended the use of Hebrew and Yiddish in the internal ledgers or records of the communities, whose writings were shifted brutally from one language to another;[11] in 1784 he suppressed rabbinical jurisdiction and introduced the obligation of military service for all;[12] in 1787 the Jews were called on to take Germanic names, both first names and family names. These decisions succeeded in antagonizing the majority of his subjects: for the adherents of traditional Judaism, these measures represented an immediate danger to the survival of traditions; for the adherents of emancipation, they were insufficient; and among Christians, it was the rare person who looked upon this social integration of the Jews with equanimity. Yet when Jewish children entered the schools, the universities half-opened their doors to them. Within the Hapsburg Empire the emancipation of the Jews would progress no further until the revolution of 1848.[13] Only in its wake would they achieve complete equality of rights. So the country that first initiated the process of Jewish emancipation was in fact the last to grant it to them and continued to maintain residence quotas and restrictions of various kinds until the middle of the nineteenth century.[14]

In quite a different domain but with the same intent, Joseph II also instituted a series of reforms regarding public health.[15] In 1783 he ordered the closing of communal graves opened in the cathedrals and other public religious buildings; in 1784 he opened the general hospital of Vienna, and his aid program addressed itself as a priority to the neediest: orphans, abandoned children, unmarried mothers, and the homeless.[16] In 1787 the ancient cemeteries situated in the town centers had to be closed, while interfaith cemeteries were established outside the towns.[17]

The majority of these reforms seem to require no comment, but one statement is made in this testimony:

> In the month of January 1781, the Emperor Joseph has decreed that all the Jews in the country must establish . . . special houses with teachers who would teach the young Israelites writing and foreign languages, calculus, and the other secular sciences. . . .
>
> Monday, the 22nd of Av 544, which is August 1784 according to their reckoning, they evoked the privilege possessed by our community for more than a hundred years, namely, of judging and condemning in cases of litigation over property and all the conflicts and disagreements between the people, of dividing the inheritance among heirs and of assigning tutors to young orphans. All this was suppressed by order of the King. . . . And this is why the magistrate has come this day to our town hall and seized the book of documents and the money for orphans. . . .
>
> Orders to bury with a delay of twenty-four hours after death. . . .

(Friday 25 Tamuz 564—31 July 1786.) Prohibition on burying the dead in the ghetto, and only during morning hours, from the opening of the gates until evening.[18]

Beyond the empire, the situation of the Jews improved in all the European countries. The spirit of tolerance toward them was at once the product of the intellectual struggle against the Church and of ideas issuing from a transformation in the perception of man. The philosophy of the Enlightenment developed the concept of the individual as a natural being, secular, social, and useful. This nonexistent man, this ideal prototype, could not come into being without the "regeneration" of his perverted model. The reverse figure of this paradigm was embodied precisely in the image of the Jew, burdened by religion, enclosed in a hermetic common language and a civil life outside the city which made him socially unproductive.

This negative vision, accompanied by the will to destroy it that appears in all the writings on Jews in the eighteenth century,[19] was perfectly reflected in the demands of enlightened Jews. Zalkind Hurwitz, one of the most active militants in the Emancipation in France, responded to the competition opened by the Academy of Metz in 1785 on the theme "How to Make the Jews Happier and More Useful in France." In the essay he writes on this occasion, he suggests, among other things, that the use of Hebrew and Yiddish should be proscribed and that the rabbis should be forbidden to force Jews to keep their beards. Although his paper is labeled an "apology for the Jews," seeking to demonstrate their resemblance to other citizens despite their mistreatment, the author does not hesitate to designate them by the term "rogues,"[20] even while arguing that only general, compulsory instruction and the supression of community power would turn them into respectable citizens. It need hardly be said that Hurwitz wanted to see the model of Jewish autonomy disappear; in 1805 he addresses a letter to the minister of religion arguing against the perpetuation of age-old practices by orthodox Jews:

Our fanatics have circumvented the prefects of their respective administrative departments and have made them believe that freedom of religion authorizes them to establish shelters for the poor, guilds, and rabbis, and grants them the power to excommunicate the recalcitrant. . . . If the prefects had consulted an enlightened Jew on this subject, they would have learned that the shelters for the poor are a misguided charity, that they favor laziness and multiply the number of vagabonds, . . . that the rabbis are hardly more useful to the Jews than the Capuchins to the Catholics; that they perform no function in the synagogue, do nothing to instruct young people, and preach neither religion nor morality.[21]

After 1789 these struggles were waged directly on the battlefield, and a great number of Jews would join the camp of the French Revolution. After 1791 the conquest of the rights of man was pursued without interruption: juridical equality followed in the wake of the Revolution and the Napoleonic wars; the Jews of Holland,[22] Rome,[23] Venice,[24] the Rhineland, Westphalia,[25] and Frankfurt[26] would be emancipated and the ghettos symbolically destroyed. Yet this backdrop does not provide a picture of the elements of internal erosion that simultaneously undermined Jewish society and were pushed by external changes until the old communities reached the breaking point. We are going to follow the course of this erosion through the challenge to community power, as well as through the transformations of the burial society and Jewish attitudes toward death.

## THE EXCLUDED

Considering the draconian conditions for admission to the ḥevra kaddisha,[27] as well as the waiting or probationary period before candidates were allowed to participate, it is likely that a great many of the Jewish Quarter's inhabitants were perforce excluded. In principle, the administration of last rites was not limited to members of the burial society: nonmembers could still obtain its services by defraying the expenses themselves.

For foreigners, whether temporary or permanent residents, the condition of poverty was more delicate. They could hope to receive some alms from the society for food and shelter, but this did not hold true for their other needs. In Prague, for example, the charity coffers were reserved, according to the rules, for local indigents. Yet with regard to the general situation of the Jews in the Ashkenazi lands in the seventeenth and eighteenth centuries, we can state without exaggeration that a great majority of them wandered from community to community, homeless and penniless. These Jewish vagabonds may have been itinerant because of their professions—musicians,[28] peddlers, or beggars—or because they had fled their own community for some reason, whether it was the pogroms of Poland and Ukraine,[29] the fact that they were excommunicated for the Sabbatian heresy,[30] or for some social deviation such as bankruptcy, the inability or refusal to participate in community tithes, or quarreling with community leaders. Clearly, this constant mass of itinerants constituted a heavy burden for the stable communities that had to welcome them, lodge them, feed them, care for them, or bury them. It will not be surprising, then, to discover in the sources that these vagabonds were not always warmly welcomed, especially when they were sick and obviously in need of care and possible burial. Nothing exceptional in itself, the situation was identical all over the Hapsburg Empire, and Christian society was familiar with the same problems of nomadism;[31] but Jews had access only to the towns in which they were admitted.

Thus the anonymous author of the following complaint carries on bitterly to one of the community leaders, describing the way he tried in 1709 to discourage the weak-willed:

> Listen, dear friends, to what happens in these times. When we poor people arrive in Frankfurt, after we vagabonds walk to Frankfurt, they do not let us through the gates. Jacob Fullwasser comes to us with his excuses; he takes us one after the other . . . and makes us enter the hall . . . there, the *gabbai'im* open the book, and Jacob Fullwasser says: "How long were you there? What is your name?" Thus we are already unwelcome, and we see what kind of feeding we will have. He lets us know that the money of the *pletn* is gone, and that it is not to be had. . . . They are so afraid that (God forfend) the wealthy of the community might disappear because of their charity. . . . And they leave us, their guests, to stand there in the sun, where we are very soon roasted and sore. . . . But in winter it is even worse for the poor people: no one is allowed to enter . . . until he is frozen . . . and cries out in shock: dear God, we are so cold. . . . And when out of great pity they let us warm ourselves, Jacob Fullwasser arrives and puts us out, one after the other. . . . And again we must stand outside the gates. One cries: "I have no dress," another: "no trousers, you wretches!"[32]

If Elhanan Kirchan[33] is accurate, the vagabonds were scarcely more welcome in the small towns than in the big cities, and the sick were all summarily turned away: "The care of a sick stranger is regarded as a chore: he is left to go his way in a wagon or cart, wandering from one town to another." He adds that because of the general indifference toward wanderers, it even happens that a sick person on the road like this would be found dead in the vehicle. The driver would then have pocketed the deceased's money and naturally dumped the body in a field.[34]

That Jewish vagabonds were unwelcome was not merely the result of indifference caused by the usual presence of itinerant masses in the German lands. In fact, many of them associated with roving bands of pillagers when they had not themselves formed their own "gang."[35] So the arrival of strangers in a place could represent a real danger to its inhabitants. The community of Karlsruhe had opened a refuge for foreigners outside the town; however, it had to close the place after a certain number of thefts had been committed by these poor people, one of whom was even caught in the act.[36] The external authorities made use of this Jewish banditry to put pressure on the communities: thus in 1727 the town of Hamburg was forbidden to grant hospitality to vagabonds, unless they were ready to take responsibility for pillaging.[37]

The process of wandering is often quite commonplace. Disfavored working-class women who did not command a dowry sufficient to marry were caught up in this phenomenon and were sent to domestic service in the communities. In the sources, servants and prostitutes are often linked. In addition to these, abandoned wives, *agunot,* who could not remarry without proof that the vanished spouse had eventually passed away or accepted a divorce, often had to resort to prostitution out of utter destitution. Although ignored by the works of codification because of the religious interdiction against them, prostitutes appear frequently in the rabbinic literature of the period, as well as in community records, such as these rulings decreed in Frankfurt in 1675:

> Society will be obliged to banish prostitutes from our community . . . in the six months to come after the publication of these ordinances, and let [none] linger or return here, under pain of excommunication, and during these six months, let them be forbidden to show themselves at their doors, and if [one among] them goes out, she will immediately be obliged to leave. And anyone whose parents have not had a religious marriage, come what may, whether boy or girl, their marriage will not be celebrated. . . . And if there is a master of the house whose daughter engages in prostitution, let the excommunication fall upon the father, and let her be expelled from here in six months. . . . And let it be forbidden to every master of the house, under pain of excommunication, to employ her as a domestic or even to keep her without pay. Unless the master of the house in question will give two *reichsthaller* each week in compensation, then he will be exempt from excommunication.[38]

Excommunication implies the casting of the individual outside Jewish society in general and the community in particular. If prostitutes thus found themselves on the roads, their only recourse was to take their chances in a new community; and similarly for the master of the house who might have lodged them. Wet nurses had to submit to a way of life that proscribed marriage, so it seems reasonable to think that only abandoned wives or widows, former prostitutes or unmarried mothers, could assume these functions. This would explain their verifiable presence in numerous Jewish homes.

In the communities, illegitimate children could be tolerated or rejected, according to local custom. They could be treated, as they were in Frankfurt, according to the law, as *mamzerim*—as bastards—and therefore goaded either to wandering or to conversion by virtue of the impurity that forbade them any legitimate Jewish marriage. In these communities, where illegitimate birth was an ineffaceable stigma, we can assume that mothers got rid of such children at birth,[39] entrusting them to Christian wet nurses. In Hamburg, the leaders of the community were required to expel young girls who had children out of wedlock.[40] In Furth, if a boy was born of an unknown father, "he was circumcised and given one of the names of the patriarchs, Abraham, Isaac, or Jacob, or the name of the mother's father, if he agreed to it."[41] But tolerance could also be extended, and as in Christian society, marriages of convenience were arranged with the avowed purpose of saving the child's faith. In this case, someone was found who was prepared, sometimes encouraged by financial compensation, to declare himself the father of the child and stand under the wedding canopy.[42]

If prostitutes could hope for more or less temporary social reintegration by taking on the function of wet nurse, making them indispensable to Jewish society, this was not the case with vagabonds and foreigners. These people provoked mistrust and ill will and could hardly claim to make a place for themselves. The rulings of the Jewish Council of the Moravian lands indicate the way they were received and especially perceived.

> On the subject of these people, prevaricators, barefoot tramps, loafers, who endanger the whole Jewish community by blaspheming publicly on market days at Kremecz and Lincz, the decision is that anyone is authorized to dispossess them of their goods and hand them over [to the civil Christian authorities]. And permission is given to expel them from the community where they live by force and violence, even if there is no unanimity in the community.[43] One is careful not to grant a night's lodging to these people who come from other countries where they can be converted. For it can be assumed that anyone [who presents himself] is also one of those who has been converted and has returned to Judaism, or has converted definitively. And if a man or a woman is found to disobey this rule, he will be punished by serious sanctions.[44]

We see that in these rulings vagabonds and foreigners incarnate danger in its pure state: as strangers, they are likely to steal, to blaspheme, and even to be converted. Under these conditions, we can understand that every poor person or foreigner who presented himself or herself at the gates of a community, before dreaming of receiving hospitality in the refuge or shelters—the pletn—where meals were provided, had to possess solid recommendations or enjoy a reputation that would allow the wanderer to be suitably welcomed. This must have been the case with Rabbi Zvi ben Samuel of Semjatitchi, who in the preface of his work describes how he was well treated by the members of the ḥevra kaddisha of Koenigsberg, who cared for him for nearly six months when he was suffering from an "internal" illness. He concludes this narrative by wishing that all communities could avail themselves of such an organization for the poor and for strangers.[45] This account bears almost no resemblance to our anonymous author's account of the welcome in Frankfurt. But should we credit this difference in treatment to changing times—the rabbi locates his account in 1786—or to the rabbi's respectability?

In the Jewish communities, the problem of strangers, like the problem of vagabondage, is closely associated with that of the "right of habitation." Indeed, to obtain the right of refuge, the poor first had to pay a certain sum for their admission into the community, for without the "right of habitation" they could not benefit from a recommendation by the guilds. As a result, most of the itinerant indigent could not hope to receive much help from communities in which they could no longer take part. The problem of these impecunious vagabonds was more acute, for their ranks were constantly swelled not only by Polish refugees but also by those members of numerous families who, lacking sufficient financial means, could neither marry nor pay for their residence rights in the community. To illustrate this point, we can cite the example of the community of Frankfurt, which in 1704 expelled from its citizenry twenty-one bankrupts and their children.[46]

Two council rulings in the Moravian lands help us to understand the treatment reserved for vagabonds and strangers in the communities of the seventeenth and eighteenth centuries. On the one hand, these rulings stipulate that whoever finds himself in a community in which a special tax exists on wine and kosher meat must pay it the same as the other inhabitants, whatever his financial means or the length of his stay.[47] This tax was identical for all, but obviously a great many of those who had to pay could hardly consume these products unless they were guests at a charity meal. On the other hand, the council judges it useful to specify to the communities within its jurisdiction that they should not exploit foreigners unreasonably in their payment of burial taxes: if it is proper to claim double the tariff applied to regular inhabitants, they must not ask more.[48] This article, considered to prevent abuses, indicates that even in matters of death and burial it was better to be able to pay the price of admission into the community than to remain outside it. It will be observed, as well, that the inflation of burial taxes is legally sanctioned: the rulings of the ḥevra kaddisha of Triesch in Moravia also ask the community leaders to be satisfied with the sum indicated by the council of the Moravian lands for foreigners.[49]

When the person buried was a "poor man," the ḥevra kaddisha generally reserved the right to take wages on behalf of his family: the family had to reimburse the loan within a certain period of time, under pain of excommunication or banishment. The ḥevra authorized itself in addition, as we have seen, to declare an individual a "rebel" against its authority, which implied that he would not have the benefit of last rites or access to the cemetery.[50] When he was thus struck down by fate, his family accompanied him in his ostracism, and they had to join the number of those who were stripped of their community citizenship or excommunicated. Impoverishment, then, could lead directly to the misery of excommunication and vagabondage.

There is no community ordinance, however, that does not emphasize the importance of works of charity: no ruling can be found that does not devote at least one or two paragraphs to the management of welfare. Thus, the council of the Moravian lands specifies,

> Every community is obliged to have welfare legislation in order to have a provisioning fund for the charitable needs of all the poor of the town [citizens] and for poor strangers and vagabonds. . . . It is for this purpose that *mitzvot* [religious duties] are put up for sale . . . and everyone should pay for them before the holiday of Passover and before *Yom Kippur*.[51]

In the text treating the collecting of the special tax for "pardon" imposed on the community of Prague,[52] we can read that the prepaid tax on burials also served to augment the funds reserved for the "poor of our city."[53]

This reveals a certain contradiction in the sources that, on the one hand, seem to be quite sensitive to the problem of indigence and constantly warn people to be mindful of the need for charitable contribution and, on the other hand, indicate that the situation of the poor, vagabonds, and strangers forbade them de facto from profiting from these funds—set aside for just such a purpose. This commits the historian to reading these texts on two levels: the first suggests that the community and the burial society oversaw the implementation of a politics of philanthropy, while the second clearly poses the limits of this politics, noting that a great number of the needy, and obviously the most wretched, were excluded. This double reading of the facts is inescapable, especially when considering the example of Passover, the holiday when ritual demands that people use kosher wine and unleavened bread.

In 1743 the members of the burial society of Triesch declared their "indignance" at the existence of "poor people" who had neither wine nor special flour and instead of seeking some, refused it. In the first instance, let us admit that the ḥevra is displaying its good intentions toward the poor while demonstrating its concern with the respect for ritual.[54] But if we take account of the particular taxes imposed on these products, we shall easily understand the problem of the indigent: their attitude was no doubt motivated more by poverty than by contempt for the holiday. In Bohemia, in addition to residence taxes and wine, the distribution of special flour for unleavened bread and kosher wine was not free. This situation was so incoherent that even to obtain emergency aid the poor were required to pay a "charity tax" or receive nothing.[55] Those unable to pay could sell some object to the community or give as a pledge the little they possessed. Thus Jacob Emden, the most famous rabbi of his time, had to resort to charity for the burial of his first wife. He tells in his autobiography that he was then obliged to make a pledge so that his wife might be buried decently.[56] But what can those who have nothing pledge? The answer comes from Poland: the most impoverished make a pledge of their *talit* (prayer shawl) and their *kittel* (ritual gown), according to Rabbi Hirsch Kaidanover.[57]

## THE HOSPICE

Considering the limits on the structures of assistance put in place to satisfy social needs, we may well wonder if these reflect a peculiarity of the Jewish communal system—which, given the limitations on Jewish residence, would call for strict preventive outlays in the face of an influx of strangers and vagabonds—or if they must be seen as reflecting the relations a society in general maintains with its poor.

In the Christian world, the models of charitable organization can be distinguished according to confessional affiliation—Catholic or Reformed. In the Catholic countries, the religious orders were concerned with dispensing aid and charity according to the model elaborated by

Saint Vincent de Paul and implemented by the "Daughters of Charity."[58] In the Reformed lands, where the Church no longer possessed property, the communities themselves took charge of managing poverty and sickness. Historical studies on poverty,[59] however, emphasize the general inadequacy of these structures of charity in relation to the enormous social needs of this period. All over Europe, from the Middle Ages until the eighteenth century, there are only constraints and laws that tend to punish begging and vagabondage, indeed to forbid them. Corporal punishments administered to beggars include yoking, whipping, cutting the hair, branding, mutilation of the ears, or even prison, the slave ships, or deportation.[60] In fact, charity was always reserved for the indigenous population: the poor were tolerated only when they were local residents.

In order to eradicate the manifestations of indigence, they were simply prohibited; to eliminate begging—and especially its outgrowth, the guilds of mendicants—it was forbidden to grant hospitality to indigent strangers and to give public alms.[61] The restrictions barring residence to strangers in Jewish society are found in Christian society as well.

> The needy man who wishes to settle in a city, a town, or a village must verify whether or not he is capable of working. He can always be expelled.[62]

We even find a Christian echo in the complaints of Kirchan:

> When a cripple or a beggar is found who cannot go on any further, the villagers (in Prussia) put him on a barrow called a *kruppelfuhre,* and he is brought to the next village; there he is again taken in hand, and thus driven from village to village until he has died or found the strength to walk, which rarely happens.[63]

Yet along with the maltreatment inflicted on vagabonds, with measures that forbid private alms yet institute compulsory taxes for indigents and stigmatize those who receive them, society is concerned with saving their souls through the intermediary of the religious orders and the brotherhoods. In a sense, the social practices reserved for the poor are related to those applied to the deranged. Poverty and illness are joined in the degradation of madness, and this combination leads society to institute a repressive politics in these areas. In this light we can see the refuges for the poor or the sick transformed, notably in Germany, into "work houses" or "houses of repentance," meant to force the poor to work or to seek the salvation of their souls through the religious orders. What until then was considered a normal state of poverty or illness would, by the last half of the eighteenth century, be progressively perceived as scandalous.[64] Just as the daily sight of the dead becomes intolerable and they are forced to leave the city,[65] the poor and the sick who are no longer welcome will increasingly be taken in hand by a system of assistance—or charity—that, while more elaborated in favor of the individual, will eliminate them from the public space.

In itself, the history of the hospital expresses the new relationship between the social body and the indigent, the sick, and the dead. By progressively determining to eliminate the external manifestations of poverty and illness, the society sought the sources of these disorders in order to absorb them by social measures. These measures mark the rupture that occurred at this moment between the medieval conceptions of poverty, as reflected in institutions, and those of the modern era. In the Jewish world, the transformations that affected the hospice illustrate the shift from older to modern conceptions. The *hekdesh,* the hospice, found in all the communities of any importance in the seventeenth and eighteenth centuries, was not identical to this institution in Christian society; intended to shelter vagabonds and the sick, it was composed of one or more rooms, sometimes as part of the community center but more often in the cemetery or else outside the boundaries of the Jewish Quarter. Its operation was typically medieval: the people who were taken in—women in labor, vagabonds, or the sick—were supposed to stay for only a brief interval of a night or two.[66] So the hospice, as it was defined, was very rudimentary: one or two bare rooms usually sufficed. Sometimes the community brought beds to accommodate travelers or servants coming from other regions. In the eighteenth century the vocation of the hekdesh was not medical aid: it was a refuge that did not claim to be a hospital, even if it offered emergency care. The aid dispensed there was reserved for strangers and the poor. The indigenous sick would never be treated there, for as the refuge of vagabonds, carriers of the most sordid poverty, this would be a sign of disgrace. In common parlance, to go to the hekdesh was synonymous with indigence in its most pejorative sense: delinquency, vagabondage, and filth.

As it is described in the texts, the hekdesh does not seem to have represented an actual social institution. Moreover, it provided a kind of minimal assistance that was not based on an elaborate model of aid or medical care. Its organization was, however, subject to the financial capacities of each locale, and consequently the quality of its welcome varied.[67] The functioning of the hekdesh adds, however, yet another paradox to the condition of the poor.

If, in fact, it was reserved for strangers, especially the indigent, access must have been barred to the local poor, who in case of illness depended essentially on the ḥevra kaddisha and on community funds. While the hekdesh was a dishonorable refuge,[68] it seems that its offer of free care and sustenance would not have been disdained by many poor people if they could have gained admittance. The problem of the indigenous needy can be read in the geographic limits placed on admission to the Furth Jewish hospice in the local rules: to be welcomed there you had to prove, in effect, that you lived at a minimum distance of ten to twenty kilometers from the community.[69] The free care and sustenance were inaccessible to others. Thus Koppel Shammash of Furth complains, in December 1783, of being abandoned, sick and starving, in his own house.[70]

## THE RUPTURE

In mapping out a general picture of the organization of Jewish society, we can discern the pressure that communal requests brought to bear on their administrators. Considering the number of constraints—laws and rulings to which administrators must bow—and the measures of excommunication that sanctioned them, it seems that a great many Jews must have found themselves on the margins of institutions, voluntarily or involuntarily excluded. These are surely the conditions that pushed so many Jews throughout the eighteenth century to create new communities, or to settle in villages where Jews did not live.[71] But when the poor had to give as pledges their ritual clothing, when they had been stripped of their citizenship, or declared rebels to the ḥevra kaddisha, what could they do? And where could they go?

Such cases must have existed, and it is tempting to think that these unfortunate people may have tried to find refuge in Christian society. It seems logical that under the gun of necessity, Jews would shave their beards and sidecurls to blend in more easily: after all, without his talit and his beard, a Jew was just a simple mortal. We know from manifold sources from the last half of the seventeenth century that the Jews of Germany began to suppress their distinctive coiffures and to "wear wigs," as Glückel reports on the subject of the Jews of Metz.[72] This fashion would grow throughout the eighteenth century and eventually affect all the communities, so that the wearing of a beard and sidecurls would become one of the criteria by which German Jews evaluated the ethics and conformity to tradition of their coreligionists.

This issue would play a singular role in the evolution of the burial societies. For along with their social vocation they would take on the preservation of orthodoxy in the communities. But do the justifications advanced by the burial societies have much to do with their true function? In fact, caring for the poor, whether healthy, sick, dying, or ready for burial, remains the fundamental mission of the ḥevra kaddisha. In the course of the eighteenth century, however, its philanthropic role was increasingly inscribed in the rules, while its exclusively funerary vocation ceased to be central. The burial societies added to their designation gemilut ḥesed shel emet the duty of bikkur ḥolim, visiting the sick. The founding charter of the burial society of Prague, dated 1564, was committed to giving charity to the poor by distributing wood and alms, as well as paying ransom for prisoners.[73] In 1702 its articles mention the brotherhood of "godfathers," whose purpose is to oversee the practice of circumcision. The various rules of the burial societies in the eighteenth century indicate the extension of the ḥevra's mission, which henceforth includes meeting the needs of the poor, raising dowries for orphans (who could not be married without one), encouraging the study of the Torah, clothing the naked, contributing financially to the construction of synagogues, sending financial aid to Palestine, paying for burials, and ensuring the study of the Mishnah for the dead and the lighting of candles in memory of the deceased.[74] The philanthropic program is vast, and nothing seems to have been left out. Yet it is impossible to explain the previous contradictions, or to understand the state of Moravia's judgment, in 1754, that the communities should be compelled to grant places in the hospices to itinerants in order to put an end to the current practices—among Jews and Christians alike—of sending the poor and the vagabond "to be buried elsewhere."[75]

The paradoxical contrast between the charitable work depicted in the rules of the burial societies and the concrete situation that seems to emerge from multiple testimonies challenges the traditional analysis of Jewish society of the past. In fact, this society was hardly closed in on itself, sealed off in perfect cultural, social, or philanthropic autonomy. On the contrary, what emerges clearly is the enterprise of community control that managed its own and ignored others, letting them escape, in their need, from Jewish society. From this perspective, the ḥevra kaddisha appears to be a supplementary structure to the community and not the autonomous and independent organization its statutes would suggest. It is remarkable, for instance, that no mention is made of the burial society in the documents concerning the plague. Yet surely the society was best qualified to meet the needs of the sick, the dying, and the dead. In his "Lamentation," Moses Eisenstadt cites only the community council, the Kahal.[76] Should we deduce from this that all the members of the ḥevra kaddisha had fled the afflicted city, in the wake of community dignitaries? Or that the ḥevra kaddisha and the Kahal overlapped and merged into a single, identical structure?

To the extent that the organization of social assistance figures in community texts—or the rules of the burial society—the terms of its philanthropic politics can be established. In the eighteenth century, this was characterized by responsibility for three specific areas:

1) ethics: by overseeing circumcisions, the dowries of orphans, and the organization of religious studies;

2) sickness: by the organization of spiritual and medical care and the development of hospitals;

3) death: by the monopoly on mortuary ritual and funerary practices, as well as the management of the cemetery.

The burial society, which takes responsibility for the charitable politics of the community, administers an important aspect of its social life, far surpassing its objective in the sixteenth century, which was limited to the management of death. At this point, the distinction between "community" and "burial society" vanishes. In the eighteenth century, with the development of asylums and hospitals, we see the reemergence of community employees: doctors, midwives, and teachers.[77] We do not know if they were employed by the ḥevra kaddisha, which administered these institutions, or by the Kahal. We must ask whether the amalgamation of funerary functions and social functions expresses an evolution in the Jews' relation to death or a transformation of the institutional framework of life in the communities.

Given the increased demand in matters of health and social welfare, the structures of social assistance in the Jewish community, as in the medieval Christian world, were entirely inadequate; hence modifications were made in the rules of the burial societies concerning care, assistance to the sick, and especially free provisions offered to members in case of illness or death. The changes that intervene in the vocation of the ḥevra kaddisha and the conceptions of the hospital are evident in the last twenty years of the eighteenth century. They indicate that the perception of relations to the body, hence to illness and death, are so transformed that they are translated by the creation of new structures of responsibility. The missionary zeal that affects the ḥevra kaddisha at the end of the eighteenth century happens at the moment when the communal system is disintegrating. In this sense it prefigures, paradoxically, the decline of what could be considered the managing institution par excellence of Jewish society.

With the dissolving of community power, burial societies would multiply within the communities. The unmarried regrouped, and to avoid the years of waiting following marriage to become members of the ḥevra kaddisha, they organized their own mutual aid and burial societies. The large communities thus saw developing in their midst a multitude of social infrastructures in which different groups managed their own needs, no longer submitting to the monolithic authority of the elders. This is the case in Vienna beginning in 1763,[78] in Frankfurt in 1786, in Prague and Dresden in 1798.[79]

Women, to whom men cannot administer the last rites, were integrated as assistants into the general societies.[80] They also had responsibility for sewing the shrouds.[81] But until the end of the eighteenth century they seem to have had no internal status. If we are to believe the rules decreed by the female burial society of Rendsburg in 1776, when they do form their own organization, they follow the path marked out by the male societies. No claim is made openly; they devote themselves to the sick and the dead and commit themselves to providing care, to visiting the sick, to making sure that the dead are overseen and purified. Even the style of writing, in Yiddish, is based on that of the male charters. "The precept says: it is the fate of man to die. That is why every being must die. . . . It is better to go into the house of mourning than into the house of celebration."[82]

This sudden necessity to constitute an autonomous organization is inscribed in the progressive breakup of a communal system, and the practice will become usual in the nineteenth century, when that system will have legally disappeared. From that time on, the moral concept of caring for the dead no longer appears to be one of the central elements of religious life, but it is integrated into a fragmented management of social needs, as are illness and poverty. From the end of the eighteenth century, then, the principle of charity conceived as an act of piety was definitively substituted for philanthropy.

## DEATH AND THE ENLIGHTENMENT

In the eighteenth century, the medical world was animated by discussions provoked by the issue of "apparent death."[83] Physicians claimed that no sign distinguishes real death from ephemeral death, or actual death from a simple swoon, other than the duration of the phenomenon. According to them, a great many people supposedly deceased would revive if people did not rush to bury them. Testimonies circulated of persons resuscitated during or after interment; others described the dead devouring themselves in their coffins or calling out in vain. In response to this, an apology for ancient funerary rituals developed which mitigated this risk by letting a certain amount of time elapse before burial. During this period the body was washed, the corpse was exhibited, and the mourners engaged in public lament. The principle culprit in hurrying its members into the ground was the Church, which, in fighting against these delaying pagan practices, neglected to take the obvious precautions in favor of human life. It was reproached for its "lack of respect" and its "negligence."[84]

Jewish doctors who studied in the Italian or German universities could not escape the agitation of their contemporary colleagues, insofar as Jews and Christians observed the same practice of burial as soon as death was verified. Despite Jewish theological considerations on the importance of prompt interment, the Jewish world was not spared the debate on apparent death.[85] Thus, as happened among the Christians, an Italian Jewish doctor demanded in his will that his burial be delayed until three days after his death.[86] Frightening accounts circulated about people buried alive, and their authors even marshaled statistics.[87] In this debate, the adherents of scientific truth, the enlightened minds, attacked the practice of immediate burial and challenged the attitude of the rabbis, just as the Christians contested their clergy on the subject.

The question of proper burial procedure became one of the most heated polemics in the Jewish communities, just as the problems of internal emancipation burst into view and gave way to theoretical struggles. This argument was privileged only by enlightened Jews, who all demanded that their burials should not take place immediately after their deaths.[88] For traditional Jews, however, this question would pit them against the state and become symbolic of tradition in combat with the outside world and the reformers. These two positions were clearly defended during the conflict that in 1772 set the community of Mecklemburg-Schwerin against the ducal authorities.

A report on apparent deaths was presented to Duke Frederick by Olaus G. Tychsen, a Hebraizing but anti-Semitic missionary, who emphasized the "cruel" and "inhuman" practices of the Jews in funerary matters. He claimed Jews usually buried their dead only three hours after death, which surely led to the interment of living persons. He added that this practice had no biblical or talmudic basis but was essentially established on the authority of the Kabbalah.[89] Despite the opposition of his cabinet, which argued that the juridical protection of the community proscribed any interference in its laws and customs and especially that rites including the preparation of the body for burial surely kept the Jews from burying the living, Frederick proposed that henceforth no one should be buried less than three days after decease. The duke considered it necessary to abolish the Jewish custom, unless someone could prove its validity, or at least its religious basis. He then commissioned a Jewish convert to Christianity to make a report on the subject. His findings were that the custom did not appear to be based on fundamental beliefs; the ducal decree was not annulled. On 15 May, a petition from the community begged him to renounce this act, explaining that Jewish tradition was opposed to his decision and suggesting that he consult two irreproachable external Jewish authorities, Rabbi Jacob Emden and the philosopher Moses Mendelssohn. To prove its good faith, the community committed itself, while awaiting their responses, to presenting a medical certificate before every burial attesting to the verification of death.[90]

Mendelssohn, unaware that Emden had also been consulted, needed to resolve a dilemma and responded step by step. First, he composed a paper addressed to the duke in which he thanked him for his attention to his subjects but did not report any biblical source supporting the practice of immediate burial. Quite the contrary, he indicated that although many Jews had long ceased any strict observance of the Mosaic law on purity, its spirit was still present in the rabbinic tradition, which required that a dead person should not be allowed to lie one night without burial. It seemed doubtful to him that this corresponded to a biblical injunction, but he was certain that the duke could not legally challenge the authority of the rabbis. He added that death had to be quite certain before people were buried and that the Jews of Schwerin could in the future remit a medical verification of death.[91] For the community, Mendelssohn appended a letter in which he commented on his position.[92] According to him, although he was not an authority on the matter, their violent reaction was unjustified, for there had been no transgression of Halakhah in delaying burial—since this was authorized anyway in case of holidays—in order to make preparations or await the presence of the family. All the more reason, surely, if death was uncertain, and even more so since no such danger had existed in ancient times when people were not put into the ground but in caves, where they were observed for three days;[93] for indeed "it happened that a man was inspected after thirty days, and he came back to life for twenty-five years, and another had sons and then died."[94] By virtue of the fact that doctors had established the absence of unquestionable signs distinguishing real death from apparent death, he counseled a return to ancient custom and judged that it was not necessary to oppose the ducal decree.[95]

In the amicable correspondence between Emden and Mendelssohn, this became a matter of lively controversy, for the Yaabets had turned to Mendelssohn to defend the side of tradition[96] and could hardly understand his point of view. Mendelssohn then answered him that he wanted to read his master's report: "For I, in my great ignorance, do not know how to justify it [this custom] nor why we have departed from the practices of our holy ancesters of blessed memory. They left their dead to lie in caves and the chambers of sepulchres where they inspected them for three days."[97] Emden then severely warned Mendelssohn against being more concerned with medical opinion than with Halakhah. He swept away his references to ancient funerary practices as fallacious justification. It seemed inconceivable to him to question a recognized and acknowledged Jewish practice in its entirety, whether Sephardic or Ashkenazi, and even more so as people who may have been buried alive must have represented very exceptional cases. He insisted, moreover, on the danger to the Jews in renouncing a practice of their own in favor of a Christian practice[98] such as the one recommended by Mendelssohn, who would have liked to have seen the kinds of funerary chambers established in cemeteries where the dead could be inspected in case a breath of life should still remain. The problem raised by the meaning of immediate interment was of the utmost importance: was this minhag, or custom, as Mendelssohn maintained—thus subject to modification—or was it *din* (law), as Emden claimed, which could not be challenged?

Jacob Emden, whom Mendelssohn certainly very much admired, was hardly a limited and conservative individual. In medical matters, he shared the preoccupations of his learned contemporaries; yet in this affair his rejection is categorical, and he bears witness, besides, to certain reticences on the "ephemeral fantasies" of doctors.[99] This is because he does not consider the debate primarily a medical problem, and he assumes this is true for Mendelssohn as well. Between the correspondents the polemic subsided, although each man remained entrenched in his position, and Mendelssohn's orthodoxy was now questioned by certain of his coreligionists. But the issue of the proper procedure for interment reappeared several years later.

In 1787, one year after Mendelssohn's death, his famous letter to the community of Schwerin was published in the *Berlinische Monatsschrift,* and the debate was revived within the community; the partisans of emancipation—advocates of the Haskalah—violently opposed the orthodox, accusing them of wanting to maintain a custom that was dangerous and unwarranted from the strictly legal point of view. The details of this debate can be followed by reading the Berlin Hebrew journal *Ha-Me'assef,*[100] an organ of the *Aufklärung* that circulated in the Ashkenazi world, spreading a polemic that would be amplified until it became the core of the battle against rabbinic and talmudic attitudes. The journal speculated publicly,

> Can one judge that there are conclusive signs of death? If the answer is positive, is it conceivable that the *ḥevra kaddisha* knows them and is able to verify them?
>
> If the answer is negative, is there really a religious reason for practicing immediate burial, despite the danger of burying people alive?
>
> If no such reason exists, would it not be logical to abolish a practice known to be dangerous?[101]

Ten years after Mendelssohn's dispute with the Yaabets, the Berlin "Society of Friends" took up the struggle for reform of the old communities. Constituted by the disciples of Mendelssohn, it united the radical partisans of the Haskalah. These young intellectuals, nourished by their traditional culture and enlightened ideas, intended by this regrouping to breach community constraints by creating their own institution. Their purpose was to offer anyone in conflict with the Kehillah the means of marginal survival without the loss of identity. The accounts of their triennial sessions bear witness to their extreme virulence on the subject of the rabbis, whom they treat as "fanatics," "dogmatists," and "swindlers," and whom they accuse of having kept the Jews in the most "benighted orthodoxy," far removed from the real beliefs of a pure faith.[102] Conscious of the ostracism that befell the *maskilim,* the "enlightened," and knowing that if one of them fell ill and found himself in need "he would find no help in the poor house" and that a fortiori "were he to die, he would not receive a decent burial,"[103] they decided to found a mutual aid society that would allow them to respond to their needs for assistance. The first and fundamental vocation of the Society of Friends was acknowledged to consist, however, in spreading the light of reason among its unfortunate coreligionists and working for their greater openness to the world.

On 10 February 1793, Doctor A. Bing alerted the society, in his capacity as secretary, to the problem posed by Jewish funerary customs and informed it of the danger inherent in premature burials. The assembly, strongly impressed by this exposé, resolved not only to do everything in its power to abolish this practice but also to demand that its members have the right to require a delayed burial for themselves and their families. Agreements of this sort would even be made with the ḥevra kaddisha, guaranteeing the Society of Friends that burial would only follow certain death. Moreover, they obtained assurance that a vigil would be kept over them until burial and that they would be left in a noisy place.[104] This second revival of the issue of the living dead marks a decisive victory for the reformers of Judaism, whose pleas were finally heard. Those who willed that their burial be delayed were the same people who demanded the secularization of their coreligionists, the suppression of community power, and the ban on Jewish vernaculars. To further the success of their struggle, they did not hesitate in the following years to knock on the doors of the powerful, writing to the authorities and taking the public stage.

An exemplary participant in this struggle on all fronts, Zalkind Hurwitz was already requesting in 1785, in Paris, "that [the Jews] be buried less rapidly;[105] in 1805 he appealed still more urgently to the minister of religion: "I would wish . . . that those of our devout be severely punished who, out of a cruel prejudice borrowed from paganism, conceive it their duty to bury their dead as soon as possible."[106] The debate over burial had clearly been transmuted into an ideological conflict.

Beyond the medical discussion, the reverberations of this affair suggest that a certain vision of Judaism was being fundamentally challenged. On the occasion of this debate over the appropriate time for burial, Moses Mendelssohn collided with the ancestral conviction that to delay the burial of a dead person was to compromise his dignity and risk the tranquillity of his soul. These conceptions, as Tychsen had informed Duke Frederick, had been spread chiefly by the Kabbalah. That Mendelssohn's position found a large audience in the Jewish communities suggests that people were no longer preoccupied with the fate of their mortal remains. In fact, it was the role and influence of Kabbalah in Jewish practice that the maskilim questioned. Indeed, the quarrel that exploded at the end of the eighteenth century was at bottom over the place reserved for Kabbalah in henceforth rationalistic conceptions of Judaism. To the extent that the influence of Kabbalah spawned mortuary practices and was propagated by institutions that claimed a monopoly on their organization, it is not surprising that the critique of Kabbalah was promulgated by the very means of its popular diffusion: the Jews' relation to death and their attitudes toward it.

I speculated earlier on the eventual definition of a popular religion within Judaism itself; an examination of the charges evident in the works of mortuary ritual published in the nineteenth century reveals the vigor and importance of the repercussions of the theological movements that shook the eighteenth century. A radical rift opened between the eighteenth and nineteenth centuries that can be read in these works of codification, which, while written by rabbis with an orthodox perception of religion, nonetheless bear witness that the spirit that dictated them had changed. Thus the *Divrei Emet,* published in 1789, is limited to surveying current precepts and rites concerning the dying and the dead for the benefit of readers who may not have access to the *Ma'avar Yabbok*. This work was no doubt reserved for members of the ḥevra kaddisha and was meant to provide minimal information, but by including only the list of established practices and the prayers that accompany them, it is denuded of all commentary of kabbalistic origin. Minimally it lingers over customs whose prescriptions recall its contents.

> During the death throes no member must faint, if a member faints, he is covered with a sheet.[107]
>
> On the sabbath and on religious holidays, one does not bury the dead but opens the window anyway.[108]

The *Sefer Zikkaron la-Yom ha-Aḥaron,* published in 1830, is presented as a complete mortuary work. The author, Wolf Jeiteles, declares that he has taken the *Ma'avar Yabbok* and the *Divrei Emet* as his sources. As secretary of the *ḥevra kaddisha,* he seeks to assemble "all the precepts and practices that concern visiting the sick, the dying, burial, and mourning."[109] The work is composed in Yiddish, for the most part in *ktav ashkenaz,* but preserves the square Hebrew script used for prayers. Jeiteles reckons, then, that all those "who do not know the sacred script well can be informed and understand."[110] He describes all the mortuary phases: the visit to the sick, the death throes, the departing of the soul, purification, clothing the corpse, interment, mourning, and finally yahrzeit. The second part of the work is entirely devoted to the collection of prayers to be recited at the graveside on visits to the cemetery that do not involve burials, in the spirit of the old *Ma'aneh Lashon.*[111] Straightaway it must be said that Jeiteles scrupulously incorporates the precepts figuring in the mortuary works of earlier centuries: the phases and sequence are identical, and the prayers, based on the recitation of the Psalms, have not been changed. The rules of the funeral ritual are given a form that seems immutable.

Thus during the death throes those present must abstain from idle chatter and pronounce only verses from the Torah or the Psalms.[112] When the dying man fails, the beadle recites aloud the Shema Yisrael, then, when the soul departs, the famous Psalm 91 (Yoshev be-Seter), the thirteen articles of faith, and so on. After the departure of the soul, a feather is placed on the lips of the deceased to confirm the absence of breath, and after at least seven and a half minutes elapse, just to be sure, the beadle covers the dead person's face that it should not be seen. Those present tear their garments and leave the deceased as he is, without moving him for at least three quarters of an hour. One of his children or one of his close relatives closes his eyes, for it was said to Jacob, "and Joseph's hand shall close your eyes."[113] The limbs of the dead man are placed together. If he is dirty, he is washed. The window is opened. The deceased is placed on the ground after being covered with a cloth. If it is a woman who died, only "pious women" of the burial society are allowed to be present. They recite Psalm 91. Water is thrown outside to notify people in the quarter that someone has died. If it is a sabbath, according to the Midrash, this does not have to be done, but if people wish "to be warned against danger, one can do it anyway" (the Midrash is not cited, nor is the danger mentioned).[114]

During the burial the mourners walk at the head of the funeral procession, just behind the bier. It is important that none of the bearers should be someone who hated the deceased while he lived. The beadle must stay beside the deceased during the entire funeral ceremony. A stop is made at the gate of the cemetery, the bier is placed on the ground, and the Ninety-first Psalm is recited by the beadle while the alms box is passed around. Then the procession moves toward the grave, where the eulogy will be said.

Fifty years later, in 1884, Brandeis published a new edition of the *Ma'avar Yabbok,* again in Prague.[115] The whole text is in German. The prayers are still in Hebrew, but they are all translated. Singularly reduced, this work, like its predecessor, conveys the chief mortuary phases. Let us follow the ceremony as it is presented in this work: the grave must be dug in a north/south alignment and must be at least two meters deep. The dead person is brought to the cemetery, the coffin covered with a black cloth. At the entrance the body is placed on the ground for the recitation of the Ninety-first Psalm.[116] Then the party makes its way toward the grave, and the psalm is recited once more. Earth is placed beneath the dead man's neck. The cloth that covered his mouth is taken off and placed between his legs; the coffin is gently lowered with ropes into the pit. Then the talit is placed on his head, halfway down the forehead, in order to leave the eyes free, on which are placed shards of glass, and on his mouth as well. On his hand is drawn the letter of the divine Name (*shin,* from *Shem* or *Shaddai*). One leg is crossed over the other. Finally, after asking absolution for the deceased, they wish him a "good rest"[117] and place the cover on the coffin. No one can leave the cemetery before the grave is filled. After the recitation of the Kaddish, those in attendance line up and say to the mourners: "May you be comforted among all the mourners of Zion and Jerusalem."[118] Before the funeral meal and during the period of mourning, the custom was to suspend a napkin in the room where the deceased died, place beside it a glass of water, and light a candle that would burn during the whole month of mourning. No one was supposed to sit in the deceased's usual chair during the first seven days.[119]

The rites are virtually identical in the two works presented here, but while Jeiteles still mentions putting earth from the land of Israel on the eyes of the corpse,[120] Brandeis no longer does. In the same way, Jeiteles specifies that the talit is arranged on the dead man "as he did in his lifetime when he prayed,"[121] while Brandeis simply describes the procedure. Let us note, again, that if Jeiteles cites the Bible, he too refrains, like Brandeis, from any commentary concerning the rites. Moreover, if the order of prayers is taken from Berachia's *Ma'avar Yabbok,* they are not accompanied by any explanation of their meaning or contents and are consequently stripped of any allusion to the Kabbalah.

The title *Ma'avar Yabbok* is no longer, as with Berachia, used to direct the vision of death to the burning purgatory of the upper worlds but to evoke a simple biblical reference,[122] recalling Jacob's battle with the angel at the ford of the Jabbok river.

These slight differences reveal another phenomenon: before disappearing, rites first lose their meaning, as illustrated by the historical vagaries of the recitation of the Ninety-first Psalm, the famous Shir Shel Pegu'im. In the fourteenth century, Aaron ha-Cohen of Lunel, one of the eminent doctors of the Provençal School, wrote,

> After burial, and after throwing in the earth and washing hands, one stands up to disengage from the bad spirits. And there are certain places where this is not done. But after washing one's hands, between each station of sitting and standing, [one says] the prayer of Moses, man of God, the entire chant, in order to recall the day of death, and *Yoshev be-Seter Elyon* [Psalm 91], which is the chant against demons, to banish evil spirits, and this is all a matter of custom.[123]

Continuously associated with the rite of sitting and standing at certain stations as the mourners file out of the cemetery, this chant is widely mentioned through the centuries in the rabbinic literature, particularly in the German lands and Italy. Joseph Yuspa Hahn recommends "the ancient custom . . . of sitting down and of standing up seven times, for seven demons . . . saying between each *vayehi no'am, yoshev* . . . in order to banish the spirits of impurity";[124] and I have dwelled on it at length here, analyzing the use Aaron Berachia made of it. In the nineteenth century the chant was still meticulously recited, but no meaning was affixed to it except the evocation of its biblical source. But what is its meaning?

> He that dwelleth in the secret place of the most High, shall abide under the shadow of the Almighty.
>
> I will say of the Lord: He is my refuge and my fortress; my God, in him will I trust
>
> Surely he shall deliver thee from the snare of the fowler, and from the noisome pestilence.
>
> He shall cover thee with his vast feathers, and under his wings shalt thou trust: his truth shall be thy shield and buckler.
>
> Thou shall not be afraid for the terror by night; nor for the arrow that flieth by day;
>
> Nor for the pestilence that walketh in darkness; nor for the destruction that wasteth at noonday.
>
> A thousand shall fall at thy side, and ten thousand at thy right hand; but it shall not come nigh thee.

Only with thine eyes shalt thou behold and see the reward of the wicked.

Because thou hast made the Lord, which is my refuge, even the most High, thy habitation;

There shall no evil befall thee, neither shall any plague come nigh thy dwelling.

For he shall give his angels charge over thee, to keep thee in all thy ways.[125]

After centuries in which commentaries and exegesis constituted the essential expression of Judaism and its meaning, the Jewish reform movement issuing from the Enlightenment challenged this singularity. These multiple rabbinic interpretations, which perpetuated precepts and customs by giving immanence to traditions, were deprived of their privileged status. If the skeletal structure of the rite persists in orthodox practice, orthodoxy itself seems transformed by renouncing all but its most fundamental features: the substance is abandoned while the form is preserved. Under the impact of the upheaval caused by the rationalist proponents of Enlightenment, the conceptual supports of the Kabbalah would henceforth be forgotten and the doctrine itself deprived of its usual domain—death. Following a similar process of symbolic loss, the burial society becomes, in the last half of the eighteenth century, a community service organization mandated to maintain the observance of rites but stripped of any esoteric prerogative.

In this way emancipation in Western Europe determined new orientations in religious matters: exegetical singularities were abandoned while ritual based on the Bible was maintained in a form that became immutable. This reduction of Jewish specificity inevitably opened the way to dialogue with the Christian world, itself in the grip of rationalism and its consequences.

But while Western Judaism was caught up in the movement of secularization sustained by the maskilim, in the same period the Judaism of eastern Europe developed its own face, the obverse side of the enlightened West, certainly, but also one that was radically new; this was embodied in the Ḥasidic revivalist movement, whose partisans were combating certain of the ancient values of Judaism and at the same time its secularization. While perpetuating the practices and conceptions elaborated by Lurianic Kabbalah, the Russian-Polish Ḥasidim would reevaluate its visions. Its doctrinal emphasis is rather on man's communion with the God of goodness and magnanimity, who wishes to be served in joy and tolerates human weakness. The ideas of the *Ba'al*

*Shem Tov*—the "master of the good name"[126]—considerably transform the meaning of transgression and guilt, while reducing the significance of sin and its corollary, repentance. The ḥasid recognizes a spiritual leader, the tsaddik, who represents the human intermediary between Heaven and earth. The place the ḥasid grants to the tsaddik allows him to participate fully in the temporal world, since he always moves under the protection of a spiritual force that scatters the malevolent presence of demons that haunt the universe.[127]

Whatever the form taken by Judaism's adaptation to modern attitudes—Haskalah or ḥasidism—these developments burgeoned from a common ground and share the transformation in the general perceptions of death. When there is no longer a monolithic belief in numerous demons attacking each other at different levels of the soul, the human being reevaluates his relation to death. The man of the Enlightenment finds himself face-to-face with finitude and not cosmogonic reunification; he is gripped by the fear of being buried alive because he must now face death alone. For the ḥasid, the summons of death necessitates the perfect completion of his terrestrial life. In both cases death disappears from daily life, and it is under the pressure of these very different attitudes that the attention paid by Jews in past centuries to the hereafter is supplanted by a concentration on the here and now.

# Afterword

Several years have passed[1] since I completed this study on sickness and death in traditional Ashkenazi society. In the meantime, in the field of Jewish Studies there has been an upsurge of interest in the history of mentalities, and other historians are discovering that the study of attitudes toward death can illuminate our understanding of attitudes toward life. It would be tempting to leave the field to them. This translation, however, offers me the opportunity to conduct a methodological evaluation as a way of concluding this project, and to that end I would like to lay out the conceptual framework for this particular historical approach and, above all, to describe the intellectual "collage" necessary in any attempt to wed the social sciences to Jewish studies.

One of the goals of the history of mentalities is to understand how the social fabric functions. In this effort historians have drawn on various disciplines, such as sociology, geography, anthropology, even philosophy and theology. What was called "new history" in the thirties later became known as "global history." Under the aegis of Marc Bloch and Lucien Febvre, themselves influenced by the works of Emile Durkheim and Max Weber, this new history focused on increasingly restricted objects of study, subdivided into ever smaller units that were nonetheless meant to serve vastly ambitious projects. And as history reached out to embrace the more precise sciences, integrating demography and economics with serial and quantitative tools, a field of research developed which concerned itself with attitudes toward life and death, kinship structures, forms of sociability, rituals and beliefs, which were studied with the help of serial and quantitative methods. As Roger Chartier affirms, the history of mentalities was constructed by applying to new objects principles of intelligibility that had already been proven with respect to economic and social history.[2] With this intellectual horizon in mind, I remodeled for my own use the definitions and analyses formulated by historians whose work I admired but whose history of the Western world left no room for Jews or any guidelines by which to situate them. Their goal was to shed light on the mental manifestations of European society over the course of time, yet they were unaware of the Jewish component, albeit a minority voice, in that history. When I decided to tackle the question of the history of mentalities, it seemed to me that the brilliance of those a priori Christian conceptions of our mental constructs was not adequate to shed light on this absence of Jewish society in the West, which is nonetheless defined as "Judeo-Christian." My efforts to adapt the results of these works to the Jewish world led me down a theoretical path that forced me either to reduce any sort of Jewish specificity to insignificance or simply to exclude Jews from any consideration of Western mental and intellectual exchange; neither option was acceptable.

While it is true that history is clearly the analysis of situations determined by time and space, attitudes toward death that particular societies developed often shed a harsh light on the beliefs of the living, on their social relations, and on their conception of the universe. These attitudes invoke key concepts that define and determine the individual as a rational being, in other words, as a being with the inclination to create and apply notions with respect to the infinite that allow him or her to act and perceive as a human being in everyday life. The belief in a form of life beyond our earthly finitude implies a series of practices whose daily exercise influences the nature of religion as well as of social relations.

In the scientific field, death is more often the province of medicine, whose aim is to push back its limits, than of the humanities. The humanities, however, in particular philosophy and anthropology, have long studied the subject of the infinite and of the rites of passage connected to it. As for Jewish Studies, problems posed by philosophical reflection refer us back to ethics, and by extension to religion, while anthropology, which traditionally studied the sacred so as to desanctify it, has only just begun to welcome certain pioneering works (those of Raphael Pataï, Harvey Goldberg, Shlomo Deshen, Jonathan Boyarin, and Nissan Rubin).[3]

Even when focusing exclusively on religious developments in the Christian world, the works undertaken in France on the history of death in the West, whether by Philippe Ariès, Pierre Chaunu, or Michel Vovelle,[4] have shown to what extent certain transformations—considered "popular" at the time—owed nothing to religious teachings but were rather perceived as emerging from "the depths of time,"[5] or venturing off the beaten parish track. A translation of Jewish attitudes toward death should by rights lead to a methodological analysis of the characteristics of Jewish society from its origins. Taking the larger perspective, we must ask what kinds of developments and discontinuities these more or less stable and coherent communities established, what constituted the basis of their authority, who comprised the elite and the scholars, what power the rabbis and masters wielded, and who Jewish society represented. In actually venturing to compare Jewish and Christian society, I found it necessary to reflect on the accepted tenets of universal history, to review the empirical facts, to subject to close scrutiny everything that might be taken for granted in order to be certain that the tool forged in this way might also be valid in the case of Jewish history.

Everyone knows that to count time is a way of expressing a precise approach to the universe: to consider the present from the moment of the creation of the world according to biblical generations, from the birth of Jesus, or from the arrival of the prophet Muhammad, gives a meaning to the temporal flow. Christians, Muslims, and Jews await the end of time, but their behavior will differ depending on whether they await the Second Coming, the Apocalypse, the coming of the Messiah, or the Last Judgment. Nevertheless, most of our attitudes in the face of death are responses to the meaning attributed to eschatological time: this is why the only possible genesis of a history of death for the Jews begins with Genesis itself. And so I began to articulate the itinerary of Jewish beliefs concerning death from the rabbinical period through Emancipation and the modern world by returning to the Bible itself. However, at first my research was stimulated by questions more concerned with the present than with the past. In fact, I had difficulty seeing whether the obvious divergences between Jewish and Christian society were superficial or indicative of deeper differences suggesting different developments within the same geographic and temporal zones. I had to ask whether the differences that separate Jewish and Christian society go beyond the simply denominational, beyond beliefs that are to all intents and purposes very close in the monotheistic religions. To answer this legitimate, if simplistic, question, I had to try to discover in their approach to death something that might distinguish Christians and Jews with respect to basic beliefs, that is, in their specific conceptions of resurrection, the afterlife, retribution, the other world, paradise and hell, or the Last Judgment. To identify norms, it was first necessary to conceive of the existence of general laws, even dogmas. Was this possible in a Judaism that defined itself by a dynamic process rather than by a series of credal affirmations? This perspective alone implied a step in the direction of a comparative history of religion, something that could not have been further from my original social preoccupations. By means of this religious approach to Jewish beliefs about death, I was trying to understand one mental construct in Jewish society that seemed to me essential inasmuch as it lay outside the realm of the conscious.

Then again, does it make sense to use the term "Jewish society" when we are faced, rather, with a vast social complex that includes Jews, among others? If I wanted my analysis to have any coherence, I first had to construct a framework for the existence of what might be considered a traditional Jewish society. This, of course, required me to identify a pattern that would permit the analysis of a Jewish society that was stable, established in time, and had roots in an ordinary, non-Jewish environment whose level of tolerance did not deviate from the prevailing norm. It would then be possible to pinpoint the transitional phenomena within a changing society in relation to these norms and to note the relevance of these internal transformations. The construction of a perfect ideal type for a case study must result in an exemplary image, or even one that might be interchangeable with other communities for the purposes of a microanalysis or a monograph. Beyond the process leading to a given body of beliefs, to the establishment of the Jews as a minority, and to the stabilization of certain specific data, the Prague community presented a convenient specimen for analysis: it had a long history, had endured as a community despite a few rare expulsions, and offered, above all, a rich social fabric that reflected the disparity between rich and poor, the tensions between community bodies and administrative authorities, political upheavals, and finally its gradual insertion into the general social structure.

One major difficulty remained, and that was to construct a history of the Jews that would be acceptable and instructive within the framework of both Jewish Studies and the social sciences, the first being more restricted but no less important than the second. While the conventional framework of Jewish Studies seemed open to all sorts of scholarly work on the Jews, it nonetheless continued to perpetuate a good number of assumptions that had governed the study of history since the previous century. For example, not long ago it was still claimed that traditional Jewish society was closely linked to its ancestral isolation, that it existed in a vacuum enabling it to preserve its institutions almost intact, or that it was at least free of any dynamic change since the "Age of the Ghetto." It was seen as a closed society, until the process of emancipation, even mute aside from rabbinical decisions, and certainly silent since it existed to all intents and purposes without any history in the schoolbooks. This history of the Jews resembled those histories of the poor, of lepers, and of women that had never managed to find their way into scholarly discourse but nonetheless had a unique, unknown, or hidden story to tell and that my generation of French students took great delight in discovering. The Jews had indeed discovered history, but since they were long considered a sect by most nations, it was written only in the passive form. The Jews had not bothered to insert it into time, and its existence depended on their social insertion into the surrounding culture. They only integrated the *Wissenschaft des Judentums* once they became caught up in the Emancipation movement and in a preoccupation with their future as Jews. A history of Jewish attitudes involved a reflection upon the Jews' place in history in general and in their environment in particular. For while we might think that since the Jews shared a certain space and time with their neighbors, Jewish attitudes should simply be included in those of the general population, a comparison of their mutual beliefs clearly showed important divergences with respect to the afterlife. It would be difficult to claim that the Jews had the same conception of history as their neighbors, however, since they had always been subject to a particular juridical status, and the legal system reserved for or granted to the Jews expressed the contradictory desires of religious and secular, seigneurial and royal authorities. History advanced within the same context, of course, but the same events could not have had the same value for Jewish actors as for Christians but instead depended on their roles as extras or protagonists. Even when they were thought to exist outside of history, before Emancipation, the Jews demonstrated over time something that strongly resembles a "culture," even a "civilization." They generated an intellectual production that was both written and oral, witness the collection of rabbinical works, responsa,[6] civil codes, codes of conduct, philosophical and theological works, and the evolution of mysticism. But how can we think in terms of a civilization to designate a society whose codes differ from those of its environment?

As everyone knows, traditional Judaism is more than a religion. It is a way of life based on the religious phenomenon; from the outset this simple fact limits the sources available to the historian. Unlike those eminent figures who wrote about death in the West, the Jewish historian was not allowed to rely on nonsacred elements or sources to prove a point. In the German, Ashkenazi world, few or no literary iconographic documents have been found, and there is a noticeable lack of poets and visual artists, which only serves to reinforce the scholastic aspect of this universe. This includes burial places as well, which seem quite sober, devoid of anything but funeral stones engraved with epitaphs and the occasional distinctive symbol. No notary acts, no declarations, a few rare wills and testaments, which are primarily ethical; the only usable sources take the form of religious texts or texts that constitute community legislation. My first task, therefore, was to transform these religious texts into major sources of information. Such a process, of course, must have constant recourse to the necessary historical context, since this alone allows us to understand the immediate issues introduced by the texts. The writers of these edifying texts inevitably share the social and conjectural preoccupations of their time. In this sense the similarities between Jewish and Christian attitudes identified throughout my research arise from the periods studied rather than from any religious interconnections. Judaism does not allow a global approach in which dogmatic decisions affect the entire social body. The Jewish communities evolved region by region, at the mercy of rabbinic influences or relationships. Ritual is one area that might be characterized by the weight of local customs, which are then transplanted into the common body of the law and enter the patrimony, Judaized along the way,[7] as "minhag." Law and custom, "din" and "minhag," are extensions of beliefs, but while *dinim* correspond to the secular beliefs of the Hebrews as they were understood by the Jews during the Mishnaic and talmudic periods, the body of minhagim accumulated throughout the centuries indicates the transformations and adaptations to which they were subject over time.

For Jews, the relationship to death is dictated by beliefs specifically linked to their conception of it at different periods, as well as by the internal community organizations they developed to deal with it. In my study of the German Ashkenazi world, seen through the community of Prague, taken as a Weberian ideal-type, the main body of sources is in part composed of classical texts: the Bible and the tractate *Semaḥot* serve as a basis for comparative analysis and the identification of changes that have occurred over the course of time; Naḥmanides' *Torat ha-Adam* and the *Shulḥan Arukh* serve as general temporal indicators. In any case, the real tools of analysis are provided by the mortuary literature, which evolved from the seventeenth century on in the wake of the *Ma'avar Yabbok,* and spread throughout the Ashkenazi communities along with the new social structure promoted by the ḥevra kaddisha. The emergence of a unique kind of religious literature within the society suggests that deep transformations were taking place. This literature must be identified in specific terms and precisely defined. At this point recourse to comparison and the tools of social science becomes important. The Ashkenazi Jews lived mainly in a Christian world and could not escape the developments that affected the attitudes and mental constructs of their neighbors; hence they created the *Sefer ha-Ḥaim* from the *Artes Moriendi,* transforming the *Art of Dying* into the *Book of Life.* What Philippe Ariès calls the "collective unconscious" refers to a system of coherent representation common to an entire society during a given period.[8] How are we to decide whether or not the Jews were part of the same society, indeed the same world, as the Christians? In spite of extremely different attitudes toward corporality, the sacred, holiness, and even the divine, not to mention conjugal, kinship, and educational structures, which would indicate totally different approaches, certain universal elements are to be found at the heart of Jewish attitudes, either simultaneously or staggered in time.

Ariès built his theory on the finding that the contemporary era had banished death from daily life. He then followed the thread of time back through those periods and stages of human history when death had been a part of life, before it was relegated to the periphery of the social network. My approach was quite different. I accepted as a postulate that there were different stages in the process of individualizing death. Personally, I found that in today's secular Jewish world, death remained the last, if not the only, reference to a form of traditional Judaism. Why make such a distinction in death? Why cling in death to a tradition that was not cherished in one's lifetime? This inquiry remained in the background during my research, since my work on attitudes toward death ended with Emancipation, with the dissolution of the community and the traditional way of life. The question nonetheless informs my essay on the history of the Jewish cemetery, in which the singularity of Ashkenazi belief and practice during the Middle Ages became apparent. During this same period Christians prayed, calmly kneeling on the flagstones that covered collective graves, wandered through the potter's field where animals stood peacefully grazing, and held dances in the cemetery. But the difference between Christian and Jewish practice in the Middle Ages is not applicable to all other times and places. It corresponds to a specific moment with respect to Christian attitudes rather than to any desire stemming from Judaism at that time, since the main themes of the Jewish relationship to funerary places seem to have been codified with the writing of the *Evel Rabbati* in the third century. It is surely no surprise to anyone that the ways Jewish society found to adapt these codifications to the social norms of the time are among the most fascinating elements of this anthropological history. Specialists have hotly debated the period in which purgatory appeared in Christian eschatological imagery, somewhere between the eleventh and thirteenth centuries.[9] With regard to Jewish eschatology, the debate could not be based on the same criteria for lack of pictorial sources, obviously, but also for lack of written dogma on the subject. The idea of an intermediate territory emerged from the biblical *she'ol*, and when Judaism introduced the notion of retribution in the other world (in the Bar Kochba period), a place of punishment also appeared. Does the Western Gehenna have an originally Jewish spatial context? The advent of the mourner's Kaddish is, for our purposes, a useful index to the temporal introduction of the possibility of recuperating lost souls. We can find references to this both in the *Sefer Ḥasidim* and codified in the thirteenth-century siddurim (prayer books). It seems, then, that the essential turning point in Jewish attitudes toward death occurred at around the time of the Crusades, and this is clearly linked not only to the transformation of the historical conditions of Jews in the Christian world but also to the mental modifications that historiographers call the "second Middle Ages." After this period the elements that come into play will become an inherent part of mortuary rituals or rituals that determined Jewish attitudes toward death.

The place death gradually assumed in everyday life becomes more apparent and the possibility of acting upon and for the other world more palpable with the writing of the Memorbuch, the rites of the hazkarat neshamot, and the recitation of the *El Male Raḥamim*, as the *Kiddush ha-Shem*, and the *Unetaneh Tokef*. This Jewish specificity is due, of course, to certain tragedies, but how do we then account for the fact that Christians picture death in the same terms? And how can we avoid comparing Ashkenazi penitential practices with those of their Christian contemporaries?

From the year A.D. 1000 until Emancipation in the eighteenth century, a number of transformations would affect Jewish attitudes toward death, but very few rituals actually stand out from the main body established at the time. The most remarkable changes would be those introduced by the spread of the Kabbalah, which reconfigured the contours of eschatological space and territory. It is hardly my purpose to gauge the accuracy of Scholem's analysis, but limiting myself to my own field I will say this: when Scholem, without ever considering questions relevant to the study of mentalities, wrote that "death, repentance and rebirth were the three great events of human life by which the new Kabbalah sought to bring man into a blissful union with God," he emphasized the way that rites of passage had the power of conferring a ritual value on mystical elements that might be useful in everyday life. If we study the *Ma'avar Yabbok* and examine the period in which it was the most popular mortuary work, we can see that for nearly a century the Kabbalah cannot be isolated from the general body of Jewish religious norms. It represents the mysterious side of these norms and is inseparable from the collection of beliefs that includes everything from the cure of Holy Names to the recitation of a "Krishmeh," the reading of the Shema Yisrael, or beatific actions after the meal. There is no problem with the Kabbalah being perceived as a tradition handed down from the beginning of time and intricately enmeshed in a diffuse, esoteric universe. Problems arise only when the myth of the origin itself is questioned during the period of the Enlightenment. It would be an arduous task for the historian of this period to distinguish within traditional Ashkenazi Jewish society those beliefs that originate in the Kabbalah from those that do not. Along with the belief in God[10] went a belief in the contiguity and interaction of the higher and lower worlds. Human actions performed in this world were supposed to have infinite repercussions, so much so that they entered into the celestial spheres either to reunite with the broken divine sparks or to send them even deeper into limbo, "*kelipot,*" and darkness. A man who breathed his last could expect the three parts of his soul (nefesh, ru'aḥ, neshamah) to separate so that, according to his worth, his neshamah might reach the Shekhinah, birthplace of his divine essence. If we were to draw a map of the Jewish hereafter, it would largely resemble the spheres of kabbalistic eschatology.

The important status gradually won by the ḥevra kaddisha in the community fabric no doubt was due to this phenomenon. This institution offers an ideal example for an analysis that can be applied to all historiographic configurations. Once I had determined the monographic nature of my work, I chose Prague as my case in point. Founded in 1564, the ḥevra kaddisha of Prague is an institution that has persisted over time, but its present nature does not begin to suggest the power it once wielded over the communities. The first burial society of the Ashkenazi region, the Prague ḥevra kaddisha, was approved by the Maharal, who signed the earliest body of rules. This "State within a State"[11] was then exported from Prague to Frankfurt in 1597 and subsequently to all the great European communities. By vocation the ḥevra kaddisha was responsible for the management of burials, cemeteries, and last rites, but it was not long before it took charge of caring for the sick, the organization of the sandakim (godfathers), the study of the Mishnah for the dead, dowries for fiancées, and matchmaking. It was also authorized to lend money, and gradually took over the social and religious life of the communities. In addition to its authority over death, it exercised authority over life, becoming the precursor to an insurance fund.

Does the ḥevra kaddisha represent power exercised by an elite over the Jews as a group? Historiography has generally convinced us that when it comes to attitudes, we can distinguish an important gap between the culture of the educated and the culture of the lower classes. How do such distinctions operate in the Jewish world?

Jewish mortuary literature since ancient times is very concerned with the way the sick are cared for, and only after dealing with this subject does it take up the matter of funerary acts, mourning rites, and anniversaries or visits to the cemetery. Jews, who were often doctors, wrote or translated an important number of works, sometimes aimed at practitioners but more often at ordinary people who had to care for themselves on their own, usually with scanty means. Zimmels's detailed work[12] on folk medicine based on the responsa enabled me to attempt an analysis. One of the insights gained by this analysis was that the formalization of the concept of learned culture as opposed to popular culture cannot be maintained within the framework of traditional Jewish society because the structure of the group depends on the accomplishment of acts related to a shared symbolism. Erudite scholars and simple, uneducated folk find their place along the same spectrum: both point in the same direction and share the same "popular" certainties and pretentions to erudition.

Accompanying the collapse of community structure, the Jewish social fabric as a whole began to disintegrate during the eighteenth century, carrying in its wake, like so much debris, the medieval fears of sin that imagined the universe populated by destructive demons, the *nezikim* and *nefilim*. With the countervailing ideas of the Enlightenment, its seemed clear that Jews and Christians, within an identical vision and perception of the universe, were pursuing different itineraries that were nonetheless characterized by the same imaginary world. As soon as enlightened Jews began to try to transform their coreligionists, they also tackled mortuary practices, including those that lay, perhaps unrecognized, at the heart of Jewish identity. Henceforth the battle of the "*halanat ha-metim*" (laying to rest of the dead) would become one of the primary goals of the activists of Emancipation.[13]

The history of ideas, of social practices, of philosophy and religion, exists simultaneously within the history of mentalities, which bows neither to linguistics nor to economics but considers itself in the larger sense to be "historical anthropology" or "cultural" or even "social" history. To make the best use of the information analyzed, data systems can be used to assemble on a larger or smaller scale all possible human attitudes. In this context, Jewish Studies can only benefit from its encounter with contemporary social science. This encounter can take place, however, only if the object of study is chosen with due care. The study of Jewish attitudes toward death is a particular test case in which, as we have seen, social science can be enriched in turn by Jewish Studies. In conclusion, I would suggest that by giving up the idea of necessary singularity by using religious documents as historical source material, we come closer to understanding the universal. The question is, will Jewish Studies be receptive, in return, to the advantages of a social scientific approach while preserving its specificity?

*Paris, June 1993*

# Appendix

RULES OF THE ḤEVRA KADDISHA OF PRAGUE 1692–1702
M. Grünwald, *Das Judische Centralblatt*

In this book:

With pens of iron and lead [they have written] the laws and customs in use, as well as the rulings for the community of the gomlei ḥasadim, for future generations. When all the laws, tentative and final, disappeared in the fire, they took heart and courageously renewed them in order to remember words pronounced, those things that underpinned and established the pillars of the Jewish Quarter. And let no word be annuled, nor a single letter of these commandments, which are pure and clear. Until the arrival of the Messiah, who will deliver us from servitude and lead us to freedom. Amen! So be it!

The sixteen [*sic*] articles recopied here on parchment are meant for the members of the ḥevra kaddisha, so that each may know which way to follow, as well as which practices to uphold, both old and new. The copy was made on the eve of Rosh hodesh [the first of the month] of Shevat 462 [1702], by the renowned and learned scribe Meir Perles, from a document written on an ancient tablet, itself written by the learned Rabbi Schmelke, our Master, son of Rabbi Haim, beadle and scribe, the grand *gaon* [spiritual leader] Schlomo Efraim of Lentschitz, our Master, *Av bet din* [president of the tribunal] and Master of our community. At the bottom of this tablet were also the signatures of Shmuel, who is called "Shmelke," son of Rabbi Efraim, beadle and scribe, Av bet din and Master of Prague.

ARTICLE 1: This is a rule from former times, that every gravedigger is obliged to go to the synagogue, morning and evening, save in a case of circumstances beyond one's control, under pain of fine.

ARTICLE 2: There is an old law that dates back many years that no gravedigger may frequent a tavern or house belonging to gentiles, and even if this is not during the time for appearing at the synagogue; and if someone does this, let him be fined. And let no gravedigger take up gambling in a Christian house, or he will lose his position as gravedigger.

ARTICLE 3: According to the majority of the Elders, it has been the usual practice, when a gravedigger does not conduct himself properly, to exclude him from the Society. And if he repents and accepts the blame leveled by the Elders, he can then be readmitted to the Society. But let this be judged, and let him return as a stranger who is being received for the first time; and let him have a complete period of probation, from beginning to end, to verify that the laws are respected. But if he begins again to fall into shame and infamy, he will be declared a "rebel" against the Elders, and will be expelled again from the Society and never readmitted. And let the punishment be 10 *hagirim* [Hungarian *gulden*], and let this not be violated.

ARTICLE 4: In case of a quarrel against one or another member of the Society, whether probational members or regular members, on the subject of the cemetery or any other subject regarding the obligation of the Society, let them all leave it to the gabbaiʾim and the mevorarim. Let it be decided according to their will. If one of them refuses to comply, the Elders have the right to levy a fine, and even to declare him a "rebel" in the Old-New Synagogue. But he will have to obey the decision of the gabbaiʾim and the mevorarim, and no rabbi or any other leader will be able to change it.

ARTICLE 5: And this issues also from the old rules. Every parnas ha-ḥodesh [administrator of the month] must call a weekly meeting of the gabbaiʾim and the mevorarim. However, this is no longer done, so that the members of the Society no longer receive any instruction and must get it from other judges. Then it was decreed, in order to prevent a case of this kind from arising [when] the beadle presents himself to the parnas ha-ḥodesh and sends to look for the mevorarim, if they are busy or if the administrator has no time, or that, if they are sent to find them and they do not come, then [in order to prevent this] let them elect people each year to resolve the quarrels among the Elders. If, however, one of the parties did not accept this procedure, let them be fined 20 hagirim [a half-gulden]. And thus the gabbaiʾim and the mevorarim will be obliged to join together. In this way, every member must submit to the legal procedure of five men, and if he does not do so, he will be decreed a "rebel" at the synagogue. If he does not submit in two weeks, he will no longer be listed among the members. And if he still refuses after these two weeks, he will be publicly excluded [from the Society] by the five Elders, before the parnas ha-ḥodesh, and he will be sent away in front of everyone.

ARTICLE 6: It was decided to extend an old article: if someone has not gone to the cemetery for a trimester, let the gabbaiʾim and the mevorarim come with five Elders to his house; if he is an *Aufgenommener* [on probation], let him be excluded; if he is a *ḥatum* [regular member], let him be demoted to probationary status; if he is an Elder, let him be demoted to the status of regular member.

ARTICLE 7: This article of the old laws was also extended: when someone is being taken to the cemetery for burial, people must go in order. First come the members of the committee [gabbaiʾim and mevorarim], then the regular members, according to their rank. And let them walk in fear, without uttering a single word that is alien [to the ritual] under pain of being fined. Then let one of the Elders or of the mevorarim lead the ceremony. And let the probationary and regular members maintain their ranks until they stand before the grave, on pain of being fined.

ARTICLE 8: If the *vokhn man* [officiant of the week] refuses to carry out a duty, whether because he scorns it or has someone do it in his stead, let him deposit 15 *tsals* [*kreuzers*] in the charity box. When the vokhn man leaves a regular member standing and honors a probationary member, he must also pay a fine of 15 tsals, unless he did not see him. In all cases, the officiant of the week must ask people if they are regular members on pain of being fined, and if not he must seat his *vokhn layt* [assistants of the week], then the Elders, then the members of the synagogue; he is also authorized to honor regular members. The vokhn man must honor a stranger [by entrusting to him] the [charity] box, even if it was not his week of service.

ARTICLE 9: It is established that when there is a burial, if the gabbai, the mevorar, or the vokhn man does not present himself, the honor of leading the ceremony reverts to an Elder, who is after him in the order. This person takes the charity box and leads the ritual. If the officiant of the week arrives during this time, he stands near the Elder whether he does or does not do him the grace [of giving him his job/role].

ARTICLE 10: This is one of the earlier laws. When there is a burial, let no gravedigger be absent. When someone dies, the gravediggers [members of the Society] carry the bier from the gate of the cemetery to the grave. And no one who is not a member of the Society. If it is an Elder who dies, all the members of the Society must come in frock coats and hats, under pain of being fined.

ARTICLE 11: It was unanimously decided, on the subject of fasting and the *meḥila* demanded in the presence of the dead, that this should always be on the day of Rosh hodesh Shevat. For this day was chosen a long time ago. By contrast, new elections will be held after the holiday of Shavuʾot, always in the synagogue of our community.

ARTICLE 12: There was also a general endorsement of an old article of ours. When there is an Av bet din functioning in the community, the gabbaiʾim and the mevorarim will go before him and choose [in his presence] from the urn seventeen members of the religious assembly; and let this article be retained as is. But if it happens that there is no Av bet din, elections will be carried out in the following way: let the names of the Elders be put into a box, and among them be chosen ten to form the gabbaiʾim and the mevorarim. Let these seventeen Elders, elected from the community, go to the synagogue and vote [on the laws] and they will be the members of the community synagogue.

ARTICLE 13: It was also voted unanimously that every year the committee will be renewed, and that seven new members will be chosen from among the Elders, or if you will, from among the gabbaiʾim and the mevorarim, but a majority of Elders must be preserved, and they will be obliged to renew the statutes each year, to maintain the laws, and to add others without annulling [the old ones].

ARTICLE 14: It was also decided that if people are elected who prove inadequate, and these people have gotten themselves elected by keeping silent about their incapacity, they will be punished by expulsion from the ḥevra kaddisha and from elections; and they will never again be trusted by the gravediggers, or even by the members of the society of sandakim [godfathers].

ARTICLE 15: This, too, is contained in the old articles. One can be elected gaon [president] after eight years as Aufgenommener. Then after another eight years as a member, one can be elected Elder. If one had been an Elder a certain time, one can become a member of the Committee, but before being gabbai, one must first have been mevorar for two consecutive years. This is the law, and it was established so that he [the gaon] should be the most competent and qualified in funeral matters among the members of the Society, and so that he can be depended upon.

ARTICLE 16: This, too, issues from the old rules. No more than forty persons can be accepted per year [as candidates] or more than four permanent members named, under pain of a fine of 10 hagirim. Moreover, the gabbai'im and the mevorarim have the right to take one kohen [priest] each year, but when they accept more than four titular members, they must take fewer.

ARTICLE 17: This, too, issues from the old rules. As for the candidacy of members of the Society of sandakim, let it be done thus: the gabbai'im and the mevorarim vote to elect nine persons, who are paid twenty-five tsals for the year, and they vote together. Three gabbai'im and mevorarim, under the supervision of the five Elders, and in addition two nonpermanent members. Second, one must have been mevorar before becoming gabbai. Before investing this trust in a new member, he must have been a gravedigger for at least four years. A kohen, however, has priority as a candidate, the same as an Elder.

ARTICLE 18: This is also an old article that we shall preserve. When a kohen is named, his function will be to make the coffin, since he does not have the right to attend burials. Let him be given the rank of Elder and let the others honor him by entrusting to him the alms box if he is officiant of the week.

ARTICLE 19: We are unanimously agreed on the fact that when an eminent person is admitted, or someone of advanced age, he is given all the privileges concerning the deceased. But he may not have the [priority] right to elections or to function in the Society. Let him be inscribed in our book, and let him sign. This decision was made because the dignitary is not versed in funerary matters.

ARTICLE 20: This, too, is an old article. From year to year, after every renewal [of the elect], let the beadles return the keys to the community that votes for a year.

ARTICLE 21: When a new member is admitted, he must, according to the old rules, first spend an entire year with the beadles, who must teach him [his duties]. And before being permanently admitted, he must answer questions before the community so that it may be judged if he is sufficiently knowledgeable in funerary matters. If he answers suitably, he will be permanently admitted; if not, he will not yet be admitted this year, and he will have to study funerary practices for another year.

ARTICLE 22: An old rule forbids members of the society of gravediggers to coerce someone in the company of a musketeer. If someone does this anyway, he can no longer be a gravedigger. Let his name be wiped off the books, and even more, let him no longer honor any burial [by conducting the ceremony] (Heaven forbid!), under pain of fine.

ARTICLE 23: This, too, is an old article that says that when there is a burial (God forbid), the beadles or the officiant of the week or his assistants must inscribe it on tablets and post it under pain of [preestablished] fine on their monthly wages.

ARTICLE 24: We have voted unanimously that as we have [at present] many poor strangers to whom our society dispenses alms, something that was not previously the case, and that because of this our funds are gone and we have nothing more to give to the poor of our community, let it be decreed that from this day and henceforth the parnas ha-ḥodesh cannot give to strangers more than five tsals (kreuzers) without the agreement of the majority of the committee. [However], if an eminent person is involved, he may be given up to fifteen tsals; and one sends gifts to a gaon as a priority, if there isn't one, to the community leader, to a learned man among the gabbaiʾim and the mevorarim, or to another among the godfathers, or to a rabbi or a physician if it comes to that. One sends gifts to these to the exclusion of all others out of the alms fund, on pain of fine.

ARTICLE 25: We have also voted unanimously no longer to tolerate the disorder of women who jostle each other at funerals and at the funeral preparations, which is a terrible thing. Let the gabbaiʾim and the mevorarim summon the *gabbaitot* and the *mevorarot* to warn them that, under pain of severe punishment, they are no longer to be found following [funerals] in the company of their assistants of the week. And also, this disorder that reigns at the burial of a *met mitsva* [an abandoned corpse], where the women rush almost into the midst of the men, which puts us in grave danger and, as a result, the men no longer attend the burials of met mitsva. Henceforth, from this day and forever, the gabbaiʾim and the mevorarim shall warn the women a first time, a second time, and even a third time, and if they are not prepared to pay attention and do not return [to the women's ranks], let their coat be seized as pledge and given to the poor. The gabbaiʾim and mevorarim shall buy two sprinklers and use them for watering and maintaining order.

ARTICLE 26: This also issues from the articles of former times: When a death occurs after noon, the procedure is as follows: one buries the same day, in summer until the twenty-first hour,* and in winter until the twentieth. If the death occurs later, burial is not the same day, except on the occasion of a Christian holiday. [In this case] the gravediggers present themselves to the administrator of the month [for his decision in the matter], and if he will attend to it that day, let the dead man be buried the same day and if not, let him not be so buried.

ARTICLE 27: This, too, is one of our old laws, that when one of our coreligionists is dying, he is sent members of the brotherhood of gravediggers to keep vigil and read to him from the *Maʿavar Yabbok*. When he expires, let him be left alone for at least a quarter of an hour, and let him be moved on after several quarter hours have elapsed, and let all those who contravene this decree be liable to a fine.

ARTICLE 28: We were also in agreement upon this fact; given that our account book was burned in the great fire and that it contained the list of all those inscribed over the years, in order that these [the inscribed] be known. Those who have claims and those who must be called to become titular members.

*Traditionally, the new day is counted from nightfall; the twenty-first hour in summer therefore corresponds to 3:00 P.M., and the twentieth in winter corresponds to 2:00 P.M.

This would be a punishment that those who must be admitted permanently wait again so long. Let the gabbai'im and the mevorarim make a list of all the inscribed, from the time of the fire until today, and let them inscribe in the records those who have been [provisionally] admitted and those who are titulary members.

ARTICLE 29: It is well known that when someone dies, one gives [money] to the fund. Let the gabbai take with him an Elder or a mevorar to receive the money, under pain of fine.

ARTICLE 30: There was unanimous agreement on this: let the gabbai'im and the mevorarim of the religious community engage two clerks to register those who go to the cemetery and those who do not attend burials, [those who are in service] must be present. When the officiant of the week is not there, or the gabbai or the mevorar stays home, let him be fined two tsals; if the assistants are not present, they must pay a fine of one tsal. The other members of the Society who would be absent [when it is their turn] would pay three pfennings. Let the gabbai and the mevorar keep track of the fines every trimester. If someone attempts to abscond and refuses to pay, then let the gabbai or the mevorar of the religious community expel him from the Society.

ARTICLE 31: This is an old rule, that the parnas ha-ḥodesh cannot hold this office more than two months. When the Rosh hodesh falls in the middle of the week, he must remit his accounts to the gabbai who replaces him. He must do his accounts in the presence of a learned man or an Elder, who will be responsible for them, until the next Christian holiday [Sunday], and this under pain of fine.

ARTICLE 32: We were also in agreement to keep this: let the money paid for the inscribing of new members and titular members to the ranks of the gabbai'im and the mevorarim of the religious community be used for the banquet [during which] people are admitted, whether candidates or permanent members. And let it remain thus. This has been decreed today, Tuesday, the sixteenth day of the month of Av, 452 [1692].

With the agreement of Zangwill, son of Josel Lipchovitch.
Prescribers: Moshe, son of Wolf, Yenkel Raussnitz.
Yeshaya, son of Rabbi Zwi Winternitz.
Yehuda Lev, son of the learned Isaac Roffe.
Yosef, son of the leader Elia Perles.
Simon Wolf Freund.
Abraham Yehuda, called Lev, son of Moshe.
Yehiel, called "Weibl Weisswasser."
Isaac, son of Rabbi Yehoshua Adeless.

The rules mentioned above, composed and recopied by the wisdom and intuition of the notables of the Burial Society, in the honor of the Holy One, blessed be He, and of his Presence, to see eternity bound to benevolence and the praise of the Throne, to charity and prayer. . . . This is why I lend my support so that this ordinance shall be decreed.

These are the resolutions held by the youth Elie, son of our father, the great Rabbi Wolf, whose memory is a beacon to us, son of the celebrated Simon Spiro, the chief rabbi, blessed be his memory. These are old resolutions, solid as a rock, that issue from the agreements of honorable masters. The leaders and worthy citizens who carefully observe the divine commandments, those who carry out the charitable good works (gomlei ḥasadim) of the holy brotherhood of gravediggers. The sages and the learned, the arbitrators and officers, authors of new rules and old, have decided, after deliberation, to sign them. After weighing them pro and con, they established after due debate to execute the will of all those who wanted to partake of the greatness. And in order to confirm and validate their words we have voted so that they are inscribed in law and [divine] dread in our community. Today, 27 Elul, "which will bless us according to the lesser calculation" [after addition of the numerical value of the initial letters = 452, that is, 1692].

Shmuel Zalman, son of our Master Abraham, may the memory of the Just be a blessing for the life of the world to come.
Uri Schraga Weibl, son of our Master Eliezer, one of the Just of blessed memory, of the Halphen family.
Yosef, son of the worthy and illustrious Zevi.
Shmuel the Small, son of the worthy Gershon Brandeis, of blessed memory.
Mordechai, son of the illustrious and celebrated David Jeiteles, of blessed memory.
Isaac, son of Rabbi Moshe Hock, of blessed memory.
Tanhum, called Neister Segal.
Natl, son of Rabbi Abraham, of blessed memory.
Moshe, son of Babriel Taussig, of blessed memory.
Moshe, son of Menahem Taussig.

## PESTILENCE

An anonymous autobiography from the seventeenth century.
A. Marx, *JQR*.

In 5440 [1680], the epidemic spread throughout Bohemia and especially in Prague. . . . During the month of Tamuz [July–August], I fell ill with definite symptoms of the plague. I ran a fever for three days and three nights and was close to death. . . . Then a bubo appeared behind my ear, on my neck, which burned like fire, and all the members of the family trembled with fear. The rabbi and his wife [who lived with us] saw it and fled from our house. . . . The epidemic was raging all around our village; the count established a lazar house, a little wooden house with two rooms, in the middle of a large forest around a kilometer from the castle. If someone fell ill in one of his villages, the sick person was ejected from his house with his belongings and had to go to this forest. The count had reserved an open space of several meters around his castle, in which only those who lived in the castle had the right to enter. He retained very few people there and shut himself in, never going out. No outside person was allowed to enter except my father, because the count loved intelligent and clever people, and he wanted my father to come every day to keep him company, but he warned all the people of his house not to go out or to let strangers in. He also warned them that if ever, God forbid, any member of his family fell ill, that he must not conceal it and that he must go, on his own initiative, taking all his goods and closing his house, come to the forest with his whole family. He had warned my father that if anyone saw that he had hidden such a thing, he would authorize the gentiles to burn the house with all its occupants. When my father realized that the plague had struck our house, he was devastated and did not know what to do; to follow the count's orders and go to the forest with the family might attract great dangers, for this would be known by the villagers, who were mostly dishonest folk, thieves and murderers, avid for blood and Jewish plunder. Even in the towns they molested them and robbed them in their own houses, and the danger was just as great that they would come and murder us in the forest. He therefore decided to keep me and hide me under the roof, in the granary, asking his father, Jacob Ha-Levy, to care for me; which he did, although he was already an old man. He did this so conscientiously that no one but he would come up to the room where I lay, in the hopes that the fire of the epidemic would not spread to the others. He did not leave my side for six days.

But one day slanderers ran to tell the count that they had seen my grandfather and another Jew, a certain Saul Pollack who lived with us with his wife, go together to other villages where the plague was raging. The count immediately decreed their explusion from the territory, on risk of their lives if they were seen there again. My grandfather was obliged to leave me alone, in my sickbed, for it would have been dangerous to hide: they would have looked for him in every room, and if I were discovered, we would all have been endangered. . . . But God took pity on me, seeing that I had no one to care for me, and he sent me a complete cure. . . . The abscesses closed up. . . . The brother of my father's wife, Rabbi Samson of Kammitz, came to our house, he told my father how to prepare a plaster out of egg whites and a little alum, the size of amut. The two elements had to be fresh and carefully mixed in a small receptacle until they became solid, and spread on the lesion; this was done, and I, although I was still only a child of twelve, and sick as well, I had to care for myself; for each thing, food or drink, they brought me on a ladder which they left near the opening [into the granary] which they closed again immediately, and I had to get out of bed to fetch them. I was alone, day and night, and all this time I had unreal visions and hallucinations. If I stayed alive, this was by the grace of God who must have taken pity and given me the strength to recover my health. The fever diminished day by day, only at the spot where the abscess was it burned like fire and my face was still red. One day, our gentile neighbors, who had noticed my absence, began to say to each other: "Look what these Jews have done: one of the children is surely dead of the plague and they have concealed it. As good servants of the count, we will go and tell him, and take our revenge on the Jews." When this rumor reached our family, my father ordered me to get dressed, to wrap my neck in a cotton cloth in such a way that people should not see the redness. He enjoined me to be brave, and to cross the garden, the fields, and return along the river, passing by the houses of the gentiles and by the castle. If they asked me where I was coming from, I had to say that I was coming home from the school where I had stayed with a schoolmaster from the village of Menain, around three kilometers away, and where I would have liked to return. I acquitted myself of this task, and thanks to God I jumped and ran like a young puppy, passing by the villages and the castle, I was seen by a great number of Christians who were ashamed, and whose conspiracy unraveled. Many of our neighbors came to my father's shop to tell him: "Your son, whom we thought dead, has returned." He answered them: "You are the dead ones, but we, we shall live for eternity."

In the year 5441 [1680], at the beginning of the month of Tishri [September], the epidemic stopped in Prague, but it spread so in the rest of Bohemia that people no longer came near each other. In our village a great number of people of the castle fell ill and died . . . By the end of Kislev [December–January], the plague had decimated our quarter of town, and many Jews were dead. In certain villages, the entire masculine population was dead and only the women remained. There was no one left to care for the dead, who could not be buried because it was winter and the ground was as hard as marble and covered with a thick layer of snow; so they covered them with snow, but the wolves often came to eat the cadavers, and sometimes dogs scratched in the snow covering the bodies. May God have pity on these souls, and may they be reunited in the light of the living with the souls of all the Just.

## RULINGS AND PRACTICES OF THE SAGES OF OUR COMMUNITY OF PRAGUE, ISSUED IN THE MONTH OF TISHRI 5372 [1611]

A Prague ruling of 1611: I. Rivkind, *Reshumot*

And here, in the month of Tishri 372, by the shorter calculation, we have gathered together to review what is happening within our holy community. For several days now we have observed a great number of misfortunes around us, as well as terrible dread, the most recent being lives cut short. For a considerable number of people and children, boys and girls, have died, and they say that surely our sins have brought this upon us. Perhaps there are hidden sins, and we have decided in God's name, and so that He may relent and take pity on those of us who remain and heal our dear ones, it has thus been decided with the consent of our holy community, to issue a law that must be respected by all those within the gates of our town who must observe it down to its precise details, which will be clarified below. Any person who would violate a single detail will be punished by terrible sanctions, by decision of the community. The beadles will go to each synagogue to declare these rulings and verify that everyone understands. When we have found in the words of our Masters that scorn for the Torah, through the commission of sins, oaths, the absence of *mezuzah* and *tsitsit* cause the deaths of young children. . . .

On this subject it was decided to expel those women who sell [their bodies]. Let them depart while they are cursed by taking out the Torah scrolls; and in the future let no woman go alone to the houses of the gentiles, nor inside houses [of prostitution] open in the street. And let [no woman] ever again go to a room. Let her refuse to go there unless her husband accompanies her inside, or at least a valet or an adolescent. And that woman who would not let the husband or adolescent accompany her inside the room, or the woman who goes into this room with her husband or an adolescent and then expels or orders them to leave; then let her leave as well and not sell the slightest thing. Let no woman go alone to the house of a gentile. Under pain of incurring all the maledictions in the Torah, and let them be formally cursed [if they do it anyway].

And if, despite this, there is still a woman who dares to transgress these rulings, let her first be punished by a heavy fine of 20 gold gulden, to which she shall be held by the directors. . . . If the adolescent has left the room and she remains there, let the adolescent be punished as well by the same sanction and held to it by the directors in the same way. . . . Therefore, if a woman is found who . . . let her also be punished and in addition cursed with all the maledictions, and let the fines be heavy enough to cause her pain. . . . And let half of this fine be immediately paid by the husband thus constrained, as if he were as guilty as she. For we have decreed and pronounced the cessation of such license. And let no one be spared who would commit these great sins. . . . And let each woman remember in the Name [of God], and her soul, her dignity, and her children. And let their husbands or their good friends keep watch that they do not transgress [this ruling]. In any event, let those women who would not respect [the ruling] or disregard it be cursed.

Regarding young girls who stroll in the street at any time of the day or night, whether they are local girls or strangers, from today and in the future they may no longer do so alone. Neither during the day and even less at night, under pain of [incurring] a heavy fine and all the maledictions in the Torah. Let them guard their dignity, modesty, and virtue. When a young girl is sent somewhere, let her not dally in the street, and let her not stay there, even to listen or speak. Therefore any girl who would be seen strolling day or night in the street, whether a local girl or a domestic, stranger or not, will be liable to a heavy sanction and a fine of ten gold hagirim. And let this girl be subjected to great humiliations, which will be painful and heavy for her. And let no one be spared, let them all be punished alike, so that no master of the house will again send a girl at night from house to distant house, and let him find another male to do it.

On the subject of prostitutes, from this day forward they may not be retained as wet nurses. Let them all leave our holy community, the eve of Rosh hodesh Heshvan 372 [the equivalent of November 1612]. And from this day forward no more of them will be found in our community. Let masters of the house who would violate this by keeping a prostitute in the house be fined ten gold hagirim for charity. And let him also be fined who would know that a prostitute is in any house of our holy community; let him denounce it to the directors. From this day forward if a prostitute is still found here, let the law be applied: let her be immediately arrested by the police and expelled from our holy community, and let her never return. And let all the people see this and know it.

Regarding those few people who abuse the law by conducting their business affairs even at the Ark. They imbibe idolatry [nonkosher wine] in our streets and frequent houses [of prostitution] and others who are not content with this but also want prostitutes in their own homes. This is no longer a simple transgression but a combination of great and serious sins [which carry] heavy consequences. These people shall not present themselves at any trial [in person], but they shall be given a real trial, and let these people be punished and let it be known what to tell them. Let fines and humiliations be inflicted on them, as well as terrible sanctions. Therefore, let these people cease these business dealings and behavior, and let them remember God, the Almighty, as well as the sanctions incurred for these sins. And let no one conceal anyone's sacrilege anywhere.

# Abbreviations

| | |
|---|---|
| *AZJ* | *Allgemeine Zeitung des Judentums* |
| *BJPES* | *Bulletin of the Jewish Palestine Exploration Society* |
| BT | Babylonian Talmud |
| *EJ* | *Encyclopaedia Judaïca* |
| *HDA* | *Handwörterbuch des deutschen Aberglaubens* |
| *HJ* | *Historia Judaïca* |
| *HUCA* | *Hebrew Union College Annual* |
| *JB* | *Judaïca Bohemiae* |
| *JGJC* | *Jahrbuch der Gesellschaft für Geschichte der Juden in der Cechoslovakischen Republik* |
| *JJLG* | *Jahrbuch der Jüdisch-literarischen Gesellschaft* |
| JMP | Jewish Museum of Prague |
| *JQR* | *Jewish Quarterly Review* (O.S. and N.S., old and new series, respectively) |
| JT | Jerusalem Talmud |
| *Jub.A* | *Jubiläumsausgabe Moses Mendelssohns gesammelten Schriften* |
| *MGJV* | *Mitteilungen der Gesellschaft für jüdische Volkskunde* |
| *MGWJ* | *Monatsschrift für Geschichte und Wissenschaft des Judentums* |
| *MJVK* | *Mitteilungen zur jüdischen Volkskunde* |
| *REJ* | *Revue des Études Juives* |
| *RHR* | *Revue de l'Histoire des Religions* |
| *ZGJD* | *Zeitschrift für die Geschichte der Juden in Deutschland* |
| *ZGJT* | *Zeitschrift für die Geschichte der Juden in der Tschechoslowakei* |

# Notes

## INTRODUCTION

1. Der Nistor, *La Famille Machber* (Paris, 1975), 2:98–102.
2. Philippe Ariès, *The Hour of Our Death* (L'Homme devant la mort), trans. Helen Weaver (New York, 1981), 573.
3. The essential works are Ariès, *The Hour of Our Death*; Pierre Chaunu, *La Mort à Paris* (Paris, 1978); Robert Favre, *La Mort dans la littérature et la pensée française au siècle des Lumières* (Lyon, 1978); Edgar Morin, *L'Homme et la mort dans l'histoire* (Paris, 1970); Louis-Vincent Thomas, *Anthropologie de la mort* (Paris, 1975); Michel Vovelle, *Mourir autrefois* (Paris, 1970).

## CHAPTER 1. FROM THE UNIVERSAL TO THE PARTICULAR

1. See Zacharia Frankel, *Entwurf einer Geschichte der Literatur der nachtalmudischen Responsen* (Berlin, 1865); Solomon B. Freehof, *The Responsa Literature* (New York, 1955).
2. French and German Responsa: *Teshuvot ḥakhmei Tsarfat ve-Loter* (1881), *Sefer ha-Yashar* (1898).
3. A decision attributed to Rabbi Gershom *Me'or ha-Golah,* the "light of the exile."
4. Moses Isserles, called the Rama (1525–1572), *Darkhei Mosheh*; A. Siev, *Ha-Rama* (1957). Bibliography of works of the Rama, in *Talpiot* (1949), 4: 743–758; (1950–1952), 5:244–287, 649–668; (1953–1955), 6:321–335, 723–729; (1964), 9:314–342.
5. Solomon ben Jehiel Luria, the *Maharshal* (1510?–1574), *Yam shel Shlomoh; Ḥochmat Shlomoh,* S. Hurwitz, *The Responsa of Solomon Luria* (New

York, 1938), Schulvas, in Israel Halperin, *Bet Yisrael be-Polin,* vol. 2 (Jerusalem, 1954). H. Tchernowitz, *Toledot ha-Poskim* (1947), 3:74–91.

6. In the rabbinic literature: *Leviticus Rabbah* 1:14; *Yevamot* 49b; *Exodus Rabbah* 29:6; *Tanḥuma,* Yitro 11. In the Mishnah, the source is *Avot* 1. JT *Shekalim* 6:49; *Sotah* 8:22d, etc. Maimonides (1135–1204), *Guide of the Perplexed* (1857, 1979). Ḥasdai Crescas (15th c.), *Bittul Ikkarei ha-Notsrim* (1451).

7. In particular, by Maimonides; on this subject, see Ralph Lerner, "Maimonides' Treatise on Resurrection," in *History of Religions* (Chicago, 1983), 23:140–155. Also, for the previous period, George F. Moore, *Judaism in the First Centuries of the Christian Era* (Cambridge, 1950); Louis Finkelstein, *The Pharisees* (Philadelphia, 1946); A. Marmorstein, *Studies in Jewish Theology* (London, 1950).

8. Mircea Éliade, *Histoire des croyances et des idées religieuses* (Paris, 1983), 163.

9. *Baba Batra* 16a.

10. Under the reign of Antiochus IV Epiphany.

11. *Sanhedrin* 10:1.

12. The blessing at the beginning of the *Amidah,* which dates from the period of the Temple, is recited at each of the three daily services.

13. JT *Kilaim* 9:4, 32c; *Ketubot* 12:3, 35b; BT *Ketubot* 11a; *Sanhedrin* 90b; see *Koheleth Rabbah* 1–4.

14. Referring again to the controversy raised by Maimonides with the *Mishneh Torah,* "*Teshuva,*" 8:2. In French, "Épître sur la résurrection des morts," in *Epîtres* (Paris, 1983), 115–158; Naḥmanides, *Torat ha-Adam*; Ḥasdai Crescas, *Or Adonai,* III, A, 4.

15. This process was defined by Gershom Scholem, *The Messianic Idea in Judaism* (New York, 1971).

16. Ariès, *The Hour of Our Death,* 29–92.

17. Jacques Le Goff, *La Naissance du Purgatoire* (Paris, 1981), 9.

18. Second and third centuries.

19. For the most part, I have used the excellent bilingual edition (English–Hebrew) by Dov Zlotnick, *The Tractate Mourning (Semaḥot)* (New Haven, 1966).

20. Éliade, *Histoire des croyances,* 163.

21. Zlotnick, *Semaḥot,* chap. 8, sec. 1.

22. Zlotnick, *Semaḥot,* chap. 6, sec. 1.

23. Zlotnick, *Semaḥot,* chap 9, sec. 2.

24. Zlotnick, *Semaḥot,* chap. 8, sec. 1–7.

25. Zlotnick, *Semaḥot,* chap. 8, sec. 7.

26. See S. Yeivin, "The Origin of an Ancient Jewish Burial Custom," *BJPS* 8, no. 1 (1940): 22–27, cited by Zlotnick, *Semaḥot,* 16.

27. G. Alon, *BJPS* 8, no. 3 (1941): 107–112, and in *Meḥkarim* 2:99–105.

28. Zlotnick, *Semaḥot,* chap. 2, sec. 2.

29. It is noteworthy that the period of one year corresponds to the period of observance of family mourning for the death of a close relative.

30. J. Finegan, *Light from the Ancient Past* (Princeton, 1946), 353–398;

A. G. Barrots, *Manuel d'archéologie biblique* (Paris, 1953), 2:274–323; Jean-Baptiste Frey, *Corpus inscriptionum iudaïcorum* (Europe) (The Vatican, 1936).

31. Yehiel M. Tukacinski, *Gesher ha-Ḥayim* (Jerusalem, 1960), 1:276–282, 2:183–191. Yekutiel Greenwald, *Kol-bo al Avelut* (Jerusalem, 1947), 1: 223–249; (1951), 2:75–94; reissued in one volume (Jerusalem, New York, 1973).

32. Zlotnick, *Semaḥot,* chap. 2, sec. 11–13.

33. The prayer Shema Yisrael, the three paragraphs of which are excerpts from the Pentateuch (Deut. 6:4–9; Deut. 11:13–21; Num. 15:37–41), proclaims the affirmation of divine unity; it is recited daily, morning and evening, and is also an integral part of the holiday services. *Tefillah* is prayer; it consists of the three daily services. Tefillin, or phylacteries, are the leather straps attached to two boxes containing four biblical texts (Exod. 13:1–10, 11–16; Deut. 6:4–9, 11:13–21) that a man winds around his left arm and forehead before reciting the morning prayers on weekdays.

34. A vaulted cave, dug in the wall of the cemetery.

35. Zlotnick, *Semaḥot,* chap. 13, sec. 1–8.

36. *Nehemiah* 2:3; JT *Sanhedrin* 10:4, 29c.

37. *Koheleth* 12:5; *Koheleth Rabbah* 10:9; *Targum Isaiah* 40:11; *Moed Katan* 80b.

38. Job 30:23.

39. JT *Shekalim* 1:1, the source of the expression "a whited sepulchre" used in the New Testament.

40. *Ḥagigah* 3b; *Nidah* 17a.

41. JT *Baba Batra* 2, 9.

42. *Baba Batra* 58a.

43. *Sanhedrin* 96b; Matthew 23:29.

44. Macc. 13:27–29; JT *Shekalim* 1:1; 2:5.

45. *Eruvim* 55b, 5a.

46. *Genesis Rabbah* 82:10; JT *Shekalim* 2:7, 47a.

47. *Horayot* 13b.

48. 1 Kings 13:30.

49. Jeremiah 22:18.

50. Zlotnick, *Semaḥot,* chap. 7, sec. 13–14.

51. The *lulav* is composed of a palm branch, accompanied by myrtle and willow, as well as by the *etrog* (citron), which form the "four kinds" used during the holiday of Sukkot, the festival of "booths."

52. G. I. Ascoli, "Inscrizioni inedite o mai note Greche, Latine, Hebraiche, di antichi sepolcri giudaici del Napolitano," *Actes du IVe Congrès des orientalistes* (Turin, 1880).

53. Moise Schwab, *Rapport sur les inscriptions hébraïques de la France. Nouvelles archives scientifiques* (Paris, 1904), 169–174.

54. Joseph Derenbourg, in *Revue des études juives* 2 (1882): 131.

55. See Schwab's inventory (see n. 53). See also Gérard Nahon, "L'Epigraphie," in *Art et archéologie des juifs en France médiévale* (Toulouse, 1980), 95–132; and Nahon, *Inscriptions hébraiques et juives de France médiévale* (Paris, 1986).

56. Reproduced by Louis Wirth, *Le Ghetto* (Grenoble, 1980), 43–44; American edition, *The Ghetto* (Chicago, 1956).

57. Nahon, "L'Épigraphie," and "Les cimetières," in *Art et archéologie,* 73, citing Eugene Bimbenet, *Histoire de la ville d'Orléans* (Orléans, 1887), 175.

58. JT *Baba Battra* 2:9.

59. BT *Baba Batra* 58a.

60. *Genesis Rabbah* 82:10; JT *Shekalim* 2:7, 47a.

61. See "*Avel*" 4:4.

62. Ariès, *The Hour of Our Death,* 47.

63. Louis De Grandmaison, "Quelques notes relatives au cimetière que les juifs possédaient à Tours au XIIIe siècle," *Bulletin de la Société archéologique de Touraine* 7 (1886–1888).

64. See the councils of Vannes in 465, of Agde in 506, of Épone in 517, of Orléans in 533, of Clermont in 535, of Mâcon in 583, etc., and Léon Poliakov, *Histoire de l'antisémitisme* (Paris, 1955), 1:43, for additional data.

65. Grégoire de Tours, *Histoire des Francs,* 2 vols. (Paris, 1963).

66. Robert Anchel, *Les Juifs de France* (Paris, 1946), 24.

67. "Épîtres antijuives," in Bernhard Blumenkranz, *Les Auteurs chrétiens latins du Moyen Age* (Paris, 1963), 152–170; Adrien Bressolles, *Saint Agobard, évêque de Lyon* (Paris, 1949).

68. Gregory of Tours cites five Jews, when he refers to "Jews," but never evokes a community. See *Histoire des Francs,* 1:7. The first numerical evaluation would be that of Benjamin of Tudela, who reckons a figure of two million souls, the majority from Islamic lands; see *Sefer ha-Massaot,* republished by A. Ben Ascher, 1840; Marcus Nathan Adler, *The Itinerary of Benjamin of Tudela* (Malibu, 1907). See Eliakim Carmoly, *Notice historique sur Benjamin de Tudèle* (Paris, 1852). A demographic table indicates 450,000 Jews in 1300 for the countries of western Europe: 100,000 in France and Avignon; 100,000 in the Holy Roman Empire; 50,000 in Italy; 150,000 in Spain, Castille, Navarre and Aragon; 40,000 in Portugal; 5,000 in Poland and Lithuania; 5,000 in Hungary. In *EJ* 13:878.

69. Wirth, *Le Ghetto.*

70. Ratisbonne: Wittmann, *Quellen und Erörterungen zur bayerischen und deutschen Geschichte,* vols. 1, 2 (1856). Cologne: Charter of the Archbishop Hermann, 9 October 1091. T. J. Lacomblet, *Niederkheim Urkundenbuch* (1850), 1:158n. 245. Worms: in *Germania judaica* (Breslau, 1934, 1963), 1:444n. 103. Nîmes: Chartulary of Nîmes, 277n. 171.

## CHAPTER 2. A DISTINCTIVE HISTORY

1. Rashi would be the best example.

2. Jean Delumeau, *La Peur en Occident* (Paris, 1978), in particular the chapter, "Les juifs, mal absolu," 273–304.

3. Fernand Braudel, *La Méditerranée et le monde méditerranéen* (Paris, 1966), 2:11. [*The Mediterranean and the Mediterranean World in the Age of Philip II,* trans. Sian Reynolds (New York, 1972).]

4. Guido Kisch, *The Jews in Medieval Germany* (Chicago, 1949); also James Parkes, *The Jew in the Medieval Community: A Study of His Political and Economic Situation* (New York, 1976).

5. Among the most widely disseminated works, we can compare two of them. The *Sachsenspiegel,* established by Eike von Repgow of Anhalt (1221–1224), was composed in two parts, constituting territorial and feudal laws. The *Landrecht,* II, 66, 1; III, 1, 2, 7, 14, deals systematically with Jewish law, demonstrating the establishment of Jews in Thuringian Saxony and their economic importance in Eastphalia in the middle of the thirteenth century. The Judaic laws of the *Miroir saxon* concern the particular position of the Jews as well as the theoretical analysis of their legal treatment and its justification, without spreading the influence of the Canon. See J. C. Hirsch, *Eike von Repgow: Der Sachsenspiegel (Landrecht), in unserer heutigen Muttersprache übertragen und dem deutschen Volke erklärt* (Berlin and Leipzig, 1936). The *Schwabenspiegel,* compiled at Augsburg in 1274–1275 is, by contrast, saturated with anti-Judaism. Its Judaic laws are based on the Canon and medieval literature, especially Franciscan, and this work is the example of the integration of the Canon into secular laws concerning the Jews. It validates the notions of *servitus judaeorum* and *servi camerae,* nonexistent in the *Sachsenspiegel.* See Wilhelm Wackernagel, *Der Schwabenspiegel in der ältesten Gestalt mit den Abweichungen der gemeinen Texte und den Zusätzen derselben* (Zurich, 1840).

6. *Meissener Rechtsbuch,* Friedrich Ortloff, *Das Rechtsbuch nach Distinctionen (Meissener Rechtsbuch) nebst einem eisenachischen Rechtsbuch* (Jena, 1836), 1: III, chap. 17.

7. Or those of Ottokar of Bohemia in 1268, of Duke Bolo I of Silesia, and of Casimir the Great in 1343.

8. Ortloff, *Meissener Rechtsbuch* 1: III, chaps. 1–3.

9. Ortloff, *Meissener Rechtsbuch* 1: III, chaps. 17–28; XVII, chaps. 36–37.

10. Ortloff, *Meissener Rechtsbuch* 1: III, chaps. 17–45.

11. Ortloff, *Meissener Rechtsbuch* 1: III, chaps. 17–45.

12. Ortloff, *Meissener Rechtsbuch* 1: III; XVII, chaps. 41–43.

13. See Wirth, *Le Ghetto.*

14. See the *Meissener Rechtsbuch* and also Julius Aronius, *Regesten zur Geschichte der Juden in fränkischen und deutschen Reiche bis zum Jahre 1273* (Berlin, 1887–1902).

15. See note 5, above.

16. *Sachsenspiegel,* 1. II, 13, 5.

17. *Schwabenspiegel,* Art. G: 207, 4; Art. L: 253a.

18. *Sachsenspiegel,* 1. II, 71, 3.

19. A. M. Habermann, *Sefer gezerot Ashkenaz ve-Tsarfat* (Jerusalem, 1946); Heinrich Graetz, *History of the Jews* (London, 1891), 3: 297–310; Ismar Elbogen, *Geschichte der Juden in Deutschland* (Berlin, 1935), 102; Marvin Lowenthal, *The Jews of Germany* (New York, 1936), 36; Leopold Zunz, *The Sufferings of the Jews During the Middle Ages* [a translation of *Die synagogale Poesie des Mittelalters* (Berlin, 1855)] (New York, 1907).

20. Adolf Neubauer and Moritz Stern, *Hebraische Berichte uber die*

*Judenverfolgerungen während der Kreuzzüge*; *Quellen zur Geschichte der Juden in Deutschland,* Fritz Isaac Baer, ed., vol. 2 (Berlin, 1892). Samuel Steinherz, "Kreuzfahrer und Juden in Prag 1096," *Jahrbuch der Gesellschaft für Geschichte der Juden in der Cechoslovakishen Republik* 1 (1929): 16; Ismar Elbogen, Marcus Brann, Aron Freimann, and Haïm Tykocinski, "Von den ätesten Zeiten bis 1238," *Germania judaica* (Breslau, 1934, 1963), 1:508–512.

21. Isaac Ben Moses of Vienna (1180–1250). (Zhitomir edition, 1862; Jerusalem, 1887–1890).

22. 1160–1230. See Aronius, *Regesten zur Geschichte der Juden,* and Habermann, *Sefer Gezerot Ashkenaz.* See the bibliography of Kisch, *The Jews in Medieval Germany,* 567–605.

23. Called the *Maharam*; see Hirsch Jacob Zimmels, *Beiträge zur Geschichte der Juden in Deutschland im 13. Jahrhundert* (Vienna, 1926).

24. Blumenkranz, *Les Auteurs chrétiens latins*; and M. Valecillo Avila, "Los judíos de Castilla en la alta Edad media," *Guadernos de Historia de España* (1950): 24.

25. Moritz Güdemann, *Geschichte des Erziehungswesens und der Cultur des Juden in Frankreich und Deutschland. (X–XV Jahrhundert)* (Vienna, 1880).

26. Johan von Buch, *Glos,* Augsburg edition, 1516, p. 125v, "Unde Juden"; K. Eckardt and A. Hubner, "Deutschenspiegel und Augsburger Sachsenspiegel," *Monumenta Germaniae historica: Fontes iuris germanici antiqui,* n.s., 3 (1933).

27. Joseph ha-Cohen, *Emek ha-Bakḥa* (1558; Vienna edition, 1852); in French, *La Vallée des pleurs,* trans. J. P. Osier (Paris, 1980).

28. Before the fall of the fortress in 72 B.C.E., the 960 Zealots who had sought refuge there committed suicide, according to the narrative of Flavius Josephus, in *The Jewish War,* 1. VII, 9, 1.

29. Hannah is one of the legendary figures among the Jewish heroic martyrs. She encouraged her seven sons to choose death rather than foreswear their convictions and submitted to the same fate herself, in 167–166 B.C.E. See 2 Macc. 7.

30. See Yosef H. Yerushalmi, *Zakhor: Jewish History and Jewish Memory.* (Seattle, 1982).

31. The shofar is the ram's horn blown by the cantor on Rosh Hashanah, Yom Kippur, and during the preceding month of Elul. The Book of Esther is read during the festival of Purim.

32. Rhindfleisch left his name to the massacres he instigated in 1298. See Heinrich B. Graetz, *Geschichte der Juden von den ältesten Zeiten bis auf die Gegenwart* (Leipzig, 1853–1875), 7:232; Simon Dubnow, *Weltgeschichte des judischen Volkes von seinen Uranfängen bis zur Gegenwart* (Berlin, 1927–1930), 5:175–176.

33. One of the three so-called pilgrim festivals, during which people came to the Temple. This is the holiday of Weeks corresponding to the Christian Pentecost.

34. The Maharil (?1360–1427) is considered, along with the Rama, Moses Isserles, to be the great codifier of the laws of Ashkenazi Judaism.

35. Siegmund Salfeld, "Das Martyrologium des nuernberger Memorbuches" (Berlin, 1898).

36. On this subject, see Israel Levi's analysis in *Revue des études juives* 29 (1894): 43, in which he shows how little proof we have of the use of this text in the Jewish customs preceding the period of the Geonim, before the second century.

37. Frey, *Corpus inscriptionum iudaïcorum,* vol. 1, no. 725, 10–11.

38. *Horayot* 6a; JT *Sanhedrin* 10:4, 29c; *Sifrei Deuteronomy* 210; *Tanḥuma Bereshit* 1.

39. *Sofrim* 10:7.

40. A collection of liturgy and codifications composed by Simḥa ben Samuel of Vitry, a contemporary of Rashi, in the twelfth century. See S. Hurwitz, ed., *Maḥzor Vitry le-rabbenu Simḥah* (1923).

41. *Sefer Ḥasidim* (Basel, 1581; Jerusalem, 1957), sec. 722; in French, see the presentation of Edouard Gourévitch, *Le Guide des Ḥassidim* (Paris, 1988).

42. See S. A. Goldberg, *Du deuil public au deuil privé,* unpublished manuscript, École des Hautes Études en Sciences Sociales (EHESS), Paris, 1982. [The burial Kaddish referred to here is no longer much used in the United States because of the difficulty of the Aramaic.]

43. Numerous examples of this expression are found in Yiddish literature. Shalom An-Ski (his real name is Solomon Zainwill Rapaport, 1863–1920), "Der Toyt in dem yiddishen Folksgloybn," in *Filologishe Shriftn,* 3, 89–100 (Vilna, 1929).

44. Moses Gaster, "The Sinner Who Was Released From Hell Through the Kaddish Prayer of His Son," in *Ma'aseh Book* (Philadelphia, 1934, 1981), 286.

45. Yehuda the ḥasid, the central character of the *Sefer,* is a descendant of the Kalonymus dynasty.

46. Fritz Isaac Baer, "Religious Social Tendancy of the Sefer Ḥassidim," in *Zion* 3 (1938): 1–50.

47. Gershom Scholem, *Major Trends in Jewish Mysticism* (New York, 1946); paperback edition, (1965), 83.

48. Scholem, *Major Trends in Jewish Mysticism,* 88.

49. Scholem, *Major Trends in Jewish Mysticism,* 92.

50. *Sefer Ḥasidim,* sec. 976.

51. *Sefer Ḥasidim,* sec. 222.

52. Gaster, "Repent One Day Before Thy Death," *Ma'aseh Book,* 13–16.

53. *Sefer Ḥasidim,* sec. 37, 53; Eleazar, *Hilkhot Teshuvah*; *Sefer Yoreh Ḥataim*; I. Nekawa, *Menorat ha-Maor,* Enelow edition, III:113–119; Scholem, *Major Trends in Jewish Mysticism,* 371.

54. *Sefer Ḥasidim,* sec. 1556. It seems generally that the popular dissemination of the teachings of the *Sefer Ḥasidim* was accomplished through collections of edifying stories such as the *Maysse Bukh,* in Yiddish, of which Gaster (see n. 44, above) has done an excellent English translation.

## CHAPTER 3. WHEN THE SPECIFIC IS THE GENERAL RULE

1. Norbert Élias, *La Solitude des mourants* (Paris, 1987), 14.

2. Schottky, "The Rights of the Jews," *Prag wie es war und wie es ist* (Prague, 1910), 315.

3. Joshua Trachtenberg, *The Devil and the Jews* (New Haven, 1943).
4. Delumeau, *La Peur en Occident,* 98.
5. Bull of 26 July 1348.
6. Chronicler of *The Life of the Emperors,* in Schottky, *Prag wie es war,* 316.
7. Decisions by the Archbishop Ernest, in 1348, ratified by the synod of Prague in 1349, in the course of which it was also decreed that the Jews could no longer serve Christians and that no additional synagogue would be constructed henceforth. See Schottky, *Prag wie is war.*
8. These engravings depict the visit of Ferdinand I to Prague in 1527.
9. Description by Aneas Sylvius Piccolomini, better known as Pope Pius II, in his *History of Bohemia.*
10. Avigdor Kara, son of Isaac Kara, president of the rabbinic court of Prague, was one of the most eminent men of his time.
11. A. Kara, *Et Kol ha-Tela'a,* cited in Anton Blaschka, "Die judische Gemeinde zur Ausgang des Mittelalters," in Samuel Steinherz, ed., *Die Juden in Prag* (Prague, 1927), 58–80.
12. See also Koppelmann Lieben, *Sefer Gal Ed* (Prague, 1856), sec. 15.
13. From which numerous historians have drawn information, although their narrative logic is not always clear and they indulge in certain chronological or historical fantasies, as G. Dobner, "Wenceslas Hajek a Liboczam," *Annales Bohemorum* (1761–1782), and Franz Palacky, "Würdignung der alten böhmischen Geschichtsschreiber," *Geschichte Böhmen* 1:84n. 30, 162, 179, have demonstrated. See Steinherz, *Die Juden in Prag,* 10n. 44.
14. The legends of the Prague Jews were collected in the nineteenth century, though it was not established whether they were all based on oral histories circulating in the community or, more prosaically, imagined by their compositor. Lowit edition, *Sippurim: Prager Sammlung Jüdischer Legenden* (Vienna and Leipzig, 1921).
15. W. Hajeck, *Böhmischer Chronik* (1541), 156, cited in Schottky, *Prag wie es war* 1:312. Also see Leopold Schnitzler, *Die prager Judendeutsch, ein beitrag zur Erforhung des Älteren Prager Jüdendeutsch in Lautlicher und insbesondere in lexikalischer Beziehung* (Munich, 1966), introduction.
16. Dalimil, "Reimschronik," 1309, in *Fontes rerum bohemicarum,* vol. 3, cited in Steinherz, *Die Juden in Prag.*
17. Cosmas, in *Monumentum Germaniae historica,* section "*Scriptores,*" 1. III: 205, in Steinherz, *Die Juden in Prag.*
18. The only earlier Jewish writings from Prague are a collection of responsa: the *Or Zarua,* which are related to the *Sefer Ḥasidim* and contain commentaries by Rashi and rabbinic responses but little historical information. See Vladimir Sadek, "Réponses de rabbins," in *Judaïca Bohemiae* 20, no. 1 (1984): 31–43.
19. Statements by Jan Huss, cited in F. Palacky, *Urkündliche Beiträge zur Geschichte des Hussitenkrieges* (Prague, 1873).
20. The Hussite credo is based on the "four articles of Prague," which demand free preaching, two kinds of communion, the repression of cardinal sins, and the secularization of Church property by confiscation. It is noteworthy, in

addition, that the term "*praguerie*" thereafter becomes synonymous, in French popular speech, with "revolution."

21. On 9 March 1422, the "tramps," taking their authority from the millenarian or chiliastic movement and entrenched at Tabor in a religious community meant to reinstitute the Empire of Christ, were defeated.

22. Procopius, Zysca's successor, was thus able to liberate the towns of Bamberg and Leipzig in 1430.

23. They would have been bought by the priest, according to Josef Macek, *Le Mouvement hussite en Bohême* (Prague, 1965).

24. I can cite the following: E. Schwartz, *JGJC* 5 (1953): 429–437; Ruth Kestenberg-Gladstein, *JGJC* 8 (1963): 25, and *JB* 4 (1968): 64–68; Salo W. Baron, *A Social and Religious History of the Jews* (New York, 1937, 1960), 2, 3:209–216; Ḥaim Hillel Ben Sasson, *Divrei ha-Akademia ha-leumit le-Madda'im* 4 (1969–1970): 66–69; Ben Sasson, "Jews and Christian Sectarians: Existential Similarity and Dialectical Tensions in Sixteenth-Century Moravia and Poland Lithuania," *Viator* 4 (1973): 369–387; Ben Sasson, "The Social Ideals of Jewry," in *A History of the Jewish People,* ed. Ben Sasson (Cambridge, 1976), 691–727.

25. See, in particular, the polemic on this subject between J. Katz, "Al Halakhah u-Derush Ke-Makor Histori," *Tarbiz* 30 (1960–1961): 62–72; and H. H. Ben Sasson, "Musagim u-Metsiut ba-Historia ha-Yehudit be-Shelahei Yemei ha-Beinaim," *Tarbiz* 30 (1960–1961): 297–312.

26. See above, notes 10, 11.

27. Ben Sasson, *Divrei.*

28. Ben Sasson, *Divrei*; the reference is to *Eḥad yaḥid meyuḥad.*

29. As does A. Blaschka, *Die judische,* 67.

30. See David Ganz, *Tsemaḥ David* (Frankfurt, 1692), and Joseph ha-Cohen, *La Vallée des pleurs,* 87–88.

31. This treatise is sometimes interpreted as a Hussite desire to convert the Jews, as their social integration can be perceived as a conversion to Christianity. On this subject, see S. A. Goldberg, "Le Concours de l'Académie de Metz," *Étude de deux cimetières juifs à Paris au XVIII*[e] *siècle,* unpublished (Paris, VIII, 1980–1981), 114–125; C. W. Dohm, *De la réforme politique des juifs* (1782; French edition: D. Bourel [Paris, 1984]).

32. Israel Isserlein (1390–1460), "Responsa" on the harmonious relations between Jews and Christians in *Pesakim u-Khetavim, Terumat ha-Deshen* (Venice, 1519); see Joseph Ben Moses, in *Leket Yosher* (Freimann edition, 1903–1904).

33. Israel Bruna (1400–1480), *Responsa* (Salonika, 1788), in *Leket Yosher.*

34. Jacob Weil (first part of 15th century), *Responsa* (Venice, 1523).

35. Yom Tov Lipman Muelhausen (14th–15th c.), noted polemicist of his era, describes and comments on the Hussite wars. *Sefer Nitsaḥon,* 1390 (Altdorf, 1644; Amsterdam, 1701); see David Kaufman, "Rabbi Yom Tov Lipman Muelhausen," *Studies in Bibliography and Booklore* 1, no. 2 (1953): 60–68; Moshe Frank, *Kehillot Ashkenaz u-Vatei Dineihen* (Tel Aviv, 1938); Shlomo Eidelberg, *Jewish Life in Austria in the Fifteenth Century* (Philadelphia, 1962).

36. Jan Herman, "La communauté juive et sa structure au commencement des temps modernes," *JB* 5 (1969): 31–70; Otto Muneles, *The Prague Ghetto in the Renaissance Period* (Prague, 1965); André Neher, *David Gans: Disciple du Maharal de Prague* (Paris, 1974).

37. Who in addition translated the *History of Bohemia* by Piccolomini and lived during the reign of Vladislav Jagellon.

38. The medieval history of the Jewish community of Prague is closely associated with its payments to the powers that be; there was a continuous struggle between the royal authorities and the civic government, each attempting to claim these revenues by turns. See S. A. Goldberg, "La communauté juive de Prague jusqu'au XVIe siècle," *Les Institutions de la mort: Perceptions, vision et gestion de l'au-dela dans la vie quotidienne des juifs avant leur emancipation (Prague jusqu'a la fin du XVIIIe siècle)* (Ph.D. diss., Paris, 1986), 67–92.

39. Ernest Denis, *Huss et les guerre des hussites* (Paris, 1890), 469–470.

40. Which augured a certain respect for their autonomy. See K. Doskocil, *Lisky a listiny/z/ dejin Ceskoslovenska,* "Nase narodni minulost v dokumenkesch," cited by V. L. Tapie, *Monarchies et peuples du Danube* (Paris, 1969), 446n. 2.

41. Ernest Denis, *La Fin de l'indépendance de la Bohême* (Paris, 1890, 1930), 2:75. According to him, the Reformation passed through Bohemia more out of dogmatic ignorance than conviction.

42. Despite Ferdinand's attempts to subject Moravia to the Counter-Reformation, it remained the home of religious tolerance, a refuge for Calixtines, Neo-Utraquists, partisans of the German or Swiss Reformation, members of the Unity of Brothers; and German, Italian, and Antitrinitarian Anabaptists. See Josef Macek and Robert Mandrou, *Histoire de la Bohême* (Paris, 1984), 167. At the time of the election of Pius IV, Ferdinand would have demanded concessions on the dogmas of two kinds of communion, the marriage of priests, the celebration of the divine service in the vernacular, and the suppression of fast days. Bovory, *Antonin Brous de Muhelnitse,* 114, sec. 73, cited by Denis, *La Fin de l'indépendance,* 199.

43. Stansky, *Les Écoles à Prague,* 321, cited by Denis, *La Fin de l'indépendance,* 399.

44. Notably, the *Czech Grammar,* by Blaoslav, completed in 1571 and published in 1857 by Jiretchek.

45. Victor-Louis Tapie, *Monarchies et peuples du Danube* (Paris, 1969), 101; also, on the complete period 1608–1619: the *Mémoires de Guillaume Slavata* (Jiretchek edition, 1866), cited by Denis, *La fin de l'indépendance,* 287.

46. Yehuda Loew Ben Betsalel, called the Maharal and also referred to as *der hohe Rabbi Loew* (1525–1609), is one of the central figures of medieval Judaism, certainly as much for the breadth of his works (*Derekh hayim* [Cracow, 1589], *Netivot Olam* [Prague, 1596], *Tiferet Yisrael* [Prague, 1593], *Netsah Yisrael* [Prague, 1599], *Be'er ha-Gola* [Prague, 1598], *Gevurot ha-Shem* [Cracow, 1582], etc.) as for the myths that surround his personality. On this discussion, the source is David Ganz, *Tsemaḥ David* (Jerusalem, 1983), 145nn. 28–29; also Otto Muneles, *Prague Ghetto in the Renaissance Period* (Prague, 1965); André Neher, *Le Puits de l'exil* (Paris, 1966).

47. Chayim Bloch, *The Golem: Legends of the Ghetto of Prague* (Vienna,

1925); Y. Herzberg, *Yosele ha-Golem ve Yotsero Maharal mi-Prag* (Tel Aviv, 1947); Friedrich Thieberger, *The Great Rabbi Loew of Prague* (London, 1954); Gershom Scholem, *Sabbatai Ṣevi: The Mystical Messiah* (London, 1973); *On Kabbalah and Its Symbolism* (New York, 1965).

48. Denis, *La Fin de l'indépendance,* 410.

49. Denis, *La Fin de l'indépendance,* 443.

50. See *Mémoires de Guillaume Slavata* [in Czech] (Prague, 1866, 1868), and Paul Skala, *Histoire de la Bohême, 1602–1623* [in Czech] (Prague, 1873), both quoted in Denis, *La Fin de l'indépendance,* 468–469.

51. Denis, *La Fin de l'indépendance,* 510.

52. Ernest Denis, *La Bohême depuis la Montagne-Blanche* (Paris, 1903), 49.

53. Bylek, *La Contre-Reforme,* 45, cited by Denis, *La Bohême,* 71. With these confiscations, a great number of knights and lords changed their status and condition. From pillaging to decrees of expropriation, Bohemia was sacked during the Thirty Years War. Tapie, *Monarchies et peuples,* 112–113.

54. On this subject, see Ben Sasson, "Jews and Christian Sectarians," 385.

55. See Kestenberg-Gladstein, "*Bassevi of Treuenberg,*" *EJ* 5: 315–316; Simon Hock and David Kaufman, *Die Familien Prag, nach den Epigraphien des alten jüdischen Friedhofs in Prag* (Prague, 1892), 61, 63, 367n.75; Gotlieb Bondy and Franz Dvorsky, *Zur Geschichte der Juden in Böhmen, Mähren, Schliesen, von 906 bis 1620* (Prague, 1906), 2: nn. 734, 818, 824, 948, 1044–1045. Käthe Spiegel, "Die prager Juden zur Zeit des Dreissigjährenkrieges," in Steinherz, *Die Juden in Prag,* 107–186.

56. Hofman, in *Zeitschrift fur die Geschichte der Juden in der Tschechoslowakei* 4 (1934): 1–5; Pollack, *ZGJT* (1930–1931), 253–256; Baron, *A Social and Religious History,* 4: 231–232.

57. See David Ganz, *Tsemaḥ David* (1983 edition), 146–147; Jacob Rader Marcus, *The Jew in the Medieval World* (New York, 1938, 1978), 323–328; Max Margolis and Alexander Marx, *History of the Jewish People* (Philadelphia, 1927, 1962), 547–548. His fate illustrates the condition of the "court Jew" who could, during his lifetime, have the same prerogatives as the Christians but could not pass them on to his heirs upon his death or in case of disgrace. Upon Meisel's death in 1601, all his goods were confiscated despite the written guarantee that the emperor had conceded to him.

58. Muneles, *The Prague Ghetto,* 62.

59. Ganz, *Tsemaḥ David*; Ben Sasson, *Tarbiz* 29 (1959–1960): 376.

60. Denis, *La Fin de l'indépendance,* 2: 548.

61. Muneles, *The Prague Ghetto.*

62. Denis, *La Fin de l'indépendance,* 2: 543.

63. Tapie, *Monarchies et peuples,* 111.

64. Maurice Popper, "Les Juifs de Prague pendant la guerre de Trente Ans," *REJ* 29–30 (1894–1895): 79–93, 127–141. See also the guarding of the Jewish quarter in 1611, in Abraham David, *Kronika Ivrit mi-Prag: Me Reshit ha-Meah ha-Shevah esie* (Jerusalem, 1985), 24.

65. *Hanusah le-Ezrah* and *Arekhu ha-Yamim.*

66. See Gustav Klemperer, "*The Rabbis of Prague,*" *HJ* 12 (1950): 66n.53.

67. Denis, *La Bohême,* 349.

68. Popper, "Les Juifs de Prague," *REJ* (1895): 79.
69. Spiegel, "*Die Prager,*" in Steinherz, *Die Juden in Prag,* 125.
70. Popper, "Les Juifs de Prague," *REJ* (1895): 80.
71. Spiegel, in Steinherz, *Die Juden in Prag,* 121.
72. Archepiscopal Archives, March 1641; M. Popper, *REJ* (1895): 86n.5. K. Spiegel, in Steinherz, *Die Juden in Prag,* 132–133.
73. Spiegel, in Steinherz, *Die Juden in Prag,* 123.
74. Spiegel, in Steinherz, *Die Juden in Prag,* 175.
75. Spiegel, in Steinherz, *Die Juden in Prag,* 176.
76. Municipal Archives 133/47; Popper, *REJ* (1895): 85.
77. The locksmiths, clock makers, and arms makers obtain the privilege of forbidding the Jews to sell or manufacture their products (Municipal Archives 133/85); and we read, "The Jews import merchandise. Although they did not have the right to manufacture the merchandise they sell, they do it all the same. Foreign buyers come to Prague, the Jews are warned in advance; they run to meet them and sell them whatever they need, so that the Christians are left with nothing but the crumbs. The Christians are therefore unable to feed their families." Municipal Archives 133/55; see Popper, *REJ* (1895).
78. Preceding the sacking of Prague and the entrance of the imperial armies, the rumor circulated that the Jews would be spared. Reformed noblemen hoping to save their goods had left them with Jews, but as this was known, the Jews had to hand them over. M. Popper, *REJ* (1894): 130; H. Pollack, *Jewish Folkways in Germanic Lands* (London, 1971), 13.
79. In the course of his life Luther modified his opinion on the Jews. He had begun by taking their side against Christianity and the Papacy in *Dass Jesus Christus ein geborener Jude sei,* in 1523. However, by 1530 he inveighed against their practices of usury. In 1543, his *Schem ha-Mephorasch* would become a repertoire of insults and accusations against them, depicting the typical medieval *imaginaire* of Jews. See Alfred Falb, *Luther und die Juden* (Munich, 1921); James Parkes, *The Conflict of the Church and the Synagogue* (London, 1934); Hirsch Jacob Zimmels, *Beiträge zur Geschichte der Juden in Deutschland im 13. Jahrhundert* (Vienna, 1926).
80. Trachtenberg, *The Devil and the Jews.*
81. Léon Poliakov, *Histoire de l'antisémitisme* (Paris, 1955).
82. In fact, the Jews marched twice: to celebrate the entrance of the Emperor Ferdinand II of Prague, on 18 April 1623, they organized a procession that was described by the chronicle of Jan Beckowsky, *Manuscript of the Cross Convent.* In Czech. Rezek edition, Prague, 1879, 1880. Popper, *REJ* (1894): 135, and *REJ* (1895): 81–82.
83. Poliakov, *Histoire de l'antisémitisme,* 1: 243.
84. Yair Bacharach (1638–1702), *Ḥavvot Yaʾir,* 185, fo. 127b, see David Kaufman, "Jair Chayim Bacharach: A Biographical Sketch," *JQR* 3 (1891): 292–313; Solomon B. Freehof, *The Responsa Literature* (New York, 1955).
85. Published by Israel Halperin, *Constitutiones Congressus generalis Judaeorum Moraviensum, 1650–1748* (Jerusalem, 1952).
86. Otto Muneles, "From the Archives of the State Jewish Museum," *Jewish Studies* 1 (1965): 100.

87. Herman Pollack, *Jewish Folkways in Germanic Lands* (London, 1971), 12.

88. S. H. Lieben, "Die prager Brandtkatastrophen von 1689 und 1754," *Jahrbuch der Judisch-literarischen Gesellschaft* 28 (1926): 190–192. For a more detailed narrative: see Sylvie Anne Goldberg, "les Institutions de la mort: Perceptions, visions et question de l'au-délà dans la vie quotidienne des juifs avant leur émancipation (Prague jusqu'à la fin du xviiie siècle)," unpublished manuscript, Paris, 1986, 169–175. See Zwi Hirsch Ashkenazi, *Ḥakham Zwi* (Furth, 1767).

89. The so-called Chmielnicki Massacres (1648–1649) provoked a long period of tribulations and pogroms, and as a result the Polish Jews flocked en masse to the gates of the Jewish communities.

90. Herman, *JB* (1969): 35–36.

91. See Graetz, *History of the Jews*; Marcus, *The Jews in the Medieval World*; Margolis and Marx, *History of the Jewish People.*

92. Kisch, *The Jews in Medieval Germany.* See S. Goldberg, "Under Princely Law: From Armor to the Yellow Badge."

93. See Jan Herman, "La Communauté juive et sa structure au commencement des temps modernes," *JB* 5 (1969): 31-70.

94. Schottky, *Prague wie es war*; Anton Blaschka, "Die jüdische Gemeinde zur Ausgang des Mittelalters," in Steinherz, *Die Juden in Prag,* 76.

95. Yiddish literature is quite prolix on this subject, and it is mentioned in an almost systematic fashion: Der Nistor; I. J. and I. B. Singer; and the *Memoirs of Glückel of Hameln.*

96. Léon Lallemand, *Histoire de la charité* (Paris, 1910); Michel Mollat, ed., *Études sur l'histoire de la pauvreté,* 2 vols. (Paris, 1974).

97. Aaron J. Gurevitch, *Les Catégories de la culture médiévale* (Paris, 1983), 207. *Categories of Medieval Culture,* trans. by G. L. Campbell (London, 1985).

98. See note 90, above, for the population figure for 1549. In 1561, the papal nuncio gives an estimate, no doubt exaggerated, of a Jewish population in Prague of 6,000 souls: Florence COD.MED., 4,482, fasc. *Germania.* See Herman, *JB* (1969).

99. S. H. Lieben, "Die prager Brandtkatastrophen von 1689 und 1754," *Jahrbuch der Judisch-literarischen Gesellschaft* 28 (1926). If one refers to the proposed world Jewish population of less than one million in the middle of the seventeenth century, the density of the Jewish population of Prague is quite striking. See Shmuel Ettinger, "Migration and Economic Activity in the Seventeenth and Eighteenth Centuries," in Ben Sasson, *A History of the Jewish People,* 733.

100. D'Elvert, *Zur Geschichte der Juden in Mähren und Oster Schliesen* (Brun, 1895).

101. Bondy and Dvorsky, *Zur Geschichte der Juden.*

102. Popper, *REJ* (1895): 89.

103. Spiegel, in Steinherz, *Die Juden in Prag,* 181.

104. Spiegel, in Steinherz, *Die Juden in Prag,* n.1.

105. Popper, *REJ* (1895).

106. Rabbi Lipman Heller's major works are *Megillat Eivah* (1618); *Tosafot Yom Tov* (1614–1617); *Ma'adanei Melekh ve-Leḥem Ḥamudot* (1628–1629). Most of his commentaries are found in Meshullam ben Joel Katz, *Ikkarei Tosafot Yom Tov* (1790), and "Responsa" in *Geonei Batrae* (1764); *Beit Ḥadash ha-Ḥadashot* (1785), and *Tsemaḥ Tsedek* (1675). Also attributed to him are the *Seliḥot* and *Piyyutim* on the massacres of 1618–1620 in Prague and of 1648 in the Ukraine; see Bet Halevy, *Rabbi Yom Tov Lipman Heller* (Jerusalem, 1954).

107. Gustav Klemperer, "The Rabbis of Prague," *HJ* 12 (1950).

108. Bassevi was also related by the marriage of one of his sons to Rabbi Yom Tov's daughter Dobrish. Spiegel, in Steinherz, *Die Juden in Prag,* 143; Ruth Kestenberg-Gladstein, *EJ* 4:317.

109. Popper, *REJ* (1895): 146.

110. Spiegel, in Steinherz, *Die Juden in Prag,* 146.

111. Moses Isserles, the Rama, *Yoreh Deah* on *Shulhan Arukh,* sec. 334–336.

112. Isserles, *Sha'are Tsedek,* 4: 5, 14.

113. See H. H. Cohn, "Herem," *EJ* 8: 352.

114. Spiegel, in Steinherz, *Die Juden in Prag,* 47.

115. Text translated and published (in French) by Popper (1895), 92–93.

116. Rabbi Jacob Levy of Moellin (?1360–1427) insists that he inflicted only one during his entire life: *Responsa Rosh,* 43: 9.

117. On this subject, see the rules for the Moravian lands in Halperin, *Bet Yisrael be-Polin,* in which every warning, interdiction, or ruling is followed by the threat of the ḥerem.

118. Klemperer, *HJ* 12 (1950): 147.

## CHAPTER 4. THE INSTITUTION OF DEATH

1. Moses Ben Maimon (Maimonides), called the Rambam (1138–1204), remains one of the great thinkers and codifiers of Judaism. The *Sefer ha-Mitsvot,* or Book of Commandments, represents his personal compilation of the 613 classic commandments, made up of 248 positive and 365 negative commandments. Translated into Hebrew by Moses ibn Tibbon (Rome, ca. 1480), edited by H. Heller (1946).

2. *Mishneh Torah* or the repetition of the Law, 14 vols. (1180), fueled over the centuries the "Maimonides" controversy concerning his choices and theological determinations.

3. "In our day . . . the commentaries and compilations of the laws and responses of the *geonim* . . . have become so unintelligible that very few individuals understand them. Consequently . . . so that the oral Law can be systematically known to all, so that the laws are accessible to young and old alike." Maimonides, *Mishneh Torah,* "Introduction," edited by A J. Friemann (1934), no. 368; edited by J. Blau (1958–1961), no. 447; (Jerusalem, 1984), 5.

4. Joseph Ben Ephraim Caro, *Shulḥan Arukh,* 1st ed. (Venice, 1564–1565).

5. For the sciences, see the attitude of Moses Isserles, the Rama, in particu-

lar concerning the study of grammar and philosophy in A. Siev, *Ha-Rama* (Tel Aviv, 1957); for that of the Maharal of Prague on education, see "The Social Ideals of Jewry at the End of the Middle Ages," in Ben Sasson, *History,* 176. Note the interest of David Ganz in the new geographic discoveries; in his *Tsemaḥ David,* he quotes the conceptions of Copernicus; see André Neher, *David Gans: Disciple du Maharal de Prague* (Paris, 1974); Mordechai Breuer, *Sefer Tsemaḥ David* (1983), which he rejects in his *Magen David* (Prague, 1612), the abridged version of his book of astronomy *Neḥmad ve-Naim* (Jesnitz, 1743).

6. On this subject, see Yosef Haim Yerushalmi, *Zakhor* (Seattle, 1982); Abraham Zacuto (1452–1515), *Sefer Yuḥasin* (Constantinople, 1566; Cracow, 1580–1581); Azaria de Rossi (1511–1578), *Meor Enayim* (Mantua, 1573); Elie Capsali (1483–1555), *Divrei ha-Yamim le-Malkhut Venezia* (1517), edited by M. Lattes, *Likkutim Shonim mi-Sefer de-Vei Eliahu* (1869); Solomon ibn Verga (end of 15th c., beginning of 16th c.), *Shevet Yehudah* (Adrianople, 1553), are the most representative, without forgetting Joseph ha-Cohen (1496–1578), *Emek ha-Bakha.*

7. The "era of the ghetto" became a paradigmatic formula (which might be summed up by the term "fossilization" of the Jews in the course of this period), used by L. Poliakov, in *Histoire,* 1:191.

8. See the works of Gershom Scholem: *Major Trends in Jewish Mysticism,* (New York, 1946); *Origins of the Kabbalah* (New York, 1987); *On the Kabbalah and its Symbolism* (New York, 1965); *The Messianic Idea in Judaism* (New York, 1971).

9. See Simḥah Assaf, *Mekorot le-Toledot ha-Ḥinnukh be-Yisrael* (Tel Aviv, 1947), 45–51; the "responsa" of the Maharal with M. Isserles.

10. Manuscript, *Jewish Museum of Prague,* no. 42842; see also some excerpts in Moses Wolf Jeiteles, *Zikkaron le-Yom ha-Aḥaron* (Prague, 1806), his "Introduction"; Otto Muneles, "From the Archives of the State Jewish Museum," *Jewish Studies* (1965).

11. "At the same period (in the year 5302 [=1542]), the Jews were banished from the province of Prague, they went away on wagons in the month of Adar and made their way to Poland, where they settled. But many of them perished on the way, and others were murdered. In the year 5319, that is, 1559, the Emperor Ferdinand banished the Jews from the realm of Bohemia. He left some, however, in Prague where around 200 families remained; the others had to leave the city. In the night of 17 Tamuz, a fire broke out in the street of the Jews, almost instantly consuming 60 houses. The whole city was seized with fear, the entire population descended on the Israelites like bears and wolves of the night and laid waste to their possessions, while the Jews fled, fearing for their very lives." Joseph ha-Cohen, *Emek ha-Bakha,* French edition (*La Vallée des pleurs*), 123–149.

12. In the Bible: Lev. 10:1–24; Num. 10:2; Rashi, *Pesaḥim* 14b, 17a; Maimonides, "*Avot, Hilkhot Tumat ha-Met*"; etc.

13. *Moed Katan* 27, 10b.

14. Naḥmanides, called the Ramban, *Torat ha-Adam* (Leaving the Body), (Warsaw edition, 1876), 46.

15. Naḥmanides, *Torat ha-Adam,* 46.
16. See chap. I, *Tractate Semaḥot.*
17. See *Moed Katan.*
18. Founding charter of the ḥevra kaddisha of Prague, sec. 1.
19. Samuel Krauss, *Talmudische Archäologie* (Leipzig, 1910–1912), 63.
20. Adolf Schmiedl, "Zur Entstehungsgeschichte der allerersten Chewra Kadisha," *Oesterreichische Wochenschrift* 10 (1893). The revolt of Bar Kokhba against the Romans dates back to 133 B.C.E.
21. Immanuel Low, "*A Szegedy Chewra,*" in *Gesammelte Schriften* (Szegedin, 1890).
22. Rashi, *Sefer ha-Tashbaz,* III n.13 on *Moed Katan* 27b: "There were organizations each of which was responsible to its members"; *Tosafot Kiddushin* 17a.
23. Rashi in *Ketubot* 8b.
24. *Baraita* in *Baba Batra* 8a.
25. *Moed Katan* 27b.
26. See Abraham A. Neumann, *The Jews in Spain: Their Social, Political and Cultural Life during the Middle Ages,* 2 vols. (Philadelphia, 1942). See also above notes 19, 20, 21.
27. Jacob Rader Marcus, *Communal Sick-Care in the German Ghetto* (New York, 1947, 1978), 56.
28. Joseph Yuspa Hahn, *Yosef Omets* (Frankfurt, 1723).
29. *Ke-met mitsvah,* according to the classic formula.
30. Hahn, *Yosef Omets,* Introduction, 4–5.
31. Marcus, *Communal,* 64.
32. Serrano Y Sanz "Origines de la dominacion española en America," *Sefarad* 8 (1918): 147–151, 369–371; see Maurice Kriegel, *Les Juifs à la fin du Moyen Age* (Paris, 1979), nn. 34, 35, p. 267.
33. Fritz Isaac Baer, *Die Juden im christlichen Spanien* (Berlin, 1936); Neumann, *The Jews in Spain.*
34. H. Pflaum, *Die Idee der Liebe, Leone Ebreo* (1926), 82.
35. Marcus, *Communal,* 64.
36. See note 8, above.
37. Particularly in Scholem's *Major Trends* and *The Origins of the Kabbalah.*
38. See Scholem's works in note 8, above; also in *EJ* 10:611.
39. See note 38, above.
40. See note 38, above.
41. JT *Souk, 4, 3; Leviticus Rabbah* 9, 3.
42. Scholem, "Kabbalah," *EJ* 10 (1972): 640.
43. Aaron Ben Moses Berachia of Modena, *Ma'avar Yabbok* (Mantua, 1626), which will be thoroughly discussed here. In the Talmud: *Ḥagigah,* 13b; JT *Ḥagigah,* 2.2, 77d.
44. It has been said that this was inspired by Dante's *Divine Comedy.* Moses Zacuto, *Tofteh Arukh* (Venice, 1715).
45. Nathan Nata Hannover, *Sha'arei Tsion* (Prague, 1662).
46. Scholem, *Major Trends,* 249.

47. The pietistic movement discussed above in chap. 2: "A Singular History: Specific Perceptions."

48. Scholem, *Major Trends,* 300.

49. On the mystical *galut: see Sefer ha-Likkutim,* fo. 89b, in Scholem, *Major Trends,* 302n.125. On *gilgul,* Ḥayim Vital, *Sefer ha-Gilgulim,* chap. 5; *Sha'ar ha-Yiḥudim, Sha'ar Tikkunei Teshuvah*; Cordovero, *Shiur Koma*; etc.

50. Midrash *Ha-Ne'elam,* in *Zohar Ḥadash,* 1885 edition.

51. See Confession of sins in *EJ* 5:879.

52. See also Idelsohn, *Liturgy,* 111, 228; Ismar Elbogen, *Der Jüdische Gottesdienst in seiner geschichtlichen Entwicklung* (Berlin, 1913), 149–151; S. Baer, *Siddur; Seliḥot, Kinot, Seder ha-Berakhot* (1858); Élie Munk, *Le Monde des prières* (Paris, 1963).

53. Maimonides, in "*Teshuvah.*"

54. On this subject, M. Benayahu, "Min ha-Ma'amadot ve-ha-Moshavot la-Met ve-ad ha-Hakkafot, ve-Issur li-Yetsiat ha-Banim Aḥarei Mitat Aviḥem," *Sinai* 92 (1983): 59–65; and his *Ma'amadot u-Moshavot* (1985).

55. Marcus, *Communal,* 67–72.

56. Marcus, *Communal,* 71: "Jews could feel free to derive inspiration from the previous pattern."

57. E. Ashkenazi (1513–1586): his chief interests were varied; he was reputed to know twelve languages. A great traveler, he found himself in Prague in 1563–1564, at the very moment of the founding of the ḥevra kaddisha, but his affinities led him toward the center of Safed. On his influence in the Ashkenazi world, see Ben Sasson, *Hagut ve-Hanhagah* (Jerusalem, 1959).

58. See the chronological list of the creation of Brotherhoods in Marcus, *Communal,* Appendix IX.

59. We can speak of a popular movement when everything involving ritual or "popular" practices is impregnated by allusions to and borrowings from Lurianic conceptions.

60. This formula is informed by the speculations of messianic anticipation; "the birth pangs" of the Messiah can take place only in the dark "night" that symbolizes it.

61. See note 10, above. M. Grünwald, "Älteste Statuten der prager Brüderschaft 1692," *Das Jüdische Centralblatt* 8 (1889), 39–57.

62. There is a symbolic correlation between the day for celebrating the giving of the Torah on Mount Sinai and the renewal of elected members entrusted with maintaining and elaborating the laws of the ḥevra. Furthermore, the holiday of Shavu'ot was traditionally the day set aside for bringing children to school—to the ḥeder—for the first time.

63. Etymologically, the term *sandak* is related to "syndic," which is nonetheless translated into English as "godfather." On the functions of the godfather, see Pollack, *Jewish Folkways,* 25.

64. Marcus, *Communal,* 95.

65. Koenigsberg: see H. Vogelstein, "Geschichte des israelitischen Vereins für Krankenpflege und Beerdigung zum Königsberg," *Festschrift zum zweihundertjährigen Bestehen des israelitischen Vereins für Krankenpflege und Beerdigung* (1904): 6, 19, 48.

66. Marcus, *Communal,* 98.

67. Boskowitz, in Heinrich Flesch, "Zur Geschichte des mährischen Heiligen Vereins (Chewra Kadischa)," *JJLG* 21 (1930): 217–258.

68. Eibenschitz, in H. Flesch, "Das alte Chewra Kadischa Protokoll der Gemeinde Eibenschitz," *Hiklis jüdischer Volkskalender für das Jähr 5684,* 23 (1923–1924): 61–71.

69. Neu-Raussnitz, in H. Flesch, "Die Statuten der Chewra Kadischa Neu-Raussnitz," *MGWJ* 70 (1926): 167–181.

## CHAPTER 5. THE RHYTHM OF DEATH

1. Ariès, *The Hour of Our Death,* 185.

2. Israel Abrahams, *Jewish Life in the Middle Ages* (London, 1932).

3. Pollack, *Jewish Folkways.*

4. The term was coined by H. Flesch, "Aus der Statuten der mährischen Beerdigung Bruderschaften," *JGJC* 7 (1933): 157–173.

5. Steinitz (1635), Heinrich Flesch, "Takkanot ha-Ḥevra Kadisha di-Kahal Steinitz bi-Medinat Maḥren," *JJLG* 19 (1928): 21–30, citation on p. 29.

6. This aphorism, which is an integral part of the daily prayers, is often cited in the rules of the burial societies.

7. Excerpt from the statutes of Steinitz, already cited, p. 100.

8. Statutes of Steinitz, already cited, p. 100.

9. The Kaddish, or sanctification, see above, "The Panegyric of Bitterness."

10. The Tehillim are the Psalms, also an integral part of the daily recitations and recited in difficult times, in cases of travel, danger, illness, birth, death, or anxiety.

11. See *Ma'aseh Book,* and chap. 2, note 114, above.

12. Joseph Caro, *Shulḥan Arukh.*

13. *Ma'aneh Lashon* (Expression of the Tongue), published in Prague around 1616. I am using here the editions from Frankfurt (1726) and Amsterdam (1723). According to Marcus, *Communal,* 228, more than forty editions of this work were published in Hebrew or in Yiddish before 1800.

14. The name *Shelah* was established on the abbreviations of the title *Shnei Luḥot ha-Berit.* We have some idea of the importance of this work from the *Memoirs* of Glückel of Hameln, whose husband, knowing he is dying, asks to read it. French edition, translated by L. Poliakov (Paris, 1971), 157.

15. Joseph Yuspa Hahn, *Yosef Omets.*

16. Isaiah Horowitz, chapter "Ner Mitsva." I am using here the Jerusalem edition (1970).

17. *Sefer ha-Ḥaim,* or the Book of Life. The principle of euphemization used here to name a mortuary manual is the same one applied to the *Evel Rabbati,* entitled "Rejoicings": *Semaḥot.* I am here using the edition published in Sulzbach in 1667. The most famous compilation was done by Simon Frankfurt, who left Poland for Amsterdam. According to Marcus (see n. 13), it was reissued at least seventeen times between 1703 and 1800, and it included a series of prayers composed by Leon of Modena as a preventive measure against any danger, physical and spiritual.

18. Naḥmanides, *Torat ha-Adam,* "Sha'ar ha-Miḥush," (Naples, 1490). I am using here the Warsaw edition (1876). See *Sota* 14.

19. I. Horowitz, *Shelah* quoting *Zohar,* "Pekudei."

20. Horowitz, *Shelah,* "Bameh Madlikin."

21. Aaron Berachia, *Ma'avar Yabbok,* "Siftei tsedek," vol. 1 (Mantua, 1626). I am also using here the other important edition published before 1800, the one from Amsterdam (1732). Excerpts from this work figure in most of the local communal burial rituals, but it is noteworthy that the abridged forms were reissued more than eighteen times in the course of the same period, if only in the German lands. These abridged editions also circulated in Poland, although the reissues were not numbered. See Meir Benayahu, *Ma'amadot u-Moshavot.*

22. Horowitz, *Shelah,* "Massekhet Pesaḥim."

23. Naḥmanides, *Torat ha-Adam,* "Sha'ar ha-Miḥush."

24. Naḥmanides, *Torat ha-Adam,* "Sha'ar ha-Sakkanah."

25. The term they use is *kavranim.* See J. R. Marcus, "The Triesch Hebra Kadisha 1628–1702," *HUCA* 19 (1945): 172.

26. See the statutes of Steinitz (1635), in Flesch, *Takkanot,* 26.

27. Marcus, *HUCA* 19 (1945), sec. 25, p. 202.

28. Horowitz, *Shelah,* "Massekhet Pesaḥim."

29. Horowitz, *Shelah.*

30. Naḥmanides, *Torat ha-Adam,* "Sha'ar ha-Sof."

31. Horowitz, *Shelah,* "Massekhet Pesaḥim."

32. Berachia, *Ma'avar Yabbok,* "Siftei Tsedek," Zohar 44, fo. 41.

33. Naḥmanides, *Torat ha-Adam,* "Sha'ar ha-Sof," Shema.

34. Berachia, *Ma'avar Yabbok,* "Seder ha-Viddui."

35. Horowitz, *Shelah,* "Massekhet Pesaḥim."

36. Berachia, *Ma'avar Yabbok,* "Seder ha-Viddui."

37. Berachia, *Ma'avar Yabbok,* "Seder ha-Viddui."

38. Article 25, in Marcus, *HUCA* 19 (1945).

39. Naḥmanides, *Torat ha-Adam,* "Inyan ha-Petirah," *Evel Rabbati* 1.

40. Naḥmanides, *Torat ha-Adam,* "Shaar ha-Miḥush," "Inyan ha-Petirah," *Shabbat* 150a.

41. Berachia, *Ma'avar Yabbok,* the prayers Shir ha-pegu'im and Be-tokh talits ve-takits.

42. Lilith is the demonic female figure; she occupies a central place in Jewish demonology by representing the female face of Satan, who attacks males in particular, both adults and children. See Gershom Scholem, *Tarbiz* 19 (1947–1948): 165–175. J. Trachtenberg, *Jewish Magic and Superstition* (New York, 1939; reprinted in New York, 1979), 36, 277.

43. Horowitz, *Shelah,* "Massekhet Pesahim," 5.

44. Horowitz, *Shelah,* "Massekhet Pesahim," 5.

45. The three specifically female commandments are *Khallah,* kneading the bread dough for the sabbath; *Niddah,* the laws of isolation during menstruation; *Hadlakah,* lighting the candles on holidays and the Sabbath. JT *Shabbat* 6, 1a.

46. Berachia, *Ma'avar Yabbok,* "Siftei Tsedek," 5.

47. Naḥmanides, *Torat ha-Adam,* "Sha'ar ha-Sakkanah."
48. Naḥmanides, *Torat ha-Adam,* "Inyan ha-Hotsa'ah," *Evel Rabbati* 11.
49. Naḥmanides, *Torat ha-Adam,* "Inyan ha-Hotsa'ah," *Evel Rabbati* 11.
50. See note 45, the laws of purity, *Niddah.*
51. Berachia, *Ma'avar Yabbok,* "Siftei Tsedek," 5.
52. On the tearing of clothing on the occasion of mourning, see: S.-A. Goldberg, "Du deuil public au deuil privé: Sive laceratione vestium apud hebraeos usitata," unpublished manuscript (Paris, 1982). "Why do we tear? Because it is as if a Torah scroll were burning," *Moed Katan,* 25; *Ma'avar Yabbok,* 3:19.
53. Naḥmanides, *Torat ha-Adam,* "Inyan ha-Keriah."
54. Horowitz, *Shelah,* "Massekhet Pesaḥim."
55. Barachia, *Ma'avar Yabbok,* "Siftei Tsedek," 32.
56. Horowitz, *Shelah,* "Massekhet Pesaḥim."
57. The prescriptions concerning periods of mourning: the seven days following burial in the course of which the mourners sit shiva, then the year during which they abstain from any manifestation of rejoicing, will be studied further on.
58. Berachia, *Ma'avar Yabbok,* "Siftei Ra'ananut," 3:9.
59. According to the rules of the burial society of Prague (1692–1702), article 27.
60. Berachia, *Ma'avar Yabbok,* "Siftei Ra'ananut," 3:9.
61. Berachia, *Ma'avar Yabbok,* "Siftei Ra'ananut," 1:26.
62. This very common usage in the Jewish communities is most often explained in a different way. It is said that the Angel of Death dips his sword in the water to clean it and that anyone who would drink it would die instantly. See Trachtenberg, *Jewish Magic*; A. P. Bender, "Beliefs, Rites and Customs of the Jews Connected with Death, Burial and Mourning," *Jewish Quarterly Review* 7 (1894): 317–347, 661–665; 8 (1895): 101–200. An-Ski, "Der Toyt in dem yiddishn Folksgloybn," *Filologische Shriften,* 3 (1929); An-Ski, *Gesammelte,* 15 vols. (Vilna, 1920–1925). H. Chajes, "Gloybungn un Minhagim in Forbindung mitn Toyt," *Filologishe Shriften* 2 (1928).
63. Berachia, *Ma'avar Yabbok,* "Siftei Ra'ananut," 2:28.
64. Berachia, *Ma'avar Yabbok,* "Siftei Ra'ananut," 3:13.
65. *Zohar,* "Vayehi," fo. 223.
66. *Devekut* is the term that signifies, precisely, the spiritual union that should be attained through prayer.
67. Berachia, *Ma'avar Yabbok,* "Sefat Emet," 2:8.
68. *Evel Rabbati* 10:3.
69. Excerpt from the rules of the burial society of Triesch, article 17, in J. R. Marcus, *The Triesch Hebra Kadisha, 1687–1828.*
70. On this subject, see the same rules, article 18.
71. Berachia, *Ma'avar Yabbok,* "Sefat Emet," 2:25.
72. Berachia, *Ma'avar Yabbok*; *Kohelet Rabbah.*
73. Berachia, *Ma'avar Yabbok,* "Sefat Emet," 2:26.
74. Again, on this subject see *Evel Rabbati* 10:6–7; 13:1–8.
75. Berachia, *Ma'avar Yabbok,* "Sefat Emet," 2:27.

76. Rules of the Prague Burial Society, article 26. The wait was three hours in Frankfurt; see Hahn, *Yosef Omets,* and Pollack, *Jewish Folkways.*

77. See Flesch, *MGWJ* 20 (1926): 22.

78. Flesch, *JJLG* 29 (1928).

79. Article 20, Marcus, *HUCA* 19 (1945).

80. See Halperin, *Constitutiones Moraviensum,* sec. 245, p. 81.

81. Marcus, *HUCA* 19 (1945), article 20.

82. Berachia, *Ma'avar Yabbok,* "Siftei Ra'ananut," 3:14.

83. Berachia, *Ma'avar Yabbok,* "Siftei Ra'ananut," 3:15.

84. The angel Michael is one of the four angels who serve the godhead. Uriel stands before the Throne, Michael at its right, Gabriel on its left, while Raphael stands behind the Throne. In Jewish demonology, angels are not objects of veneration. According to the *Zohar* (I, pp. 11, 45), they live in the seven "corridors" or "palaces" of Heaven, the *hekhalot.* Each angel plays a particular role. See Reuben Margulies, *Malakhe Elyon* (Jerusalem, 1945, 1964); Eisenstein, *Otsar ha-Midrashim,* vol. 1 (New York, 1915).

85. Berachia, *Ma'avar Yabbok,* "Siftei Ra'ananut," 3:16.

86. Berachia, *Ma'avar Yabbok,* "Siftei Ra'ananut," 3:10.

87. "Sakkanat Nefesh," in Marcus, *HUCA* 19 (1945), article 26.

88. *Sefer ha-Ḥaim* 84.

89. See articles 7, 9, and 10 of the rules of the Prague Burial Society.

90. As above, articles 8 and 9.

91. Naḥmanides, *Torat ha-Adam.*

92. Barachia, *Ma'avar Yabbok,* "Siftei Ra'ananut," 3:17, 18.

93. Berachia, *Ma'avar Yabbok,* "Siftei Ra'ananut," 3:18.

94. Prov. 10:4; also 11:4. This maxim is always inscribed on the alms boxes. At Triesch, the beadle moved toward the procession of women in order to prevent them from approaching the men. Marcus, *HUCA* 19 (1945), art. 26.

95. Berachia, *Ma'avar Yabbok,* "Siftei Ra'ananut," 3:20.

96. "*Vayehi no'am yoshev be-seter Elyon,*" Psalms 90, 91.

97. These are the essential texts of the Kabbalah. The *Sefer Yetsirah,* or Book of Creation (1894 edition), one of the oldest, dates back to the first centuries of our era (between the second and the sixth centuries); the Midrash *ha-Ne'elam,* although initially independent, was integrated into the *Zohar* in *Zohar Ḥadash.*

98. Joseph Ben Ephraim Caro, *Shulḥan Arukh.*

99. Horowitz, *Shelah Massekhet Ḥulin.*

100. Berachia, *Ma'avar Yabbok,* "Sefet Emet," 2:17. Cordovero, on Midrash *Rabbati,* 66.

101. *Shelah,* "Ner Mitsvah."

102. Ariès, *The Hour of Our Death,* 301.

103. Ariès, *The Hour of Our Death,* 303–304.

104. *Sefer ha-Ḥaim* 2.

105. *Evel Rabbati* 12:5.

106. Horowitz, commentaries on *Massekhet Pesaḥim.*

107. One does not take on mourning for a newborn less than thirty days

old. *Tosafot Yevamot* 36, 5a; JT *Yevamot* 11, 10b; BT *Shabbat* 135. And of course the same is true for a stillborn or premature birth, a *nefel.* Children less than twelve years old, for whom mourning is performed, are not buried clothed in shrouds but only in a white sheet.

108. Yehiel M. Tukacinsky, *Gesher ha-Ḥaim* (Jerusalem, 1960), 2:135.

109. Yekutiel Y. Greenwald, *Kol-bo al Avelut* (Jerusalem, 1973), 262; *Minhag Israel,* 1:377, 140; Maurice Lamm, *The Jewish Way in Death and Mourning* (New York, 1969), 102–104.

110. Greenwald, in *Kol-bo,* according to the *Ḥatam Sofer,* on JT *Moed Katan* 3:5; see also Taylor, "The Dirge of Koheleth," *JQR* 4:539; Bender, "Beliefs, Rites and Customs of the Jews Connected with Death, Burial and Mourning," *JQR* 8:117.

111. Cited by Greenwald in *Kol-bo* 262.

112. Berachia, *Ma'avar Yabbok,* "Sefat Emet," 2:15.

113. See Prov. 20, 27.

114. Greenwald, *Kol-bo,* 4, 9:261.

115. "Those in mourning and the excommunicated are authorized to wear their shoes when they travel a main road, but to remove them when they enter the quarter. And this applies also on *Tisha b'Av* or a public fast" (*Evel Rabbati* 5:12).

116. "*Yad Shaul,* on *Yoreh Deah,*" 400; see *Yosef Omets*; Joseph ben Moses Kosman, *Noheg katson Yosef* (Hanau, 1718), fo. 67b, on the Ninth of Av.

117. As the books of customs have it, the Ninth of Av is a day of public mourning, which everyone must respect. On Tisha b'Av, see above, chap. 2.

118. After the fall of the Second Temple, a group called the "Mourners of Zion" was formed, which devoted itself to the commemoration of the mourning of Jerusalem and to the prayers for its redemption. Goldberg, "Si je t'oublie Jerusalem, un concept, une histoire," *Communauté Nouvelle* 30 (1987): 139–149. In addition, it is interesting to note that this vestimentary practice is generally described for marriages; see Pollack, *Jewish Folkways,* 37n. 122.

119. Berachia, *Ma'avar Yabbok,* "Siftei Ra'ananut," 3:19.

120. *Moed Katan* 27.

121. *Perishah* 378; Greenwald, *Kol-bo,* 272.

122. Rama, on *Orah Ḥaim,* 552.

123. *Ma'avar Yabbok,* "Sefat Emet," 2:22.

124. *Shulḥan Arukh, Kitsur,* CCV, sec. 1.

125. Greenwald, *Kol-bo* 261–266n. 17, C. Tcherniak, *Mishmeret Shalom* (Warsaw, 1928), 24.

126. Job 2:13.

127. *Kol-bo* 4:259.

128. Berachia, *Ma'avar Yabbok,* "Sefat Emet," 2:19.

129. JT *Moed Katan* 3:3.

130. Berachia, *Ma'avar Yabbok,* "Sefat Emet," 2:19.

131. Glückel of Hameln, *Memoirs,* 152–153.

132. BT *Moed Katan* 27b.

133. At the time of the destruction of the Temple, as a sign of mourning

people shaved their heads and beards, going against the usual practice. See Rashi, in Greenwald, *Kol-bo,* 350 n. 1.

134. *Sefer ha-Ḥaim* 84.

135. *Shulḥan Arukh,* "Even ha-Ezer," 132.

136. BT *Moed Katan* 22b.

137. Naḥmanides, *Torat ha-Adam,* 40:72.

138. Rama, 389; Radbaz, 454.

139. See above, chap. 2, "Panegyric of Bitterness."

140. Berachia, *Ma'avar Yabbok,* 2:29.

141. Greenwald, *Kol-bo,* 366.

142. *Noda bi-Yehudah*; *Oraḥ Ḥaim*; *Tenina.* See the Responsa of Bacharach, on the subject of a Jew from Amsterdam, who, having no son, had asked that his daughter be allowed to recite his Kaddish. Yair Bacharach, *Ḥavvot Ya'ir,* n. 222, fo. 208a, cited by Pollack, *Jewish Folkways,* 44n. 179.

143. Greenwald, *Kol-bo,* 366.

144. According to the Talmud, *Rosh ha-Shanah* 16a–17a; *Avot de-Rabbi Nathan* 41:15.

145. Talmud, *Rosh ha-Shanah.*

146. Rama, 402, 12.

147. *Sefer Ḥasidim* 231.

148. *Mo'ed kol ḥai* 81.

149. *Rama,* 368; in *Mishmeret Shalom,* "Avelut," "Bet kevarot," 11.

150. The days reserved for "going up" to the Torah are Monday, Thursday, and Saturday.

151. See above, chap. 2, "Panegyric of Bitterness," and Greenwald, *Kol-bo,* 389.

152. *Mo'ed kol ḥai,* quoted in Greenwald, *Kol-bo,* 398.

153. Rama, quoted in Greenwald, *Kol-bo,* 610. On hazkarat neshamot on Yom Kippur, see also "Siddur Rashi," in *Maḥzor Vitry,* 392.

154. Rama, *Darkhei Moshe,* after Mahariv.

155. Greenwald, *Kol-bo,* 402, according to *Minhagim of Rabbi Tyrnau* (Schick edition), fo. 51b. From Isaac Tyrnau, *Minhagim shel Kol ha-Medinot* (Amsterdam, 1708).

156. Mordekhai Jaffe, *Levush* (Prague, 1646; Berdiczew, 1819), 347.

157. *Yevamot* 107.

158. *Sefer ha-Ḥaim* 60.

159. *Midrash Tanḥuma*; *Ha'azinu.*

160. *Genesis Rabbah* 11:5.

161. Tcherniak, "Ge'ulat Yisrael," *Mishmeret Shalom,* Introduction; "Avelut," 10:13.

162. Berachia, *Ma'avar Yabbok,* 2:7.

163. Berachia, *Ma'avar Yabbok,* 2:19.

164. See the rules of the Prague Burial Society, article 22.

165. On this subject, see Marcus, *Communal,* 102.

166. Two brothers, Zelig and Feibush, were excluded from the burial society of Triesch in 1726. Although the reason for this punishment had not been specified, the act was noted in the records with the indication that they would

not be allowed a religious burial. Cited in Marcus, *The Triesch Hebra Kadisha,* 187.

## CHAPTER 6. THE LAW AND THE LETTER

1. See H. Chajes, "Gloybungen un Minhagim in Forbindung mitn Toyt," *Filologishe Shriftn* 2 (1928): 295.
2. M. Benayahu, *Ma'amadot u-Moshavot* (Jerusalem, 1985).
3. *Seder Tefillot ve-Pizmonim u-Teḥinot ve-Kinot* (Venice, 1572), by Rabbi Schneur Ben Yehuda Falcon.
4. See above, chap. 5, "The Secret of the Tree of Life."
5. According to the Midrash, see Benayahu, "Min ha-Ma'amadot," *Sinai* 92 (1983): 59.
6. "Lo Yatsu ha-Hakkafot mi-Yedei Peshutan," Benayahu, *Sinai* 92 (1983): 60.
7. The three chief propagators of this custom would be Rabbi Abraham Saba, in *Tseror Hamor* (Venice, 1523), to whom this custom was "well known" from the rabbinic literature; Rabbi Yehuda Ḥalowa, who asserts in *Tsofnat Pa'anéaḥ* (in manuscript) that these harmful beings form the "seven kinds of impurity"; and David Zimra (1479–1573), the Radbaz, in *Magen David* (Amsterdam, 1713), who, though he does not base this custom on rabbinic codifications, grants it a profound and hidden meaning—*a segulah*—in relation to the number seven, which he does not relate to the seven malevolent forces. See Benayahu, in *Sinai* and in *Ma'amadot u-Moshavot,* 105–113.
8. *Shelah,* "Tovlei Yom," *Massekhet Pesaḥim* 5.
9. *Ta'ame ha-Mitzvot* (Lublin, 1571), by Menahem ha-Babli, who lived in Safed and Hebron in the middle of the sixteenth century (d. 1571).
10. See note 7, above.
11. See the central notebook, B. Picart (1673–1733) also reproduced numerous Jewish customs.
12. For example, *Tsidduk ha-Din* (Venice, 1738); *Seder Berakhot* (Amsterdam, 1687).
13. Glückel, "*Memoirs,*" 152.
14. Isaiah Horowitz was rabbi of Prague between 1614 and 1621.
15. The Jewish State Museum of Prague (JMP) has preserved many engravings and pictures representing the ḥevra kaddisha and the different stages of its activities, from deathbed to grave. One book brings these together: *The Precious Legacy, Judaic Treasure,* edited by D. Altshuller (New York, 1983). See iconography. See also S. A. Goldberg, *L'Art de bien mourir* (Paris, 1995).
16. See An-Ski, *Der Toyt.*
17. "In the house of the dead, the dead person is circled seven times"; Der Nistor, *La famille Machber,* 2:103.
18. Sulzbach edition, 1667, title page of Part Two.
19. Yair Bacharach, *Ḥavvot Ya'ir,* #222, fo. 228, in Pollack, *Jewish Folkways,* 45n. 175; 231.
20. A. Margarita, *Der gantz jüdisch Glaub* (Augsbourg, 1530). Notably, this work particularly inspired Luther in his *Schem ha-Mephorasch.*

21. Is this the house of the *Tsidduk ha-Din*?

22. The retranscription of this did not seem necessary, since it accords with and integrates Naḥmanides' formula: "Let my death be the remission of all my sins," etc. On this subject, see Azriel Shoḥat, *Im Ḥillufei Tekufot* (Tel Aviv, 1967), 46 n. 123, on penitence.

23. This is supported by the survival of the tradition of presenting the rabbi with notes (tseytl) in which people formulate questions or submit a personal problem.

24. See An-ski, *Der Toyt.*

25. J. Trachtenberg, *Jewish Magic.*

26. "But as I lay sound asleep, three knocks resounded on my door, as though the whole house were tumbling in," Glückel, *Memoirs,* 120–121.

27. Stauben, *Scènes de la vie juive en Alsace* (1860), 89.

28. An-Ski, *Der Toyt.*

29. Seven times in *Kol-Bo,* 164; three times in *Yosef Omets,* 986.

30. See "Measuring the Cemetery," in *Ba'er Heytev* on *Yoreh De'ah* 37b, sec. 4.

31. *Ta'anit* 16a, 23b; *Sota* 34b. E. Gourévitch calls our attention to the Midrash in Deuteronomy 21:8, in which it is said that Caleb, one of the twelve scouts who survived with Joshua, went to prostrate himself on the graves of the patriarchs, in order to ask for success in the conquest.

32. The Maharam (1215–1293), *Meir ben Baruch Responsa* (Lemberg, 1860), n. 164, fo. 13a.

33. See in the preceding chapter the general ideas developed in the Jewish mortuary manuals.

34. *Shelah* (Isaiah Horowitz), *Shnei Luḥot ha-Berit* (Amsterdam, 1649), "Massekhet Rosh ha-Shanah," 54.

35. Isidor Kracauer, *Die Geschicte der Judengasse in Frankfurt am Main* (Frankfurt, 1925–1927), 336; Oksman, in *Reshumot* 3:100; Dubnow, *Weltgeschichte,* 8:170; Julius Hulsen, *Der alte Judenfriedhof in Frankfurt am Main* (Frankfurt, 1932), 10.

36. J. Bergl, "Die Ausweisung der Juden aus Prag im Jahre 1744," in Steinherz, *Die Juden,* 242.

37. *Shelah,* see note 34, above.

38. Naḥmanides, *Torat ha-Adam,* "Inyan ha-Hotsa'ah," 48.

39. Trachtenberg, *Jewish Magic,* 64n. 6; 285.

40. *Ta'anit* 16a, Max Grünbaum, *Judischdeutsche Chrestomathie* (1882), 571–572.

41. The Maharam, see above, note 32; Pollack, *Jewish Folkways,* 48–49.

42. Moses ben Abraham Mat of Prezmilav (1551–1606), *Mateh Mosheh,* (Cracow, 1590).

43. I am using the Frankfurt edition (1720), sec. 738, 789, 839.

44. Notably Jacob ben Moses Moellin (1360–1427), *Sefer ha-Maharil* (1874), 37a; Abraham ben Shabbetai Sheftel Horowitz, *Emek ha berakha* (Amsterdam, 1729), sec. 6, p. 74b, cited in Trachtenberg, *Jewish Magic,* 285n. 6.

45. See articles 11 and 32 of the rules of the Prague Burial Society (appendix).

46. Ariès, *The Hour of Our Death,* 116.

47. The dance of death by Niklaus Manuel (1516–1517, 1519–1520) is found at the Dominican cloister in Berne; see Reinhold Hammerstein, *Tanz und Musik des Todes: Die Mittelalterlichen Todtentaïnz und ihre Nachleben* (Berne and Munich, 1980). See iconography.

48. Glückel, *Memoirs,* 99, where this passage is translated into English without the final phrase.

49. Shlomoh Rubin, "Meḥolot ha-Mavet," in *Ha-Shaḥar* (1877), 8: 16–90.

50. *Birkat ha-Kohanim.*

51. "After the dance had become known in Germany, it was introduced as Jewish festivities"; Pollack, *Jewish Folkways,* 38n. 133; 225; see Rubin's introduction to *Meḥolot Ha-Mavet,* 3.

52. Purim is a more recent holiday (around the 2d c. B.C.E.) preceded by a day of fasting and followed by lively rejoicing, during which the scroll of the Book of Esther is read to celebrate the deliverance of the Jews from a sentence of death. This holiday traditionally provides the occasion for dressing in costume and getting drunk, while authorizing public joking (Druyanow, *Reshumot* 1:2). The communities also used to compose Purim Shpiln, plays that were often parodic and irreverent, performed with masks. See *Yiddisher Folklor* (1938), 219–274. For the "barber's dance," see M. Grünwald, "Trachten und Sitten," *MGWJ* (1898): 39.

53. Franz Magnus Bohme, *Geschichte des Tanzes in Deutschland* (Leipzig, 1886) 1: 69, 210, 322n. 6. This work also contains the musical accompaniment for the dance.

54. See, however, the customary practices of dances at the court of this period in Azriel Shoḥat, *Im Ḥillufei,* 37–39, 162–163.

55. M. Grünwald, see above, note 52.

56. A Gleichen-Russwurm, *Die gotische Welt: Sitten und Gebräuche im späten Mittelalter* (Stuttgart, 1919), 243–244; Bohme, *Geschichte des Tanzes,* 1: 60, 322; cited in Pollack, *Jewish Folkways,* 38n. 132; 225.

57. Bernard Wachstein, "Pinqas Runkel," in *ZGJD* 4 (1932): 139, sec. 35, cited in Pollack, *Jewish Folkways,* 39n. 136; 225.

58. Ezekiel Landau, *Derushei ha-Tselah* (Warsaw, 1886), no. 23, fo. 35b, sec. 19.

59. See the ethical testament of Abraham ben Shabbetai Sheftel Horowitz, *Yech Noḥalim* (Amsterdam, 1701), sec. 17.

60. According to Pollack, *Jewish Folkways,* 36n. 122; 223; I. Abrahams, *Jewish Life,* 203.

61. Jacob Moellin, *Sefer ha-Maharil,* fo. 82b, sec. 1556.

62. Pollack, *Jewish Folkways,* 224n. 124.

63. An-Ski, *Tsvishn Tsvey Veltn* (*Der Dibek*), performed in Yiddish in Vilna, 1920, and translated into Hebrew by H. Bialik in *Ha-tekoufah* 1 (1918).

64. "It was recommended to the community to beg for mercy from the Almighty by a virtuous act, such as marrying a very poor boy and girl at the cemetery. The most impoverished, the lowliest, the most despairing were chosen." I. J. Singer, *The Sinner* (Yoshe Kalb), trans. Maurice Samuel (New York, 1933).

## CHAPTER 7. BODY AND SOUL

1. For example, see J. Saugnieux, *Les Danses macabres de France et d'Espagne* (Paris, 1972); Edelgard Dubruck, *The Theme of Death in French Poetry of the Middle Ages and the Renaissance* (The Hague, 1964).

2. For the mourning cowl, see Adolf Wuttke, *Der deutsche Volksaberglaube der Gegenwart* (Berlin, 1869), 206–207, sec. 31; 317, 346, sec. 558; see Wultke, *HDA* 4 (1931–1932): 153, sec. 2.

3. Cited by Isidore Simon, "La médecine hébraique," in *Histoire de la médecine* (Paris, 1978), 68.

4. Maimonides (1135–1204): on the circulation of the blood, *Fusūl Musa*; medications, *Sarḥ asmā̧ al-ʿuqqar*; asthma, *Maqāla fi al-Rabw*; poisons, *Kitab al-sumūm wa-al Mutaḥarriz*. Furthermore, a medallion with his portrait can be seen at the medical school in Paris, rue des Saints-Pères, which shows the mythical aspect of his medical character.

5. See Abrahams, *Jewish Life*, 255.

6. Karl Opitz, "Avicenna, das Lehgedicht über die Heilkunde (canticum de medicina)," *Quellen und Stadien zur Geschichte der Naturwissenschaft und der Mëdizin* (1940), 7: 173, 175, 320.

7. See Yair Bacharach (1638–1702), *Ḥavvot Yaʾir*, no. 106, fo. 104b; Jacob Emden, the *Yaʿabets* (1697–1776), *Sheʾelot Yaʿabets*, no. 41, fo. 70a; Ezekiel Landau (1713–1793), *Noda bi-Yehudah*, in Shlomo Wiener, "Sheelot u-teshuvot Nodah bi Yehudah betokh mekor letoledot Yisrael," *Ḥoreb* 10 (1948): 76n. 82; Pollack, *Jewish Folkways*, 286.

8. The rabbinic literature is rife with information concerning doctors and their role; I have freely borrowed from an excellent study devoted to this subject by Hirsch Jacob Zimmels, *Magicians, Theologians, and Doctors; Studies in Folk Medicine and Folklore as Reflected in the Rabbinical Responsa* (London, 1952).

9. Joseph Nathanson, *Shoʾel u-meshiv* (Lemberg, 1868–1890), III: n. 44; I. Melzer, *Otsar ha-Poskim* (Jerusalem, 1947), 1: 249; Zimmels, *Magicians*, 181n. 108.

10. Jacob Ettlinger, *Binyan Zion*, Vol. III (Altona, 1868); Jacob Reischer, *Shevut Yaʿakov* (Lemberg, 1897), III: n. 75; Zimmels, *Magicians*, 181n. 109.

11. Samson ben Zaddok, *Tashbets* (Warsaw, 1902), 3: 82; Zimmels, *Magicians*, 181n. 10.

12. Eleazar Rokeaḥ, *Rokeaḥ ḥil Teshuvah* (Zolkiew, 1866), n. 21; *Sefer Ḥasidim*, n. 176; Rabbi Israel Al Nakawa, *Menorat ha-Maʾor*, 3:116; Zimmels, *Magicians*, n. 111.

13. Reischer, *Shevut Yaʿakov*, I: n. 86; Eleazar Fleckeles, *Teshuvah me-Ahavah*, vol. 3 (Prague, 1819); Hahn, *Yosef Omets*, 76, sec. 380.

14. Opinions are divided on this subject: Rabbi Jacob Zaḥalon, *Otsar ha-Ḥaim* (Venice, 1783); Sinai Schiffer, *Sitri u-Magini* (Tyrnow, 1932–1933); I: 44n. 8; Zimmels, *Magicians*, 182n. 114.

15. Ḥayim Halberstam, "Oraḥ Ḥayim," in *Divrei Ḥayim*, (Bardiov, 1902), II: n. 25; Zimmels, *Magicians*, n. 114.

16. Zvi Hirsch Chajes, *Darkhei Oraha* (Zolkiev, 1843), no. 1; Moses Sofer, *Ḥatam Sofer* on *Yoreh Deah* (Vienna, 1855), no. 338; Zimmels, *Magicians,* n. 116.

17. Abraham Samuel Benjamin Sofer, *Ketav Sofer* (Presburg-Drohobycz, 1873–1894), no. 16; Rabbi Jehuda Assad, *Responsa Oraḥ Ḥayim,* no. 47; Zimmels, *Magicians,* n. 117.

18. Rabbi Meyer of Rothenburg, the Maharam, *Responsa* on *Yoreh Deah,* no. 343; Zimmels, *Magicians,* n. 118.

19. Elia Montalto, "Responsum," in Cecil Roth, *REJ* 94 (1933): 113.

20. Gershon Ashkenazi, *Avodat ha-Gershoni* (Frankfurt: 1699), I: no. 123; Zimmels, *Magicians,* n. 121.

21. "Ha-rofeh melekh neʾeman ve-raḥman gaʾon ha-muflah," Rabbi Asher Ben Yeḥiel, *Responsa* (Vilna, 1885), 103b.

22. Meir Margulies, "Muflag ba-Torah," in *Meir Netivim* (Polnoi, 1792), no. 75.

23. "Ha-muflah ba-Torah u-va-ḥasidut," Meir of Lublin, *Responsa* (Metz, 1769), no. 111.

24. "Rofeh Shinayim," in Schiffer, *Sitri u-Magini,* I: no. 61.

25. "Rofeh Mumḥeh le-rabim she-osek be-taḥluei nashim," *Ḥatam Sofer,* no. 15.

26. "Rofeh ha-mitaseq bi-refuot eynayim," in Nissim H. Moses Mizraḥi, *Admat Kodesh* on *Oraḥ Ḥayim* (Constantinople: 1560), no. 6.

27. Jews could study medicine at the medical school in Mantua and, beginning in the eighteenth century, in Prague.

28. D. Kaufman, *Zikhronos Moras Glikl Hamil mi Shenos, 1647–1719* (Frankfurt, 1896), 86. See Marvin Lowenthal, *The Memoirs of Glückel of Hameln* (New York, 1932, 1977).

29. Tobias ha-Cohen, *Maʾaseh Toviah* (Jesnitz, 1721), II: Introduction.

30. Jona Landsoffer, *Meʾil Tsedakah* (Prague, 1757), no. 34; Menaḥem Krochmal, *Tsemaḥ Tsedek* (Furth, 1766), no. 86; *Mishkenot Yaakov,* no. 42; cited in Zimmels, *Magicians.*

31. See Charles Singer, *A Short History of Medicine* (Oxford, 1928), 163.

32. Paul Portal, *La Pratique des accouchements* (Paris, 1682); Didelot, *Instructions pour les sages-femmes* (Nancy, 1770); P. Peu, *La Pratique des accouchements* (Paris, 1694); G. Mauquets de la Motte, *Traité des accouchements* (Paris, 1765); M. Dumont, P. Morel, *Histoire de l'obstétrique et de la gynécologie* (Lyon, 1968); Jacques Gelis, *L'Arbre et le fruit* (Paris, 1984).

33. *Ḥatam Sofer* on *Yoreh Deah,* no. 131.

34. According to E. Landau, *Noda bi-Yehudah,* nos. 44, 49; Zvi Hirsch Spiro, *Darkhei Teshuvah* on *Yoreh Deah* (Vilna, 1892), chap. CXCVI, no. 6; *Ḥatam Sofer,* no. 174; *Shevut Yaakov,* no. 42; Zimmels, *Magicians,* 192–193, nn. 166–172.

35. Léon Poliakov, *Les Mémoires de Glückel Hameln* (Paris, 1971), 154–155.

36. Excerpt from the manuscript of Mordechai of the Rabbinical School of Paris, in Wellesz in *MGJV* 35, no. 1 (1910): 117–118; J. Trachtenberg, *Jewish Magic,* 200; 304n. 14.

37. Samuel Aboab, in *Devar Shemuel* (Venice, 1702), no. 359.

38. A. Rapoport, *Eitan ha-Ezraḥi* (Ostrow, 1796), no. 21; Zimmels, *Magicians,* 193n. 191.

39. Rabbi Akiba Egger, *Responsa,* Vol. I (Warsaw, 1835); (Vienna, 1889), II: no. 74.

40. See H. Leitner, *Bibliography to the Ancient Medical Authors* (1973).

41. Ezekia Silva, *Peri Ḥadash* on *Oraḥ Ḥayim* (Karlsruhe, 1787), no. 428; Zimmels, *Magicians,* 219n. 36. We can also observe the correlation with the Midrash, see above chap. 5, "Crossing the Jabbok," which maintains that the Angel of Death plunges his sword into the water and, in so doing, poisons it.

42. *Shabbat* 2b; *Gittin* 68a; *Sotah* 21a; etc.

43. Matthew 10:1.

44. *Sefer Ḥasidim* 975, sec. 1170.

45. Deut. 28:10–11.

46. I. Isserlein, *Pesakim u-Khetavim* (Furth, 1778), 96.

47. S. Luria, *Responsa* (Lublin, 1575), 998, sec. 3; Trachtenberg, *Jewish Magic,* 199n. 14.

48. Jacob Coblenz, *Mafteaḥ ha-Yam* on *Shulḥan Arukh*; *Ketubot* 19a.

49. Trachtenberg, *Jewish Magic,* 202.

50. Trachtenberg, *Jewish Magic.*

51. Like the curious *Neue Hauss-Apothek* (17th c.), which was widely disseminated in Christian society and recorded all the medical treatments current at the time.

52. Jacob Reischer, *Shevut Ya'akov,* Vol. II (Lemberg, 1897), no. 70, fo. 11a. See Pollack, *Jewish Folkways,* 75, 295.

53. Eliakim Goetz, *Even ha-Shoḥam u-Meirat Einayim,* Vol. I (Dyhenfurth, 1733), no. 30, fo. 14b.

54. Menaḥem Mendel Krochmal was rabbi of Nikolsburg in Moravia in the sixteenth century when he wrote *Tsemaḥ Tsedek* (Furth, 1766), no. 13, fo. 13b.

55. J. Emden, *She'elot Ya'abets* (Lemberg, 1884), 1: no. 41, fo. 70b.

56. Glückel, *Memoirs,* 12–13.

57. Rabbi Eliezer Ben Eliyah Ashkenazi, *Ma'aseh ha-Shem, Ma'asei Avot* (Venice, 1583), chap. 27, 73a. Zimmels, *Magicians,* 128n. 39.

58. Zimmels, *Magicians,* 126–127; Rabbi David Zimra, *Responsa* (1882), III: 44b (548), no. 979.

59. Zimra, *Responsa,* III.

60. Abraham ben Mordechai ha-Levy, *Ginnat Veradim* (Constantinople, 1716–1717), on *Yoreh Deah* I, no. 4; Rabbi Judah Rosanes, *Mishneh la-Melekh* on *Mishneh Torah* and *Evel,* III and I, 14 and 21. On prohibitions: *Ḥillul, Ma'akhalot Asurot,* 8 and 18.

61. Zimmels, *Magicians,* 126–128.

62. *Ma'avar Yabbok,* "Siftei Ra'ananut," sec. 25, p. 128. Joseph Ben Moses, *Leket Yosher,* II (Berlin, 1903–1904), no. 87. Abraham Danzig, *Ta'amei ha-Minhagim* (Lemberg, 1911–1912), no. 43.

63. Zimmels, *Magicians,* 116, on Avigdor Cohen Tsedek in *Abhandlungen zur Erinnerung an Hirsch Perez Chayes* (1933), 206.

64. *Shabbat* 75b, and Rashi's commentary.

65. C. F. Leyel, *The Magic of Herbs* (London, 1932), 97.

66. Talmud and Tosefta *Baba Kama* VIII; Naḥmanides, *Responsa,* no. 206.

67. Moses Teomim, *Devar Moshe* (Lemberg, 1864), nos. 8, 9; and his *Oryan Telitai* (Lemberg, 1880), no. 159.

68. *Binyan Tsion,* no. 49; *Darkhei Teshuvah,* 155, cites *Naḥameh Afarseman, Yoreh Deah,* no. 143; in modern medicine, see David Zvi Hofmann, *Melammed le-Hoil* (Berlin, 1926–1932), V: no. 33.

69. Samson Morpurgo, *Shemesh Tsedakah* (Venice, 1743), on *Yoreh Deah,* no. 29; *Darkhei Teshuvah,* 81, no. 1; *Otsar ha-Ḥayim,* II: no. 17, p. 18b; Daniel Terni, *Ikkarei Dinim* (Florence, 1803), XV: no. 3. Human or donkey urine: Rabba, *Responsa,* 1: no. 577; Radbaz, II: no. 739.

70. *Oryan Telitai; Ketav Sofer, O.H.,* no. 22; *Ḥatam Sofer, Y.D.,* no. 73; *Melammed le-Hoil,* 5: no. 33; *Darkhei Teshuvah,* 115, no. 22. Abraham Yizḥaki, *Zera Abraham,* on *Yoreh Deah* (Smyrna, 1733), no. 26; *Ikkarei Dinim,* 15, 5–8.

71. Ishmael ben Abraham ha-Cohen, *Zera Emet* (Livorno, 1786–1796), (Reggio, 1815), no. 47; *Darkhei Teshuvah,* 155, no. 22.

72. Asher ben Yeḥiel, *Bessamim Rosh* (Berlin, 1793), no. 1.

73. *Bessamim Rosh,* no. 171; *Leket Yosher,* I: 40.

74. Maharam, *Responsa,* no. 179.

75. Manasseh ben Israel, *Nishmat Ḥayim* (Stettin, 1861), III: 14.

76. *Zera Emet,* no. 30.

77. Abraham ben Samuel Meyuḥas, *Sedeh ha-Arets,* I, II (Salonika, 1784–1798); III (Livorno, 1788) on *Oraḥ Ḥayim,* no. 16; Radbaz, III, no. 1062.

78. *Zera Emet,* no. 48; cited in *Darkhei Teshuvah,* 155, no. 116.

79. Jacob Hagiz, *Halakhot Ketanot* (Venice, 1704), no. 20.

80. *Darkhei Teshuvah,* 155.

81. *Ḥavvot Yair,* no. 105; *Sefer Zekhirah* (1709) 32a.

82. *Shemesh Tsedaka* on *Yoreh Deah,* no. 29.

83. *Ikkarei Dinim,* 15, 3. Galen also recommends this treatment; see Lynn Thorndyke, *A History of Magic and Experimental Science During the First Sixteen Centuries of Our Era* (New York, 1923, 1958), I: 170; C. F. Leyel, *The Magic of Herbs* (London, 1932), 278; Zimmels, *Magicians,* 245n. 50.

84. On the "evil eye," Maharam, *Responsa,* no. 40; Tachbets, no. 60.

85. S. Luria, *Responsa,* no. 47.

86. Solomon Kluger, *Tuv Ta'am va-Da'at* (Podgorz, 1900), 2: no. 47.

87. Ephraim ben Jacob ha-Cohen, *Sha'ar Efraim* (Lemberg, 1887), no. 90.

88. *Divrei Ḥayim,* on *Even ha-Ezer* (Jacob ben Asher, *Arba'ah Turim,* III, Vilna edition, 1900), no. 13; Isaac Spektor, *Ein Yitsḥak* (Vilna, 1889–1895), on *Even ha-Ezer,* no. 20.

89. *Shevut Ya'akov,* II, no. 50; *Shabbat* 66b.

90. Ḥayim Azulai, *Birkhei Yosef* (Vienna, 1859), on *Oraḥ Ḥayim,* 301n. 6, cited in *Zera Emet* III, no. 214.

91. *Shevut Ya'akov,* II: no. 50; *Shabbat* 66b.

92. *Shemesh Tsedakah,* no. 29.

93. *Ma'aseh Tovia,* III, 19, p. 109b; it seems that a flourishing trade in belts made of human skin, taken from soldiers who died in combat or from anatomical dissections, did exist. *She'elot Ya'abets,* I, no. 41; Eliya ben Samuel of Lublin, *Yad Eliahu* (Amsterdam, 1712), no. 66, cited in *Yad Efraim* on *Yoreh Deah* 17, no. 1, according to Zimmels, *Magicians,* 136.

94. See Robert Blaser, *Paracelse et sa conception de la nature* (Geneva, 1950). Alexandre Koyre, *Mystiques, spirituels, alchimistes du XVI*[e] *siècle allemand* (Paris, 1955, 1970).

95. S. Morpurgo, *Divrei ha-Ḥakhamim*; *Sedeh Emet,* no. 125. Excerpt from Zimmels, *Magicians,* 122–123.

96. Glückel, *Memoirs,* 87–88.

97. See Glückel, *Memoirs,* 67, 180.

98. John MacManners, *Death and the Enlightenment* (Oxford, 1981), 25.

99. Glückel, *Memoirs,* 128.

100. See Trachtenberg, *Jewish Magic,* 157.

101. Ps. 20.

102. See above, chap. 5, "Mortuary Literature," n. 42 on Lilith.

103. In I. Holzer, "Aus dem Leben der alten Jugengemeinde zu Worms nach dem Minhagbuch des Juspa Shames" in *ZGJD* 5 (1935): 71.

104. According to *Sanhedrin* 10a and Rashi. Trachtenberg, *Jewish Magic,* 203.

105. Margulies, *Sefer Ḥasidim,* sec. 382; sec. 441.

106. Menahem Ziyuni, *Tsefunei Tsiyuni* (Lemberg, 1882), 20a; Trachtenberg, *Jewish Magic,* 233n. 6, 310.

107. *Shelah,* in *Massekhet Ḥullin* 91a.

108. Raben, *Sefer Even-ha-Ezer* (1926).

109. In *Or Zarua,* sec. 164.

110. See Adolf Lowinger, *Der Traum in der jüdischen Literatur,* Leipzig, 1908.

111. Glückel, *Memoirs,* 13.

112. *Nedarim,* 8a.

113. The "*Ta'anit Ḥalom*" in *Shelah, Massekhet Shabbat,* II: 85; *Maggid Mesharim* on *Isaiah,* chap. 40 (1929), 135; *Zerah Emet,* III: no. 63; *Ikkarei Dinim,* on *Oraḥ Ḥayim,* 30, 94; on the eve of Pesach *Ikkarei Dinim* 171; Saturdays *Leket Yosher,* I, 41; Menaḥem Recanati, *Piskei rabbi Menaḥem Recanati* (Bologne, 1538), no. 178, etc.

114. Trachtenberg, *Jewish Magic,* 51.

115. *Benjamin Ze'ev* (Venice, 1539), no. 126; Zimmels, *Magicians,* 222, no. 99.

116. Also called *koltunes* in *Ma'aseh Tovia,* II: 84c; see M. Freudenthal, "Leon Elias Hirsch," *MGWJ* 50 (1906): 436, in Zimmels, *Magicians,* 228n. 33.

117. See Trachtenberg, *Jewish Magic,* 156.

118. *Shelah, Massekhet Ḥullin* 90a.

119. See above, chap. 4, "The Period of Rupture," n. 45; Nathan Nata Hannover, *Sefer Sha'arei Tsion ve-Tikkun Se'uda ve-Sefer Yetsirah* (Venice, 1736).

120. *Sefer Yetsirah*.

121. In the Lurianic literature, Samuel Vital, *Sha'ar ha-Gilgulim* (Cairo, 1666), 1903 edition; Ḥayim Vital, *Sefer ha-Ḥezyonot* (Damascus, 1598; published 1954); "*Sha'ar ha-Gilgulim*" in *Ets ha-Ḥayim* (1660; Jerusalem, 1863–1898); *Nishmat Ḥayim* III: 10, 4; Moses Graff of Prague, *Kuntres Ma'asei ha-Shem Ki-nora Hu* (Furth, 1696); see M. Weinreich, *Bilder fun der yiddisher Literaturgeschichte* (Vilna, 1928); Gedalia Nigal, *Sippurei Dibbuk be-Sifrut Yisrael* (Jerusalem, 1983).

122. The *Pidyon Nefesh*.

123. Azulai, *Avodat ha-Kodesh* (Jerusalem, 1841), 103b.

124. Luncz, *Jerusalem* (Vienna, 1882), I: 19.

125. *Ikkarei Dinim,* I, on *Oraḥ Ḥayim, Din Yom Tov,* 83a, n. 22; Zimmels, *Magicians,* 255n. 243.

126. *Ma'aseh Tovia, Beit Ḥadash,* IV: 96, 188.

127. Trachtenberg, *Jewish Magic,* 204n. 21, 304.

128. Excerpt from the *Memorbuch of Vienna,* 1669, in Moritz Stern, "Memorbuch ha-Yashan de-Kehillat Vina Lifneh ha-Gerush," in *Berliner's Festschrift* (Frankfurt, 1903).

129. *Rosh ha-Shana* 16b; *Genesis Rabbah* 44, 10.

130. I. Isserlein, *Terumat ha-Deshen* (Venice, 1519; Furth, 1778), n. 234; *Leket Yosher,* II, n. 83.

131. Moses ben Jacob of Coucy (13th c.), *Sefer Mitsvot Gadol (Semag),* II: 16, Kopys, 1807. See also the formula for the buying back of the soul in the *Tikkun Nefesh* of E. Landau (Prague, 1786).

132. *Ḥatam Sofer* III; *Ma'avar Yabbok,* "Sefat Emet," sec. 13: 176.

133. R. Yona Navon, *Neḥpah ba-Kessef* (Constantinople, 1748), on *O.H.*, n. 4; Zimmels, *Magicians,* 143n. 221, 253.

134. See the description of the ceremony in Trachtenberg, *Jewish Magic,* 205.

135. The Yersin factor, Leonard Fabian Hirst, *The Conquest of the Plague* (Oxford, 1953).

136. Anton Margarita, "Von der Juden Krankheiten," in *Der gantz jüdisch glaub* (Augsburg, 1530) (unpaginated).

137. Daniel Defoe, *A Journal of the Plague Year in London* (New York, 1992), 21.

138. Moses ben Ḥayim Eisenstadt, *Ayn naye Klaglied,* in manuscript, Oxford, Opp. 8, 643 (4).

139. The four exiles mark the chronological ordering of the world, according to the Tradition, from the book of Daniel: Egypt, Babylon, Persia, and Edom.

140. The month of Av is called *menaḥem Av* (which consoles), according to the principle of euphemization frequently mentioned here. Av is a month of mourning, symbolizing all the calamities that have befallen the Jewish people since the destruction of the Temple.

141. The Rabbinic School.

142. The Community Council.

143. The month of Ellul is a penitential period preceding the "days of

awe" that begin with the new year (Rosh Hashanah) and conclude with the Day of Atonement (Yom Kippur).

144. The joyful holiday celebrating the Torah which marks the beginning of the annual cycle of weekly readings from the Hebrew Bible.

145. The pharmacy in Prague is the oldest Jewish pharmacy in the German lands, apparently dating back to 1633. See B. Kisch, "The History of the Jewish Pharmacy in Prague," *HJ* 8: 149–180; M. Grunwald, "Aus Hausapotheke und Hexenküche," *MGJV* 5 (1900); n.s., 30 (1927–1928): 27–29, 178–226; see Grünwald also in *Jahrbuch für jüdische Volskunde* 1 (1923): 178–226.

146. See 2 Sam. 24.

147. See the precipitous departure in 1607 of the Grand Rabbi of Prague, Ephraim Lenczycz, accompanied by all the community notables, while the epidemic ravaged the city, in E. Lenczycz, introduction to *Amudei Shash*; and Gustav Klemperer, "The Rabbis of Prague," *HJ* 12 (1950): 46; compare with the flight of the prelates in C. Carrière, M. Courdurie, and F. Rebuffat, *Marseille ville morte, la Peste de 1720* (Marseille, 1968), 66.

148. Before this epidemic the plague also occurred in Prague in 1613 and in 1679–1680, which would explain the rigorous organization put in place for the management of the disease. *Shevut Yaakov,* II: no. 84 and 97; III: no. 30; Pollack, *Jewish Folkways,* 131; Reisher, on *Yoreh Deah,* 362, 1–2.

149. See the fires in Jean Noel Biraben, *Les Hommes et la peste en France et dans les pays européens et méditerranéens* (Paris, 1975).

150. Manzoni, cited by Delumeau, *La Peur en Occident,* 114n. 87.

151. Isaac Masran, *Ha-Galut ve-ha-Pedut* (Venice, 1634), 10.

152. A practice condemned elsewhere in the 19th century. Hayim Palaggi, *Ḥayim be-Yad* (Smyrna, 1878) on *Yoreh Deah,* no. 81; Zimmels, *Magicians,* 100n. 81, 230.

153. *Ma'aseh Toviah,* II: 101b; the question remains whether or not it is relevant to flee from an epidemic, for either one is condemned—in which case flight is useless—or one is not—in which case it is judicious. See Rabbi Simon Duran, *Responsa* no. 195, which suggests nonetheless to save oneself at all costs; *Shivḥei ha-Ari* 34a.

154. Defoe, *Journal,* 132.

155. The columns of the plague in Marseille, in Carrière et al., *Marseille ville morte,* 123; J. N. Biraben, *Les Homme et la peste,* II: 65–69.

156. Leon of Modena, *Ḥayyei Yehudah* (Kiev edition, 1913), 51. On collective fasts, see also Marcus, *Communal,* 218.

157. Delumeau, *La Peur en Occident,* 136–137, and 433n. 190: in particular the attitude of Luther, "*Ob man vor dem Sterben fliehen moege,*" Martin Luther, *Sammtliche Werke* 22 (Weimar, 1883–1948): 323–386.

158. See above, Moses Eisenstadt's second piece of advice.

159. M. N. Adler, *The Itinerary of Benjamin of Tudela*; see *Massaot shel Rabbi Benjamin. Itinerarium D. Beniaminus cum Versione et Notis Constantini l'Empereur ab. Oppyck Iudyum Batavorium* (1633).

160. Hahn, *Yosef Omets,* 205.

161. Trachtenberg, *Jewish Magic,* 65–66n. 33.

162. Delumeau, *La Peur en Occident,* 233.

163. Delumeau, *La Peur en Occident,* 369.

164. See particularly in the Talmud, *Shabbat* 2b; *Gittin* 68a; *Megillah* 2b; *Sotah* 21a.

165. *Yoma* 20a.

166. *Genesis Rabbah* 38:7; JT *Berakhot* 1:1; *Shabbat* 2:6.

167. *Zohar,* 44, fo. 41; *Shelah,* "Massekhet Pesaḥim" 5; *Maʾavar Yabbok,* "Siftei tsedek," chap. 1, 55.

168. *Sefer Ḥasidim* (Margulies), sec. 605.

169. See, for example, in Jehiel Epstein, *Kitsur Shelah* (Berlin, 1715), fo. 57a; Zacharia Plangian, *Sefer Zekhirah* (Hamburg, 1709), fo. 9a; the *Testament of Sheftel Horowitz,* already cited, and in *JQR* 3 (1891): 479; Gudemann, *Geschichte,* I: 203–204, 215.

170. Who is called *Mekhashef.* See Lynn Thorndike, *A History of Magic and Experimental Science during the First Sixteen Centuries of Our Era,* 8 vols. (New York, 1923, 1958); James George Frazer, *The Golden Bough* (England, 1890); Yossi Dan, "Magic," *EJ* 11: 703–715.

171. Aaron J. Gurevitch, *Les Catégories de la culture médiévale* (Paris, 1988), 9; *Categories of Medieval Culture* (London, 1985).

172. Hahn, *Yosef Omets,* 203.

173. *Tsefunei Tsiyuni.*

174. See the Florentine circles of Christian Kabbalah around Giovani Pico della Mirandola, the Jewish convert Samuel ben Nissim Abulafaraj, and Raymond Moncada. See Jean Reuchlin, *De Verbo mirifico* (1494), and *De Arte cabbalistica* (1517).

175. Cornelius Agrippa of Nettesheim, *De Occulta Philosophia* (1531); the term of practical Kabbalah distinguishes this from the theological doctrine.

176. Ernest Bax, *German Culture, Past and Present* (New York, 1915), 118.

177. Cited by Pollack, *Jewish Folkways,* 118.

178. See Trachtenberg, *The Devil and the Jews,* 81–87.

179. Re: The medieval assimilation of the "Jew" to the "sorcerer." Suspicion or condemnation for "sorcery" should not be minimized. When a Jew was suspected or condemned for sorcery, it was most often Judaism that was on trial, and we can cite, for example, the case of a woman called Judith Franchetti who, at the age of 77, was burned at the stake as a sorceress in Mantua in 1600, for having incited a nun to embrace Judaism. The special targets of the Inquisition were the "new Christians," constantly suspected of heresy and apostasy, who were often fodder for the pyres. Accusations of ritual murder, of profanation of the host, and so on, are all related to those of sorcery, except that they are addressed specifically to Jews and do not require a return to the category of "black" magic. On this subject, see H. C. Lea, *A History of the Inquisition in the Middle Ages* (New York, 1911).

180. Anonymous extract, in Gedalia Nigal, *Sippurei Dibbuk, be-Sifrut Yisrael* (Jerusalem, 1983), 106–107.

181. Jacques Le Goff, *L'Imaginaire médiéval* (Paris, 1985), 139.

182. Le Goff, *L'Imaginaire médiéval,* 139.

## CHAPTER 8. SICKNESS AND DEATH

1. Barukh Mevoraḥ, "Ma'aseh ha-Hishtadlut be-Eropa li-Meniyat Gerusham shel Yehudei Bohemia u-Moravia, 1744–1745" *Zion* 28 (1963): 124–164.

2. Mevoraḥ, *Zion* 28: 136. On the activities of the English community, see C. Roth, *A History of the Jews in England* (Oxford, 1949).

3. The decree of expulsion also indicates the shift from a religious anti-Judaism to "political" anti-Semitism as it manifests itself during the Napoleonic period of the convocation of the "Great Sanhedrin" in France and Germany. The first, anonymous edition of the *Protocols* came out in Paris in the last years of the nineteenth century. It was disseminated in Russia in 1905 and was widely diffused in the years from 1920–1930. It became a famous centerpiece of the Nazi regime.

4. The diplomatic negotiations spread over several years.

5. On Josel of Rosheim, see Marcus, *The Jew in the Medieval World,* sec. 41, p. 198; Lowenthal, *The Jews of Germany,* 161–173. For his role in Prague in the sixteenth century, see Goldberg, *Les Institutions de la mort,* 1:88.

6. A tax of 204,000 guldens was imposed on the new community, which had to be annually augmented by 1,000 guldens after the first five years. See *EJ* 10:157; Josef Bergl, "Die Ausweisung der Juden aus Prag im Jahre 1744," in Steinherz, *Die Juden in Prag,* 187–247.

7. Guido Kisch, "The Yellow Badge in History," in *HJ* 4 (1942): 95–144.

8. See J. Bergl, "Die Ausweisung," in Steinherz, as above, note 6.

9. Compare with the statements of Father Gregory in his essay for the meeting of the Academy at Metz in 1787. C. W. Dohm, *Ueber die buergerliche Verbesserung der Juden* (Berlin, 1781).

10. The taxes of Leibmaut and Leibzoll.

11. In the records of the ḥevra kaddisha of Prague, the language shifts without transition from Hebrew writing to German. *Records,* ms., *JMP* 46595, Jerusalem HM 3827, HM 3927.

12. J. Prokes, "Die prager Judenkonskription vom Jahre 1729," *JGJC* 4 (1932): 297–332.

13. See Ruth Kestenberg-Gladstein, "The Jews Between Czechs and Germans in the Historic Lands, 1848–1918," in *The Jews of Czeckoslovakia* (Philadelphia, 1968), I: 21–71; and Kestenberg-Gladstein, in *Neuere Geschichte der Juden in den Bohmischen Landern* (Tubingen, 1969), 341–349.

14. See above, chap. 3, "A Community and Its Environment."

15. Henry E. Strakosch, *State Absolutism and the Rule of Law: The Struggle for Codification of Civil Law in Austria 1753–1811* (Sydney, 1968); H. Benedikt, "Der Josephinismus vor Joseph II" in *Oesterreich und Europa,* 183–201; Victor-Louis Tapie, *Monarchies et peuples du Danube* (Paris, 1969); and his *L'Europe de Marie-Thérèse du Baroque aux Lumières* (Paris, 1973).

16. Léon Lallemand, *Histoire de la charité* (Paris, 1910), 4:73.

17. The German procedure of closing the intraurban cemeteries is characteristic of the period. See Ariès, *The Hour of Our Death,* 479–496.

18. Vladimir Sadek, "La Chronique hébraique des Juifs pragois de la deuxième moitié de XVIIIe siècle," *JB* I (1956): 59–68.

19. From Voltaire to Mendelssohn, by way of Dohm and Mirabeau, it is clear that the Jews' achievement of full citizenship is unimaginable without the intervention of drastic transformations.

20. Zalkind Hurwitz's report is found in the library of Metz, ms. 1349, fos. 549–594, and in *La Révolution française et l'émancipation des juifs* (Paris: EDHIS; 1968), 4:1–2, 335–340.

21. Hurwitz's letter dated 20 *ventose,* year 13. A. N. F 19/11030, cited in S. A. Goldberg, "Étude de deux cimetières juifs à Paris au XVIIIe siècle" (unpublished, 1981), 197–198.

22. The emancipation of the Jews of Holland: 1796.

23. Rome: 1798.

24. Venice: 1797.

25. Rhineland, Westphalia: 1807.

26. Frankfurt: 1811.

27. See chap. 4, "The Community and the Burial Society."

28. The "Jewish musician," like the peddler, is one of these archetypal figures of an older society. He was itinerant, going from community to community, also playing on occasion for Christians. See above, chap. 3, "The Jews and Christians of Prague."

29. On this subject, see Simon Dubnow, *History of the Jews of Russia and Poland Until the Present Day* (Philadelphia, 1916); S. W. Baron, *A Social and Religious History of the Jews* (New York, 1952–1983).

30. The purposes of this study do not lend themselves to a discussion of the Sabbatian heresy. In the eighteenth century, the communities of central Europe were torn apart by Sabbatianism, and a great number of excommunications were linked to the suspicion that pervaded Jewish society. No one was spared; rabbis and scholars were equally incriminated in the heresy. On this subject, see Jacob Emden, *Torat ha-kena'ot* (Altona, 1752), and *Sefer Hit'abkut,* (Altona, 1762); Jonathan Eybeschutz, *Luḥot Edut* (1775); H. B. Graeṭz, *Geschichte der Juden* 7: 428–524; G. Scholem, *Sabbatai Sevi* (Princeton, 1973); Scholem, "The Sabbatian Movement in Poland," in *RHR* (1953–1955): 43–44.

31. See Lallemand, *Histoire de la charité.*

32. Excerpt from the anonymous "Ayne Klaglied oyf a meshores fun Frankfurt," [Aron Freimann, ed.,] *Filologishe Shriftn* (1928), 2:170–173.

33. Elḥanan Kirchan, *Simḥat ha-Nefesh* (1726–1727), in Shatzky, ed. (New York, 1926), 2:36, fo. 17b, and introduction.

34. See Kirchan, as above, and see also Pollack, *Jewish Folkways,* 163n. 6; 322.

35. A. Shoḥat, *Im Ḥillufei,* 153–161.

36. Georg Liebe, *Das Judentum in der deutschen Vergangenheit* (Leipzig, 1903).

37. Berthold Rosenthal, *Heimatsgeschichte der badischen Juden* (1927), sec. 209; H. Kottek, *Geschichte der Juden von Bad Homburg v.d. Hoehe,* sec. 5, cited by A. Shoḥat, as in note 35, above: 311, n. 135.

38. *Pinkas kehillat Frankfurt* (community records), fo. 141, sec. 20, 30, 46 and in Shoḥat, *Im Ḥillufei,* 166.

39. See Ezekiel Katznellenbogen, *Knesset Yeḥezkiel* (Altona, 1732), sec. 73; J. Eybeschutz, *Sefer Hit'abkut,* sec. 21, fo. 2; *Shevut Yaakov,* III, sec. 129; Shoḥat, *Im Ḥillufei,* 169. See the decree of the Lithuanian Jewish National Council of 1637, and also F. Wettstein, *Kadmoniyyot mi-Pinkessa'ot Yeshanim le-Korot Yisrael be Polin bi-khelal ve-bi Cracow be prat* (1892), 42–48; and Wettstein, *Devarim Attikim mi-Pinkessei ha-Kahal bi-Cracow* (1901), V, n. 5.

40. Max Grunwald, "Hamburgs deutsche Juden bis zum Auflosung der Dreigemeinde, 1811," *MGJV* 12 (1903): sec. 125, 16; *MGJV* 13 (1911): sec. 27.

41. *Sefer Minhagim di-Kehilateynu* (Furth, 1767): 2; Shoḥat, *Im Ḥillufei* 168, n. 38.

42. Shoḥat, *Im Ḥillufei.*

43. Israel Halperin, *Constitutiones Congressus Generalis, Judaeorum Moraviensum, 1650–1748* (Jerusalem, 1952), 265, 267, p. 88.

44. The Jews had the opportunity to convert in Holland and in England.

45. Rabbi Zvi ben Samuel of Semjatitchi, in the introduction to *Margaliot ha-Torah* (Poryck, 1788), 3a, cited in Marcus, *Communal,* 124.

46. *Pinkas Kehillat Frankfurt,* 176, fos. 1–2, cited in Shoḥat, *Im Ḥillufei,* 120.

47. Halperin, *Constitutiones Congressus,* sec. 196, p. 65.

48. Halperin, *Constitutiones Congressus,* sec. 245, p. 81.

49. J. R. Marcus, "The Triesch Hebra Kadisha," *HUCA* 19: see article 20 and see above, chap. 5, "The Secret of the Tree of Life," nn. 79 and 81.

50. See above, chap. 5, "From Affliction to Sorrow."

51. Halperin, *Constitutiones Congressus,* sec. 201, p. 67.

52. This special tariff for "pardon" was instituted in 1624. The alms boxes were then sealed in the south wall of the main synagogue, the Alt-Neue Schul; see Milada Vilimkova, "Seven Hundred Years of the Alt-Neue Synagogue," *JB* 5 (1965): 72.

53. The text written on this occasion exists in manuscript, entitled *Prague Pardon: Tikkunim Meyusharim Yesdom Ḥakhamim di-Kehillateynu Prag,* Oxford, Opp. 4/557 (5), sec. 38.

54. This is how J. R. Marcus regards it in "The Triesch Hebra Kadisha."

55. *Sefer Berakh le-Avraham ben Meir ha-Levi* (Prague, 1735), unpaginated; in A. Shoḥat, *Im Ḥillufei,* 121n. 157.

56. Jacob Emden, *Megillat Sefer* (1896), 151.

57. Zvi Hirsch Kaidanover, in *Kav ha-Yashar* (Sulzbach, 1705), sec. 9. In this work intended to present the torments of the soul of sinners in hell, Kaidanover also sketches a picture of community oppression, of religious laxness, and of the difficult economic and intellectual conditions of Jewish society in the wake of "Sabbatianism." See also Avigdor Tcherikover, *Jiwobleter* (1932), 4: 159–167.

58. On this subject, see also Jean Bayer, *Les Instituts séculiers* (Paris, 1954); Max Heimbucher, *Die Orden und Kongregationen der Katholischen Kirche* (Paderborn, 1907–1908); Jean Houlier, *Histoire du droit et des institutions de*

*l'Église en Occident* (St. Armand-Moutrond, 1974); Michel Mollat, *The Poor in the Middle Ages,* trans. Arthur Goldhammer (New Haven, 1986).

59. In particular among the studies on poverty, see Lallemand, *Histoire de la charité*; and Mollat, ed., *Études sur l'histoire de la pauvreté* (Paris, 1974); Erich Maschke, *Pauvres urbains et pauvres ruraux dans l'Allemagne médiévale,* Sorbonne notebooks, Vol. I, no. 7; Bronislaw Geremiek, *La Potence ou la pitié* (Paris, 1987).

60. A repertory of the punishments inflicted on the poor was reported by Lallemand, *Histoire de la charité,* 4: chap. 3.

61. Lallemand, *Histoire de la charité,* 4: 207–214; and in Maschke, *Pauvres urbains et pauvres ruraux.*

62. Lallemand, *Histoire de la charité,* 4: 240.

63. *Recueil des établissements d'humanité,* 66, in Lallemand, *Histoire de la charité,* 4: 241; compare with above, n. 33.

64. See Michel Foucault, *Discipline and Punish,* trans. Alan Sheridan Smith (New York, 1979), and *The Birth of the Clinic,* trans. Smith (New York, 1975).

65. See Philippe Ariès, *Western Attitudes Towards Death* (Baltimore, 1974); and his *Hour of Our Death.*

66. See Marcus, *Communal,* 169.

67. There could be several *hekdeshim* in the large communities: there were two in Lissa, Posen, Breslau, Hanover, Vienna, and Berlin and three in Frankfurt. See Louis Lewin, *Geschichte der Juden in Lissa* (Pinne, 1904); J. Grätzer, *Geschichte der Israelitischen Kranken-Verpflegungs-Anstalt und Beerdigungs-Gesellschaft zu Breslau* (Breslau, 1841); "Seder ha-Takkanot ha-Ḥadashot Ḥevra Kadisha Gemilut Ḥasadim u-Bikkur Holim de Kehilat Kodesh Breslau," *Kitsur Maavar Yabbok* (Dyhernfurth, 1797); W. Hanauer, *Festschrift zur Einweihung des neuen Krankenhauses der israelitischen Gemeinde zu Frankfurt am Main* (Frankfurt, 1914); L. Ronne and H. Simon, *Die früheren und gegenwärtigen Verhältnisse der Juden in den sammtlichen. Landestheilen des preussischen staates* (Breslau, 1843); Max Grünwald, *Vienna* (Philadelphia, 1936); Samuel Meyer, *Geschichte des Wohltatigkeitsvereins der Synagoguen-gemeinde Hannover* (Hanover, 1862).

68. Marcus, *Communal,* 188–194.

69. *Takkanot Fiurda,* sec. 220, manuscript, Hebrew Union College, sec. 220, cited in Marcus, *Communal,* 187, and Andreas Würfel, *Historische Nachricht von der Judengemeinde in dem Hofmarkt Furth unterhalb Nurnberg* (Frankfurt, 1754), 24–38.

70. Marcus, *Communal,* 193.

71. See also A. Shoḥat, *Im Ḥillufei,* 121.

72. Glückel, *Les Mémoires* (French edition), 246. [This passage is not included in the Lowenthal edition—trans.]

73. See above, chap. 4, "The Institution of Death."

74. Excerpt from the rules of the Burial Society of Vienna, 1763; also Marcus, *Communal,* 117.

75. Lallemand, *Histoire de la charité,* 4: 241.

76. See above, chap. 7, "Pestilence."

77. B. Kisch, "The History of the Jewish Pharmacy in Prague," *HJ* 8 (1946): 149–180; and G. Kisch, "Die prager Universität und die Juden 1348–1848," *MGWJ* 79 (1935): 270–363; *JGJC* 8 (1936): 130.

78. On the burial society of Vienna, see Bernhard Wachstein, *Die Gründung der wiener Chewra Kadischa im Jahre 1763* (Presburg, 1910).

79. On the burial society of Frankfurt, A. Sulzbach, "*Ein alter frankfurter Wohltatigkeitsverein*" *JJLG* 2 (1904): 241–266; of Prague, J. Diamant and B. Glaser, "Statuten einer Chewrah Kadischa für Jügendliche in Prag zum Ende des 18. Jahrhunderts" *ZGJD* 4 (1938): 13–22; of Dresden, Emil Lehmann, "In Festlichen Stundenfestrede zur Feier des 125 jahrigen Bestehens der israelitischen Beerdigungsbrüderschaft und Krankenverpflegungsgesellschaft am 13. Februar 1875," in *Gesammelte Schriften* (Berlin, 1899), 39–53.

80. Rules of the Prague Burial Society (1692), article 25.

81. See above, note 76.

82. Rule of the female burial society of the community of Rendsburg. Transcription made by Hadassa Assouline, from the manuscript in the Jerusalem Archives. GA/Rendsburg 18.

83. On this subject, see Ariès, *The Hour of Our Death,* 389–405.

84. Ariès, *The Hour of Our Death,* 398.

85. This subject has been analyzed by Moshe Sammet, *Halakhah ve-Reformah,* unpublished doctoral dissertation (Hebrew University, Jerusalem, 1967), 76–172.

86. Sammet, *Halakhah ve-Reformah,* 77–78.

87. Statistics on apparent deaths in Finkel, *Mi-Tsarei Shaul* 46; Emil Altschul, *Kol Korei Kritisches Sendschreiben ueber das bisherige Verfahren mit dem Sterbenden bei den Israeliten* (Prague, 1846), 64, cited in Sammet, 21n. 13.

88. Jacob Katz, *Massoret u-Mashber* (Tel-Aviv, 1958), 301.

89. See in Alexander Altmann, *Moses Mendelssohn: A Biographical Study* (Birmingham, 1973), 288–295.

90. Altmann, *Moses Mendelssohn,* 288; S. A. Goldberg, "La Bible dans les attitudes juives face à la mort," in Y. Belaval and Dominique Bourel, eds., *Le Siècle des Lumières et la Bible* (Paris, 1986), 397–414.

91. S. Silberstein, "Mendelssohn und Mecklenburg," *ZGJD* I (1929): 233–244, 278–286.

92. The text of this letter appears in Silberstein, "Mendelssohn und Mecklenburg," 284; Mendelssohn's correspondence in *Jubiläumsausgabe Moses Mendelssohns Gesammelten Schriften* (Stuttgart, 1971), *Jub. A,* 16, letter 133, p. 157.

93. See above, chap. 1, "Rejoicing."

94. Zlotnick, *The Tractate Mourning (Semaḥot),* 8: 1, see chap. 1, n. 21.

95. On this subject, see also Meyer Kayserling, "Die Begrabnissfrague," in *Moses Mendelssohn sein Leben und seine Werke* (Leipzig, 1862), 276–280; Moses Mendelssohn, "Von Schenkungen Todes halber und im gefunden Zustande," in *Gesammelten Schriften,* 6:33–47. Mendelssohn relies also on *Yoma,* 86, and *Nidah* 69b, 96. *Jub. A* 16, letter 134, p. 157.

96. *Jub. A* 16, letter 134, p. 157.

97. *Jub. A* 16, letter 135, p. 159.

98. *Jub. A* 16, letter 162.

99. Jacob Emden, *Iggeret Bikkoret* (Zhitomir, 1868), 41b, 47b.

100. The journal appeared for the first time in 1783 in Koenigsberg. Its founders were Isaac Euchel and Naftali Wessely, who were engaged in all the polemics supported by the progressives. See also J. Katz, *Massoret u-Mashber,* 301.

101. The Berlin Hebrew journal, *Ha-Meʾassef,* 1788.

102. Ludwig Lesser, *Chronik der Gesselschaft der Freunde in Berlin* (Berlin, 1842), 3.

103. Lesser, *Chronik,* 5–6.

104. Lesser, *Chronik,* 23–28.

105. Zalkind Hurwitz, *Apologie des juifs*; see above, note 20.

106. Hurwitz; see above, note 21.

107. Lipmann Bash, *Sefer Divrei Emet* (Prague, 1789), sec. 3.

108. *Sefer Divrei Emet,* sec. 12.

109. Moses Wolf Jeiteles, *Zikkaron le-Yom ha-Aḥaron* (Prague, 1830–1860), introduction.

110. Jeiteles, *Zikkaron le-Yom ha-Aḥaron.*

111. See above, "Mortuary Literature," chap. 5, n. 13.

112. Jeiteles, *Zikkaron le-Yom ha-Aḥaron,* 16.

113. Gen. 46:4.

114. Jeiteles, *Zikkaron,* 20.

115. Jacob B. Brandeis, *Maawar Jabok, Sefer Maʿavar Yabbok Gebete bei Kranken, Sterbenden und im Trauerhause* (Prague, 1884).

116. Brandeis, *Maawar Jabok,* 108.

117. Brandeis, *Maawar Jabok,* 93.

118. The Hebrew and German translations of the words of comfort are "*Ha-makom yenaḥem otkḥem betokh sheʾar avelei Tsion vi-Yerushalayim*"; and "*Der Herr mog trusten mit den ubrigen Leidtragenden Zions und Jerusalem,*" from Brandeis, *Maawar Jabok,* 99.

119. Brandeis, *Maawar Jabok,* 109–110.

120. Jeiteles, *Zikkaron,* 58.

121. Jeiteles, *Zikkaron,* 58.

122. Gen. 32:23.

123. Aharon Ha-Cohen, *Oreḥot Ḥayim,* M. Schlesinger, ed. (Berlin, 1902), 2: 575; see also Benayahu, *Maʿamadot u-Moshavot* (Jerusalem, 1985), 39–40.

124. Hahn, *Yosef Omets,* "Leaving the Body," 327.

125. Ps. 91:1–11.

126. Israel ben Eliezer, called the Besht or the Baʾal Shem Tov (1700–1760), founded a new religious order on an oral tradition. His personality and the legends surrounding it constitute the essential elements of a new approach to the religious universe based on charisma. With this movement, the "simple" man of pure faith—as opposed to the austere, cold man of learning—was glorified, taking traditional study to a secondary level through fervor. In the Polish communities, the new sect, which challenged the spiritual authority of the communities, provoked a schism and the group was excommunicated, which

neither halted its development nor prevented it from becoming the richest and most popular religious wellspring in the course of the nineteenth century, before it came to represent the bastion of a Judaism that was henceforth considered "conservative." See Israel Jaffe, *Shivḥei ha-Besht* (Kapust, 1814–1815). In English: D. Ben Amos and J. R. Mintz, *In Praise of the Baʾal Shem Tov* (1970); Jacob Joseph of Polonnoye, *Toledot Yaakov Yosef, Tsofenat Paʾaneah* (Korets, 1780); E. Steinman, *Rabbi Yisrael Baʾal Shem Tov* (1960); Martin Buber, *Hasidism and Modern Man* (New York, 1958); Buber, *Pardes ha-Ḥasidut* (Jerusalem, 1945); Simon Dubnow, *Geschichte fun Chassidism* (Vilna, 1931–1933); J. De Menasce, *Quand Israel aime Dieu* (Paris, 1931); B. Weinryb, *The Jews of Poland* (New York, 1972).

127. *Keter Shem Tov* (Korzec, 1797); (Lvov, 1865), 5a; Ephraim of Sadilkow, *Degel Maḥaneh Efraim* (Zhitomir, 1850), 79, 179; *Tsavvaʾat Haribach* (Lemberg, 1865), 2b, 6b.

AFTERWORD

1. My thesis dates from 1986; the work derived from it, *Les Deux Rives du Yabbok,* was published in 1989.

2. See R. Chartier's article, "Le monde comme représentation," *Annales, ESC,* November–December 1989, entitled *Histoire et Sciences Sociales, un tournant critique.*

3. See Howard Eilberg Schwartz, *The Savage in Judaism* (Bloomington, 1990), and *Jewish Life in Muslim Libya, Rivals and Relatives* (Chicago, 1990); Harvey Goldberg, *Judaism, Viewed from Within and Without* (New York, 1987); and his various articles; Nissan Rubin, *A Sociological Analysis of Jewish Mourning Patterns in the Mishnaic and Talmudic Periods,* Ph.D. dissertation (Bar Ilan University, Tel Aviv, 1977); Shlomo Deshen, Robert Graves, and Raphael Pataï, *Les Mythes hébreux* (Paris, 1987), etc. And in another area of anthropology, see Joelle Bahloul, *Le Culte de la table dressée* (Paris, 1983), and *La Maison de Mémoire* (Paris, 1992); and Jonathan Boyarin, *Polish Jews in Paris* (Bloomington, 1991), and *Storm from Paradise: The Politics of Jewish Memory* (Minneapolis, 1992).

4. P. Ariès, *Essais sur l'histoire de la mort en Occident* (Paris, 1975); *L'Homme devant la mort* (The Hour of Our Death) (Paris, 1977); P. Chaunu, *La mort à Paris* (Paris, 1978); M. Vovelle, *Visions de la mort et de l'au-delà en Provence d'après les autels des âmes du Purgatoire* (Paris, 1970); Vovelle, *Mourir autrefois* (Paris, 1974).

5. Jacques Le Goff, *La Naissance du Purgatoire* (Paris, 1981), 9.

6. Ever since the publication of the works of Haim Solovetchik, *The Use of Responsa as Historical Source* (Jerusalem, 1990).

7. See the article since written on this subject by H. Goldberg, about another population in quite another context and independent of any previous discussion on this mode of integrating foreign accretions in Judaism. "The Zohar in Southern Morocco: a Study in Ethnographic Texts," *History of Religions* 29 (1990).

8. P. Ariès, *Essais de mémoires,* ed. R. Chartier (Paris, 1993), 35.

9. I refer especially to the discussion between Ariès, A. Gurevitch, Chaunu, and Le Goff about the emergence of the "third site" situated between the world here below and the other world, or heaven.

10. G. Scholem, *Major Trends in Jewish Mysticism,* chap. 7, 249.

11. H. Flesch, "Aus der Statuten der mahrischen Beerdigung Brüderschaften," *JGJC* 7 (1933): 157–173.

12. H. J. Zimmels, *Magicians, Theologians and Doctors: Studies in Folk Medicine and Folklore as Reflected in the Rabbinical Responsa* (London, 1952).

13. On this subject, see the Ph.D. dissertation by Moshe Sammet, "Halakhah ve-Reforma" (Jerusalem, 1967); and a more recent dissertation by M. E. Panitz, "Modernity and Mortality: The Transformation of Central European Jewish Responses to Death, 1750–1850" (Jewish Theological Seminary of America, 1989).

# Bibliography

Aboab, Samuel. *Devar Shemuel.* Venice, 1702.
Abrahams, Beth Zion. *Life of Glueckel of Hameln, 1646–1724.* London, 1962.
Abrahams, Israel. *Hebrew Ethical Wills.* Philadelphia, 1926.
———. *Jewish Life in the Middle Ages.* London, 1932.
Adler, Marcus Nathan. *The Itinerary of Benjamin of Tudela.* Malibu, 1907.
Agrippa, Cornelius. *De Occulta Philosophia.* Cologne, 1531–1533.
Alon, G. "Lemokoro shel minhag kvurat kodem be-Yisreal."*BJPS* 8, no. 3 (1941): 107–112.
Altmann, Alexander. *Moses Mendelssohn: A Biographical Study.* Birmingham, 1973.
Altschul, Emil. *Kol Korei Kritisches Sendschreiben ueber das bisherige Verfahren mit dem Sterbenden bei den Israeliten.* Prague, 1846.
Altshuller, David, ed. *The Precious Legacy: Judaic Treasure.* New York, 1983.
An-Ski, Shalom [Solomon Zainwill Rapaport]. *Tsvishn Tsvey Veltn.* Translated into Hebrew by Hayim Nahman Byalik, "Bein Shnei Olamot." *Hatekufah* 1 (1918): 222–296.
———. *Gesammelte Shriften.* 15 vols. Vilna, 1920–1925.
———. "Der Toyt in dem yiddishen Folksgloybn." *Filologishe Shriftn* 3 (1929).
Anchel, Robert. *Les Juifs de France.* Paris, 1946.
Ariès, Philippe. *Essais sur l'histoire de la mort en Occident.* Paris, 1975. English edition, *Western Attitudes Towards Death.* Baltimore, 1974.
———. *L'Homme devant la mort.* Paris, 1977. English edition, *The Hour of Our Death.* Translated by Helen Weaver. New York, 1981.
———. *Essais de mémoires.* Edited by R. Chartier. Paris, 1993.
Aronius, Julius. *Regesten zur Geschichte der Juden in fränkischen und deutschen Reiche bis zum Jahre 1273.* Berlin, 1887–1902; Hildesheim, 1970.
Aronstein, R. P. "Notes on the History of the Jews of Germany in the Seventeenth and Eighteenth Centuries." *Tarbiz* 17 (1946): 105–109.
Ascoli, G. I. "Inscrizioni inedite o mai note Greche, Latine, Hebraiche, di antichi

sepolcri giudaici del Napolitano." In *Actes du IVe Congrès des orientalistes.* Turin, 1880. Also in *REJ* 2 (1882): 131.
Asher Ben Yeḥiel. *Bessamim Rosh.* Berlin, 1793.
———. *Rabbénou Acher.* Vilna, 1885.
———. *Responsa.* Vilna, 1885.
Ashkenazi, Eliezer Ben Eliyah. *Maʿaseh ha-Shem, Maʿasei Avot.* Venice, 1583.
Ashkenazi, Gershon. *Avodat ha-Gershoni.* Frankfurt, 1699; Lemberg, 1861.
Ashkenazi, Zwi Hirsch. *Ḥakham Zwi.* Furth, 1767.
Assad, Jehuda. *Yehudah Yaʿale.* Lemberg, 1873.
Assaf, Simhah. *Mekorot le-Toledot ha-Ḥinnukh be-Ysrael.* Tel Aviv, 1947.
"Ayne Klaglied oyf a meshores fun Frankfurt." Anonymous. Edited by Aron Freimann. *Filologishe Shriftn* 2 (1928): 170–173.
Azaria de Rossi. *Meor Enayim.* Mantua, 1573.
Azulai, Ḥayim Joseph. *Avodat ha-Kodesh.* Jerusalem, 1841.
———. *Birkhei Yosef.* Vienna, 1859.
Baas, Karl. "Jüdische Hospitaler im Mittelalter." *MGWJ* 57 (1913): 452–460.
Bacharach, Yair. *Ḥavvot Yair.* Frankfort, 1699; Lemberg, 1896.
Baer, Fritz Isaac. *Hebraische Berichte über die Judenverfolgungen während der Kreüzuge. Quellen zur Geschichte der Juden in Deutschland,* vol. 2. Berlin, 1892.
———. *Die Juden im christlichen Spanien.* 2 vols. Berlin, 1926–1936. English edition, *A History of the Jews in Christian Spain.* 2 vols. Philadelphia, 1961, 1978, 1983.
———. "Der Ursprung der Chewra." *Zeitschrift für jüdische Wohlfahrtspflege* 1 (1929).
———. "Religious Social Tendancy of the Sefer Ḥassidim." *Zion* 3 (1938): 1–50.
Bahloul, Joelle. *Le Culte de la table dressée.* Paris, 1983.
———. *La Maison de mémoire.* Paris, 1992.
Baron, Salo W. *A Social and Religious History of the Jews.* New York, 1937.
———. *Histoire d'Israël.* Paris, 1964.
Barrots, A. G. *Manuel d'archéologie biblique.* Paris, 1953.
Bash, Lipmann. *Sefer Divrei Emet.* Prague, 1789.
Bax, Ernest. *German Culture, Past and Present.* New York, 1915.
Bayer, Jean. *Les Instituts séculiers.* Paris, 1954.
Beckowsky, Jan. *Manuscript of the Cross Convent.* In Czech. Prague, 1879, 1880.
Ben Amos, D. , and J. R. Mintz. *In Praise of the Baʿal Shem Tov.* New York, 1970.
Ben Sasson, Ḥaim Hillel. *Hagut ve-Hanhagah.* Jerusalem, 1959.
———. "Musagim u-metsiut ba-Historia ha-Yehudit be-Shelahei Yemei ha-Beinaim." *Tarbiz* 30 (1960–61): 297–312.
———. "Ha-yehudim mul ha-reformatsia." *Divrei ha-Akademia ha-leumit le-Maddaʿim* 4 (1969–1970): 66–69.
———. "Jews and Christian Sectarians: Existential Similarity and Dialectical Tensions in Sixteenth-Century Moravia and Poland Lithuania." *Viator* 4 (1973): 369–387.
———. *A History of the Jewish People.* Cambridge, 1976.

Benayahu, Meir. *Sefer toledot ha-Ari.* Jerusalem, 1967.
———."Min ha-Maʾamadot ve-ha-Moshavot la-Met ve-ad ha-Hakkafot, ve-Issur li-Yetsiat ha-Banim Aḥarei Mitat Avihem." *Sinai* 92 (1983): 59–65.
———. *Maʾamadot u-Moshavot.* Jerusalem, 1985.
Bender, A. P. "Beliefs, Rites and the Customs of the Jews Connected with Death, Burial and Mourning," *JQR* 7 (1894): 317–347; 8 (1895): 661–665.
Benjamin of Tudela. *Massaot shel Rabbi Benjamin. Itinerarium D. Beniaminus cum Versione et Notis Constantini l'Empereur ab. Oppyck Iudyum Batavorium.* Lipsiae, 1633.
———. *Sefer ha-Massaot.* Edited by A. Ben Ascher. London, 1840.
*Benjamin Zeʾev.* Anonymous. Venice, 1539.
Berachia, Aaron Ben Moses. *Maʾavar Yabbok.* Mantua, 1626.
Bérenger, Jean. *Finances et absolutisme Autrichien dans la deuxième parties du dix-hirtième siècle.* Lille, 1970, 1975.
Bergl, Josef. "Die Ausweisung der Juden aus Prag im Jahre 1744." In *Die Juden in Prag,* edited by Samuel Steinherz. Prague, 1927.
Bet Halevy, Israel David. *Rabbi Yom Tov Lipman Heller.* Jerusalem, 1954.
Bimbenet, Eugene. *Histoire de la ville d'Orléans.* Orléans, 1887.
Biraben, Jean Noel. *Les Hommes et la peste en France et dans les pays européens et méditerranéens.* Paris, 1975.
Blaschka, Anton. "Die judische Gemeinde zur Ausgang des Mittelalters." In *Die Juden in Prag,* edited by Samuel Steinherz. Prague, 1927.
Blaser, Robert. *Paracelse et sa conception de la nature.* Geneva, 1950
Bloch, Chayim. *The Golem: Legends of the Ghetto of Prague.* Vienna, 1925. French edition, *Le Golem: Légendes du ghetto de Prague.* Strasbourg, 1928.
Blumenkranz, Bernhard. *Les Auteurs chrétiens latins du Moyen Age sur les Juifs et le Judaïsme.* Paris, 1963.
———. *Juifs et chrétiens dans le monde Occidental, 430–1096.* Paris, 1960.
Bohme, Franz Magnus. *Geschichte des Tanzes in Deutschland. Beitrag zur deutschen Sitten, Litteratur, und Musikgeschichte. Nach dem Quellen zum erstenmal bearbeitet und mit alten Tanzliedern und Musik proben.* Leipzig, 1886.
Bondy, Gotlieb, and Franz Dvorsky. *Zur Geschichte der Juden in Böhmen, Mähren, Schliesen, von 906 bis 1620.* Prague, 1906.
Boyarin, Jonathan. *Polish Jews in Paris.* Bloomington, 1991.
———. *Storm from Paradise: The Politics of Jewish Memory.* Minneapolis, 1992.
Brandeis, Jacob B. *Maawar Jabok, Sefer Maʾavar Yabbok Gebete bei Kranken, Sterbenden und im Trauerhause.* Prague, 1884.
Braudel, Fernand. *La Méditerranée et le monde méditerranéen.* Paris, 1966. English edition, *The Mediterranean and the Mediterranean World in the Age of Philip II.* Translated by Sian Reynolds. New York, 1972.
Bressolles, Adrien. *Saint Agobard, évêque de Lyon.* Paris, 1949.
Breuer, Mordechai. *Magen David.* Prague, 1612. Abridged version of *Neḥmad ve-Naim.* Jesnitz, 1743.
———. *Sefer Tsemaḥ David.* Jerusalem, 1983.
Bruna, Israel. *Responsa.* Salonika, 1788.
Buber, Martin. *Die Chassidischen Bücher.* Hellereau, 1928.

———. *Pardes ha-Ḥasidut.* Jerusalem, 1945.
———. *Die Erzaehlungen der Chassidism: Tales of the Hassidim.* Translated by Olga Marx. New York, 1947–1948.
———. *Hasidism and Modern Man.* New York, 1958.
———. *Récits hassidiques.* Paris, 1963.
Capsali, Elie. *Divrei ha-Yamim le-Malkhut Venezia* (1517). In *Likkutim Shonim mi-Sefer de-Vei Eliahu,* edited by M. Lattes. Padua, 1869.
———. *Seder Eliyahu Zutah.* 3 vols. Edited by Meir Benayahu, Arieh Shmuelovitz, and Shlomoh Simonson. Tel Aviv, 1975–1983.
Carmoly, Eliakim. *Histoire des médecins juifs, anciens et modernes.* Brussels, 1844. English edition, *History of the Jewish Physicians.* Translated by J. R. Dunbar. Baltimore, 1845.
———. *Notice historique sur Benjamin de Tudèle.* Paris, 1852.
Caro, Joseph Ben Ephraim. *Shulḥan Arukh.* Venice, 1564–1565.
Carrière, C., M. Courdurie, and F. Rebuffat. *Marseille, ville morte, la Peste de 1720.* Marseille, 1968.
Chajes, H. "Gloybungen un Minhagim in Forbindung mitn Toyt." *Filologishe Shriftn* 2 (1928): 282–327.
Chajes, Zvi Hirsch. *Darkhei Oraha.* Zolkiev, 1843.
———. *Tiferet le-Mosheh.* Zolkiew, 1843.
———. *Responsa.* Zolkiew, 1850.
Chartier, R. "Le Monde comme représentation." *Annales E.S.C.,* November–December 1989, 1505–1520.
Chaunu, Pierre. *La Mémoire et le sacré.* Paris, 1977.
———. *La Mort à Paris.* Paris, 1978.
Coblenz, Jacob. *Mafteaḥ ha-Yam.* Offenbach, 1788.
Cohen, B. *Kuntres ha-Teshuvot.* Budapest, 1930.
Cordovero, Moshe. *Pardes Ha-rimmonim.* Krakow, 1592.
———. *Shiur Koma.* Warsaw, 1883.
Crescas, Ḥasdai. *Bittul Ikkarei ha-Notsrim.* Translated by Joseph ben Shem Tov. Alcala de Henares, 1451; Frankfort, 1860. Edited by E. Deinard, 1904.
———. *Or Adonai.* Ferrare, 1555.
D'Elvert, Christian Ritter. *Zur Geschichte der Juden in Mähren und Oster Schliesen.* Brun, 1895.
Danzig, Abraham. *Ta'ame ha-Minhagim.* Lemberg, 1911–1912.
David, Abraham. *Kronika Ivrit mi-Prag: Me Reshit ha-Meah ha-Shevah esre.* Jerusalem, 1985.
Defoe, Daniel. *A Journal of the Plague Year in London.* New York, 1992.
Delumeau, Jean. *La Peur en Occident.* Paris, 1978.
———. *La Péché et la peur.* Paris, 1983.
De Menasce, J. *Quand Israel aime Dieu.* Paris, 1931.
Denis, Ernest. *La Fin de l'indépendance de la Bohême.* Paris, 1890, 1930.
———. *Huss et les guerre des hussites.* Paris, 1890.
———. *La Bohême depuis la Montagne-Blanche.* Paris, 1903.
Derenbourg, Joseph. "Les anciennes épitaphes des Juifs dans l'Italie méridionale." *REJ* 2 (1882): 131–134.
Der Nistor. *La Famille Machber.* Paris, 1975. English edition, *The Family Mashber.* Translated by Leonard Wolf. New York, 1987.

de Rossi, Azaria. *Meor Enayim*. Mantua, 1573.
Deshen, Shlomo, Robert Graves, and Raphael Pataï. *Les Mythes hébreux*. Paris, 1987.
Diamant, J. , and B. Glaser. "Statuten einer Chewrah Kadischa für Jügendliche in Prag zum Ende des 18. Jahrhunderts." *ZGJD*, n.s., 4 (1938): 13–22.
Didelot. *Instructions pour les sages-femmes*. Nancy, 1770.
Dobner, G. "Wenceslas Hajek a Liboczam." In *Annales Bohemorum*. Prague, 1761–1782.
Dohm, Christian Wilhelm. *Uber die buergerlich Verbesserung der Juden*. Berlin, 1781.
———. *De la réforme politique des juifs*. Paris, 1782, 1984.
Dubnow, Simon. *History of the Jews of Russia and Poland Until the Present Day*. Philadelphia, 1916–1920.
———. *Weltgeschichte des judischen Volkes von seinen Uranfängen bis zur Gegenwart*. Berlin, 1927–1930.
———. *Geschichte fun Chassidism*. Vilna, 1931–1933.
Dubruck, Edelgard. *The Theme of Death in French Poetry of the Middle Ages and the Renaissance*. The Hague, 1964.
Dumont, Louis. "Les Pauvres dans la prière de l'Eglise." *Sorbonne Notebooks*, vol. 7. Paris.
Dumont, M. , and P. Morel, *Histoire de l'obstétrique et de la gynécologie*. Lyon, 1968.
Duran, Simon ben Tsemah. *Responsa Tashbetz*. Amsterdam, 1738–1741.
———. *Magen avot*. Livourne, 1785.
Eckardt, K., and A. Hubner. "Deutschenspiegel und Augsburger Sachsenspiegel." *Monumenta Germaniae historica: Fontes iuris germanici antiqui*, n.s., 3 (1933).
Egger, Akiba. *Responsa*. Vol. I. Warsaw, 1835; vol. 2, Vienna, 1889.
Eidelberg, Shlomo. *Jewish Life in Austria in the Fifteenth Century, as Reflected in the Legal Writings of Rabbi Israel Isserlein and His Contemporaries*. Philadelphia, 1962.
Eidelstein, Jacob Elaezer, ed. *Tsavaot ve-divre qedoshim*. Varsovie, 1878.
Eisenstadt, Moses ben Ḥayim. *Ayn naye Klaglied*. Manuscript. Oxford National Library, Opp. 8/643(4).
Eisenstein, J. D. *Otsar ha-Midrashim*. New York, 1915.
———. *Otsar Dinim u-minhagim*. New York, 1917.
Elbogen, Ismar. *Der Jüdische Gottesdienst in seiner geschichtlichen Entwicklung*. Berlin, 1913.
———. *Geschichte der Juden in Deutschland*. Berlin, 1935.
———. *A Century of Jewish Life*. Philadelphia, 1944.
Elbogen, Ismar, Marcus Brann, Aron Freimann, and Haïm Tykocinski. *Germania Judaica. Von den ältesten Zeiten bis 1238*. Breslau, 1934; Tubingen, 1963.
Éliade, Mircea. *Histoire des croyances et des idées religieuses*. 3 vols. Paris, 1983. English edition, *History of Religious Ideas*. 3 vols. London, 1975–1985.
Élias, Norbert. *La Solitude des mourants*. Paris, 1987.
Eliya ben Samuel of Lublin. *Yad Eliahu*. Amsterdam, 1712.

Emden, Jacob. *Torat ha-kena᾽ot*. Altona, 1752.
———. *Sefer Hit᾽abkut*. Altona, 1762.
———. *Iggeret Bikkoret*. Zhitomir, 1868.
———. *She᾽elot Ya᾽abets*. Lemberg, 1884.
———. *Megillat Sefer*. Krakow, 1896; New York, 1956; Jerusalem, 1979.
Ennemoser, Joseph. *The History of Magic*. London, 1894.
Ephraim of Sadilkow. *Degel Maḥaneh Efraim*. Zhitomir, 1850.
Epstein, Abraham. "Die wormser Minhagbücher, Literarisches und Kulturehistoricsches aus denselben." In *Gedenkbuch zur Erinnerung am David Kaufmann*. Breslau, 1900.
Epstein, Jehiel. *Kitsur Shelah*. Berlin, 1715.
Esse, C. H. *Das neue Krankenhaus der jüdischen Gemeinde zu Berlin*. Berlin, 1861.
Ettinger, Shmuel. *Toledot Israel be-et ha-ḥadash*. Jerusalem, 1969.
———. "Migration and Economic Activity in the Seventeenth and Eighteenth Centuries." In Ben Sasson, *A History of the Jewish People*. Cambridge, 1976.
Ettlinger, Jacob. *Binyan Zion*. Altona, 1868.
Eybeschutz, Jonathan. *Luḥot Edut*. Lemberg, 1775.
Falb, Alfred. *Luther und die Juden*. Munich, 1921.
Falcon, Schneur Ben Yehuda. *Seder Tefillot ve-Pizmonim u-Teḥinot ve-Kinot*. Venice, 1572.
Falke, Jacob. *Die deutschen Trachten und Modenwelt: Ein Betrag zu deutschen Culturgeschichte*. 2 vols. Leipzig, 1858.
Favre, Robert. *La Mort dans la littérature et la pensée française au siècle des Lumières*. Lyon, 1978.
Feuerwerker, David. *L'Emancipation des juifs en France*. Paris, 1976.
Finegan, Jack. *Light from the Ancient Past: The Archaelogical Background of Judaism and Christianity*. Princeton, 1946.
Finkelstein, Louis. *Jewish Self-Government in the Middle Ages*. New York, 1924.
———. *The Pharisees*. Princeton, 1946.
Fishman, Isidore. *The History of Jewish Education in Central Europe, from the End of the Sixteenth to the End of the Eighteenth Century*. London, 1944.
Fleckeles, Eleazar. *Teshuvah me-Ahavah*. Prague, 1819.
Flesch, Heinrich. "Das alte Chewra Kadischa Protokoll der Gemeinde Eibenschitz." *Hiklis jüdischer Volkskalender für das Jähr 5684* 23 (1923–1924): 61–71.
———. "Die Statuten der Chewra Kadischa Neu-Raussnitz." *MGWJ* 70 (1926): 167–181.
———. "Takkanot ha-Ḥevra Kadisha di-Kahal Steinitz bi-Medinat Maḥren." *JJLG* 19 (1928): 21–30.
———. "Zur Geschichte des mährischen Heiligen Vereins (Chewra Kadischa)." *JJLG* 21 (1930): 217–258.
———. "Aus der Statuten der mährischen Beerdigung Brüderschaften." *JGJC* 7 (1933): 157–173.
Foucault, Michel. *Naissance de la clinique*. Paris, 1963. English edition, *The Birth of the Clinic*. Translated by Alan Sheridan Smith. New York, 1975.

———. *Surveiller et punir*. Paris, 1975. English edition, *Discipline and Punish*. Translated by Alan Sheridan Smith. New York, 1979.
Frank, Moshe. *Kehillot Ashkenaz u-Vatei Dineihen*. Tel Aviv, 1938.
Frankel, Zacharia. *Entwurf einer Geschichte der Literatur der nachtalmudischen Responsen*. Berlin, 1865.
Frazer, James George. *The Golden Bough*. England, 1890.
———. *La Crainte des morts*. Paris, 1937.
Freehof, Solomon B. *The Responsa Literature*. New York, 1955.
Freimann, Aron, and Isidor Kracauer. *Frankfort*. Philadelphia, 1929.
Freudenthal, Max. "Leon Elias Hirschel ein judischen arzt." *MGWJ* 50 (1906): 426–443.
Frey, Jean-Baptiste. *Corpus inscriptionum iudaïcorum. Recueil des inscriptions juives qui vont du III^e^ siècle avant J.C. au VII^e^ siècle de notre ère*. The Vatican, 1936.
Friedenwald, Harry, ed. *The Jews and Medicine*. 2 vols. Baltimore, 1944.
Friedlander, Hermann. "Notes on the History of the Jewish Hospitals." In *The Jews and Medicine*, vol. 2. Edited by Harry Friedenwald. Baltimore, 1944.
Frisch, Ephraim. *An Historical Survey of Jewish Philanthropy from the Earliest Times to the Nineteenth Century*. New York, 1924.
Frommann, Friedrich, ed. *Juiläumsausgabe von Moses: Mendelssohns Gesammelten Schriften*. 15 vols. Stuttgart, 1971.
Ganz, David. *Magen David*. Prague, 1612.
———. *Tsemaḥ David*. Frankfurt, 1692.
———. *Neḥmad ve-naïm*. Jesnitz, 1743.
———. *Sefer Tsemaḥ David*. Edited by Mordechai Breuer. Jerusalem, 1983.
Gaster, Moses. *Ma'aseh Book*. Philadelphia, 1934, 1981.
Geiger, Abraham. "Die Krankenpflege bei den Juden." *Jüdishe Zeitschrift für Wissenschaft und Leben* 6 (1868): 277–279.
Geiger, Ludwig. "Kleine Beiträge zur Geschichte der Juden in Berlin, 1701–1817." *ZGJD* 4 (1890): 29–65.
Gelis, Jacques. *L'Arbre et le fruit*. Paris, 1984.
Geremiek, Bronislaw. *La Potence ou la pitié*. Paris, 1987.
Ginzberg, Louis. *Jewish Folklore, East and West*. Cambridge, 1837.
———. *The Legends of the Jews*. 7 vols. Philadelphia, 1909–1938.
Gleichen-Russwurm, Alexander. *Die gotische Welt: Sitten und Gebräuche im späten Mittelalter*. Stuttgart, 1919.
Goetz, Eliakim. *Even ha-Shoḥam u-Meirat Einayim*. Dyhenfurth, 1733.
Goldberg, Harvey. *Judaism, Viewed from Within and Without*. New York, 1987.
———. *Jewish Life in Muslim Libya: Rivals and Relatives*. Chicago, 1990.
———. "The Zohar in Southern Morocco: A Study in Ethnographic Texts." *History of Religions* 29 (1990): 233–258.
Goldberg, Sylvie-Anne. "Étude de deux cimetières juifs à Paris au XVIII^e^ siècle." Unpublished manuscript, 1981.
———. "Du deuil public au deuil privé: Sive laceratione vestium apud hebraeos usitata." Unpublished manuscript, 1982.
———. "La Bible dans les attitudes juives face à la mort." In *Le Siècle des Lumières et la Bible*, edited byY. Belaval and Dominique Bourel. Paris, 1986.

———. *Les Institutions de la mort: Perceptions, visions et question de l'au-délà dans la vie quotidienne des juifs avant leur émancipation (Prague jusqu'à la fin du xviii^e siecle)*. Paris, 1986.
———. "Si je t'oublie Jerusalem, un concept, une histoire." *Communauté Nouvelle* 30 (1987): 139–149.
———. *L'Art de bien mourir*. Paris, 1995.
Gourévitch, Edouard. *Le Puits de l'exil*. Paris, forthcoming.
———. *Le Guide des ḥassidim*. Paris, 1988.
Graetz, Heinrich B. *Geschichte der Juden von den ältesten Zeiten bis auf die Gegenwart*. Leipzig, 1853–1875.
———. *History of the Jews*. 6 vols. London, 1891.
Graff, Moses. *Kuntres Ma'asei ha-Shem Ki-nora Hu*. Furth, 1696.
Grandmaison, Louis de. "Quelques notes relatives au cimetière que les juifs possédaient à Tours au XIII^e siècle." *Bulletin de la Société archéologique de Touraine* 7 (1886–1888).
Grätzer, J. *Geschichte der Israelitischen Kranken-Verpflegungs-Anstalt und Beerdigungs-Gesellschaft zu Breslau*. Breslau, 1841.
Graves, Robert, and Raphael Patai. *Hebrew Myths*. London, 1964, 1985.
Greenwald, Yekutiel. *Kol-bo al Avelut*. Jerusalem, 1947–1951; Jerusalem, New York, 1973.
Grégoire de Tours. *Histoire des Francs*. 2 vols. Paris, 1963.
Grun, Nathan. "Sage und Geschicte aus der Vergangenheit der israelitischen Gemeinde in Prag." *Das jüdische Centralblatt* 5 (1888): 3–25.
Grünbaum, Max. *Judischdeutsche Chrestomathie*. Leipzig, 1882.
Grunwald, Max. *Geschichte der Juden in Boehmen*. Pisek, 1885.
———. "Älteste Statuten der prager Brüderschaft 1692." *Das Jüdische Centralblatt* 8 (1889): 39–57.
———. "Spiele." *MGJV* 3 (1898): 34–40.
———. "Trachten und Sitten. Aus der Dreigemeinde Hambourg, Altona, Wansbeck vom Jahre 1726." *MGJV 3* (1898): 29–33.
———. "Aus Hausapotheke und Hexenküche." *MGJV 5* (1900): 1–73; n.s., 30 (1927–1928): 27–29, 178–226.
———. "Hamburgs deutsche Juden bis zum Auflosung der Dreigemeinde, 1811." *MGJV* 12 (1903): 1–124; subsequently published, Hamburg, 1904.
———. "Die Statuten der Hambourg-Altonae Gemeinde von 1726." *MGJV* 11 (1903): 1–64.
———. "Beiträge zu den Memoiren der Glückel von Hameln." *MGJV* 44 (1915): 63–70.
———. "Altjudisches Gemeindeleben. Bestimmungen der Chebra kaddischa, Horn 1784." *Menora* 4 (1926): 599–604; *MGJV* 39 (1926).
———. *Geschichte der Wiener Juden, bis 1914*. Vienna, 1926.
———. "Fünfundzwanzig Jahre jüdische Volksunde." *Jahrbuch für Jüdische Volskunde* 1 (1923): 1–23.
———. *Vienna*. Philadelphia, 1936.
———, ed. *Die Hygiene der Juden. Im Anschluss an die Internationale Hygiene-Austellung Dresden 1911*. Dresden, 1911.
Güdemann, Moritz. *Geschichte des Erziehungswesens und der Cultur des Juden in Frankreich aund Deutschland (X–XV Jahrhundert)*. Vienna, 1880.

Gurevitch, Aaron I. *Les Catégories de la culture médiévale.* Paris, 1983. English edition, *Categories of Medieval Cultures.* Translated by G. L. Campbell, London, 1985.
ha-Babli, Menahem. *Ta'ame ha-Mitzvot.* Lublin, 1571.
Habermann, Abraham Meir. *Sefer gezerot Ashkenaz ve-Tsarfat.* Jerusalem, 1946.
Ha-Cohen, Aaron. *Oreḥot Ḥayim.* Edited by M. Schlesinger. Berlin, 1902.
ha-Cohen, Ephraim ben Jacob. *Sha'ar Efraim.* Lemberg, 1887.
ha-Cohen, Ishmael ben Abraham. *Zera Emet.* Livorno, 1786–1796; Reggio, 1815.
ha-Cohen, Joseph. *Emek ha-Bakḥa.* Vienna, 1852. French edition, *La Vallée des pleurs.* Trans. J. P. Osier. Paris, 1980.
ha-Cohen, Tobias. *Ma'aseh Toviah.* Hesnitz, 1721.
Haggard, Howard D. *Devils, Drugs and Doctors.* London, 1929, 1946.
Hagiz, Jacob. *Halakhot Ketanot.* Venice, 1704.
Hahn, Joseph Yuspa. *Yosef Omets.* Frankfurt, 1723.
Hajeck, W. *Böhmischer Chronik.* 1541.
Halberstam, Ḥayim. *Divrei Ḥayim.* Bardiov, 1902
ha-Levy, Abraham ben M. *Ginnat Veradim.* Constantinople, 1716–1717.
Halperin, Israel. *Constitutiones Congressus Generalis Judaeorum Moraviensum, 1650–1748.* Jerusalem, 1952.
———. *Bet Yisrael be-Polin.* Jerusalem, 1954.
Hammerstein, Reinhold. *Tanz und Musik des Todes: Die Mittelalterlichen Todtentaïnz und ihre Nachleben.* Berne, 1980.
Hanauer, W. *Festschrift zur Einweihung des neuen Krankenhauses der israelitischen Gemeinde zu Frankfurt am Main.* Frankfurt, 1914.
Hannover, Nathan Nata. *Sefer Sha'arei Tsion ve-Tikkun Se'uda ve-Sefer Yetsirah.* Prague, 1662; Venice, 1736.
Heimbucher, Max. *Die Orden und Kongregationen der Katholischen Kirche.* Paderborn, 1907–1908.
Herman, Jan. "La Communauté juive et sa structure au commencement des temps modernes." *JB* 5 (1969): 31–70.
Hermann, L., J. Teiger, and Z. Winter. *Das Prager Ghetto.* Prague, 1903.
Herzberg, Y. *Yosele ha-Golem ve Yotsero Maharal mi-Prag.* Tel Aviv, 1947.
Higger, Michael, ed. *Massekhet Semaḥot.* New York, 1931.
Hirsch, J. C. *Eike von Repgow: Der Sachsenspiegel (Landrecht), in unserer heutigen Muttersprache übertragen und dem deutschen Volke erklärt.* Berlin, Leipzig, 1936.
Hirst, Leonard Fabian. *The Conquest of the Plague.* Oxford, 1953.
Hock, Simon, and David Kaufman. *Die Familien Prag, nach den Epigraphien des alten jüdischen Friedhofs in Prag.* Prague, 1892.
Hofmann, David Zvi. *Melammed le-Hoil.* Berlin, 1926–1932.
Holzer, Isaac. "Aus dem Leben der alten Judengemeinde zu Worms nach dem Minhagbuch des Juspa Shames." *ZGJD*, n.s., 5 (1935): 169–186.
Horodetzki, S. A. *Torat ha-Kabbalah shel Rabbi Itshak Ashkenazi ve-Hayim Vital.* Tel Aviv, 1947.
Horowitz, Abraham ben Shabbetai Sheftel. *Emek ha berakha.* Amsterdam, 1729.
Horowitz, Isaiah ben Abraham. *Shnei Luḥot ha-Berit.* Amsterdam, 1649.

———. *Yech Noḥalim.* Prague, 1615; Amsterdam, 1701.
Houlier, Jean. *Histoire du droit et des institutions de l'Église en Occident. L'Age classique 1140–1378.* St. Amand-Moutrond, 1974.
Hulin, Michel. *La Face cachée du temps.* Paris, 1985.
Hulsen, Julius. *Der alte Judenfriedhof in Frankfurt am Main.* Frankfurt, 1932.
Hurwitz, Simon. *The Responsa of Solomon Luria.* New York, 1938.
Hurwitz, Zalkind. *La Revolution française et l'émancipation des juifs.* Paris, 1968.
Idelsohn, Abraham Zwi. *The Ceremonies of Judaism.* Cincinnati, 1930.
Isaac ben Moses of Vienna. *Or zaruʾa.* Zhitomir, 1862; Jerusalem, 1887–1890.
Isaie of Janov. *Tsavvaʾat ha-Ribash.* Lemberg, 1865.
Isserlein, Israel. *Pesakim u-Khetavim.* Furth, 1778.
———. *Terumat ha-Deshen. Venice, 1519;* Furth, 1778.
Isserles, Moses. *Darkhei Mosheh.* Amsterdam, 1711.
Jacob ben Asher. *Arbaʾah Turim.* Piove di Sacco, 1675; Vilna, 1900.
Jacob Joseph of Polonnoye. *Toledot Yaakov Yosef, Tsofenat Paʾaneah.* Korets, 1780.
Jacobovits, Immanuel. *Jewish Medical Ethics: A Comparative and Historical Study of the Jewish Religious Attitudes to Medicine and Its Practice.* New York, 1959.
Jaffe, Israel. *Shivḥei ha-Besht.* Kapust, 1814–1815.
Jaffe, Mordekhai. *Levush.* Prague, 1646; Berdiczew, 1819.
Jeiteles, Moses Wolf. *Zikkaron le-Yom ha-Aḥaron.* Prague, 1806.
Johnston, William M. *The Austrian Mind: An Intellectual and Social History 1848–1938.* Berkeley, 1972, 1983.
Joseph Ben Moses. *Leket Yosher.* Edited by Freimann. Berlin, 1903–1904.
Kaidanover, Zvi Hirsch. *Kav ha-Yashar.* Sulzbach, 1705; Vilna, 1925.
Katz, Jacob. *Massoret u-Mashber.* Tel-Aviv, 1958.
———. "Al Halakhah v-derush kemekor histori." *Tarbiz* 30 (1960): 62–72.
———. "Marriage and Sexual Life among the Jews at the Close of the Middle Ages." *Zion* 10 (1970): 21–54.
———. *Out of the Ghetto: The Social Background of Jewish Emancipation, 1770–1870.* New York, 1978.
———. *Exclusiveness and Tolerance: Studies in Jewish-Gentile Relations in Medieval and Modern Times.* Oxford, 1981.
———. *Al Halakhah ve-Kabbalah.* Jerusalem, 1984.
Katz, Meshullam ben Joel. *Ikkarei Tosafot Yom Tov.* 1790.
Katznellenbogen, Ezekiel. *Knesset Yeḥezkiel.* Altona, 1732.
Kaufman, David. "Jair Chayim Bacharach: A Biographical Sketch." *JQR* 3 (1891): 292–313, 485–536.
———. *Zikhronos Moras Glikl Hamil mi Shenos, 1647–1719.* Frankfurt, 1896.
———. *Gesammelte Schriften von David Kaufman.* Frankfort, 1908.
———."Rabbi Yom Tov Lipman Muelhausen." *Studies in Bibliography and Booklore* 1, no. 2 (1953): 60–68.
Kayserling, Meyer. *Moses Mendelssohn, sein Leben und seine Werke.* Leipzig, 1862.

Kestenberg-Gladstein, Ruth. "Hussitentum und Judentum." *JGJC* 8 (1936): 1–26.
———. "Difference of Estates within Preemancipation Jewry." *Journal of Jewish Studies* 5 (1954): 156–166; 6 (1955): 35–49.
———. "A Voice of the Prague Enlightenment." In *Yearbook of the Leo Baeck Institute*. London, 1964.
———. "The Jews Between Czechs and Germans in the Historic Lands, 1848–1918." In *The Jews of Czeckoslovakia,* vol. 1. Philadelphia, 1968.
———. "Cechen und Juden in altväterischer Zeit." *JB* 4 (1968): 64–72.
———. *Neuere Geschichte der Juden in den Bohmischen Ländern.* Tubingen, 1969.
———. "Bassevi of Treuenberg." *EJ* 4 (1972): 315–316.
*Keter Shem Tov.* Anonymous. Korzec, 1797; Lvov, 1865.
Kirchan, Elḥanan. *Elḥanan Haenle, Simḥat ha-nefesh.* Sulzbach, 1798.
———. *Simḥat ha-Nefesh: An Exact Facsimile Reproduction of the First and Only Edition Published in Furth, in the Year 1727.* Edited by Shatzky. New York, 1926.
Kisch, Bruno. "The History of the Jewish Pharmacy in Prague." *HJ* 8 (1946): 149–180.
Kisch, Guido. "Die prager Universität und die Juden 1348–1848." *MGWJ* 79 (1935): 270–363.
———."The Yellow Badge in History." *HJ* 4 (1942): 95–144.
———. *In Search of Freedom: A History of American Jews from Czechoslovakia.* London, 1949.
———. *The Jews in Medieval Germany: A Study of Their Legal and Social Status.* Chicago, 1949.
———. "Jewish Historiography in Bohemia, Moravia, Silesia." In *The Jews of Czechoslovakia,* vol. 1. Philadelphia, 1968.
*Kitsur Maʾavar Yabbok.* Anonymous. Dyhernfurth, 1797.
Klemperer, Gustav. "The Rabbis of Prague." *HJ* 12 (1950): 33–82.
Kluger, Solomon. *Tuv Taʾam va-Daʾat.* Podgorz, 1900.
Kobler, Franz. *Letters of Jews through the Ages.* 2 vols. New York, 1952, 1978.
*Kol-bo.* Anonymous. Venice, 1574.
*Kol-bo.* Anonymous. Furth, 1782.
Kosman, Joseph ben Moses. *Noheg katson Yosef.* Hanau, 1718.
Kottek, H. *Geschichte der Juden von Bad Homburg v.d. Hoehe.* Frankfurt, 1915.
Koyre, Alexandre. *Mystiques, spirituels, alchimistes du XVIe siècle allemand.* Paris, 1955, 1970.
Kracauer, Isidor. "Beiträge zur Geschichte der FrankfurterJuden im dreissigjharigen Krieges." *ZGJD* 3 (1889): 130–156, 337–372.
———. "Die Juden Frankforts im Fettmilschen Zusstand 1612–1618." *ZGJD* 4 (1890): 127–169, 319–365.
———. *Die Geschichte der Judengasse in Frankfurt am Main.* Frankfort, 1925–1927. Reprint of *Fesstschrift zur Jahrundertfeier der Realschule der Israelititidchen Gemeinde zur Fankfurt am Main* Frankfort, 1904, 307–453

Krauss, Samuel. *Talmudische Archäologie*. Leipzig, 1910–1912.
Kriegel, Maurice. *Les Juifs à la fin du Moyen Age*. Paris, 1979.
Krochmal, Menaḥem Mendel. *Tsemaḥ Tsedek*. Furth, 1766.
*La Révolution française et l'émancipation des juifs* (Paris, 1968)
Lacomblet, T. J. *Niederkheim Urkundenbuch*. N.p., 1850.
Lallemand, Léon. *Histoire de la charité*. Paris, 1906–1910.
Lamm, Maurice. *The Jewish Way in Death and Mourning*. New York, 1969.
Landau, Alfred, and Bernhard Weinreich. *Jüdische Privatbriefe aus dem Jahre 1619*. Vienna, 1909.
Landau, Ezekiel. *Noda bi-Yehudah*. Prague, 1776; New York, 1985.
———. *Derush Hesped*. Prague, 1781.
———. *Tikkun Nefesh*. Prague, 1786.
———. *Derushei ha-Tselah*. Warsaw, 1886.
Landsoffer, Jona. *Me'il Tsedakah*. Prague, 1757.
———. *Kanfei Yona*. Prague, 1822.
Le Goff, Jacques. *La Naissance du Purgatoire*. Paris, 1981. English edition, *The Birth of Purgatory*. Translated by Arthur Goldhammer. Chicago, 1984.
———. *L'Imaginaire médiéval*. Paris, 1985. English edition, *The Medieval Imagination*. Translated by Arthur Goldhammer. Chicago, 1988.
Lea, Henri Charles. *A History of the Inquisition in the Middle Ages*. New York, 1911.
Lehmann, Emil. *Gesammelte Schriften*. Berlin, 1899.
Leitner, Helmut. *Bibliography to the Ancient Medical Authors*. Bern, 1973.
Leon of Modena. *Ḥayyei Yehudah*. Kiev, 1913.
Lerner, Ralph. "Maimonides' Treatise on Resurrection." In *History of Religions*. Chicago, 1983.
Lesser, Ludwig. *Chronik der Gesselschaft der Freunde in Berlin*. Berlin, 1842.
Levi, Israel. "Le Repos sabbatique des âmes damnées." *REJ* 25 (1892): 1–13; 26 (1893): 131–135.
———. "Si les morts ont conscience de ce qui se passe ice-bas." *REJ* 29 (1894): 69–94.
———. "L'Intercession des vivants en faveur des morts." *REJ* 47 (1903): 214–220.
Levy, Abraham ben Mordechai. *Ginnat veradim*. Constantinople, 1716.
Lewin, Louis. *Geschichte der Juden in Lissa*. Pinne, 1904.
———. *Geschichte der israelitischen Krankenverpflegungsanstalt und Beerdigungsgelsellschaft zu Breslau 1726–1926*. Breslau, 1926.
Leyel, C. F. *The Magic of Herbs*. London, 1932.
Liebe, Georg. *Das Judentum in der deutschen Vergangenheit*. Leipzig, 1903.
Lieben, Koppelmann. *Sefer Gal Ed*. Prague, 1856.
Lieben, Salomon Hugo. "Die prager Brandtkatastrophen von 1689 und 1754." *JJLG* 28 (1926): 175–191.
Lipman Heller, Yom Tov. *Tosafot Yom Tov*. Prague, 1614–1617.
———. *Megillat Eivah*. Breslau, 1618.
———. *Ma'adanei Melekh ve-Leḥem Ḥamudot*. Prague, 1628–1629.
———. *Tsemaḥ Tsedek*. Amsterdam, 1675.
——— "Responsa." In *Geonei Batrae*. Turka, 1764.
———. *Beit Ḥadash ha-Ḥadashot*. Koretz, 1785.

Lipman Muelhausen, Yom Tov. *Sefer Nitsaḥon.* Altdorf, 1644; Amsterdam, 1701, 1827.
Loew Ben Betsalel, Yehuda. *Gevurot ha-Shem.* Cracow, 1582.
———. *Derekh ḥayim.* Cracow, 1589.
———. *Tiferet Yisrael* . Prague, 1593.
———. *Netivot Olam.* Prague, 1596.
———. *Be'er ha-Gola* . Prague, 1598.
———. *Netsaḥ Yisrael* . Prague, 1599.
Low, Immanuel. *Gesammelte Schriften.* Szegedin, 1890.
Lowenstein, Leopold. "Die Chewra Kadischa speciell eine jüdische Institution." *Die Neuzeit* 24 (1888): 238.
Lowenthal, Marvin. *The Memoirs of Glückel of Hameln.* New York, 1932, 1977.
———. *The Jews of Germany.* New York, 1936.
Lowinger, Adolf. *Der Traum in der jüdischen Literatur.* Leipzig, 1908.
Luncz, Abraham Moses. *Jerusalem.* Vienna, 1882.
Luria, Salomon ben Ashkenazi. *Shulḥan Arukh shel ha-Ari.* Amsterdam, 1709.
Luria, Solomon ben Jehiel. *Responsa.* Lublin, 1575.
——— *Yam shel Shlomoh.* Stettin, 1861.
Luther, Martin. *Sammtliche Werke.* Weimar, 1883–1948.
———. *Martin Luthers Werke.* Weimar, 1901.
*Ma'aneh Lashon.* Anonymous. Prague, 1616.
Macek, Josef. *Le Mouvement hussite en Bohême.* Prague, 1965.
Macek, Josef, and Robert Mandrou. *Histoire de la Bohême.* Paris, 1984.
MacManners, John. *Death and the Enlightenment.* Oxford, 1981.
Maimonides [Moses Ben Maimon]. *Responsa.* Vienna, 1519; Zolkiew, 1798.
———. *Guide des Egarés.* Translated by Salomon Munk. Paris, 1857. English edition, *Guide of the Perplexed.* Translated and annotated by Shlomo Pines. Chicago, 1963–1979.
———. *Sefer ha-Refuot.* London, 1900.
———. *Sefer ha-Mitsvot.* Translated into Hebrew by Moses ibn Tibbon, edited by H. Heller. Jerusalem, 1946.
———. *The Code of Maimonides.* 13 vols. New Haven, 1949–1975.
———. *Epîtres.* Paris, 1983. English edition, *Crisis and Leadership: Epistles of Maimonides.* Translated by Abraham Halkin. Philadelphia, 1985.
———. *Mishneh Torah.* 14 vols. Edited by A J. Friemann and J. Blau. Jerusalem, 1984.
Manasseh ben Israel. *Nishmat Ḥayim.* Stettin, 1861.
Marcus, Ivan G. *Piety and Society: The Jewish Pietits of Medieval Germany.* Leyne, 1981.
Marcus, Jacob Rader. *The Jew in the Medieval World.* New York, 1938, 1978.
———. "The Triesch Hebra Kadisha 1628–1702." *HUCA* 19 (1945): 169–204.
———. *Communal Sick-Care in the German Ghetto.* New York, 1947, 1978.
Margarita, Anton. *Der gantz jüdisch Glaub.* Augsburg, 1530.
Margolis, Max, and Alexander Marx. *History of the Jewish People.* Philadelphia, 1927, 1962.
Margulies, Meir. *Meir Netivim.* Polnoi, 1792.

Margulies, Reuben. *Malakhe Elyon*. Jerusalem, 1945, 1964.
Marmorstein, Arthur. *Studies in Jewish Theology*. London, 1950.
Marx, Alexander. "A Seventeenth-Century Autobiography: A Picture of Jewish Life in Bohemia and Moravia." *JQR* 8 (1918): 269–304.
Maschke, Erich. *Pauvres urbains et pauvres ruraux dans l'Allemagne médiévale*. Sorbonne notebooks, vol. 1, no. 7. Paris.
Masran, Isaac. *Ha-Galut ve-ha-Pedut*. Venice, 1634.
Mat, Moses ben Abraham. *Mateh Mosheh*. Cracow, 1590.
Mauquets de la Motte, G. *Traité des accouchements*. Paris, 1765.
Meir ben Gedalia of Lublin. *Responsa*. Metz, 1769.
Melzer, Isser Zalman. *Otsar ha-Poskim*. Jerusalem, 1957.
*Mémoires de Guillaume Slavata*. Anonymous. Edited by Jiretchek, Prague, 1866, 1868. Also in Paul Skala, *Histoire de la Bohème 1602–1623*. 5 vols. Prague, 1873.
Menasce, Jean de. *Quand Israel aime Dieu*. Paris, 1931, 1992.
Mendelssohn, Moses. *Moses Mendelssohn's Gesammelten Schriften*. 7 vols. Leipzig, 1843–1845.
———. *Jubiläumsausgabe Moses Mendelssohns Gesammelten Schriften*. Edited by F. Bamberger et al. 15 vols. Stuttgart, 1971.
Mevoraḥ, Barukh. "Ma'aseh ha-Hishtadlut be-Europa li-Meniyat Gerusham shel Yehudei Bohemia u-Moravia, 1744–1745." *Zion* 28 (1963): 124–164.
Meyer, Samuel. *Geschichte des Wohltatigkeitsvereins der Synagoguen-gemeinde Hannover*. Hanover, 1862.
Meyer of Rothenburg. *Meir ben Barukh Responsa*. Cremona, 1557; Prague, 1608; Lemberg, 1860.
Meyuḥas, Abraham ben Samuel. *Sedei ha-arets*. Salonika, 1784–1798; Livorno, 1788.
Minkoff, Nokhem B. *Glikl Hameln*. New York, 1952.
———. "Old-Yiddish Literature." In *The Jewish People, Past and Present*, vol. 3. New York, 1952.
Mizraḥi, Nissim H. Moses. *Admat Kodesh, Orekh Ḥaïm*. Constantinople, 1560.
Moellin, Jacob ben Moses. *Sefer ha-Maharil*. Warsaw, 1874.
Moellin, Jacob Levy. *Responsa Rosh*. Cracow, 1881.
Mollat, Michel. *Les Pauvres au Moyen Age*. Paris, 1978. English edition, *The Poor in the Middle Ages*. Trans. Arthur Goldhammer. New Haven, 1986.
———, ed. *Études sur l'histoire de la pauvreté*. 2 vols. Paris, 1974.
Moore, George F. *Judaism in the First Centuries of the Christian Era*. Cambridge, 1950.
Morin, Edgar. *L'Homme et la mort dans l'histoire*. Paris, 1970.
Morpurgo, Samson. *Shemesh Tsedakah*. Venice, 1743.
Moses ben Jacob of Coucy. *Sefer Mitsvot Gadol*. Kopys, 1807.
Moses Ben Maimon. See under Maimonides.
Muneles, Otto. *Bibliograficky Prehled Zidovske prahy*. Prague, 1952.
"From the Archives of the State Jewish Museum." *Jewish Studies* 1 (1965): 100.
———. *The Prague Ghetto in the Renaissance Period*. Prague, 1965.
Munk, Élie. *Le Monde des prières*. Paris, 1963.

Naḥmanides, *Torat ha-Adam,* Naples, 1490; Warsaw, 1876.
Nahon, Gérard. "Les Cimetières." In *Art et archéologie des juifs en France médiévale.* Toulouse, 1980.
———. "L'Epigraphie." In *Art et archéologie des juifs en France médiévale.* Toulouse, 1980.
———. *Inscriptions hébraiques et juives de France médiévale.* Paris, 1986.
Nathanson, Joseph. *Sho'el u-meshiv.* Lemberg, 1868–1890.
Navon, R. Yona. *Neḥpah ba-Kessef.* Constantinople, 1748.
Neher, André. "The Humanism of the Maharal of Prague." *Judaism* 14, no. 3 (1965): 292–304.
———. *Le Puits de l'exil.* Paris, 1966.
———. *David Gans: Disciple du Maharal de Prague.* Paris, 1974.
Neubauer, Adolf, and Moritz Stern. *Hebraische Berichte uber die Judenverfolgerungen während der Kreuzzüge: Quellen zur Geschichte der Juden in Deutschland.* 2 vols. Berlin, 1892.
Neumann, Abraham A. *The Jews in Spain: Their Social, Political and Cultural Life during the Middle Ages.* 2 vols. Philadelphia, 1942.
Neusner, Jacob. *The Evidence of the Mishna.* Chicago, 1981.
Nigal, Gedalia. *Sippurei Dibbuk be-Sifrut Yisrael.* Jerusalem, 1983.
Opitz, Karl. "Avicenna, das Lehgedicht über die Heilkunde (canticum de medicina). Aus dem Arabischen über setzt." *Quellen und Stadien zur Geschichte der Naturwissenschaft und der Médizin* 7 (1940): 150–220.
Ortloff, Friedrich. *Das Rechtsbuch nach Distinctionen (Meissener Rechtsbuch) nebst einem eisenachischen Rechtsbuch.* Jena, 1836.
Palacky, Franz. *Geschichte von Böhmen.* 5 vols. Prague, 1845–1874.
———. *Urkündliche Beiträge zur Geschichte des Hussitenkrieges.* Prague, 1873.
Palaggi, Hayim. *Ḥayim be-Yad.* Smyrna, 1878.
Panitz, Michael E. *Modernity and Mortality: The Transformation of Central European Jewish Responses to Death, 1750–1850.* Ph.D. dissertation, Jewish Theological Seminary of America, 1989.
Parkes, James. *The Conflict of the Church and the Synagogue.* London, 1934.
———. *The Jew in the Medieval Community: A Study of His Political and Economic Situation.* London, 1938; New York, 1976.
Peu, P. *La Pratique des accouchements.* Paris, 1694.
Pflaum, H. *Die Idee der Liebe, Leone Ebreo.* Tubingen, 1926.
Plangian, Zacharia. *Sefer Zekhirah.* Hamburg, 1709.
Polak-Rokykana, Jaroslav. "Die Häuser des Jacob Bassevi von Treuenberg." *ZGJT* 1 (1931): 41–50.
Poliakov, Léon. *Histoire de l'antisémitisme.* 3 vols. Paris, 1955. English edition, *The History of Antisemitism.* London, 1974–1985.
———. *Les Mémoires de Glückel Hameln.* Paris, 1971.
Pollack, Herman. *Jewish Folkways in Germanic Lands.* London, 1971.
Popper, Maurice. "Les Juifs de Prague pendant la guerre de Trente Ans." *REJ* 29 (1894): 79–93; 30 (1895): 127–141.
Portal, Paul. *La Pratique des accouchements.* Paris, 1682.
Pritzker, Asher. "Burial and Mourning Customs." *Yeda Am* 3 (1955): 115–117; 4 (1956): 38–40.

Prokes, J. "Die prager Judenkonskription vom Jahre 1729." *JGJC* 4 (1932): 297–332.
Rapoport, Abraham. *Eitan ha-Ezraḥi*. Ostrow, 1796.
Recanati, Menaḥem. *Piskei rabbi Menaḥem Recanati*. Bologne, 1538.
Reischer, Jacob. *Shevut Ya'akov*. Lemberg, 1897.
Riemer, Jack. *Jewish Reflections on Death*. New York, 1974.
Rivkind, Isaac. "Kuntres Takkanot Prag: A Codex of Prague 1611." *Reshumot* 4 (1925): 345–352.
Rokeaḥ, Eleazar. *Rokeaḥ ḥil Teshuvah*. Zolkiew, 1866.
Ronne, Ludwig, and Heinrich Simon. *Die früheren und gegenwärtigen Verhältnisse der Juden in den sammtlichen Landestheilen des preussischen staates*. Breslau, 1843.
Rosanes, Salomon. *Divrei yemi Yisrael be Togarma*. Sofia, 1934–1935.
Rosenberg, Yudel. *Niflaot Maharal, ha-golem mi-Prag*. Varsovie, 1909.
Rosenthal, Berthold. *Heimatsgeschichte der badischen Juden*. Baden, 1927.
Roth, Cecil. "Elie Montalto et sa consultation sur le sabbat." *REJ* 94 (1933): 113–136.
———. *A History of the Jews in England*. Oxford, 1949.
Rubin, Nissan. *A Sociological Analysis of Jewish Mourning Patterns in the Mishnaic and Talmudic Periods*. Ph.D. dissertation, Bar Ilan University, Tel Aviv, 1977.
———. *Rechit ha-ḥayim*. Tel Aviv, 1995.
Rubin, Shlomoh. "Meḥolot ha-Mavet." *Ha-Shaḥar* 8 (1877): 16–90.
Saba, Abraham. *Tseror Hamor*. Venice, 1523.
Sadek, Vladimir. "La Chronique hébraique des Juifs pragois de la deuxième moitié de XVIIIe siècle." *JB* I (1956): 59–68.
———. "Réponses de rabbins." *Judaïca Bohemiae* 20, no. 1 (1984): 31–43.
Salfeld, Siegmund. "Das Martyrologium des nuernberger Memorbuches." In *Quellen zur Geschichte der Juden in Deutschland,* vol. 3. Berlin, 1898.
Sammet, Moshe. "Halakhah ve-Reforma." Ph.D. dissertation, Hebrew University, Jerusalem, 1967.
Saugnieux, Joel. *Les Danses macabres de France et d'Espagne*. Paris, 1972.
Schiffer, Sinai. *Sitri u-Magini*. Tyrnow, 1932–1933.
Schmiedl, Adolf."Zur Entstehungsgeschichte der allerersten Chewra Kadisha." *Oesterreichische Wochenschrift* 10 (1893): 133–135.
Schnitzler, Leopold. *Die prager Judendeutsch. Eine beitrag zur Erforshung des Älteren Prager Judendeutsch in Lautlicher und insbesondere in lexikalisher Beziehung.*. Munich, 1966.
Schwarzbaum, Haim. *Studies in Jewish Folklore*. Berlin, 1968.
Scholem, Gershom. *Major Trends in Jewish Mysticism*. New York, 1946, 1965.
———. "Perakim ḥadashim me'inianei Ashmodai ve Lilit." *Tarbiz* 29 (1947–1948): 160–175.
———. "Le mouvement sabbataïste au Pologne." In *RHR* 142 (1952): 30–90; 143 (1953): 42–77, 209–233.
———. *On the Kabbalah and Its Symbolism*. New York, 1965.
———. *The Messianic Idea in Judaism*. New York, 1971.
———. "Kabbalah." *EJ* 10 (1972): 489–653.

———. *Sabbatai Sevi: The Mystical Messiah, 1626–1676*. Princeton, 1973. French edition, *Sabataï Tsevi*. Lagrasse, 1982.
———. *Origins of the Kabbalah*. New York, 1987.
Schottky, Julius Max. *Prag wie es war und wie es ist*. Prague, 1910.
Schwab, Moise. *Rapport sur les inscriptions hébraïques de la France*. Special issue of *Nouvelles Archives Scientifiques*. Paris, 1904.
Schwartz, Emanuel. "Zur geschichte der Juden von Prag unter könig Wenzel IV." *JGJC* 5 (1953): 429–437.
Schwartz, F. "Ueber der Ursprung der Chewra Kadischa." *Die Neuzeit* 20 (1888): 196–197.
Schwartz, Howard Eilberg. *The Savage in Judaism*. Bloomington, 1990.
Schwartzbaum, Haïm. *Studies in Jewish Folklore*. Berlin, 1968.
*Seder Berakhot*. Anonymous. Amsterdam, 1687.
*Seder Tefillot ve-Pizmonim u-Tehinot ve-Kinot*. Anonymous. Venice, 1572.
*Sefer Berakh le-Avraham ben Meir ha-Levy*. Anonymous. Prague, 1735.
*Sefer derekh tovim*. Frankfort, 1717.
*Sefer divrei emet*. Anonymous. Prague, 1789.
*Sefer ha-Ḥayim*. Anonymous. Sulzbach, 1667. Edited by Simon Frankfurt, Amsterdam, 1703.
*Sefer Ḥasidim. Yehudah he-ḥassiol*. Anonymous. Basel, 1581. Edited by Wistinecki, Berlin, 1892; edited by Margolis, Jerusalem, 1957.
*Sefer Minhagim di-Kehilateynu*. Anonymous. Furth, 1767.
*Sefer Tsidduk ha-Din*. Anonymous. Venice, 1738.
Serrano Y Sanz. "Origines de la dominacion española en America." *Sefarad* 8 (1918): 147–151, 369–371.
Shoḥat, Azriel. "Hitorerut chel Yehudei Germania bi-sevivatam im peros ha-haskala." *Zion* 21 (1957): 207–235.
———. *Im Ḥillufei Tekufot*. Tel Aviv, 1967.
Siev, A. *Ha-Rama*. Tel Aviv, 1957.
Silberstein, S. "Mendelssohn und Mecklenburg." *ZGJD* I (1929): 233–244, 278–286.
Silva, Ezekia. *Peri Ḥadash*. Karlsruhe, 1787.
Simon, Isidore. "La Médecine hébraique." In *Histoire de la médecine*. Vol. 3. Edited by J. Poulet, J.C. Sournia, and M. Martigny. Paris, 1978.
Simḥa Vitry. *Maḥzor Vitry le-rabbenu Simḥah*. Edited by Simon Hurwitz. Nuremberg, 1923.
Singer, Charles. *A Short History of Medicine: Introducing Medical Principles to Students and Non-Medical Readers*. Oxford, 1928.
Singer, Israel Joshua. *The Sinner* (Yoshe Kalb). Translated by Maurice Samuel. New York, 1933. French edition, *Yoché le Fou*. Paris, 1984.
*Sippourim Prager Sammlung Jüdischer Legenden in neuer Auswald und bearbeitung*. Anonymous. Vienna, 1921.
Skala, Paul. *Histoire de la Bohême, 1602–1623*. Prague, 1873.
Sofer, Abraham Samuel Benjamin. *Ketav Sofer*. Presburg-Drohobycz, 1873–1894.
Sofer, Moses. *Ḥatam Sofer*. Vienna, 1855.
Soloveitchik, Hayim. *The Use of Responsa as Historical Source*. Jerusalem, 1990.

Spektor, Isaac. *Ein Yitsḥak*. Vilna, 1889–1895.
Spiegel, Käthe. "Die prager Juden zur Zeit des Dreissigjährenkrieges." In *Die Juden in Prag*. Edited by Samuel Steinherz. Prague, 1927.
Spiro, Zvi Hirsch. *Darkhei Teshuvah*. Vilna, 1892.
Stannard, David E. *The Puritan Way of Death: A Study in Religion, Culture and Social Change*. New York, 1977.
Stauben, Daniel. *Scènes de la vie juive en Alsace*. Paris, 1860. English edition, *Scenes of Jewish Life in Alsace*. Translated by Rose Choron. Malibu, 1991.
Steinherz, Samuel. "Die einwanderung der Juden in Böhmen." In *Die Juden in Prag*. Edited by Samuel Steinherz. Prague, 1927.
———. "Kreuzfahrer und Juden in Prag 1096." *JGJC* 1 (1929): 1–32.
———, ed. *Die Juden in Prag: Bilder aus ihrer tausendjahrigen Geschichte. Festgaber der Loge Praga des Orden*. Prague, 1927.
Steinman, Eliezer. *Rabbi Yisrael Ba'al Shem Tov*. Jerusalem, 1960.
Steinschneider, Moritz. *Allgemeine Einleitung in die Jüdische Literature des Mittelalters*. Jerusalem, 1938.
Stern, Moritz. "Memorbuch ha-Yashan de-Kehillat Vina Lifneh ha-Gerush." In *Berliner's Festschrift*. Frankfurt, 1903.
Strakosch, Henry E. *State Absolutism and the Rule of Law: The Struggle for Codification of Civil Law in Austria 1753–1811*. Sydney, 1968.
Sulzbach, Abraham. "*Ein alter frankfurter Wohltatigkeitsverein.*" *JJLG* 2 (1904): 241–266.
Tapie, Victor-Louis. *Monarchies et peuples du Danube*. Paris, 1969.
———. *L'Europe de Marie-Thérèse du Baroque aux Lumières*. Paris, 1973.
Tcherikover, Avigdor. "Die geshikhte fun a literarishn plagiat (ver is gevn der emter mehber fun Kav hayosher)." *Jiwobleter* 4 (1932): 159–167.
Tcherniak, Chekhna. *Mishmeret Shalom*. Warsaw, 1928.
Tchernowitz, Hayim. *Toledot ha-Poskim*. New York, 1947.
Teomim, Moses. *Devar Moshe*. Lemberg, 1864.
———. *Oryan Telitai*. Lemberg, 1880.
Terni, Daniel. *Ikkarei Dinim*. Florence, 1803.
Thieberger, Friedrich. *The Great Rabbi Loew of Prague*. London, 1954.
Thiers, J.B. *Superstitions anciennes et nouvelles*. Paris, 1733.
Thomas, Louis-Vincent. *Anthropologie de la mort*. Paris, 1975.
Thorndike, Lynn. *A History of Magic and Experimental Science during the First Sixteen Centuries of Our Era*. 8 vols. New York, 1923–1958.
Trachtenberg, Joshua. *Jewish Magic and Superstition: A Study in Folk Religion*. New York, 1939, 1979.
———. *The Devil and the Jews*. New Haven, 1943.
Tukacinski, Yehiel M. *Gesher ha-Ḥayim*. Jerusalem, 1947, 1960.
Twerski, Isadore. *Introduction to the Code of Maïmonides (Mishneh Torah)*. New Haven, 1980.
Tyrnau, Isaac. *Minhagim shel Kol ha-Medinot*. Amsterdam, 1708.
Urbain, Jean Didier. *La Société de conservation*. Paris, 1978.
Valecillo Avila, M. "Los judíos de Castilla en la alta Edad media." In *Guadernos de Historia de España*. 1950.
Van Gennep, Arnold. *Manuel de folklore français contemporain*. Paris, 1980.
Verga, Solomon ibn. *Shevet Yehudah*. Adrianople, 1553.

Vilimkova, Milada. "Seven Hundred Years of the Alt-Neue Synagogue." *JB* 5 (1965): 31–72.
Vital, Ḥayim ben Joseph. *Sefer ha-Ḥezyonot.* Damascus, 1598; edited by Z. Ascoly, 1954.
———. *Sefer ha-Gilgulim.* Frankfort, 1684; Przemysl, 1875.
———. "Sha'ar ha-Gilgulim." In *Ets ha-Ḥayim.* Jerusalem, 1863–1898.
Vital, Samuel ben Ḥayim. *Sha'ar ha-Gilgulim.* Cairo, 1666; Jerusalem, 1903.
Vogelstein, Hermann. "Geschichte des israelitischen Vereins für Krankenpflege und Beerdigung zum Königsberg." In *Festschrift zum zweihundertjährigen Bestehen des israelitischen Vereins für Krankenpflege und Beerdigung.* Koenigsberg, 1904.
von Buch, Johan. *Glos.* Augsburg, 1516.
Vovelle, Gaby, and Michel Vovelle. *Visions de la mort et de l'au-delà en Provence d'après les autels des âmes du Purgatoire.* Paris, 1970.
Vovelle, Michel. *Mourir autrefois.* Paris, 1974.
Wachstein, Bernhard. *Die Gründung der wiener Chewra Kadischa im Jahre 1763.* Presburg, 1910.
———. "Die prager Takanot fun 1767, kegn luxus." *Yivo Bletter* 4 (1931): 335–354.
———. "Pinqas Runkel." In *ZGJD* 4 (1932): 129–149; *Yivo Bletter* 6 (1934): 84–116.
Wackernagel, Wilhelm. *Der Schwabenspiegel in der ältesten Gestalt mit den abweichungen der gemeinen Texte und den Zusätzen derselben.* Zurich, 1840.
Weil, Jacob. *Responsa.* Venice, 1523.
Weinreich, Max. *Bilder fun der yiddisher Literaturgeschichte fun di onheybn bis Mendele Moykher Sforim.* Vilna, 1928.
———. *History of the Yiddish Language.* Chicago, 1980.
Weinryb, Bernard D. *The Jews of Poland: A Social and Economic History of the Jewish Community in Poland from 1100 to 1800.* New York, 1972.
Wellesz, J. "Volkmedizinisches aus dem jüdischen Mittelalter." *MGJV* 35 (1910): 117–120.
Wettstein, F. "Kadmoniyyot mi-Pinkessa'ot yeshanim le-korot Yisrael be Polin bi-khelal u-bi Cracow be prat." *Otsar ha-Sifrut* 4 (1892): 577–642.
———. *Devarim attikim mi-Pinkessei ha-kahal bi-Cracow.* Krakow, 1901.
Wiener, Shlomo. "Sheelot u-teshuvot Nodah bi Yehudah betokh mekor letoledot Yisrael." *Ḥoreb* 10 (1948): 57–76.
Wirth, Louis. *The Ghetto,* Chicago, 1956.
Wittman, ***. "Urkunden und Aktenstucke zur geshichte der Juden in Regensburg 1453–1732." In *Quellen und Erörterungen zur bayerischen und deutschen Geschichte,* vols. 1, 2. Edited by Raphael Strauss. Munich, 1960.
Wolf, Gerson. *Die jüdische Friedhöfe und die Chewra Kadischa.* Vienna, 1879.
———. "Die Juden in Prag unter der Kaiser Maria Theresa nach deren Wiederaufnahme im Jähre 1748." *AZJ* 51 (1887): 676–679.
———. "Der Ursprung die Chewra Kadischa." *Die Neuzeit* 21 (1888): 208.
———, ed. *Die alten Statuten der jüdischen Gemeinden in Mähren samt der nachfolgenden Synodalbeschlüssen.* Vienna, 1880.
Würfel, Andreas, ed. *Historische Nachricht von der Judengemeinde in dem*

*Hofmarkt Furth unterhalb Nurnberg. In das Teutsche übersetzt und mit Anmerkungen erläuter*. Frankfurt, 1754.
Wuttke, Adolf. *Der deutsche Volksaberglaube der Gegenwart*. Berlin, 1869.
Yeivin, Shmuel. "The Origin of an Ancient Jewish Burial Custom," *BJPS* 8, no. 1 (1940): 22–27.
Yerushalmi, Yosef Haim. *Zakhor: Jewish History and Jewish Memory*. Seattle, 1982.
Yizḥaki, Abraham. *Zera Abraham*. Smyrna, 1733.
Zacuto, Abraham. *Sefer Yuḥasin*. Constantinople, 1566; Cracow, 1580–1581. Edited by Freimann, 1963.
Zacuto, Moses. *Tofteh Arukh*. Venice, 1715.
Zaddok, Samson ben. *Tashbets*. Warsaw, 1902.
Zaḥalon, Jacob. *Otsar ha-Ḥaim*. Venice, 1783.
Zimmels, Hirsch Jacob. *Beiträge zur Geschichte der Juden in Deutschland im 13. Jahrhundert*. Vienna, 1926.
———. *Abhandlungen zur Erinnerung an Hirsch Perez Chayes*. Berlin, 1933.
———. *Magicians, Theologians, and Doctors: Studies in Folk Medicine and Folklore as Reflected in the Rabbinical Responsa*. London, 1952.
Zimra, David. *Magen David*. Amsterdam, 1713.
———. *Responsa*. Warsaw, 1882.
Zinberg, Israel. *Di Geshikhte fun der Literatur bay yidn*. Vilna, 1908–1935.
Ziyuni, Menahem. *Tsefunei Tsiyuni*. Lemberg, 1882.
Zlotnick, Dov. *The Tractate Mourning*. New Haven, 1966.
*Zohar*. Anonymous. Munkacz, 1911.
Zunz, Leopold. *Die synagogale Poesie des Mittelalters*. Berlin, 1855–1959. English edition, *The Sufferings of the Jews During the Middle Ages*. Revised and edited by George Alexander Kohot. New York, 1907.
Zvi ben Samuel of Semjatitchi. *Margaliot ha-Torah*. Poryck, 1788.

## MANUSCRIPTS

"Account Book and List of New Members of the Burial Society, Covering Dates 1691–1846." Archives of the Holy Brotherhood of Prague, Jewish Museum of Prague, 46595; Jerusalem, Archives of the Jewish People, HM 3827.
"Ayn naye klaglied." Amsterdam, 1680. Oxford Bodleian Library, Opp. 8/632.
"Ipush lied fun Prag." Prague, 1714. Oxford Bodleian Library, Opp. 8/643(4).
"Judicial Protocol: Minute Book of the Prague Jewish Court 1714–1718." Archives of the Jewish People, Jerusalem, HM 2/3299.
"Register of Deceased 1787–1846." Archives of the Jewish People, Jerusalem, HM 3927.
"Statutes of the Holy Brotherhood of Prague 1564–1754." Jewish Museum of Prague, 42842.
"Tikkunim Meyusharim Yesdom Ḥakhamim di-Kehillateynu Prag" (The Prague Pardon). Prague, 1624. Oxford Bodleian Library, Opp. 4/557 (5).

# Index

Compositor: Prestige Typography
Text and Display: Sabon
Printer: Thomson-Shore, Inc.
Binder: Thomson-Shore, Inc.